STRANGE CRIMES AND CRIMINALS

Carl Sifakis

Checkmark Books®

An imprint of Facts On File, Inc.

Strange Crimes and Criminals

Checkmark Books
An imprint of Facts On File, Inc.
132 West 31st Street
New York NY 10001

Library of Congress Cataloging-in-Publication Data

Sifakis, Carl.
Strange crimes and criminals / Carl Sifakis
p. cm.
Originally published as part of: The encyclopedia of American crime.
New York: Facts On File, 2000, in series: Facts On File crime library.
Includes bibliographical references and index.
ISBN 0-8160-4424-4 (alk. paper)
1. Crimes—United States—Encyclopedias. I. Sifakis, Carl. Encyclopedia of American Crime. III. Title.
HV6789 .S543 2001
364.973—dc21   2001028661

Checkmark Books are available at special discounts when purchased in bulk quantities for
businesses, associations, institutions or sales promotions. Please call our
Special Sales Department in New York at (212) 967-8800 or (800) 322-8755.

You can find Facts On File on the World Wide Web at http://www.factsonfile.com

Text design by Cathy Rincon
Cover design by Nora Wertz

Printed in the United States of America

VB FOF 10 9 8 7 6 5 4 3 2 1

This book is printed on acid-free paper.

Contents

Introduction

As these selections from *The Encyclopedia of American Crime* demonstrate, the strange crimes and criminals that tread across the national stage are limitless in their bizarre, weird and almost unimaginable behavior. Oddly, or perhaps not, many are forgotten, or sometimes more accurately repressed, in the American psyche because of their sheer horror.

Certainly that could be said of the Bath, Michigan school bombing in which 37 schoolchildren were slain by Andrew Kehoe in what was undoubtedly the most horrendous taxpayer revolt in history. A farmer, Kehoe could not pay an increase of $300 in his house taxes for a new schoolhouse, and he faced imminent loss of his property. Night after night, Kehoe slipped into the schoolhouse planting dynamite in safe hiding places. Then on the morning of May 18, 1927, the whole building shook under a massive explosion, crushing the first floor in an avalanche of wreckage, killing the school children and one teacher and leaving 43 others very seriously injured.

Sitting across the street in his car, Kehoe watched the unfolding slaughter. But he still wanted two more victims. He saw the head of the school board on the scene and called him over. He was the man Kehoe held most responsible for the new school. As the stunned official placed his foot on the running board, Kehoe turned a switch and a second violent explosion killed the last two victims of the mad bomber of Bath, the school board head and himself.

There is an almost endless stream of quaint characters to be portrayed here—within the context of quaintness set by the bizarre borders of criminal behavior. Old New York was home to Gallus Mag. a six-footer known as the Queen of the Waterfront who held sway at the legendary Hole-In-Wall Saloon on Water Street where more men were robbed and killed than in any other watering hole of the day. If someone was robbed without the specific approval of Mag, he would be put out of commission with a vicious swipe of a mallet she always carried. When Mag had a victim of her own, she took him out and to make sure he would not err by returning to protest, she would bite his ear off and add it to her collection in a jar she kept behind the bar as a showcase. Once she fought a bitter feud with Sadie the Goat, who always lowered her head and butted out a robbery victim, hence her nickname. She tried to butt out Gallus Mag but got the mallet treatment instead, and also lost her ear in the process. After a few years, a chastened Sadie the Goat returned to Water Street and accepted Mag's primacy. The surrender so impressed Gallus Mag that she magnanimously fished around in her alcohol jar of ears and returned Sadie's severed member to her.

It would be an impossible task to attempt to categorize the villains or their crimes in this collection. They are all startlingly different. Such certainly was the murder of Philip Peters by a mysterious figure who became known as Denver's Spiderman of Moncrieff Place. He was a tramp who entered the house to rob it when he witnessed Peters rush into his car to visit his wife in a hospital. The Spiderman was looking to steal food and whatever else he could find, but then he noticed a trap door that led to a narrow attic cubbyhole. Rounding up some food, some rags to use for bedding and a crystal radio, he took up residence. When Peters was out, the Spiderman roamed the house, using the bathroom, shaving and judiciously appropriating some food. After about a month, Peters unexpectedly came home early and gaped at the mysterious intruder. They fought and the Spiderman killed him. Still, the Spiderman did not leave the house. He had no safer place to go. The Spiderman continued in residence for almost another year, even after the victim's wife finally returned from the hospital. Then, when she and the housekeeper started hearing noises and decided it was the ghost of the departed Mr. Peters, they left for good, insisting the police keep checking the house. Finally officers making a random search heard the click upstairs and got there just in time to see a pair of legs climbing into the attic cubbyhole. The Spiderman of Mon-

crieff Place was caught, ending the saga of Denver's strangest murder case.

Others in the amazing cast of characters include such outlandish members of the law, as New York's celebrated Izzy and Moe, possibly the only two honest revenue agents in the city during Prohibition, who enthralled newspaper readers with their comic exploits in catching bootleggers, as well as Howe and Hummel, the notorious legal sharks who got guilty clients off with remarkable cunning. On these pages the reader will meet the real Mickey Finn and the proprietor of New York's McGuirk's Suicide Hall, a low class dive, who boasted that more women had killed themselves in his place than in any other place in the world.

There are many fleshpots of the country, such as San Francisco's "Municipal Brothel" of the early 20th century, so named for the common knowledge that the profits from the establishment flowed into the pockets of city officials and their sponsors. Whenever a stranger inquired of a policeman where women could be found, the officer was required to send them off to the Municipal Brothel at 620 Jackson Street—or face suspension for failing to do so. Trolley conductors cooperated as well and the brothel was a regular stop for Jackson Street trolleys, and if no ladies were aboard, the conductors shouted, "All out for the whorehouse!"

Americans always had a certain degree of tolerance on sexual matters, more so in the West. In Cripple Creek, Colorado, train travelers passing through town were treated to a full view of Myers Avenue and its "line," replete with signs such as "MEN TAKEN IN AND DONE FOR." A leading muckraker of the turn of the 20th century, Julian Street, wrote a searing article in *Colliers* magazine exposing the shame of Myers Avenue as a disgrace for the entire nation. The outraged city fathers of Cripple Creek fought back by bestowing a special honor on the journalist—they renamed Myers Avenue "Julian Street."

Entries A - Z

Aldermen's Wars Chicago political killings

Even for Chicago, a city noted for its gang-land killings and battles, the so-called Aldermen's Wars, between 1916 and 1921, stand out for sheer savagery. In all, 30 men died in the continuous five-year battle fought for control of the 19th, or "Bloody," Ward, which encompassed the city's Little Italy. The political forces that controlled the 19th were entitled to the huge payoffs coming out of Little Italy for various criminal enterprises. With the coming of Prohibition, the production of moonshine alcohol became the area's "cottage industry" and an important source of illicit alcohol for the entire city.

The 19th had been controlled by Johnny "de Pow" Powers, an incorrigible saloon-keeper, protector of criminals and graft-taking alderman from the 1890s on. Despite the transition of much of the area from Irish to Italian, Powers was able to maintain his control and met no serious challenge until 1916, when Anthony D'Andrea mounted a bid against James Bowler, junior alderman from the 19th and a Powers henchman. D'Andrea was less than a pillar of civic virtue

himself, although he was a prominent leader in many Italian fraternal societies and a labor union official. The *Chicago Tribune* reported: "Anthony Andrea is the same Antonio D'Andrea, unfrocked priest, linguist, and former power in the old 'red light' district, who in 1903 was released from the penitentiary after serving 13 months on a counterfeit charge. D'Andrea's name has also been connected with a gang of Italian forgers and bank thieves who operated at one time all over the country."

The killings commenced in February 1916. Frank Lombardi, a Powers ward heeler, was shot dead in a saloon. D'Andrea lost his election battle that year, as well as another one in 1919 and a final one in 1921, a direct race against Powers. During all that time, corpses of supporters on both sides filled the streets, and a number of bombings took place, including one set off on the front porch of Powers' home. The Powers forces retaliated with the bombing of a D'Andrea rally, severely injuring five persons. There were subsequent bombings of D'Andrea's headquarters and the home of one of his lieutenants.

One day in March 1921, Paul Labriola, a Powers man who was a court bailiff, walked to work with some apprehension because his name had been listed on the Dead Man's Tree, a poplar on Loomis Street on which both factions had taken to posting the names of slated victims, a grim form of psychological warfare. At Halsted and Congress, Labriola passed four D'Andrea gunmen; as he started across the intersection, he was cut down by a volley of shots. One of the four gunmen walked over to their victim, straddled his body and pumped three more revolver shots into him. Later that day the same four gunmen killed cigar store owner Harry Raimondi, a former D'Andrea man who had switched sides. While the killings and bombings continued, Alderman Bowler declared:

> Conditions in the 19th Ward are terrible. Gunmen are patrolling the streets. I have received threats that I was to be "bumped off" or kidnapped. Alderman Powers' house is guarded day and night. Our men have been met, threatened and slugged. Gunmen and cutthroats have been imported from New York and Buffalo for this campaign of intimidation. Owners of halls have been threatened with death or the destruction of their buildings if they rent their places to us. It is worse than the Middle Ages.

The killings continued after D'Andrea's third election defeat, despite his announcement that he was through with 19th Ward politics. In April 1921 a man named Abraham Wolfson who lived in the apartment across the hall from D'Andrea got a threatening letter that read in part: "You are to move in 15 days. We are going to blow up

the building and kill the whole D'Andrea family. He killed others and we are going to do the same thing. We mean business. You better move and save many lives."

Wolfson showed the note to D'Andrea and then moved out. This gave D'Andrea's enemies what they wanted, an empty apartment from which to watch him. On May 11, just after his bodyguard had driven off, D'Andrea was gunned down as he was about to enter his building.

D'Andrea was the wars' 28th victim. There were to be two more, Andrew Orlando and Joseph Sinacola, D'Andrea's Sicilian "blood brother," both of whom had sworn to avenge their boss' death. Orlando was killed in July and Sinacola in August.

There was only one prosecution for any of the 30 murders committed during the Aldermen's Wars, that of Bloody Angelo Genna for the street corner slaying of Paul Labriola. But nothing much came of it. The numerous witnesses to the murder belatedly realized they hadn't seen a thing.

See also: DEAD MAN'S TREE.

Allison, Dorothy (1925–1999) crime-solving psychic

Among the various psychics who have made the popular press in recent years, one American psychic, a housewife from Nutley, N.J., ranked above all others as having some apparent crime-solving ability. Dorothy Allison's visions of peaceful landscapes containing unfound bodies have turned out to be, as *Newsweek* labeled them, "close approximations of grisly reality." In the past dozen years or so, Mrs. Allison had been consulted by police in well over 100 cases and, by her own count, had helped solve 13 killings and find more than 50 missing persons. Many police departments expressed wholehearted, if befuddled, gratitude. "Seeing is believing," said Anthony Tortora, head of the missing persons division of the Bergen County, N.J. sheriff's office. "Dorothy Allison took us to within 50 yards of where the body was found. She's quite a gal."

Some of Mrs. Allison's "finds" have been accident victims and others have been the victims of foul play. In September 1977 two of her finds turned up in different states just one day apart. She pinpointed a swamp area in New Jersey where 17-year-old Ronald Stica would be found and was able to tell police prior to the discovery of the body that he had been stabbed to death. The day before, the body of 14-year-old Susan Jacobson, missing two years, had turned up inside an oil drum in an abandoned boat yard in Staten Island, N.Y. Mrs. Allison had described the corpse site—although she had never been to Staten Island—as a swampy area, with "twin church steeples and two bridges—but one not for cars" nearby. She said she also saw the letters M A R standing alone. All the elements were there, including the letters M A R painted in red on a nearby large rock.

Perhaps Mrs. Allison's most amazing case was one that began at about 6:30 P.M. on Thursday, July 22, 1976, when Deborah Sue Kline left her job as a hospital aide, got in her car and started for her home in Waynesboro, Pa. She never got there. Months of police investigations proved fruitless. Jane Kline, the girl's mother, finally contacted Mrs. Allison, who agreed to come to Pennsylvania. Quite naturally, the first thing the mother asked was if her daughter was still alive. By the end of the day, Mrs. Allison told her the answer: Debbie was dead. Mrs. Allison put on Debbie's graduation ring "to help me feel

her presence." She toured the area with police, reporters and a friend of the Klines.

After a while, she was able to reconstruct the crime. She saw Debbie driving home from the hospital and two cars, a yellow one and a black one, forcing her off the road. According to a local newspaper account: "She was taken from her car in one of the other cars to a place where she was molested. She was taken to another place where she was killed with a knife wound. I saw [at the death site] yellow signs, a dump, burnt houses and a swimming pool. I could see her skeleton. It was not underground. The word 'line' or 'lion' came to me."

On January 26, 1977, three days after Dorothy Allison had returned home, police located the body of Debbie Kline. It was not buried and was in an area where junk was dumped. There were no "burnt houses" but the spot was just off the Fannettsburg–Burnt Cabins Road. In the area were yellow traffic signs warning motorists of steep grades on the road. Near the body was a discarded plastic swimming pool. There was no "lion" but there was a "line"—150 feet away was the line between Huntington and Franklin Counties. And Debbie had been stabbed to death.

Then the police confronted a suspect, in jail at the time on another rape charge. His name was Richard Lee Dodson. Dodson broke down and led them to where the body had been found. He and another man, Ronald Henninger, were charged with the crime. Ken Peiffer, a reporter for the *Record Herald,* said: "She told me, among other clues later proven accurate, the first names of the two men involved, Richard and Ronald. She even told me that one of the men had a middle name of Lee or Leroy."

The police of Washington Township, who were in charge of the case, made Dorothy

Allison an honorary member of the police department. The citation given to her reads in part, "Dorothy Allison, through psychic powers, provided clues which contributed to the solving of the crime."

Of course, not all of Dorothy Allison's efforts had been triumphs. She was the first psychic called in by Randolph Hearst after daughter Patty disappeared in Berkeley, Calif. Mrs. Allison turned up little of value while on the West Coast. Still, Hearst did not scoff. "Dorothy couldn't locate Patty," he said, "but she is honest and reputable. I wouldn't laugh at it." Allison died December 1, 1999.

Alta, Utah   lawless mining town

For a time, Alta, Utah Territory sported a sign that read, "WELCOME TO THE MEANEST LITTLE TOWN IN THE WEST." The small silver-mining town in the foothills of Utah's Rustler Mountains lived up to its motto. In its heyday during the 1870s, Alta had 26 saloons and a cemetery touted as the largest in any town of that size.

While avalanches claimed the lives of many miners, the largest contingent of corpses buried in the Alta cemetery were the more than 100 victims of gun battles. In 1873 a stranger dressed in black came to town and announced he had the power to resurrect all of the town's dead gunmen. The miners, a superstitious lot, speculated that such a development would only lead to a lot of bullets flying about in vengeance shoot-outs and opted for the status quo. They raised $2,500 in a community collection as a gift for the "resurrection man" contingent on his leaving Alta permanently.

By the early 1900s Alta was a ghost town, its ore mined out, but today it thrives in a new reincarnation as a popular ski resort.

animal criminals

The history of crime and justice in America is replete with examples of dumb animals being charged and often punished for alleged illegal acts. Perhaps the most famous episode occurred in Erwin, Tenn. in 1916, when a circus elephant named Mary was charged with murder after running amok and killing a man. The dumb beast was hanged from a railroad derrick before a cheering crowd of 5,000 persons. Whether Mary deserved capital punishment might be legally debated on the grounds that she did not know right from wrong, but there are numerous cases of animals being trained to follow a life of crime.

In Chicago in 1953, a resourceful bird fancier trained her pet magpie to enter rooms in a nearby hotel and bring back any bright object it found. The heavy jewelry losses were driving the house detectives crazy, but they were unable to turn up any leads. If not for the fact that one day the magpie entered the room of a woman guest who was a particularly light sleeper, the bird fancier and her pet might have continued their winged larceny for years. The woman, taking a nap after lunch, was awakened by a low noise. She saw a bird flying around the room as though looking for something. It swooped down and picked up a diamond ring lying on a table. When the bird flew out the window, the woman jumped up and got to the window in time to see the bird flying into a neighboring flat. She told her story to the police, and although dubious, they raided the apartment. Their doubts were allayed when they found a fortune in jewelry. The lady bird-lover tearfully admitted all. She had spent arduous years training her bird because magpies, although notorious thieves, can seldom be taught to bring what they steal to a specific spot. Usually they drop their loot in any place that strikes their fancy.

Then there was the case of the chimp cat-burglar. For months in 1952 householders in a New York City neighborhood were being plagued by a series of odd burglaries. In some instances the victims lived in apartments 15 stories up and there seemed to be no means of entry other than a window. One day the son of a city detective happened to see a small figure round a rooftop corner. At first he thought it was a child, but when he looked around the corner, he saw an ape. The boy watched the animal climb through the open skylight of a shop. When it emerged within a matter of seconds, it was carrying a sack; around its neck, packed nearly full. The boy followed the chimp and saw it disappear into a run-down house on another street. He ran home and told his father. Shortly thereafter, the owner of the long-armed, light-fingered animal stood before a judge and told a strange story.

While abroad he had bought a chimpanzee for his children. Chimps are probably the brightest of animals next to humans and his was one of the smartest, he said. He named the chimp Socrates. But then his fortunes took a sudden dive, and it became difficult to provide for his family's needs. One day Socrates went foraging by himself. When he returned, he was munching on a piece of bread and carrying a bagful of pastries. Realizing what had happened, the owner decided to exploit the chimp's latent talents. Socrates was a quick learner, and his master designed a special sack he could use to carry the swag in. Before long, Socrates had the family back in the chips again. The upshot of the case was jail for the chimp owner and a zoo for Socrates.

See also: ANIMAL LYNCHING.

Further reading: *The Criminal Prosecution and Capital Punishment of Animals* by E. R. Evans.

animal lynching

The lynching of animals—cats, dogs, horses, cows, bulls, etc.—has a long and brutal history in the United States, but on September 13, 1916 an all-time low in man's inhumanity to beast was reached when Mary, a circus elephant that had killed three men, was hanged from a railroad derrick in Erwin, Tenn. The first attempt to lynch the animal ended after two hours when the derrick's steel cable broke and Mary came crashing down to earth. The second try was successful, and much to the satisfaction of 5,000 spectators, the dumb beast paid the human price demanded for its crimes.

It was not uncommon in the West to kill horses or cattle deemed to have been responsible for the loss of human life. And even the Chicago underworld got into the act. When the celebrated Nails Morton was thrown by a riding horse and killed in Lincoln Park in 1924, his buddies in Dion O'Banion's gang abducted the animal from its stable at gunpoint and took it to the spot where Nails had been killed. There the poor creature was executed, as each of the gangsters solemnly shot it in the head.

During the last century more restraint was shown toward a steer over which an argument regarding its ownership had arisen. Shooting broke out and when the smoke cleared, six men were dead or dying. Because the incident was such a tragedy, it was felt that something other than death was required. The animal was branded with the word MURDER and allowed to live on as a grim reminder of the awful occurrence.

Apache gangs   mythical Indian outlaw bands

Without doubt one of the most fertile subjects for foreigners' misconceptions of conditions in America has always been crime. This has been true not merely because of purple reporting by several popular writers but also because of the inaccurate opinions of many experts. Typical was the work of Dr. Edmond Locord, one of the great criminologists of France in the early part of this century. Writing in the preface of a book on crime in 1925, Locard discussed crime in various parts of the world; of America he said: "In Texas and California even today one meets roving bands of redskins who live by extortion, pillage, and rapine. They are the Apaches." Thus, foreigners visiting the United States in that period spoke fearsomely of traveling in "Apache Gang" country.

The "Apache dancers," depicting the ways of the brutal French underworld, also derived their name from popular 19th-century misconceptions of the generally peaceful Apache.

Arnold, Stephen (c. 1770–?) murderer

Men and women suffering from varying degrees of lunacy have committed murders, and depending on the prevailing mores of their societies, they have received varying punishments. Stephen Arnold, in an event marked by high drama, was one of the first in America to win leniency due to insanity. As a thirtyish schoolteacher in Cooperstown, N.Y., he was a perfectionist who would fly into a mad rage whenever a pupil made a spelling error. When in 1805 his six-year-old niece, Betsy Van Amburgh, misspelled *gig*, Arnold lost all control of himself, seized a club and beat her to death. Then comprehending what he had done, he fled Cooperstown for Pittsburgh, Pa., where he took up a new identity. Caught later that year, he was returned to

Cooperstown to be tried for murder. Since his lawyer could not dispute the obvious facts of the crime, Arnold was convicted in short order and sentenced to be hanged.

Arnold's execution day was a banner event in Cooperstown, with thousands from the surrounding area converging on the town for the big show. According to a contemporary account, marching bands, a company of artillery and a full battalion of infantry led Arnold to the gallows. Flowers and bunting decorated the caissons and even the gallows. While Arnold stood with the noose around his neck, a minister launched into an hour-long sermon on the sins of men letting their tempers race unchecked. Much of the admonishments were quotations from Arnold himself. Now, with the obligatory matters taken care of, the hangman stepped forward—the crowd tensed . . . suddenly the sheriff moved to the condemned man and ceremoniously flung the noose from Arnold's neck. Before the stunned onlookers, the sheriff then read a reprieve for Arnold that he had received from the governor earlier in the morning. The sheriff had let the execution charade continue for three reasons: to show his disagreement with the chief executive's act; to force Arnold to experience the terror of execution for his murderous sin; and not to disappoint entirely the thousands gathered for the event. The crowd's disappointment was great nonetheless, and there was some speculation that the sheriff had acted as he did only so that the local merchants and tavern keepers could still profit from what would prove to be a nonevent. Amidst all the bickering on that point, the concept of temporary insanity and the pros and cons of it were lost on most of the crowd. Arnold was later pardoned for the same reason.

Astor Place Riots

One of the worst riots in New York City's history started on May 10, 1849, ostensibly as an outgrowth of a rather silly theatrical feud between the English tragedian William Charles Macready and the American actor Edwin Forrest. Actually, the riots were fomented by a notorious political rogue, Capt. Isaiah Rynders, who capitalized on the poor's general class hatred and anti-British feeling to regain a measure of public power following the unexpected defeat of his Democratic Party in 1848.

Macready had been chosen instead of Forrest to perform in *Macbeth* at the Astor Place Opera House. When the English actor appeared on stage, he was met by a mob who had gathered in response to a fiery tirade by Capt. Rynders and one of his chief lieutenants, Edward Z. C. Judson, better known as Ned Buntline. Rynders' thugs broke up the performance by hurling rotten eggs, pennies and even chairs onto the stage. Others threw pieces of paper filled with gunpowder in the chandeliers. Macready was driven from the stage but no one was injured. The noted actor was induced by the righteous element, led by Washington Irving and other prominent citizens to try once more on May 10, but Rynders was again prepared.

Offering free drinks, passes and rabble-rousing handbills, Rynders produced a crowd of 10,000 to 15,000. Twenty of Rynders' thugs entered the theater with orders to kidnap the hated foreigner right off the stage. However, the police foiled the plot and locked them all up in the basement, where they unsuccessfully tried to burn down the building. Meanwhile, the mob outside was running wild. They bombarded the barricaded windows of the theater with cobble-stones gathered from a nearby sewer excavation and ripped down street lamps to use as clubs, plunging the area into darkness.

The police managed to evacuate the building and got Macready out wearing a disguise, but they couldn't contain the rioting. When Edward Judson was arrested, the mob turned even more violent. Officers were stoned to their knees, and the Seventh Regiment was called into action. Even the cavalrymen were knocked off their horses, and the infantry fell back on the sidewalk on the east side of the opera house. When the crowd tried to seize their muskets, the soldiers were ordered to fire, and several volleys tore into the rioters, who fell by the dozens. Twenty-three persons were killed, and the injury list on both sides totaled more than 120.

The mobs returned the following night determined to wreck and burn the opera house, but they were driven off by reinforced troops and artillery, which had been set up to sweep Broadway and the Bowery. For several days thereafter, crowds gathered in front of the New York Hotel, where Macready had been staying, calling on him to come out and be hanged. However, the actor had rushed to New Rochelle on May 10 and gone on by train to Boston, where he sailed for England, never to return to America.

For his part in fomenting the trouble, Edward Judson was fined $250 and sentenced to a year in the penitentiary. Rynders also was tried for inciting to riot. At the farcical trial, prosecution witnesses retraced the genesis of the plot back to Rynder's Empire Club, where the original plotting had been done, but they could not recall anything involving him directly. The jury acquitted Rynders in two hours and 10 minutes.

Aurora, Nevada   lawless mining town

As far as gold-mining towns went, Aurora, Nev. may not have been much more violent than others, but because accurate records were kept in Aurora, statistics offer considerable evidence on how wild the West really was. Founded in 1860, Aurora's heyday lasted only four years and then the gold seams ran out, but in that time, it managed to bury exactly 65 persons in its graveyard. Half were described as the victims of gunshot, and the rest expired of such afflictions as knife wounds, mining mishaps and "accidents." Aurora lasted another 90 years as a ghost town; the last of its buildings were vandalized in the 1950s.

B

Baca, Elfego (1865–1945) gunfighter and lawman
In his native New Mexico Territory, Baca, at 19, was the chief participant and main target of one of the truly memorable gun battles of the frontier West. At the time, Frisco, a town in western New Mexico, was constantly being terrorized by cowboys from the Slaughter spread. Among other things the cowhands castrated a Mexican for a prank and then used another man for target practice when he tried to intervene. These stories were told to Baca by his brother-in-law, who was deputy sheriff of Frisco.

Enraged, Baca put on his brother-in-law's badge and on November 30, 1884 headed for Frisco. He found the town living in terror and being constantly shot up by cowboys. When one of them shot Baca's hat off, the self-appointed deputy promptly arrested him. The next day 80 cowboys descended on Frisco to get the "dirty little Mex." Baca placed all the women and children in the church and prepared to meet his attackers in an ancient adobe hut. The gunplay started at 9 A.M. and continued for 36 hours, during which time an estimated 4,000 bullets were poured into the shack. The plucky Baca killed four of his assailants, wounded eight others and came through the battle unscathed. When two regular lawmen appeared, the remaining cowboys retreated and Baca was placed under arrest. Baca was tried twice in connection with the great shoot-out, but even in the Anglo courts, he was found innocent. A hero to his people, Baca was later elected sheriff of Socorro County and enjoyed a political career of 50 years.

Badman from Bodie western bogeyman
During the last three decades of the 19th century, western mothers would scare their mischievous children into line by invoking the specter of the "Badman from Bodie," who had to have a victim every day. Unlike the more traditional bogeyman, the Badman from Bodie was rooted in reality. Bodie, Calif. was one of the West's most lawless towns reportedly averaging at least one killing a day for 20 years. Even if that estimation was somewhat off, threatening nasty children with the Badman from Bodie was

apparently an effective instrument of parental control.

See also: BODIE, CALIFORNIA.

Baker, Rosetta (1866–1930) murder victim

Few murder trial verdicts were ever based so much on racial stereotypes as that in the Rosetta Baker case, although this was one of the few times the decision went in favor of a member of a minority.

A wealthy San Francisco widow in her sixties, the woman was found dead by her Chinese houseboy, Liu Fook. In the course of their investigation, detectives zeroed in on Liu Fook, who was about the same age as the victim, as the only logical suspect. Witnesses revealed that Liu Fook and his "boss missy" had quarreled often, and on the day of the murder, he had scratches on his face and an injured finger—as though it had been bitten. In addition to that, a broken heel and a shirt button found on the floor beside the body belonged to the houseboy.

In spite of this and still more incriminating evidence, the jury at Liu Fook's trial in 1931 acquitted him. Some of the jurors said they had simply been swayed by the defense lawyer's repeated insistence that Liu Fook could not have been guilty because no Chinese employed in this country had ever murdered his employer. Immediately after the trial, Liu Fook took a fast boat for Hong Kong.

Banditti of the Plains, The book

Probably the most explosive book ever to come out of the West, *The Banditti of the Plains* by Asa C. Mercer was a hard-hitting account of the brutal Johnson County War in 1892 between cattlemen and homesteaders.

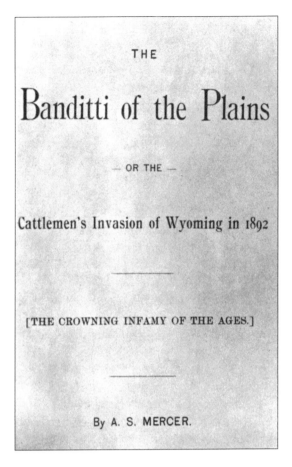

THE

Banditti of the Plains

— OR THE —

Cattlemen's Invasion of Wyoming in 1892

[THE CROWNING INFAMY OF THE AGES.]

By A. S. MERCER.

Title page of *The Banditti of the Plains*, which charged some of Wyoming's greatest cattlemen with mass murder. The book was ruthlessly suppressed and even the copy at the Library of Congress vanished.

Mercer, born in 1839, was a longtime editor, author and lawmaker on the frontier. In *Banditti* he placed the blame for the war on some of the richest and most powerful cattlemen of Wyoming, various state officials and even President Benjamin Harrison, whom he accused of being in sympathy with the stockmen. He charged that many important men—naming names and supplying details—

were guilty of a long list of crimes from bribery to genocide.

The book itself had a most violent life from the time it appeared in the winter of 1893. It was ruthlessly suppressed and its plates were destroyed. Copies of the book were burned and even the one in the Library of Congress disappeared. At one point, Mercer was jailed for a time for sending "obscene matter" through the mails. Somehow a few copies survived over the years, and in 1954 the University of Oklahoma Press reprinted the book. Thanks to that printing, it can be found today in many libraries. The motion picture *Shane* has been described as being "straight out of *The Banditti of the Plains*."

As for Mercer, he wrote other books and pamphlets but nothing as potent as *Banditti*. He died in relative obscurity in 1917.

See also: JOHNSON COUNTY WAR.

bank robberies—bounties

In 1928 a strange invitation to murder was unwittingly issued by a group dedicated to the prevention of crime. At the time, Texas was being plagued by a rash of bank robberies that law enforcement officials were unable to solve. Finally, the state's desperate bankers came up with what was thought to be the perfect deterrent. The Texas Bankers Association had printed and posted in every bank in the state a notice that read:

REWARD
$5,000 for Dead Bank Robbers
Not One Cent For Live Ones

In short order, several bank robbers turned up very dead and rewards were paid out to the local lawmen who brought in the bodies in what was very much a throwback to the bounty system of the Old West. The bankers were happy, and the lawmen were happy. But a Texas Ranger named Frank Hamer, who was to win fame later as the stalker and killer of outlaws Bonnie Parker and Clyde Barrow, was unhappy. Hamer wondered why all the bank robbers had been killed late at night. He also wondered why local lawmen were making all the kills rather than Texas Rangers or U.S. marshals, both of whom had a fairly good record of bringing bank robbers to justice.

Hamer dug into the background of a number of cases and found the "bank robbers" were types such as loners, town bums, drifters passing through or young men who had been drunk earlier in the evening of their demise. The ranger unearthed evidence that these so-called bank robbers had been framed and murdered by crooked lawmen who then collected the rewards. It soon became apparent that there were "murder rings" at work collecting the rewards. When Hamer went to law enforcement officials with his findings, he met with stubborn disbelief. He tried appealing to the Texas Bankers Association for a withdrawal of the reward system. Again, he was rebuffed.

Hamer took his findings to the leading newspapers of the state, including an accusation that the bankers were "bringing about the execution of men by illegal means and for money." The ensuing headlines broke the scandal wide open and led to a grand jury investigation that handed down indictments against two men accused of being the leaders of one of the several murder rings. Hamer arrested them and they subsequently confessed. Only then did the bankers admit their scheme had caused the death of innocent men; the terms of the reward offer were changed to require positive proof that a bank robbery had taken place.

Barbe, Warren Gilbert (?–1925) murder victim

To his neighbors in Berkeley, Calif., Charles Henry Schwartz was a remarkable individual. He was a master chemist and during World War I he'd been a spy in Germany for the Allies. After the war he'd taken an important post in a German chemical plant, where he had discovered a process for the manufacture of artificial silk. He smuggled the process into the United States and set up a hush-hush experimental laboratory, in which he often worked into the night. It sounded impressive, but it was all hogwash. Least of all was he a master chemist. But Schwartz found plenty of people willing to give him money in exchange for a piece of the process. When he produced no silk, however, some of his backers started to grumble and talk of fraud.

In 1925 Schwartz began to take an avid interest in a different science—human anatomy. He cultivated a friendship with a traveling evangelist named Warren Gilbert Barbe. Although the facial features of the two men were very dissimilar, they were of the same overall size. Late in July, Barbe disappeared from his usual haunts, but no one gave it a thought. He most likely got the "call" and had "gone into the wilderness" to preach. Meanwhile, Schwartz was very busy in his laboratory. He said he was almost finished with his process and he worried that some international cartel might try to stop his work. He took out a $200,000 insurance policy on his life and allowed no one to enter the laboratory.

In the lab he was very busy altering the dead evangelist into a stand-in corpse for himself. He burned away a section of the corpse's chest because he had a scar in his own chest. He pulled out two teeth from the upper jaw to match his own dental characteristics. He punctured the eyeballs to solve the problem of different color eyes. But all these he regarded as extra precautions, since he planned to blow up his laboratory in order to really make the corpse unidentifiable. In fact, he believed the entire building would be destroyed in the explosion. He soaked the laboratory with several gallons of benzol which, when detonated, would take care of the building and the evidence. Schwartz set up a timing device and left. He couldn't afford to be seen at the site of the explosion. But he stayed close enough to hear the clanging fire trucks approaching as he stepped into a taxi.

Hiding out in Oakland, Schwartz was shocked to discover he was wanted for murder. The body, hardly singed, had been identified. Even three religious pamphlets bearing Barbe's name had survived the blaze. An incompetent chemist, Schwartz didn't realize that benzol fumes rise very slowly. Several more minutes would have been needed to set off the fire properly. A flop as a chemist, an anatomist and a murderer, Schwartz did better in his final endeavor: suicide.

See also: INSURANCE FRAUDS—FAKED DEATHS.

Barrie, Peter Christian "Paddy" (1888–1935) horse race fixer

Without doubt the most successful horse race fixer in the United States was Paddy Barrie, a skilled "dyer" who applied his handiwork to swindle bettors out of some $6 million from 1926 to 1934.

Barrie's system was perhaps the simplest ever used to fix races. He would buy two horses, one with a very good record and the other a "dog." Then he would "repaint" the fast horse to look like the slow one and enter it in a race under the latter's name. Based on the past performance record of the slow horse, the ringer would generally command odds of 50 to one or even more; because it really outclassed its opponents, the horse would usually win the race easily. Using stencils, bleaches, special dyes and dental instruments, Barrie changed the identity of a champion horse, Aknahton, and ran it under three less-distinguished names at four tracks—Havre de Grace, Agua Caliente, Bowie and Hialeah. The horse made five killings for a gambling syndicate Barrie was working with. It was a feat that led the gamblers to call him "Rembrandt."

The Pinkerton Detective Agency finally unmasked Barrie following an investigation that was started after a leader in the betting syndicate, Nate Raymond, made a drunken spectacle of himself in Broadway clubs and was heard bragging about a "bagged race" worked by an "artist" from England named Paddy. The Pinkertons queried Scotland Yard and learned that a master dyer named Paddy Barrie had disappeared from the British Isles some years previous. An alert went out for Barrie, but he managed to elude capture for another two years by doing the same thing to himself that he did to horses, adopting disguises and changing his name frequently. One day a Pinkerton operative recognized him at Saratoga race track in New York, and he was bundled off to jail.

Oddly, the laws on horse race gambling and fixing were rather lax and Barrie appeared to have broken no law other than having entered the United States illegally. He was deported back to his native Scotland, where he died less than six month later of a "broken heart," according to a sensational British tabloid, due to constant surveillance aimed at guaranteeing he would never be able to ring another horse.

Because of Barrie's depredations, American tracks adopted such precautions as lip tattoos and other methods of identification to make the ringing in of other horses almost impossible. However, since foreign horses have not been so identified they have been used as ringers in recent years. The disclosure of such fixes has led to close checks on the identification of foreign horses.

Barter, Rattlesnake Dick (1834–1859)
stagecoach robber

Few criminal reputations in the Old West were more enhanced by the Eastern writers whose flowery prose graced the pages of such 19th-century publications as *New York Weekly, Harper's Monthly* and the torrent of dime novels and paperbacks than Rattlesnake Dick's.

The real-life Rattlesnake Dick Barter was more wooly than wild and, alas, hardly an archbadman of the West. Barter was, on the whole, quite incompetent. According to the legend-makers, he was named Rattlesnake Dick because he was so dangerous and devious. No doubt the fact that he was an Englishman operating outside the American law was enough to give him a certain romantic aura. However, Rattlesnake Dick was downright prosaic in comparison with many native American badmen of the period. The real story behind his name was that he had prospected for a short time at Rattlesnake Bar in the Northern Mines area of California. Rattlesnake Dick soon decided, however, that it was easier to steal gold than to dig for it. Here the legend-makers were right, although they failed to note that Rattlesnake Dick had never made a dime at his digs. In 1856, after some small-time stage holdups, Barter hit on what was to prove the most brilliant and, at the same time, most comic criminal scheme of his career. To give him credit due, he masterminded the $80,000 robbery of the Yreka Mine's mule train and managed to organize a gang for that purpose. Rattlesnake Dick did not take part in the actual robbery, which was left to George Skinner and some others, possibly explaining why that part of the scheme worked so well. The Yreka Mine mule train had been regarded as immune from robbers because the mules would always tire out halfway down the mountains and thus make pursuit too easy. Rattlesnake Dick's plan called for him and George Skinner's brother, Cyrus, to meet the robbers on the mountain trail with fresh mules. Clever though the plan was, it left the execution of this phase to Rattlesnake Dick. When George Skinner and his gunmen reached the rendezvous point, there was not a fresh mule in sight. It developed that Rattlesnake Dick and Cy Skinner were already in jail. They had been caught, drunk, trying to steal some mules.

Under the circumstances all George Skinner could think to do was bury most of the stolen gold nuggets and then head off with his crew for some high living over at Folsom. That's where Wells Fargo agents caught up with them. George Skinner was shot dead while in bed with a screaming prostitute and the rest of the gang was similarly liquidated. But with them died the secret of where the stolen gold was buried. Shortly thereafter, Rattlesnake Dick and Cy Skinner broke jail by walking out an open door and went looking for the buried loot. Following an unsuccessful search for it, the pair returned to the stagecoach-robbing

business. After some of their hold-ups netted the pair less than $20, Cy Skinner decided he had had enough of the criminal genius of Rattlesnake Dick and went his separate way. Barter continued his bush-league hold-ups until he was shot and killed by a pursuing posse in July 1859. But the legend of Rattlesnake Dick as California's worst bandit between the eras of Murieta and Vasquez lives on, enhanced by the fact that today treasure hunters still scour the California hills for Dick's buried gold.

Bass, Sam (1851–1878) outlaw

Sam Bass was born in Indiana, it was his native home;
At the age of seventeen young Sam began to roam.
Sam first came out to Texas, a cowboy for to be—
A kinder-hearted fellow you seldom ever see.

From "The Ballad of Sam Bass"

Kinder-hearted or not, Sam Bass was an outlaw. While he "came out of Texas, a cowboy for to be," young Bass found life dull and soon opted for crime. He and two other characters, Joel Collins and Jack Davies, went in for some "easy rustling," taking on 500 cattle on consignment, driving them to market in Kansas in 1876 and then neglecting to settle up with the Texas ranchers who had hired them. With their loot as capital, the trio became pimps and opened a whorehouse in Deadwood, Dakota Territory, a place described as "the most degraded den of infamy that ever cursed the Earth." With that sort or recommendation, the brothel did a thriving business. Nonetheless, Bass, Collins and Davies drank and gambled away their income faster than their prostitutes could

Photograph shows outlaw Sam Bass (center), although its authenticity has been disputed.

make it, so the trio and three of their best bordello customers, Bill Heffridge, Jim Berry and Tom Nixon, formed an outlaw gang and held up a number of stagecoaches. On September 19, 1877 the gang made a big score, robbing a Union Pacific train of $60,000.

With a $10,000 stake, Bass returned to Denton County, Tex. and started a new gang, becoming a folk hero in the process. While he was not exactly a Robin Hood, Bass was loose with the money he stole and if there was one way for a gunman to become popular in Texas, it was for him to be a free spender. For a time, Bass proved to be a real will-o'-the-wisp, impossible for the law to corner and remarkably skillful at extracting hospitality from Texans who looked upon him with affection. As the reward money

mounted, however, Bass became a marked man. Finally, one of his own band, Jim Murphy, whose family often gave Bass refuge on their ranch, betrayed him by informing the law that the gang planned a bank robbery in Round Rock. While Murphy ducked for shelter, ambushers killed an outlaw named Seaborn Barnes and shot Sam Bass off his horse. Another outlaw, Frank Jackson, rode back through a fusillade of fire to rescue Bass and carry him out of town.

Bass was found by pursuers the next day; he was lying under a tree, near death. While he clung to life, Texas Rangers questioned him about his accomplices and the location of the loot he was believed to have buried. Bass would not respond, saying only: "Let me go. The world is bobbing around." He died on his 27th birthday. Some treasure hunters still search for the Bass loot, although it is more than likely that the dying Bass told Jackson where to find it. The "Ballad of Sam Bass" is still a Texas favorite, and the outlaw's grave at Round Rock remains an attraction.

Bassity, Jerome (1870?–1929) whoremaster
During the long history of prostitution in San Francisco's Barbary Coast, Jerome Bassity stands out as perhaps the owner of more brothels than any other single person in that city. Although he was described by the press as being a "study in depravity" with an intelligence only slightly higher than that of a chimpanzee, Bassity was the veritable lord of the red-light district. In the heyday of the corrupt Ruef machine, especially during the three terms of Mayor Eugene Schmitz from 1901 to 1907, Bassity, whose real name was said to be Jere McGlane, was far and away the most potent figure in the San Francisco underworld.

The newspaper singled him out for special condemnation. The *San Francisco Bulletin* invited its readers to "look at the low, cunning lights in the small, rapacious, vulture-like eyes; look at that low, dull-comprehending brow; the small sensual mouth; the soft puffy fingers with the weak thumb, indicating how he seeks ever his own comfort before others, how his will works only in fits and starts." Despite such publicity, Bassity operated with little or no restraint, from about the turn of the century until 1916, save for two years— 1907 to 1909—during a reform administration. In 1909 Mayor P. H. McCarthy took office on a platform designed to "make San Francisco the Paris of America." Bassity aided that cause by operating a 100-cubicle brothel called the Parisian Mansion. While McCarthy was in office it was openly acknowledged that the city was really ruled by a triumvirate: the mayor, police commissioner and bar owner Harry P. Flannery, and Bassity.

In addition to his brothels, Bassity owned dance halls and other dives, including a notorious Market Street deadfall called the Haymarket that even the streetwalkers refused to enter. Bassity had an interest in the income of at least 200 prostitutes and his own income was estimated to be around $10,000 a month, no trifling sum for the period. A dandy dresser and "diamond ring stud," Bassity reportedly went to bed with a diamond ring on each of his big toes. In his own brothels he claimed and exercised his seigniorial rights whenever a young girl or virgin arrived, but by and large, Bassity patronized his competitors' establishments. His patronage practically amounted to sabotage since he was generally drunk, always armed and frequently concluded a night of debauchery by shooting out the lights or seeing how close he could fire shots to the harlots' toes.

Bassity bragged that he squandered most of his income on clothes, jewelry and debauchery, but he predicted the flow of money would never end. In 1916, foreseeing the success of reform efforts to shut down the Barbary Coast, Bassity retired from the sex racket and headed for Mexico, where he unsuccessfully attempted a takeover of the Tijuana race track. He was later charged but not prosecuted for a swindle in California. When he died in 1929, after what was described as "California's most sinful life," he left an estate of less than $10,000.

Bath, Michigan   school bombing

One of the most hideous crimes ever committed in America was the slaying of 37 schoolchildren in 1927 by Andrew Kehoe, the mad bomber of Bath, Mich.

The background to the case was pieced together by the police after the fact, because Kehoe himself did not survive the crime. Kehoe was a farmer, but not a very successful one, barely scraping by even in boom years. When the community of Bath decided to build a new schoolhouse, property owners were assessed a special levy. Kehoe's tax bite came to $300. After he paid up, he no longer could meet his mortgage and faced imminent loss of his house. "It's that school tax," he would tell anyone who would listen. "If it hadn't been for the $300 I had to pay, I'd have the money. That school never should have been built."

Kehoe feuded with school board officials, accusing them of squandering the taxpayers' money. He started telling people he'd have his revenge for that. Night after night Kehoe would be seen near the school. It turned out that he was sneaking in the building and spending hours planting dynamite in safe hiding places.

At 9:43 A.M. on May 18, 1927, the whole building shook. The second floor of the north wing rose in the air and came down, crushing the first floor in an avalanche of battered wreckage. In all, 37 schoolchildren and one teacher died, and some 43 others were very seriously injured.

The explosion brought the townspeople running, while Andy Kehoe sat and watched the whole horrible scene from his parked car. Among the rescuers was the head of the school board, heroically risking his life to bring injured children out of the tottering wreckage. He kept at it until Kehoe beckoned him over to his car. Andy Kehoe still had one more murder card to play. As the school official placed his foot on the running board of the car, Kehoe turned a switch and a violent explosion killed the last two victims of the mad bomber of Bath.

Beadle, William (?–1782) murderer

As a murderer, Wethersfield, Conn.'s William Beadle achieved lasting local notoriety not only because of the horrendous nature of his crime but also because of the way he kept coming back to remind local residents of what he'd done. It appeared later that William had planned to wipe out his family—his wife and five children, aged six to 11—for some time. Finally, one night as they slept, he crept upstairs, struck each in the head with an ax and then cut their throats. After this bloodletting, Beadle returned to the kitchen downstairs and sat in a chair at the table. He picked up two pistols, placed one in each ear and pulled both triggers at the same time. The victims were all buried in the town cemetery, but the townspeople had to decide what to do with Beadle. They determined he should be buried secretly and a grave was dug in the frozen December ground down by the river. However, an overflow the following spring disinterred the body. Beadle was again buried secretly, but this time a dog dug up the corpse. Finally, on the third try, the murderer's body stayed buried.

Bean, Roy (c. 1825–1902) saloonkeeper and judge

Billing himself as the "law west of the Pecos," Roy Bean of Texas was without question the most unusual and colorful jurist ever to hold court in America. Bean dispensed justice between poker hands in his saloon-courtroom. He would open a proceeding by declaring: "Hear Ye! Hear Ye! This honorable court's now in session and if any galoot wants a snort before we start, let him step up and name his pizen."

A native of Kentucky, Bean had been a trader, bartender and Confederate guerrilla during the Civil War. (He organized the Free Rovers in the New Mexico Territory, which local residents soon began calling the Forty Thieves, an indication of how much of the booty went to the Confederate cause.) In his late fifties, fat, bewhiskered and whiskey sodden, Bean ambled into the tent town of Vinegaroon in 1882 and got himself appointed justice of the peace, perhaps because he had a copy of the 1879 *Revised Statutes of Texas*. When the road gangs moved on from Vinegaroon, Bean went to Langtry, a stopover point on the Southern Pacific. Here Bean, first by appointment and then by elections held in his saloon, was to dispense his bizarre justice for 20 years.

Judge Bean had all sorts of profitable lines. He got $5 a head officiating at inquests, $2 performing marriages and $5 granting divorces. When higher-ups informed him he did not have the authority to divorce people, he was unimpressed. "Well, I married 'em, so I guess I got a right to un-marry 'em if it don't take." When a railroad man with a good record, meaning he was a regular paying customer at Bean's saloon, was hauled in for killing a Chinese laborer, the judge leafed through his dog-eared legal guide and then released the prisoner, ruling, "There ain't a damn line here nowheres that makes it illegal to kill a Chinaman." And when another friend of the judge was charged with shooting a Mexican, Bean's finding was that "it served the deceased right for getting in front of a gun."

Having himself appeared in other courts on occasion, Bean knew that judges from time to time made very flowery speeches, and he endeavored to do the same, adding a flourish or two of his own. Passing sentence on a cattle rustler once, he intoned:

You have been tried by 12 good men and true, not of your peers but as high above you as heaven is of hell, and they have said you are guilty. Time will pass and seasons will come and go. Spring with its wavin' green grass and heaps of sweet-smellin' flowers on every hill and in every dale. Then sultry Summer, with her shimmerin' heat-waves on the baked hori-zon. And Fall, with her yeller harvest moon and the hills growin' brown and golden under a sinkin' sun. And finally Winter, with its bitin', whinin' wind, and all the land will be mantled with snow. But you won't be here to see any of 'em; not by a damn sight, because it's the order of this court that you be took to the nearest tree and hanged by the neck till you're dead, dead, dead, you olive-colored son of a billy goat.

In 1896 a lamentable oversight occurred in Bean's reelection campaign. He ended up with more votes than there were eligible vot-ers, and as a result, the authorities awarded the office to his hated opponent, Jesus P. Tor-res. Bean was undaunted by this develop-ment and continued to handle cases that originated on his side of town. He died in 1902, a victim of his own rum as much as old age.

See also: BENEDICT'S SENTENCE.

Beckett sisters   white slave kidnap victims

During the early 1800s, no kidnapping of young girls by the infamous Mississippi River procurers excited the American public as much as that of two teenage sisters, Rose and Mary Beckett of St. Louis, who were abducted by the notorious Sam Purdy gang.

It was the custom of these river procurers to buy up young girls from their impover-ished parents and transport them down the Mississippi by flatboat to Natchez, where they were sold at auction to whoremasters from various Southern cities. Only when they could not find enough willing girls available to be "sold down the river"—hence the ori-gin of the phrase—did the procurers go in for actual kidnapping. Such was the fate of the Beckett girls, who wound up at Natchez in early 1805 and were sold off after spirited bidding by various bordello keepers and "floating hog pen" operators. The girls were sold as a set for $400 to the proprietor of a notorious New Orleans establishment called The Swamp.

Here the girls were incarcerated, and here they would have remained had it not been for a reformer named Carlos White, who had tracked the Purdy gang from St. Louis and scoured the New Orleans fleshpots for the Beckett sisters. A man of action, White used force to rescue the two sisters from The Swamp, shooting one of their guards to death and pistol-whipping another while the girls climbed out a window and escaped.

White eventually reunited the pair with their parents and, unlike the fate of most "ruined girls," the Beckett sisters became famous heroines of the day.

Beidler, John X. (1831–1890) Montana vigilante hangman

In the 1860s John Beidler's "long rope" became the terror of Montana's badmen, and Beidler became known as the most zealous vigilante that ever looped a noose. In one six-week period 26 outlaws were hanged, and Beidler's rope did the job in every case.

Beidler, a plump, walrus-faced man, was born in Montjoy, Pa. of German stock. Even to his friends in the West, he was known as a rather joyless person. Some biographers are unsure how much of Beidler's appetite for hanging sprang from a respect for law and order and how much from a morbid pleasure in hanging people. But whatever else was said about Beidler, he was certainly brave enough in taking credit for his acts. He never wore a mask, as did so many other vigilantes. If some of the "boys" ever wanted to get even with him, they knew where to find him.

Beidler's first vigilante act took place in Kansas, where, as the head of a posse, he disabled a gang of lawbreakers by firing a howitzer loaded with printer's type at them. In contradiction to the general description of his somberness, Beidler said, as the victims painfully dug the type slugs out of their bodies, that he saw no need for a necktie party, pointing out they could become good citizens now that "they have the opportunity to learn to read." A few years later, in the Alder Gulch–Bannack area of lawless Montana, Beidler came to the fore as the hanging vigilante. His victims included all the important badmen in the area. Beidler's style was casual in most cases: a handy tree limb or corral gate, the noose tightened and a box kicked out from under the victim's feet. With the coming of more organized law and order, the need for Beidler's long rope ended, and he became a businessman and saloon keeper, later serving as collector of customs for Idaho and Montana. He held that post until his death on January 22, 1890 in Helena.

Bell, Tom (1825–1856) outlaw doctor

Known as the Outlaw Doc, Tom Bell, whose real name was Thomas J. Hodges, is believed to have been the only physician to ride the western bandit trail. On a criminal job he would carry as many implements as a doctor would carry on a house visit, in one case totaling up to six revolvers and a like number of knives and, presumably because of his superior medical knowledge, a chest protector fashioned from sheet iron.

Born in Rome, Tenn., Bell took part in the Mexican War. During that period he was trained as a doctor and emerged as a fully qualified practitioner. Bell followed the '49ers to California in search of gold but came up empty. He supported himself by gambling at cards, now and then taking time out to treat a gunshot victim. Exactly how or why he turned to crime is not known, but in 1855 he was doing time for theft in Angel Island Prison. There he befriended a vicious criminal named Bill Gristy, and within a matter of weeks the pair engineered an escape. The two then organized their own outlaw gang with five other hard cases and began pulling stage holdups.

On August 12, 1856 Bell and his confederates attempted to hold up the Camptonville-Marysville stage, which had $100,000 in gold bullion aboard. They killed a woman passenger and wounded two men but were beaten back by the stage's shotgun guards who killed two of them. The murder of the woman passenger sparked a huge manhunt for the bandits. There were legal posses under assorted lawmen and illegal posses of vigilantes who vowed to reach the killers first and mete out fast western justice. By the end of September, Gristy had been arrested and, under threat of being handed over to a lynch mob, had turned stoolpigeon in his jail cell, identifying Doc Bell as the main culprit. The official and unofficial posses were quickly back on the trail in a race to locate Bell first. The sheriff of Stockton came in a close second. He found Doc on October 4, 1856 dangling from a tree on the Nevada City road.

Benedict's Sentence   judge's speech

Probably the most famous judicial speech ever made in the Old West was the death sentence pronounced by Judge Kirby Benedict and referred to with solemn awe as Benedict's Sentence.

Benedict was an extremely learned man who was appointed to the Supreme Court of New Mexico by President Franklin Pierce in 1853. Previously, he had spent all his adult life in Illinois, where he was a highly regarded member of the bar and a friend of both Abraham Lincoln and Stephen A. Douglas. On the New Mexico bench, Benedict handed down several opinions that are often cited as examples of fine judicial writing, but he is unquestionably best remembered for his sentencing in Taos of Jose Maria Martin. Martin had been convicted of a particularly heinous murder, a verdict with which Benedict fully concurred. Judge Benedict addressed the prisoner as follows:

Jose Maria Martin, stand up. Jose Maria Martin, you have been indicted, tried and convicted, by a jury of your countrymen, of the crime of murder, and the Court is now about to pass upon you the dread sentence of the law. As a usual thing, Jose Maria Martin, it is a painful duty for the Judge of a court of justice to pronounce upon a human being the sentence of death. There is something horrible about it, and the mind of the Court naturally revolts at the performance of such a duty. Happily, however, your case is relieved of all such unpleasant features and the Court takes the positive pleasure in sentencing you to death!

You are a young man, Jose Maria Martin; apparently of good physical condition and robust health. Ordinarily, you might have looked forward to many years of life, and the Court has no doubt you have, and have expected to die at a green old age; but you are about to be cut off in consequence of your own act. Jose Maria Martin, it is now the springtime, in a little while the grass will be springing up green in these beautiful valleys, and, on these broad mesas and mountain sides, flowers will be blooming; birds will be singing their sweet carols, and nature will be pleasant and men will want to stay; but none of this for you, Jose Maria Martin; the flowers will not bloom for you, Jose Maria Martin; the birds will not carol for you, Jose Maria Martin; when these things come to gladden the senses of men, you will be occupying a space about six feet by two beneath the sod, and the green grass and those beautiful flowers will be growing about your lowly head.

The sentence of the Court is that you be taken from this place to the county jail; that you be kept there safely and securely confined, in the custody of the sheriff, until the day appointed for your execution. (Be very care-

ful, Mr. Sheriff, that he have no opportunity to escape and that you have him at the appointed place at the appointed time); that you be so kept, Jose Maria Martin until—(Mr. Clerk, on what day of the month does Friday about two weeks from this time come? "March 22nd, your honor.") Very well, until Friday, the 22nd day of March, when you will be taken by the sheriff from your place of confinement to some safe and convenient spot within the county (that is in your discretion, Mr. Sheriff, you are only confined to the limits of this county), and that you there be hanged by the neck until you are dead, and the Court was about to add, Jose Maria Martin, 'May God have mercy on your soul,' but the Court will not assume the responsibility of asking an all-wise Providence to do that which a jury of your peers has refused to do. The Lord couldn't have mercy on your soul. However, if you affect any religious belief, or are connected with any religious organization, it might be well for you to send for your priest or minister, and get from him—well—such consolation as you can, but the Court advises you to place no reliance upon anything of that kind! Mr. Sheriff, remove the prisoner.

The only footnote to Judge Benedict's sentence was that Jose Maria Martin did escape and never paid the supreme penalty.

See also: ROY BEAN.

Berman, Otto "Abbadabba" (1889–1935)
policy game fixer

Few rackets have ever produced as much money for underworld coffers as the numbers game, and although the profit slice is 40 percent or more, crime bosses have always searched for ways to give the suckers even less of a break.

Otto "Abbadabba" Berman was for a time a magician at this, as his nickname indicates. During the 1930s Berman devised a system for rigging the results of the game so that only a lesser-played number would win. He worked for Dutch Schultz, the crime czar who controlled the bulk of the numbers game in New York, including most of the action in black Harlem. At the time, the winning number was derived from the betting statistics at various race tracks. The underworld could not control the figures at the New York tracks, but during the periods when those courses were closed, the number was based on the results from tracks that the underworld had successfully infiltrated, such as New Orleans' Fair Grounds, Chicago's Hawthorne and Cincinnati's Coney Island. Berman was able to figure out how much money to put into the mutual machines to have a low-played number come out. It was estimated that Abbadabba's magic added 10 percent to every million dollars a day the underworld took in.

In 1935 Dutch Schultz was assassinated by vote of the Luciano-Lansky national crime syndicate, allegedly because Schultz had announced he intended to kill Thomas E. Dewey, whose racket-busting activities were hampering underworld operations. Luciano especially was concerned about the ramifications of killing a man of Dewey's stature. His concern, however, was no doubt heightened by the opportunity he saw to take over the Schultz numbers racket. Schultz and three of his favorite underlings were cut down at the Palace Chophouse in Newark while having dinner. Unfortunately for the mob, one of those shot with Schultz was Berman. His loss was to cost the mob literally millions of dollars a year, for while others tried to imitate the technique of what Luciano's aide, Vito Genovese, called "the Yid adding machine," few approached even a fraction of his results.

Bethea, Rainey (1914–1936) last publicly executed man

The last public execution in America was held in 1936. The victim was a 22-year-old black man named Rainey Bethea, and his execution at Owensboro, Ky. remains one of the most shameful episodes in U.S. history.

Because Rainey had killed a 70-year-old white woman, public opinion was at a fever pitch, and the county sheriff, a woman named Florence Thompson, decided to stage the execution in an open field so that thousands of witnesses could be accommodated. By the night before the execution, Owensboro was swamped with visitors from all over the country; by dawn more than 20,000 persons had gathered at the execution site. Only six blacks were present—virtually all the local blacks had fled the town during the previous night's drunken revelry, which was punctuated by calls for a mass lynching. Each time the hangman tested the scaffold, it snapped open to the appreciative cheers of the crowd. Bethea reached the scaffold at 5:12 A.M. and the execution moved briskly, authorities now fearing the crowd might get out of hand. When the bolt snapped, a joyous roar swept over the field and the crowd surged closer. Souvenir hunters almost immediately attacked the dangling, still-warm body, stripping off pieces of the condemned man's clothing and in some instances trying to carve out chunks of flesh. Meanwhile, doctors fought their way through the melee to certify Bethea's death and then cried out that his heart was still beating. The spectators groaned and pulled back, waiting. Bethea was finally pronounced dead at 5:45, and once more the souvenir hunters charged forward, a great scuffle taking place for possession of the death hood.

See also: EXECUTIONS, PUBLIC.

Biddle brothers murderers and death-row escapees

Ed and Jack Biddle escaped from the Allegheny County Jail on January 30, 1902, 16 days before they were to be executed for the killing of a store owner and a police detective. When details of the escape became known, it scandalized Pittsburgh and much of the rest of the country since the escape was engineered by 26-year-old Katherine Scoffel, the warden's wife. She had come to their death cells a month earlier, as was her custom, to try to bring religion to doomed men and had fallen in love with Ed Biddle, eight years her junior. Mrs. Scoffel supplied the brothers with guns and hacksaws and led them to freedom through the warden's home, which had a private entrance to the institution. She had drugged her husband so he would be asleep and made sure their four children were not home at the time.

Two guards were shot superficially and another was overpowered during the breakout; when they were found, the alarm was sounded. The warden, apprised of the facts, notified the police of the Biddle brothers' escape and told them to arrest his wife as an accomplice. Then he wrote a letter of resignation, gathered up his children and left the prison for the last time.

Meanwhile, the three fugitives made it as far as Butler, Pa., switching from the carriage Mrs. Scoffel had secured for them to a stolen sleigh. They were stopped by a seven-man roadblock, and in a furious gun battle 26-year-old Jack Biddle was shot dead. Ed Biddle was hit three times in the lung. As he was dying, Katherine Scoffel begged him to shoot her. He did so, but while Biddle died a few hours after being taken into custody, Mrs. Scoffel survived. When she recovered, she was tried and sentenced to serve two years in the penitentiary of which she had once been the first lady. Asked during her trial how a woman of her standing could love a vicious criminal like Ed Biddle, she said: "I can forgive anything he's done. Except one. I can forgive his killings, his robberies, anything. But I cannot forgive him for failing to kill me so that I could be with him forever in death."

Katherine Scoffel was released from prison in 18 months and lived until 1926, ostracized and in disgrace. Often through the years, she would see an advertisement in a newspaper for a performance of a melodrama about the case. It was called *The Biddle Boys* and played to capacity houses for many years.

Biler Avenue Chicago vice district

From the 1870s until the turn of the century, Pacific Avenue, nicknamed Biler Avenue, was "one of the most disreputable streets in the city, built up with hastily constructed tenements which were occupied by the most depraved of men and women, black, white and mixed." Yet it was still held in particular fondness by the reigning political powers. Biler Avenue and its side streets were filled with bordellos of the lowest class and lowest price in the city. A typical establishment was Dan Webster's big groggery and bagnio at Nos. 130–132, which the *Chicago Times* called an "infernal hell hole. There it is that the rottenest, vilest, filthiest strumpets, black and white, reeking with corruption, are bundled together, catering indiscriminately to the lust of all." What made the activities of the establishment most noteworthy was, as the *Times* discovered, that the building was owned by Michael C. Hickey, the superintendent of police. Because of the stir caused by the *Times* exposé, Hickey was hauled before the Police Board for trial, but he was

acquitted of any wrongdoing since there was no way a superintendent of police could possibly have known about the character of his tenants. An even more startling revelation was that an entire block on Harrison Street was the property of Mayor Carter Harrison.

"Our Carter" the *Times* said, "owns the entire block between Clark Street and Pacific Avenue. On the corner of Clark, and running west to the middle of the block, stands a hotel. The other half of the block is occupied by four or five ordinary frame houses. One is used for a lager-beer saloon, another for a restaurant, still another for a tobacco store, a fourth as a hotel on a small scale, and right among these, as snug as a bug, Our Carter has allowed a number of gay damsels to nestle down, and they are rather homely ones at that."

Even that last withering comment was not enough to keep Carter Harrison from becoming a five-term mayor. Biler Avenue thus typified Chicago's tolerance of political venality, an attitude that was to last for many decades.

See also: CARTER HARRISON.

Billee, John (?–1890) western murderer

The idea of bringing in a badman dead or alive was an Old West concept that did not usually apply to deputy federal marshals. For each prisoner brought back, the marshal was paid the sum of $2 plus a mileage allowance of 6¢ per mile going and 10¢ coming back provided he had his man. Out of this sum, the marshal had to pay all his own expenses and feed his prisoner. However, if he lost his prisoner or was forced to kill him, the lawman lost his fee and mileage allowance! The system encouraged marshals to try their best to keep their quarry alive.

A noted case that underscored the point involved John Billee, who killed a man named W. P. Williams in April 1888 and buried the corpse in a ravine in the Kiamichi Mountains. Federal deputies caught up with Billee in a wide sweep during which they also netted four other wanted men. On their way back to Fort Smith, deputies Perry DuVal, Will Ayers and James Wilkerson stopped with their prisoners to spend the night at a deserted two-room cabin outside Muskogee, Okla. in Indian Territory.

Deputy Ayers, with three prisoners chained to him, bedded down in the front room along with Deputy DuVal, who had Billee in tow. Deputy Wilkerson and the fifth prisoner slept in the small rear room of the cabin. About 3 A.M. Billee worked out of one of his handcuffs and managed to reach DuVal's revolver. He fired but in the darkness only succeeded in wounding DuVal in the head. He then turned the gun on Ayers before the deputy had a chance to react out of his sleep, shooting him in the right nipple. Meanwhile Wilkerson had rolled over into a sitting position in the doorway of the next room and Billee put a shot into his back. Ayers then lunged at the outlaw and battled Billee to keep him from getting off another shot. While this was going on, Wilkerson leveled his own gun and aimed carefully at the outlaw, trying to get off an incapacitating, rather than a fatal, shot, which he did. By keeping Billee alive long enough for him to meet his doom on the gallows at Fort Smith on January 16, 1890, the three wounded deputies were able to collect their fee for the outlaw.

Billy the Kid (1859–1881) outlaw

There has probably been more written about Billy the Kid than any other outlaw, which

Famous "flopped," i.e., reversed, portrait of Billy the Kid started the legend that he was left-handed.

perhaps explains why so little of his true story can be accurately reconstructed.

Hyperbole has been added to lies until we are left with a portrait of a young outlaw said to have killed 21 men during his 21 years. The number is an exaggeration. He did not kill a man at the age of 12 for insulting his mother as is often stated. Probably the first man the New York–born youngster— whose real name is believed to have been either William Bonney or Henry McCarty— killed was a bully named Frank "Windy" Cahill, who had called him a "pimp and a son of a bitch." Billy gunned him down on the spot. He was arrested but almost immediately escaped from jail. In fact, he frequently escaped from jails, which probably helped to give him a romantic air. There was certainly nothing romantic about his looks. He was small, with prominent front teeth and a short, fuzzy upper lip, almost a harelip, which gave him a perpetual smile. He smiled when he killed and his smile made him look pathological, which he probably was. One moment he was good natured and the next he displayed an explosive temper.

Beginning in his early teens, Billy supported himself by gambling and, when the cards ran wrong, by stealing anything from clothes to cattle. After his mother died in 1874, Billy was completely on his own. Following the Cahill killing and a few others, according to some historians, Billy hired out as a cowboy to an English gentleman rancher, John Tunstall. It was a smart move by Tunstall since Billy had been stealing his stock. Billy looked upon the Englishman as a father figure, even though Tunstall was only five or six years older. Tunstall, on the other hand, said he saw good in Billy and was determined to make a man out of him. When the Lincoln County War for much of the New Mexico Territory backcountry and the Pecos Valley broke out soon afterwards, Tunstall became a leading figure on one side. Allied with Alexander McSween and cattle king John Chisum against the business interests of the county dominated by Lawrence G. Murphy, James J. Dolan and James H. Riley,

Tunstall turned out to be the first major casualty, shot down in February 1878 by gunmen supposedly deputized to arrest him on a trumped up charge.

Billy saw the killing from a distance but could do nothing about it. He was deeply affected by Tunstall's murder. "He was the only man that ever treated me like I was free-born and white," he said. Over Tunstall's grave he swore, "I'll get every son-of-a-bitch who helped kill John if it's the last thing I do."

With that pledge Billy the Kid became the chief killer of the Lincoln County War, lining up with McSween. When the opposing forces besieged the town of Lincoln for several days, Billy killed numerous enemies. McSween was murdered during the siege and his death ended the war, as Chisum saw he lacked the power to win by himself. Billy the Kid went back to rustling and organized a gang of gunfighters and cutthroats. He robbed Chisum's cattle as well as others'. Eventually, Gov. Lew Wallace offered an amnesty to all participants in the Lincoln County War, and for a time, Billy considered accepting it. But he was leery of the "formality" of the trial he would have to face and stayed on the loose. He permanently lost his chance to go straight after killing a lawman.

Billy and his gang killed several more men over the next year or so but suffered their losses as well. Sheriff Pat Garrett stalked Billy and in one ambush killed Billy's close friend Tom O'Folliard, whom he mistook for the Kid. In December 1880 Charlie Bowdre died in an ambush at Stinking Springs, New Mexico Territory. Trapped by Garrett and his posse, Billy and several of his confederates were forced to surrender. Billy was convicted of the murder of Sheriff William Brady and sentenced to hang. Confined in a top-floor room of the Lincoln County Courthouse, he made a sensational

An enthusiastic *Police Gazette* artist was so awed by the Kid's exploits that he awarded him two right hands.

escape, killing deputies James Bell, whom he liked, and sadistic Bob Olinger, whom he hated. He shot Olinger down like a dog in the street outside the courthouse and fled.

Billy was a hero to those who shared his sympathies in the Lincoln County War and to Mexicans, among whom he often hid out.

Finally, Garrett located Billy the Kid hiding at old Fort Sumner. When Billy walked into a darkened room, Garrett shot him down without giving him a chance to surrender. He was buried in a common grave with his two buddies, O'Folliard and Bowdre. The gravestone bore the inscription "Pals."

After Billy the Kid died, the legend-makers went to work. The first book about him appeared three weeks after his death. Most of his biographers probably had never been west of New York. Sheriff Garrett contributed a volume, which greatly built up Billy and in the process, of course, the man who had gotten him. Serious students of Billy the Kid have been mystified by his place in the folklore of the country. His crimes were largely unimaginative and cold blooded. He lacked the verve and style that marked Jesse James, for instance, and seldom inspired the loyalty that James did.

Bird Cage Theatre   Tombstone night spot and "shooting gallery"

One of the more wicked establishments in Tombstone, Ariz. during the 1880s was the Bird Cage Theatre. A performance of *H.M.S. Pinafore* might grace its stage while harlots plied their trade in 12 tiny balcony boxes. An act more in keeping with the place was the appearance of Fatima, who belly-danced to raucous western acclaim in 1882.

The owners of the theater, Bill and Lottie Hutchinson, made it a rule that the audience had to check their shooting irons upon entering, but unfortunately, the regulation was not always obeyed, often with tragic consequences. In one wild shoot-out 12 men were reportedly left dead. Care was required in the selection of the repertoire, since if too evil a villain appeared on the stage, he might soon be forced to dodge lead from outraged members of the audience. There is no accurate record of the numbers of fatalities that occurred in the Bird Cage, but while it never equaled the fabulous Oriental Saloon as a shooting gallery, it certainly provided the setting for a good many death scenes on both sides of the footlights.

Bismarck Hall   New York dive

Of all the vicious establishments that abounded in New York's Bowery in the post–Civil War period, one that had a uniquely Old World flavor was Bismarck Hall. Low physically as well as morally, the Hall had an annex in a string of cavelike rooms buried under the sidewalk where ladies employed in the dive could entertain gentlemen. Following an Old World custom, the operator of the dive supposedly often "bought" his inmates by paying them a small sum of money binding them to him for several years. While such an agreement, of course, would have had little standing in court, its terms were quite well enforced; the girls were not allowed off the premises unless they left a "deposit" that guaranteed their return. Bismarck Hall achieved a measure of renown when Grand Duke Alexis of Russia, visiting it in the 1870s while slumming, or, as the practice was then known, "elephant hunting," recognized a Russian countess who had fallen on hard times and was working there as a "waiter girl." According to the story, he bought the freedom of this unnamed noblewoman and took her back to Russia and her former position of grace.

Black Bart (1830–1917?) stagecoach robber

One of the most colorful, daring and unconventional bandits of the Old West was Charles E. Bolton, better known as Black Bart, the poet laureate of outlawry. By the best count, he pulled 27 stagecoach holdups in California from 1874 to 1883. But he prided himself on never robbing a stagecoach passenger. After each robbery Black Bart would send the coach on its way and then stroll off on foot, since he greatly disliked horses. Wearing a duster and a flour-sack mask and carrying an empty shotgun, he would step out into the road and shout to the stage driver, "Throw down your box or die." Sometimes he would issue orders to his men in the bushes to open fire if the driver refused. The driver would see a half-dozen rifles in the shadows and would do as he was told. Actually, the rifles were never more than broomstick handles. After each holdup Black Bart would leave behind bits of doggerel that won him a reputation as a poet. One typical poem read:

> Here I lay me down to sleep
> To await the coming morrow
> Perhaps success, perhaps defeat
> and everlasting sorrow
>
> I've labored long and hard for bred [sic]
> For honor and for riches
> But on my corns too long you've tred
> You fine-haired Sons of Bitches
>
> Let come what will, I'll try it on
> My condition can't be worse
> And if there's money in that box
> 'Tis munny in my purse.
> Black Bart, the Po-8.

Black Bart was captured on November 3, 1883, after a robbery that had netted him $4,800. A rider came by during the robbery and fired at the outlaw, forcing him to flee so rapidly he dropped his handkerchief. Detectives traced the laundry mark, F.O.X. 7, until it led them to a man named Charles E. Bolton in San Francisco. The *San Francisco Bulletin* described him as "a distinguished-looking gentleman who walked erect as a soldier and carried a gold-knobbed cane." At first, Bolton denied being Black Bart but finally confessed. He was sentenced to 10 years in San Quentin but was released on January 21, 1888, with time off for good behavior. When a reporter asked him if he intended to go on writing poetry, Black Bart snapped, "Young man, didn't you just hear me say I will commit no more crimes?" According to the report, which had a romantic air, Wells Fargo settled an annuity on Black Bart for his agreement to rob no more stagecoaches. There is no additional information about him. One account had him living out his days in Nevada, and another said he died in 1917 in New York City.

Black Dahlia (1925–1947) murder victim

The 1947 case of Elizabeth Short, better known as the Black Dahlia, is unsolved but still actively pursued, principally because it has had more "confessions" than any other case in California history.

In a sense, Elizabeth Short was typical of the young girls who flooded Los Angeles: she was from a broken home, with an unhappy lovelife, consumed with a desire for a Hollywood career. She had, as they said in Hollywood, a gimmick. She always dressed completely in black. It was one way to grab attention, but she certainly had others. She understood the meaning of the casting couch and would go to bed with any man who had even the most tenuous connection with the studios. They started calling her the Black Dahlia, and in the zany world of moviemaking, she might eventually have gained enough of a reputation to make it despite a lack of acting ability.

On January 15, 1947 her nude corpse was found in a garbage-strewn vacant lot in a Los Angeles suburb. She had been badly mutilated and her body had been crudely cut in half. Deep into the thigh of the 22-year-old victim, the killer had carved the initials "BD," presumably for Black Dahlia. It took the police some time to identify the severed corpse as Elizabeth Short, or the Black Dahlia, but no time at all to make several arrests. The murder seemed to excite the public and produced a rash of confessions. In fact, the police were overwhelmed by men and women coming forward to claim credit for the brutal act. Most of the confessions were soon discounted because the self-proclaimed murderers demonstrated a lack of knowledge about various aspects of the case. Yet, still more confessors came forward. One woman walked into a station house and said "The Black Dahlia stole my man, so I killed her and cut her up." A husband whose wife had deserted him said he was the killer in the hope that if he made himself notorious and got his picture in the papers, his wife would return to him. Another sent the police a letter made out of pasted-up letters from magazines, offering to meet them and give them information. He signed the message "Black Dahlia Avenger." But he never kept the rendezvous. Another writer sent a message reading: "Here are Dahlia's belongings. Letter to follow." Enclosed were Elizabeth Short's Social Security card and birth certificate and her address book—with one page missing. Unfortunately, no letter followed. The most promising confession appeared to be that made by a 29-year-old army corporal, who talked loudly and convincingly of knowing her. He appeared quite knowledgeable about the facts of the case and insisted, "When I get drunk, I get rough with women." After an intensive investigation, the police wrote him off as an unbalanced personality. As the confessions continued to pour in, all efforts to keep an accurate count were dropped, and to this day the Black Dahlia case remains unsolved.

Bliss Bank Ring criminal-police alliance

Crime's golden age in America started with the end of the Civil War, as thousands of wastrels and rogues schooled in the rough-and-tumble of wartime criminality came home determined never to work for a living again. While great gangs had existed in the cities long before the war, the crime specialist emerged during the postwar period. Mobs formed to practice one particular brand of crime, and among the most highly rewarded were the bank burglar gangs. Since the great street gangs had often allied themselves with political protectors and carried out many chores for them, such as winning elections through voter intimidation, it was only logical that the new crime mobs would work with the authorities.

The Bliss Bank Ring, bossed by two leading thieves, George Miles Bliss and Mark Shinburn, was probably the biggest bank mob to appreciate the virtue of working with the law. It was common practice for the Bliss gang to pay off the police with about 10 percent of the loot, somewhat less if the score was exceptionally large. "If we spoil them with too much money," Shinburn said, "they won't be hungry for more."

They hardly needed to worry. The appetite of the police seemed insatiable, and they often squabbled about their individual shares. Capt. John Young, chief of the Detective Bureau of the New York Police Department, finally quit in disgust rather than share the $17,500 cut given him by the Bliss forces for one robbery. The extent of the gang's involvement in police bribery was perhaps best exhibited after Young's departure. Bliss lobbied openly for Detective Jim Irving to be put in charge of the bureau, personally stating his case to Boss Tweed of Tammany Hall. The friction over bribes within the bureau was such, he warned, that some disgruntled member might go to reform-minded Samuel Tilden with the facts. "Put Detective Jim Irving at the head of the Detective Bureau," Bliss told Tweed, "and you'll switch the whole business to safety. If not, I can't say what will happen."

Tweed saw the merits in Bliss' argument, and Irving was given the post, whereupon the bank ring entered its most prosperous period. With the cooperation of the police, the ring pulled off the famous $2.75 million raid on the Ocean Bank located at Fulton and Greenwich Streets, in 1869. The breakdown of bribes paid to police was revealed later by confessions:

James Irving, head of Detective Bureau	$17,000
John McCord, detective	$17,000
George Radford, detective	$17,000
James Kelso, detective	$17,000
Philip Farley, detective	$17,000
John Jordan, captain of the Sixth Precinct and later superintendent of police	$17,000
George Elder, detective	$17,000
Inspector Johnson	$1,800
One other detective	$1,000
Frank Houghtaling, clerk of Jefferson Market Police Court	$10,000
John Browne	$500
Total	$132,000

For this sum of money the police not only did not harrass the Bliss gang but also performed yeoman service in trying to pin the job on the George Leonidas Leslie gang, an outfit notorious for being niggardly in the payment of bribes.

The Bliss Ring survived even the fall of Boss Tweed in 1873, but when Thomas F. Byrnes became head of the Detective Bureau in 1880 and outlawed the alliance between the police and the bank burglars, the gang fell apart. Many members were arrested, and Bliss himself was captured and sentenced to prison for the robbery of a Vermont bank. Penniless when released, he spent his final years writing exposés of crime.

Only Shinburn survived the ring's demise, fleeing to Europe, where for years he lived the life of a count, having bought the title with the proceeds of some of his crimes.

Bloody Angle   New York murder site

During the great tong wars fought in the early 20th century in New York's Chinatown, the area became an armed camp. Mott Street became the stronghold of the On Leong Tong, while Pell Street belonged to the Hip Sing Tong. Doyers Street was a sort of no-man's-land with a certain sharp turn that journalists labeled the Bloody Angle. The police later estimated that more men were murdered there than at any other spot in New York City and most likely the entire United States. Only the foolhardy ventured past it after dark. The Bloody Angle was ideal for an ambush, with too abrupt a turn for a pedestrian to see ahead. Armed with a snickersnee, or hatchet, sharpened to a razor's edge, a *boo how doy*, or hatchet man, could strike before the victim had time to cry out, lay the weapon across his throat and flee through an arcade to safety.

See also: BOW KUM, MOCK DUCK, TONG WARS.

Bodie, California   lawless gold-mining camp

Gold placers were first discovered in Bodie in 1859, but since the town was isolated on the eastern slope of the Sierra Nevada, it didn't boom until 1870, when rich veins started showing up. The population quickly mushroomed to some 15,000, drawn by what would eventually prove to be some $100 million worth of ore over the next two decades. With fortunes to be made and stolen overnight, Bodie became perhaps the most lawless, corrupt and vice-ridden town in the West. Three breweries working 24 hours a day, were needed to service some 35 saloons. There were also some 60 bordellos in action on a 24-hour basis, home, according of one historian's account, to no less than 1,800 prostitutes. With a total population of only 15,500, it was clear what the remaining 13,200 were doing when they weren't drinking, digging or killing each other. Violent deaths in such an atmosphere were understandably frequent, and in fact, it was said that Bodie always had "a man for breakfast." Men were killed for their gold in arguments over who paid for the last beer, for being line-jumpers at brothels and, now and then, in disputes about the facts of some previous killing. When one entire Sunday passed without a fatality, folks in Bodie spoke with pride of the "Christian spirit" that had overtaken the town.

Bodie did not live long enough to be tamed. After 1880 the gold finds became less lucrative and by the turn of the century much of the town was empty and forlorn. Some slight mining activity continued up to World War II, but most of the town's well-preserved but unused wooden structures were burned in a fire in 1932. Today Bodie is nothing more than a ghost town with a bloody past.

See also: BADMAN FROM BODIE.

Bonnet, Jeanne (1841–1876) gangster
Also known as the Little Frog Catcher, Jeanne Bonnet was a bizarre character who founded one of California's strangest criminal gangs, composed only of women. Jeanne got her nickname from the way she made an honest living—catching frogs in the marshes of San Mateo County. She had other unusual habits, including wearing men's clothing and regularly visiting the leading bagnios of the Barbary Coast. Whether her interests were truly or solely sexual became a cloudy issue in view of later events. She formed a gang of women recruited from the brothels, from which they all fled on a single night. A dozen of them joined her, holing up in a shack on the San Francisco waterfront south of Market Street. They lived by robbing, stickups, shoplifting and other forms of thievery, swearing off prostitution completely and having nothing to do with men, except, of course, as victims. The gang crumbled in less than a year, however, when Jeanne Bonnet was found shot to death with a bullet through her heart. The police concluded she had been murdered by one or more of the pimps whose ladies she had taken, thus ending an early, if criminal, experiment in women's liberation.

book whippings
During colonial days books that were deemed offensive were also considered "criminal" in themselves and therefore subject to criminal punishment in addition to being burned. In a typical Massachusetts case, a book was sentenced "to be publicly whipt with 40 stripes, save one, and then burnt." In 1754 the hangman was assigned to perform that same task on a pamphlet that criticized the court. The public punishment was carried out in the middle of Boston's King Street.

Boot Hill
Almost all Americans believe that every gunslinging western community had its Boot Hill, where all the victims of lead poi-

soning were buried. The fact is that the "Boot Hill industry" is a 20th-century development. There really was only one Boot Hill and that was at Dodge City. The name referred to a slight rise used as a temporary burial spot and alluded to the custom of burying a corpse there with his boots curled up and placed under his head as a sort of permanent pillow. In due course, Dodge's Prairie Grove Cemetery was completed, and in 1879 the 25 or so inhabitants of Boot Hill were transferred to the new burial grounds.

Most communities didn't know they were supposed to have a Boot Hill until they read modern western novels and saw movies about the Wild West and became aware of the demands of the tourist industry. Along with newly christened Boot Hills came such graveyard graffiti as "Died of lead poisoning" and, for a cattle rustler, "Too many irons in the fire." One of the superattractions of the West is the 20th-century Boot Hill in Tombstone, Ariz., where visitors are welcomed to the burial sites of Tom and Frank McLowery and Billie Clanton, who all died in the famous gunfight at the O.K. Corral. With a certain pride it is claimed that among the graveyard's residents are Dan Dowd, Red Sample, Tex Howard, Bill DeLaney and Dan Kelly, all of whom were "hanged legally," an accomplishment of sorts. In one of the more exploitative events at Tombstone, one promoter tried to sell square-inch plots of Boot Hill cemetery but was squelched by the city council.

Bordenmania   impact of Lizzie Borden case

No murder case in American history caused more public repercussions than that involving Lizzie Borden, the 32-year-old spinster who was tried and acquitted of killing her father and stepmother with an ax in their home in Fall River, Mass. in 1892. The case was the subject of an endless number of books, magazine articles and newspaper accounts. Edmund Pearson explained the public's fascination with the case may have resulted from its very "purity." The murders, and Lizzie's guilt or innocence, were uncomplicated by such sins as ambition, robbery, greed, lust or other usual homicidal motives. Innocent or guilty, Lizzie became an American hero.

The verse and doggerel on the case varied from the anonymous children's jump rope rhyme:

> *Lizzie Borden took an ax*
> *And gave her mother forty whacks;*
> *When she saw what she had done,*
> *She gave her father forty-one.*

to A. L. Bixby's almost endearing:

> *There's no evidence of guilt,*
> *Lizzie Borden,*
> *That should make your spirit wilt,*
> *Lizzie Borden;*
> *Many do not think that you,*
> *Chopped your father's head in two,*
> *It's so hard a thing to do,*
> *Lizzie Borden.*

The *New York Times* informed its readers that controversy over Lizzie Borden's innocence or guilt was directly responsible for 1,900 divorces. Such was the grip of "Bordenmania" on the entire nation.

Bowery Boys   early New York gang

One of the toughest gangs in New York during the early 1800s was the famed Bowery Boys, who, as native Americans, did battle with the dreaded Irish gangs, especially the Dead Rabbits and their satellites. On occasion, they also fought the police.

Unlike the other great gangs, the Bowery Boys were not loafers and bums—except on Sundays and holidays. Nor were they criminals, except once in a while, until the Civil War. The average Bowery Boy was a burly ruffian who worked as a butcher or apprentice mechanic or perhaps a bouncer in a Bowery saloon or dance cellar. Almost always, he was a volunteer fireman, an avocation that gave the Bowery Boys important political pull since the firemen were strong allies of Tammany Hall and thus had important influence on the running of city government. The Bowery Boys were especially valuable allies on election day when their rough activities often determined voting results.

The Bowery Boys' hatred of Irish gangs and of foreigners in general was implacable, and they campaigned strongly for those candidates who ran against naturalization laws and favored their repeal so that Irish voters could be stripped of their citizenship. The Bowery Boys worked on behalf of such candidates with blackjacks in hand and voted early and often themselves in every election.

The Bowery Boys' greatest fight was a two-day battle on July 4 and 5, 1857, when allied with forces of the anti-Irish Native American Party, they withstood an invasion of the Bowery by the Dead Rabbits and the Plug Uglies and other gangs from the Five Points area. With more than 1,000 combatants taking part, the police lacked sufficient manpower or backbone to stop the fighting throughout the first day and much of the second. Officially, eight gang members died and another 100 were injured, but it was known that both sides dragged off a considerable number of corpses for secret burials in their own bailiwicks.

During the Draft Riots the Bowery Boys took part in much of the criminality loosed on the city. After that, the gang splintered into various smaller groups, almost all involved in illegal pursuits.

See also: DEAD RABBITS, DRAFT RIOTS.

Bow Kum (1889–1909) murder victim

Bow Kum, meaning "Little Sweet Flower," was a beautiful slave girl of 15 when she was illegally brought into the United States by a wealthy San Francisco Chinese, Low Hee, who had paid a Canton slave merchant the unheard of sum of $3,000 for her. The American authorities found out about Bow Kum some three years later and despite Low Hee's valid bill of sale, placed her in a home. Bow Kum was finally released when she married another man, Tchin Len, who took her to New York. A dispute broke out between Low Hee and Tchin Len on the matter of compensation and soon involved three groups: the On Leong Tong, an alliance of the Hip Sing Tong and a fraternal organization called the Four Brothers. These groups were already at odds on such matters as the control of gambling in various parts of New York's Chinatown. As the dispute appeared beyond settlement, the On Leongs murdered Bow Kum on April 15, 1909, and the first of Chinatown's great tong wars broke out.

One typical killing spree took place in the venerable Chinese Theater on Doyers Street on New Year's night during a supposed truce in the fighting that had been arranged for the biggest Chinese celebration of the year. The performance went along smoothly until a celebrant in the audience suddenly tossed a bunch of lighted firecrackers into the air. This caused a brief commotion before things quieted down. As the audience filed out at the end of the performance, five men remained in their seats. They all had bullets in their heads. The banging of the firecrackers had drowned out the cracks of the revolvers of five Hip Sings behind five On Leongs.

Police estimates of casualties during the war were put at about 350 before the tongs came to a peace settlement in late 1910 and the war over Little Sweet Flower ended.

See also: BLOODY ANGLE, MOCK DUCK, TONG WARS.

branding   punishment for crime

Branding as a punishment for crimes was never as widely used in the New World as in Europe, but it was a standard form of punishment in colonial America. In the Massachusetts colony the wearing of signs or initials on a person's outermost garment was in effect a method of symbolic branding. Thus, in Boston in 1639 Richard Wilson had to wear a T for theft of "money and diverse small things" from his master, and about the same time in Plymouth, Katheren Aines, a married woman, was required to wear a B for bawd "for her unclean and laciviouse behavior with . . . William Paule."

A number of crimes were considered so heinous that branding was mandatory even for a first offense. Burglary of a dwelling house called for the letter B to be branded on a culprit's forehead. A second such offense required a second branding and whipping. A third offense called for the death penalty. Counterfeiting was considered such a danger that the offender was branded on his right cheek with an F for forger. It was presumed that such a branding would be proper warning to any potential victims to beware of their money or supposed legal records.

With proper application, branding of course produced a permanent scar, but the punishment was considered so awesome that several constables took to using a light touch or an iron not heated sufficiently to destroy the tissue.

Officially, the branding iron was last used on Jonathan Walker, who in 1844 had the letters S.S. (for slave stealer) burned into the palm of his right hand; however, the practice of branding continued as an acceptable form of punishment in the informal miners courts in the West and in the military, especially during the Civil War. On October 10, 1863 a Union artillery brigade held a mass branding of those being drummed out of the service for deserting their batteries. The brigade was assembled in the form of a hollow square facing inward, with a battery forge in the center. A battery blacksmith heated irons, and the letter D was burned into the convicted men's left hips. Significantly, the army had by this time restricted branding to relatively unseen parts of the body. Miners courts, acting in a lawless environment, were not as lenient. Generally, these courts believed in only two penalties, hanging and expulsion from the community. When this later punishment was decreed, the convicted man was often branded on the forehead, face or hands to give due warning to other communities of his unsavory character. This extralegal form of punishment disappeared by the 1880s and 1890s.

Bras Coupe (?–1837) slave outlaw

In the 1820s one of the most famous slaves in New Orleans was Squier, an exceptionally talented Bamboula dancer. His master was Gen. William de Buys, well known as an indulgent slave owner. The general was all the more indulgent of a famous slave like Squier. He taught Squier to shoot and let him go hunting alone in the forests and swamps. A big and powerful man, Squier became adept at firing a rifle with either hand, something that would stand him in good stead later on. He also became accustomed to the feeling of freedom. So much so, that he ran away. When he was caught, he escaped again. In 1834 Squier was shot by a patrol of planters hunting slaves in the swamps, and his right arm was amputated. As soon as his wound had healed, Squier ran away again, determined never to be retaken. He organized a gang of escaped blacks and—what truly terrified New Orleans—some renegade whites. Now known as Bras Coupe, the escaped slave led his gang on frequent robbery and murdering raids around the outskirts of New Orleans. For nearly three years Bras Coupe was the scourge of New Orleans, a hobgoblin used by mothers and nurses to frighten their children. The New Orleans *Picayune* described him as "a semi-devil and fiend in human shape" and called his life "one of crime and depravity." What frightened the slave owners most, of course, was the fact that Bras Coupe became a hero to the other blacks. They endowed Bras Coupe with superhuman powers. In the instant folklore that sprung up around him, the veritable superman was fireproof and, having now lost his one weak arm, invulnerable to wounds. Hunters who tried to take him in the swamp stood in awe as their bullets flattened against his chest while he laughed. Sometimes the bullets whizzed off Bras Coupe's chest and came flying back at the hunters.

When a detachment of soldiers invaded his lair, they were swallowed up in a cloud of mist and never seen again. Bras Coupe was said to paralyze with a mere glance and to nourish himself on human flesh.

Bras Coupe's mythic qualities were tarnished on April 6, 1837, when he was shot by two hunters. But he escaped and it was assumed, would surely survive since he knew all the miraculous herbs that could be found in the swamps. On July 19 of the same year, the legend came to a tawdry end. A Spanish fisherman, Francisco Garcia, long considered to be in league with the slave-outlaw, brought Bras Coupe's body into New Orleans on a mule-drawn cart. He said Bras Coupe had fired on him from the shore of the Bayou St. John. Infuriated, Garcia said he had come ashore and beat the slave renegade's brains out with a club. The weight of evidence, however pointed to the conclusion that Bras Coupe had been murdered as he slept in Garcia's hut. Garcia demanded the $2,000 reward that had been posted for the outlaw; but however much the whites had feared the man they called the Brigand of the Swamp, they had little stomach for the Spaniard's act. He was given only $250 and told to leave. The body of Bras Coupe was displayed for two days in the Place d'Armes so that several thousand slaves could be brought to view it as an object lesson.

Briggs, Hattie (c. 1880–1890s) madam
In vice-ridden Chicago during the 1880s and 1890s, the most famous madams were Carrie Watson and Lizzie Allen, but a black madam ("as ugly as anyone could imagine," according to one contemporary account) named Hattie Briggs enjoyed almost equal notoriety,

being the subject of a never-ending string of newspaper articles.

Six feet tall and weighing about 225 pounds, Hattie cut an arresting figure in the long scarlet coat she always wore. She ran two brothels, one on Clark Street and another on Custom House Place, where her girls were available for 25¢. However, rare indeed was the customer who got out of either of these dens without being robbed. Scorning such slow-moving, indirect robbery methods as the sliding panels used in some other establishments, Hattie's technique was quick and most direct. She would simply seize a customer and slam him up against a wall a few times, strip him of his money and toss him out into the street. Although Hattie was raided several times a week, she got off with minor fines; few victimized customers cared to appear in court to testify against her.

While the newspapers constantly wrote exposés of her activities, it took the police some 10 years to drive her from the city; some cynical newsmen saw this as proof of police corruption. Indeed, Hattie's downfall resulted more from her insulting the police than from her breaking the law. In the early 1890s Hattie took a young black thief and gambler, William Smith, as a lover. She set him up in the saloon business and dressed him gaudily in patent-leather shoes with white spats, lavender pants, white vest, yellow shirt, bright blue coat and, of course, a silk hat. She adorned him with diamond pins and rings. Smith soon became very "big for his britches" and bragged that Hattie intended to make him the "biggest black boy in Chicago." Indeed, Hattie announced that she was making so much money she intended to buy up all the brothels and saloons in the city's vice centers for Smith, elect him mayor and abolish the police force.

This may have been the insult the police could not abide because a force of 20 patrolmen raided Smith's main saloon and, following a desperate battle, arrested the great man and 22 of his henchmen. After Smith's liquor license was revoked, the still-smarting police turned their rage on Hattie Briggs, arresting her 10 to 20 times a day with blanket warrants. After lasting about half a month, Hattie finally hired a moving van and shipped off her girls and their bedding to a new place in suburban Lemont. According to later reports, Hattie moved south to a place where the law was said to be more considerate of hard-working madams.

Brink's robbery

The Great Brink's Robbery of 1950 was two years in the making. For 24 months, 11 middle-aged Bostonians, seven of them heretofore no more than petty thieves, worked on the robbery of the Brink's North Terminal Garage. They entered the garage at night and walked about in their stocking feet, measuring distances, locating doors, determining which way they opened, all beneath unsuspecting guards. On one occasion they removed the locks from the doors, fitted keys to them and then replaced the locks. They even went so far as to break into a burglar alarm company in order to make a closer study of the alarm system used by Brink's. In December 1949 they ran through a complete dress rehearsal. Finally, they decided they were ready.

On the appointed day, January 17, 1950, the bandits entered the garage dressed in simulated Brink's uniforms, rubber Halloween masks, and crepe-soled shoes or rubber overshoes. They made their way to the counting

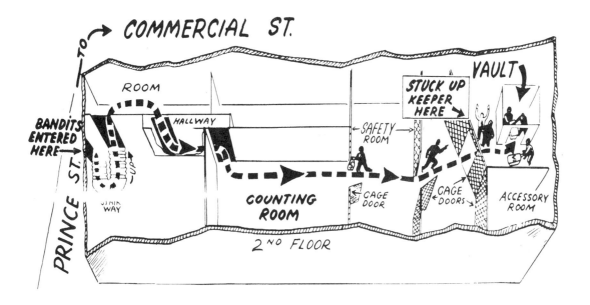

A diagram shows the route taken by the bandits in the Great Brink's Robbery in 1950, which netted them $2.7 million in cash, checks and securities.

room and relieved five very surprised employees of $2.7 million in cash, checks and securities. The cash alone came to $1,218,211. In less than 15 minutes they were gone.

The plan had been to keep a low profile for six years until the statute of limitations ran out, but one of the bandits, Joseph "Specs" O'Keefe, felt he had been gypped out of his fair share. He demanded another $63,000. The others refused but then started worrying he would turn informer. A professional hit man, Elmer "Trigger" Burke, was assigned to shut O'Keefe up permanently. Burke chased O'Keefe through the streets of Boston in a wild nighttime shoot-out, firing at him with a machine gun. O'Keefe was wounded in the arm and chest but escaped, although Burke was sure he had finished him off. The hit man was seized by police before he could correct his error.

O'Keefe took offense at the effort to kill him and eventually started talking to the law; by then the FBI had spent $25 million investigating the caper. As a result of O'Keefe's talking to the police, eight of the plotters were convicted and given life sentences.

In 1980 an $18 million movie titled *The Brink's Job* was released. It was played partly for laughs. On hand for the showing in Boston were two of the three surviving members of the original bandit group. Both had served 14 years for the crime before being released.

"I'm glad they made something light out of it," said 72-year-old Thomas "Sandy" Richardson. "Yeah, people need a few laughs these days."

Seventy-year-old Adolph "Jazz" Maffie wasn't completely sold. "I thought it was all right. But only thing is that it wasn't that much fun. That was hard work, that kind of job."

"Yeah," Sandy said.

Byrnes, Thomas F. (1842–1910) New York police inspector

Although he served briefly as chief of police in New York City, Thomas F. Byrnes really made his mark while serving as chief of detectives and chief inspector of the force in the 1880s and 1890s, during which time he was easily the most renowned American policeman of the era. What he lacked in honesty he more than made up for in flamboyance. It has been said that Byrnes embodied all that was good and all that was bad in the 19th-century policeman.

Born in Ireland in 1842, he was brought to New York as a child. During the Civil War he fought for two years in the Union Army before joining the police force in 1863. By 1870 he had moved up to captain, a rank generally achieved only by playing according to the accepted rules, which meant collecting bribes and passing along the proper share to police higher-ups and to the right politicians at Boss Tweed's Tammany Hall. In 1880 Byrnes became head of the Detective Bureau after solving the record $3-million robbery of the Manhattan Bank. He had rounded up most of the loot and several of the burglars and been applauded by Tammany for his work, especially since the Leslie mob, which pulled the job, had neglected to fork over the standard police-politician cut for such a caper, generally 10 percent of the take.

As head of the Detective Bureau, Byrnes outlawed such cooperation between crooks and police and set as his first goal the elimination of bank robberies in the Wall Street area. He had received more than acclaim after solving the Manhattan Bank job. Several grateful bankers had gotten together and "invested" a large sum of money for him from which he collected the profits. This was not to be considered a reward because rewards had to be approved by and shared with police superiors, not to mention that a certain percentage of rewards had to be given to the police pension fund. Byrnes appreciated the sentiments of the bankers and decided to show his gratitude by ordering all professional criminals to stay out of the Wall Street area. To enforce this edict, he ordered his men to arrest or at least blackjack any professional thief found south of Fulton Street, the demarcation known to criminals as Byrnes' Dead Line.

Byrnes further aided the prominent bankers and stockbrokers by always proving cooperative in hushing up any personal scandals. If he reduced the incidence of major crimes in the Wall Street area, Byrnes was also responsible for a novel treatment of crime elsewhere in the city. He more or less legalized crime, or more precisely, he kept it within acceptable limits by using some criminals to oversee or suppress other criminals, giving each a protected area in which to operate. In return, for this right, the criminals paid Byrnes far less than the previous levels of graft but were required to perform certain other duties on request. For instance, if a prominent person had his pocket picked or was robbed by foodpads, all Byrnes had to do was ask for the return of the loot and it was on his desk within 24 hours.

A gullible public regarded such feats as examples of keen detective work, and overall, Byrnes' stature was enhanced. Byrnes appreciated the value of public relations and became a romantic figure in print. He collaborated on a number of books, and one of his own, *Professional Criminals of America* became a best-seller. In his day, Byrnes got as much mileage out of denouncing foreign-born anarchists as did J. Edgar Hoover upon his discovery of the communist menace.

Byrnes realized that if he catered to a privileged few, he had carte blanche to do whatever he wished with all others. In the 1880s he was considered second only to Inspector Alexander "Clubber" Williams in his devotion to the practice of the third degree. Byrnes was, to journalist Lincoln Steffens, "Simple, no complication at all—a man who would buy you or beat you, as you might choose, but get you he would."

Byrnes' downfall came about in the mid-1890s because of the opposition of reformer Theodore Roosevelt, at the time a member of the four-man board of police commissioners, and because of the findings of the Lexow Committee. Writing to Henry Cabot Lodge, Roosevelt announced: "I think I shall move against Byrnes at once. I thoroughly distrust him, and cannot do any thorough work while he remains. It will be a hard fight, and I have no idea how it will come out."

As it was, Byrnes retired about a month later, in June of 1895. He had had a particularly trying time before the Lexow Committee, which heard testimony indicating that Byrnes permitted widespread corruption within the Detective Bureau. His men were notorious for refusing to undertake robbery investigations unless the victim first posted a reward. Byrnes was personally pressed to explain how he had accumulated $350,000 in real estate, $292,000 in his wife's name. His top salary had been $5,000 a year and no more than a quarter of his huge estate could be attributed to the "gratuities" of the Wall Street crowd.

Despite these embarrassments, Byrnes made a pitch at staying on as chief of police, assuring Roosevelt and the other reformers that he could run a department free of all corruption. His own failings, he said, were due to being trapped in a foul system. His offer was rejected.

See also: BLISS BANK RING, DEAD LINE.

Calamity Jane (1852–1903) woman "outlaw"
Few works touching on female criminality in America and especially in the West fail to include Martha Jane Cannary, best known as Calamity Jane. However, her inclusion in such studies is a miscarriage of justice, since it has been clearly demonstrated that the extent of her lawless behavior was limited to disorderly conduct, drunkenness and stints of prostitution, such as her 1875 tour of duty at E. Coffey's "hog farm" near Fort Laramie.

Calamity's "autobiography" is full of shoot-'em-up exploits and, of course, a torrid love affair with Wild Bill Hickok. Actually, it is doubtful that Hickok ever considered this muscular, big-boned girl who dressed like a man anything other than an occasional member of his entourage. After Hickok's death in 1876, Calamity Jane became a living legend: "the White Devil of the Yellowstone," as one dime novel called her. The last 25 years of her life were spent peddling her autobiography and other books about her for a few pennies, whoring and appearing in various Wild West shows, from which she was invariably fired for drunkenness. In 1900 a newspaper editor found her sick in a brothel and nursed her back to health. Calamity was dying in a hotel room in Terry, not far from Deadwood, S. Dak. in the summer of 1903. On August 2 her eyes fluttered open and she asked the date. Upon being told, she nodded and said: "It's the 27th anniversary of Bill's [Hickok's] death. Bury me next to Bill." They did and recorded her death on August 2, although she had not died until August 3. But then the facts never have been permitted to cloud the Calamity Jane legend.

See also: JAMES BUTLER "WILD BILL" HICKOK.

Calico Jim (?–1897?) shanghai operator
Shanghaiing of men was an old San Francisco custom and one of its most proficient practitioners, along with the infamous Shanghai Kelly, was Calico Jim. A Chilean whose real name was said to be Reuben, Jim ran a saloon and crimping joint at Battery Point, from which a great many men were sent on long sea voyages. During the 1890s the San Francisco police received so many

Public drunk and prostitute Calamity Jane picked up occasional change in her last years posing for tourists at the gravesite of her "lover," Wild Bill Hickok.

complaints against Jim that they began paying him close attention. Evidently not close enough, however, because a policeman sent to arrest him didn't come back. Another tried and also never returned. A total of six police officers went to the saloon and disappeared; all had taken a sea cruise, compliments of Calico Jim. Feeling now that his days in the business were limited, Jim sold out and returned to his native Chile.

It was many months before the policemen made their way back to home port. It has been said that they pooled their money, drew lots and sent one of their number off to Chile to hunt down Calico Jim. After many months of hunting, according to the story, the policeman found Jim on a street corner in Callao, Chile and shot him six times, one for each officer he had shanghaied. There is some doubt about the truth of this account, although it gained a great deal of currency. For years the police department insisted there was no record of six officers being shanghaied. But jaded citizens of San Francisco contended they knew a cover-up when they heard one.

See also: SHANGHAI KELLY.

Canal Street Buffalo vice center

"For sheer wickedness, vice and crime there is no need to go any further west than here," a 19th-century historian said of Canal Street in Buffalo, N.Y. It was quite a claim to make about a thoroughfare but two blocks long.

Born with the Erie Canal, Canal Street was set off on a jutting piece of land, segregated from the rest of Buffalo by 40 feet of murky water. On quiet summer nights Buffalonians could stroll casually along the canal and gaze across at the street that never lost its light from dusk to dawn. They could hear boisterous noises of ribaldry and wonder if at that moment, somewhere on Canal Street, someone was in the process of being killed, a likely occurrence on a street that boasted 93 saloons, three combination grocery-saloons and 15 dives known as concert halls. More than half these establishments had portions of their premises given over to prostitution, with an estimated 400 practitioners of that art on hand around the clock.

Canal Street grew up with the Erie Canal, which cut across New York State and linked up the Hudson with the Great Lakes. The street sucked gold from the rugged sailors of the Lakes and the lusty canalers and in return provided a bawdiness unrivaled even in the tenderloin sections of far bigger cities. An early clergyman thundered from his pulpit that it should be called Market Street because the fruits of any vice could be purchased along its cobble-stoned length. The ladies of Canal Street knew how to get a man's money, and they were not averse to slitting his throat if need be. In the end, the residents of the street usually got every penny a man had, leaving him without even enough with which to buy a mug of beer. Canal Street was said to be the birthplace of the word *mugging*. When a man had been so sheared that he did-

n't even have the price of a mug of beer, he would walk outside and waylay a passerby or "mug" him.

The worst dives on Canal Street were those places on the East Side whose rear areas extended on wooden pilings over the canal. Unsuspecting canalers and lakers were hustled there by painted women who charged exorbitant prices for their services. However, if a man had money, but was uncooperative about parting with it, he was fed an overdose of knockout drops. He then was hauled into a backroom, stripped of all his clothes and dumped naked down a slicked wooden chute into the canal with hardly an incriminating splash. Eventually he would turn up floating face down in the murky water. The police would know no more than that he had been killed in one of about 100 places and listed the victim as a "floater." In one week in 1863 no less than 14 floaters were fished out of the canal, five on one morning alone.

Canal Street lived on protection. One time there was a report, undoubtedly true, that several leading politicians had had a little two-day party in one of the street's leading bordellos, which helped explain why no concerted effort was made to drive out the scarlet women. For many years about all the politicians would grant the citizens of Buffalo was a segregation ruling that denied such ladies the right to go any further uptown than the liberty pole, which marked the entrance to Buffalo proper in those days. So long as the prostitutes remained in the Canal Street area, they were safe.

In 1870 a young reformer named Grover Cleveland was elected sheriff of Erie County after making campaign promises to clean up Canal Street. Cleveland tried to keep his word but was singularly ineffective. The saloon keepers and brothel owners of the street paid out so much money to the right political forces in Buffalo that Cleveland's campaign was fruitless. If he made arrests, politically controlled judges immediately released the prisoners for "lack of evidence." Cleveland went on to become president of the United States. He was once asked what was the greatest disappointment of his life; he stated that it was not failing to be reelected president in 1888 but rather being unable to wipe out the scourge of Canal Street.

Both before and after Cleveland, Canal Street went its own murderous way, regarding all type of crime as hardly worthy of special notice. When Fat Charley Ott, the proprietor of The Only Theater, a sort of combination concert hall, saloon, dance hall and assignation hotel, came to a bad end, the street handled it in typical fashion. Fat Charley had a propensity for padding the bill of a client who appeared in possession of less than all his faculties. One sweltering night in the 1890s, he made the mistake of trying it on a certain bearded laker. After letting out an angry howl that filled the Only, the laker reached across the bar, seized Fat Charley by the hair and with brute force hauled Charley to him. Like many a lakeman, he carried a Spanish knife, a nasty, two-edged slicer that was worn up the sleeve, attached by a leather thong. He whipped it out. Fat Charley struggled to get loose, but his unhappy patron wasn't letting go. At the time, there were some two dozen other patrons in the Only. They gaped in motionless horror as the bearded lakeman decapitated Charley Ott with one swipe.

The murderer strode out of the Only as the other customers froze. Someone allowed that perhaps the police should be informed.

Others agreed but suggested that perhaps they should have a drink in memory of the dear departed. They had one, another and then another. When in due course the police arrived, the Only was empty save for the two parts of Fat Charley, a looted till and scores of empty liquor bottles. And some wag had even left a sign on the door that read CLOSED ON ACCOUNT OF ILLNESS.

It was said, not without good reason, that the females of Canal Street were far more deadly than the males. There was, for instance, Gallow May Moore, a blond hellion who could throw her garter stiletto with unerring accuracy; any man who tried to leave her without paying the premiums could count on awesome retribution. Her favorite trick was to pin an unchivalrous gentleman to a wall with a stiletto, empty his pockets, kiss him goodbye and leaving him dangling as she went out to live it up on his roll, with enough set aside for a new knife.

Then there was Frosty Face Emma, described as a handsome woman much sought after by men. She had, however, one disconcerting habit. For a time she could drink liquor as though she had a hollow leg, and a gentleman would wait impatiently for her to enter a more compliant phase, which unfortunately never happened. At a certain level of consumption, she turned into a vicious man-hater. A man's only hope was that he had not as yet adjourned with her to a more secluded atmosphere before she exploded. Otherwise, there was little chance he would be seen alive again. One historian states Emma assassinated at least seven lovers and cut up many others. The law never did get anything on Emma, however. Her victims couldn't or wouldn't talk, and Canal Street had its own rules: nobody ever told anything to the law about anybody.

Fittingly, Emma got her just deserts in a knife battle with a redhead called Deadly Dora. If there was one thing Dora wouldn't tolerate, it was another woman stealing a man from her. She had latched on to a blue-eyed Swedish sailor for whom she developed a genuine affection. Emma tried to cut in and knives flashed. They fished Emma's body out of the canal a few days later.

A time came when Buffalonians could thank the girls of Canal Street for preventing the city from being overrun by prostitutes. It happened during Pan-American Year, when all Buffalo was in a Mardi Gras spirit in celebration of the turn of the century. Up till then the several hundred prostitutes in and around Canal Street had the territory to themselves, but with the celebration hundreds of sinful ladies from New York City headed for the bonanza town of the North. One day, bag and baggage, they poured from a train at the Terrace railroad station, directly across from the canal, and attempted to move in.

The women were all colorfully dressed, and canalers paused in their labors to give them a cheering welcome. They circulated among the men with friendly words that happy days had indeed come to Buffalo. The gay arrival, however, also had been seen by the women of Canal Street, and like an army, they swarmed out of the dives and bordellos to descend on the train station. Many carried stillettos, clubs, planks or chairs.

It was a battle the likes of which Buffalo had never seen before. Before it was over, close to 100 ladies were in various degrees of undress. A dedicated reporter counted eight females stripped totally raw. Two dozen girls had to be hospitalized, many with awful knife slashes across their faces. The paddy wagon made a total of 32 trips to the Franklin Street Station, hauling off battling participants. By nightfall the battle was over, and the New York ladies, no match for the denizens of Canal Street, jammed back into the station and took the next train out.

Pan-American Year was the last really big one for Canal Street. Buffalo was changing. Erie Canal traffic was dipping, and as the railroads took over more, fewer and fewer Great Lakes freighters docked. Consequently, fewer sailors and canalers hit Canal Street. The joints began to shutter. In 1908 a citizens' movement increased the pressure on the police to clean up Canal Street once and for all. Raids increased, and foreign immigrants began to flood into Canal Street, soon outnumbering the criminal element. In 1915 the name of the street was changed to Dante Place. In peculiarly American style, the area became an ordinary slum, breeding its own type of vice and crime. But the whores and whoremasters were gone, and Canal Street, with its incredible century of murder, mayhem, vice and corruption, was just a memory.

See also: YORKY OF THE GREAT LAKES.

Car Barn Gang

The Car Barn Gang, the last gang in America to declare open war on the police, was clearly an organization born in the wrong era. The Car Barners harkened back to the post–Civil War days when criminal bands operated in most big cities on the basis of pure terror and often engaged in pitched battles or vindictive strikes against the police. Organized in late 1911 in New York City, the Car Barners recruited mostly the young toughs who infested the East River docks, fighting, stealing and rolling drunks. As a gang, they became vicious gunmen and highwaymen, staging daring daylight robberies and holding up trolley cars with the same Wild West techniques used in earlier days on stagecoaches.

The first the police knew of the existence of an organized gang was the appearance of placards near the old car barns around Second Avenue and East 97th Street. The signs read:

Notice
COPS KEEP OUT!
NO POLICEMAN WILL
HEREAFTER
BE ALLOWED IN THIS
BLOCK
By Order of
THE CAR BARN GANG.

The police soon learned the Car Barners were most serious about their edict after a half-dozen officers who had ventured into the forbidden zone were either stabbed or had their skulls fractured. Following that, the police never patrolled the area in groups of less than four or five, leading to the vaudevillian comic's famous joke that the police were insisting on police protection.

The primary captain of the Car Barners was one Big Bill Lingley, widely renowned as a burglar and desperado. He seldom ventured forth with less than two revolvers, a blackjack and a slungshot, which he used to attack a likely citizen or a police officer. Big Bill's principal confederate was Freddie Muehfeldt, a youth who, although from a good family and a background of considerable Sunday School work, at age 17 had taken up a wastrel life on the docks. Big Bill determined to make over Muehfeldt, who became known as the Kid, in his own image. They became the twin terrors of the Car Barners' domain from East 90th Street to 100th and from Third Avenue to the East River. Almost by themselves, they were said to make the

area as unsafe for honest folk as the notorious Hell's Kitchen section.

The Car Barn Gang ranged far afield in their depredations and would often make an incredible sweep robbing saloons from Manhattan's 14th Street all the way up to the Bronx. The Kid would simply walk behind the bar and tap the till while Big Bill and a dozen or so stalwarts isolated the bouncers. If a barkeep objected to the Kid's action, he would receive a liquor bottle across his skull from the teenaged gangster. Often the saloon keepers who got advanced warning of the approach of the Car Barners, realizing that resistance was foolhardy, would reduce the amount of cash in the till and hope the gangsters would be mollified with their take.

Meanwhile, the war between the Car Barners and the police raged on. Finally, the police strong-arm squad was sent into the area to clean out the gang. They clubbed the gangsters unmercifully, but neither side could get the better of the other as long as Big Bill and the Kid were in the forefront of the battles. Eventually, however, the pair killed a Bronx liquor dispenser making a valiant effort to protect his receipts and were arrested for murder.

Big Bill and the Kid, not yet 21, were executed for the crime, and by the onset of World War I, the dispirited Car Barners collapsed under persistent police attacks.

card trick suicide   inventive way of avoiding execution

William Kogut, San Quentin death row convict #1651, is seldom remembered today except in the folklore of the notorious prison he inhabited, but his final exploit would alter the practices followed in numerous death rows around the country.

When Kogut entered San Quentin Penitentiary in 1930 sentenced to death by hanging for the lethal stabbing a woman, he openly boasted he would never be executed, that he would instead die by his own hand. The sentencing judge did not dismiss the threat but instead warned authorities to deprive him of all weapons or tools that would facilitate a suicide attempt. In San Quentin the guards kept an unusually close watch on Kogut, whose only diversion was playing solitaire with one of the two decks of cards he was permitted to keep in his cell.

One Sunday morning not long before his scheduled execution, the prison was ripped by a terrific explosion. Guards rushed to death row and discovered Kogut lying in a pool of blood, his face little more than a blob. It took the coroner and a group of chemists several days to figure out how Kogut had managed to kill himself. He had in days previous been playing solitaire—or so it seemed. Unobserved by guards, he was busily scraping off all the red spots on the cards—the hearts and diamonds—with his thumbnail. Then he soaked that residue in water in his tin cup, producing a wet pulp. This he poured into a hollow knob from his cot and then he plugged the knob with a second knob. Now Kogut had what he wanted—a potential deadly bomb. The bits of playing cards were made of cellulose and nitrate, and when mixed with a solvent formed pyroxylin, an explosive that could be set off by heat. What he had was a primitive homemade pipe bomb.

On the night of October 9, 1930 Kogut put his bomb in his tin cup and placed it on the small heater in his cell. Then he laid his head on the cup and waited for the inevitable explosion that cheated the hangman.

Kogut's card suicide trick can never be duplicated in San Quentin or, in fact, any other death row. Condemned prisoners are still allowed playing cards, but the decks are routinely collected and checked.

Carlton, Handsome Harry (?–1888)
murderer

Handsome, blue-eyed Harry Carlton was a dapper murderer who had a date with the hangman late in 1888. However, after his sentence had been pronounced, the New York legislature decided that no convicted murderer would be hanged after June 4, 1888 and that from January 1 of the following year on, the state would use the electric chair for capital punishment. The lawmakers' intention was that anyone with a death sentence who was still alive on June 4 would be executed the next year in the electric chair. But that was not the way they had written the statute. Instead, the law was phrased to say that nobody could be hanged after June 4, 1888 and that "electrocution shall apply to all convictions punishable by death on or after January 1st." Carlton's lawyer was quick to spot the loophole. He demanded that Handsome Harry be freed. Death happened to be the only punishment on the books for murder—unless the jury recommended mercy, which in Handsome Harry's case it had not. If a person committed murder, as Harry had, and got no sympathy from the jury, he or she had to die. However unintentionally, the language of the new law stated that persons who committed murder before June 4, 1888 not only could not be hanged but moreover could not be punished at all.

Handsome Harry became an instant worldwide cause célèbre and his case shook the very foundation of law in New York State. If he were let go, it would mean that for a seven-month period murder was legal in the state! The dispute was rushed to the Supreme Court. In a marked departure from the High Court's traditional respect for legalisms, it ruled that while the interpretation of the law by Carlton's attorney might be technically correct, no slipup by the legislature could be allowed to endanger human lives. Hanging, the Supreme Court held, remained in force until replaced by the electric chair. On a gray morning two days before Christmas, Carlton swung from the gibbet in the Tombs courtyard in New York City. After the execution a newspaper commented, "We are not at all sure that this hanging was entirely legal but it certainly was justice."

See also: HOWE AND HUMMEL.

Catania curse   fate of Mafia victim's family
A Sunday supplement phrase invented to describe the sorry plight of the Catanias, father and son, who met the same fate at the hands of Mafia executioners 29 years apart, it nevertheless reflects the primitive law of survival pervading that criminal organization.

Joe Catania was a Mafia capo who ran the southern Brooklyn docks area in 1902. This position made him extremely valuable to New York's first Mafia family, the Morellos, in their counterfeit money distribution setup. The bogus money was printed in Sicily and then concealed in olive oil shipments that were sent to Catania's piers. From there the bills went to Pittsburgh, Buffalo, Chicago and New Orleans, where they were passed by Mafia organizations. The only threat to the arrangement was Catania himself, whose increasing addiction to the bottle weakened his sense of discretion. When his saloon remarks became too open, Catania was sub-

ject to a special Mafia trial—one that the defendant knew nothing about—and his execution was ordered. His body was found near the Gowanus docks inside a barrel, his throat slit from ear to ear. He had also been so savagely beaten that all major bones in his body were broken, a clear Mafia signal for all to maintain silence.

At the time of his father's assassination, Joseph "Joe the Baker" Catania was only a babe in arms. He grew up in the rackets, as was his right since he was related by blood to the Morello family. On February 3, 1931, just after he kissed his wife good-bye, Joe the Baker was gunned down in the Bronx by Joe Valachi and the mysterious "Buster from Chicago." Much was made about Joe the Baker being a victim of the Masseria-Maranzano war for control of New York, but the fact was that Catania had been marked for death when his father died. It was a Mafia custom that members of a family were supposed to avenge killings of their kin. Joe the Baker, therefore, was supposed to kill his father's assassins. On the other hand, when someone in the Mafia had cause to eliminate Joe the Baker for reasons unrelated to his father's killing, in this case his hijacking of certain bootleg whiskey trucks, they found ready allies among the kin of old Joe Catania's murderers.

Cattle Kate (1862–1889)   prostitute and alleged rustler
Ella Watson, known as Cattle Kate, was an enterprising young prostitute from Kansas who settled in the Wyoming cow country. With a partner of sorts, Jim Averill, she did a thriving business in cattle, which was the coin of the realm for cowboys paying her for services rendered.

It would of course have been highly unusual if the cowboys limited their payments to cows they held clear title to. For a time, Cattle Kate was tolerated by all, including the big stockmen, who understood that men on the range needed certain diversions and cattle losses of this sort were merely the price of doing business, that era's equivalent of cheating on expense accounts. However, the blizzards of 1888 thinned out the herds, and the big stockmen felt they could no longer stand such losses. One July day in 1889 a wealthy and arrogant cattleman named Albert Bothwell and 10 others decided to do something about the matter. They kidnapped Cattle Kate from her cabin, picked up Averill, who had become something of a spokesman for the small homesteaders fencing off the wide-open range, and threatened to hang them. It appears there was no real plan for a lynching but rather just a desire to frighten the duo. Unfortunately for them, neither Cattle Kate nor Averill took the threats seriously, even when nooses were put around their necks. They were then shoved into space, apparently just to carry the scare tactics a step further. But as the pair slowly strangled, no one made a move to cut them down. The lynchings stirred up an outcry from citizens that Bothwell and his friends had not anticipated, but Bothwell's fellow stockmen hastily came up with a new justification for the act. Stories were planted in the friendly Cheyenne press that Cattle Kate was a mean, gun-toting bandit queen and Averill her business manager. They were accused of systematically looting the range, with her red-light activities a mere cover for their crimes. Cattle Kate became a criminal adventuress worthy of front-page coverage in even the *Police Gazette*. The *Cheyenne Weekly*

Rendering of the lynching of Cattle Kate and Jim Averill appeared in a publication sympathetic with the interests of the big cattlemen.

Mail observed that the lynchings indicated the time had come "when men would take the law into their own hands." The whitewash, the cattle barons soon saw, was effective enough cover for them to launch a major attack on the homesteaders in Johnson County, Wyo. Others were accused of running rustling operations similar to Cattle Kate's and, it was said, would have to be dealt with. Thus, the lynching of a 26-year-old prostitute provided the rationale for what was to become the Johnson County War.

See also: JOHNSON COUNTY WAR.

cave-in-rock pirates

The great commercial route that opened the frontier in the early 15th century was down the Ohio and Mississippi Rivers to the port of New Orleans. The two rivers teemed with pirates who falsely marked the channels so that rafts and keelboats would run aground or crash into the rocks. When this wasn't practical, the boats were attacked in skiffs and canoes. The most treacherous stretch was on the Kentucky shore of the Ohio from Red Bank to Smithland, where the king of the local pirates was Bully Wilson.

A Virginian, Wilson set up his headquarters in a cave near the head of Hurricane Bars. Beckoning thirsty travelers to shore was the following sign:

WILSON'S LIQUOR VAULT
and
HOUSE FOR ENTERTAINMENT

The unwary who paused there rarely resumed their voyage. Wilson's place was known as Cave-in-Rock, and the only visitors who could stop there in safety were pirates, robbers, slave stealers and murderers. And if they were alone and were known to have a hoard of loot with them, they were not particularly safe either. But the main purpose of Cave-in-Rock was to prey on river traffic, and Bully Wilson always had 80 to 100 men ready to swoop down on helpless vessels. Whenever a craft was taken, all aboard were killed, and the boat, manned by a pirate crew, would sail on to New Orleans to sell its goods. The river pirates dominated the waterways until the mid-1820s, when the boatmen organized to fight back.

In July 1824 the crews of about a dozen flatboats, about 80 men in all, hid in the cargo box of a single boat and floated down the river. The boat was soon attacked by a force of about 30 pirates, coming out in canoes and skiffs. As the pirates swept aboard the flatboat, the hidden men stormed out of the cargo box. Ten pirates were killed and another 12 captured. They were blindfolded and forced to walk the plank in 20 feet of water. As the helpless men surfaced, crewmen armed with rifles stood on the cargo box and shot them. The end result of such punitive expeditions finally broke the power of Bully Wilson and other pirates, so that the waterways were relatively free of piracy and safe for commerce after 1825.

Chappleau, Joseph Ernst (1850–1911)
murderer

Joseph Chappleau was the first man sentenced to die in the electric chair, but he escaped that fate in 1889 when the newfangled instrument of death was not completed in time for his execution, and his sentence was commuted to life imprisonment. In his memoirs, the famous warden of Sing Sing, Lewis E. Lawes, later credited Chappleau with doing more to shape his philosophy of modern penology than any other man. While Lawes was a rookie guard at Clinton Prison in New York in 1905, Chappleau was credited with saving his life in a prison yard melee.

A New York farmer, Chappleau had been found guilty of the murder of a neighbor named Tabor over some poisoned cows. The real motive for the murder, according to local gossip, was not the poisoning of the cows but an affair between Tabor and Chappleau's wife. Once his sentence had been commuted, Chappleau became a prisoner uniquely popular with other convicts and the guards. None regarded him as a true criminal but rather a man trapped by fate. Lawes came to regard Chappleau as the perfect example of a murderer not likely ever to commit another crime and perhaps the best possible argument against capital punishment, a penalty Chappleau had escaped for purely technical reasons. When Chappleau died in the prison hospital at Clinton in 1911, guards and prisoners alike declared their happiness that he had been released from the burdens of his life.

Charlton Street Gang Hudson River pirates

In early New York virtually all pirate activity was restricted to the East River, where the prime loot was the stores of relatively small craft. On the West Side, only a daring bunch of ruffians called the Charlton Street Gang worked the Hudson River, but they did it with a vengeance, actually flying the Jolly Roger and making forays as far upriver as Poughkeepsie, attacking riverside mansions and even kidnapping men, women and children for ransom. In the 1860s the Charlton Streeters found the pickings on their side of Manhattan slim because the Hudson piers were reserved for ocean vessels and shippers kept an army of watchmen on duty to protect their property. With looting in the immediate city area not very rewarding, gang leaders were forced to cast their eyes upstream. It is doubtful if their ambitions would ever have become as grandiose as they did without the inspiration of an attractive but deadly harridan named Sadie the Goat. She convinced them in 1869 that to be successful river pirates, they had to have a first-class sloop of their own, one that could outrun pursuers. The gang promptly went out and stole one.

The gang flew the Jolly Roger from the masthead, finding that its appearance frightened residents along the Hudson from the Harlem River to Poughkeepsie and tended to encourage flight rather than resistance. The Charlton Streeters soon had a lucrative enterprise going, looting farmhouses and mansions. Learning that Julius Caesar had once been held for ransom by pirates, Sadie involved the gang in kidnapping. She cut a sinister figure pacing the deck, issuing orders. According to the sensationalist press of the day, Sadie on several occasions made men walk the plank in proper piratical style.

After a number of murders had been committed, the desperate riverside residents finally organized vigilante posses to battle the pirates. Their ranks thinned by a number of musket battles, the Charlton Streeters returned to their home base and restricted their activities to more ordinary urban crimes. Sadie the Goat left the group in disgust with its timidity.

See also: GALLUS MAG.

Cherry Hill Gang   Gay Nineties criminals

A vicious bunch of thieves and killers, the Cherry Hill Gang were the "dandies" of the New York underworld in the 1890s. Members of the gang were seldom seen in other than dress suits and often carried walking sticks, metal-weighted of course. Disguised in the height of fashion, they found it easy to get within striking range of a well-heeled gentleman and attack before their victim had a chance to be alarmed.

The Cherry Hillers were also responsible for provoking others to crime out of envy. Other gangs often tried to match their sartorial splendor and would go to any lengths to do so. When the Batavia Street Gang announced plans to hold a ball at New Irving Hall, the Cherry Hillers announced they were obtaining new wardrobes for the occasion. As hosts, the Batavians felt required to match or surpass the Cherry Hillers in dress. To raise funds the night before the gala social affair, the gangsters smashed a window of Segal's jewelry store on New Chambers Street and carried off 44 gold rings. They sold them the following morning, but more than a dozen of the gangsters were caught by police as they were being fitted for new suits at a Division Street tailor shop. On the night of the big event, the leading lights of the Batavia Street Gang languished in the Tombs while the elegant dandies of Cherry Hill were once again the hit of the ball.

Chicago fire looting

Without question the greatest rampage of criminality sparked by an American disaster occurred during the 24 hours of the Great Chicago Fire on October 8–9, 1871.

The *Chicago Post* perhaps best set the scene:

The people were mad. Despite the police—indeed, the police were powerless—they crowded upon frail coigns of vantage, as fences and high sidewalks propped on wooded piles, which fell beneath their weight, and hurled them, bruised and bleeding, in the dust. They stumbled over broken furniture and fell, and were trampled under foot. Seized with wild and causeless panics, they surged together, backwards and forwards, in the narrow streets, cursing, threatening, imploring, fighting to get free. Liquor flowed like water; for the saloons were broken open and despoiled, and men on all sides were to be seen frenzied with drink. . . . Everywhere dust, smoke, flame, heat, thunder of falling shouts, braying of trumpets, wind, tumult, and uproar.

And into this human cauldron the criminals swarmed. Hoodlums, prostitutes, thieves hunting alone or in packs snatched all they wanted from drays and carriages. They broke into stores and homes and stuffed their pockets with money and jewelry. Men ran about wearing as many as a dozen women's rings and bracelets. They broke into saloons and guzzled down liquor to fortify their criminal daring. "They smashed windows with their naked hands," the *Post* reported, "regardless of the wounds inflicted, and with bloody fingers rifled till and shelf and cellar, fighting viciously for the spoils of their forage. Women, hollow-eyed and brazen-faced, with filthy drapery tied over them, their clothes in tatters and their feet in trodden-over slippers, moved here and there—scolding, stealing, fighting; laughing at the beautiful and splendid crash of walls and falling roofs."

When the courthouse caught fire, guards released 350 prisoners from the basement jail and then watched helplessly as they descended in a single horde on a jewelry store and looted every stone, every watch in the place. William Walker, a Chicago reporter, added his eyewitness account:

As the night wore on, and the terrors aggregated into an intensity of misery, the thieves, amateur and professional, dropped all pretense at concealment and plied their knavish calling undaunted by any fear of immediate retribution. They would storm into stores, smash away at the safes, and if, as happily was almost always the case, they failed to effect an opening, they would turn their attention to securing all of value from the stock that could conveniently be made away with, and then slouch off in search of further booty. The promise of a share in the spoils gave them the assistance of rascally express-drivers, who stood with their wagons before doors of stores, and waited as composedly for a load of stolen property to be piled in as if they were receiving the honestly-acquired goods of the best man in town. . . . The scenes of robbery were not confined to the sacking of stores. Burglars would raid into the private dwellings that lay in the track of the coming destruction, and snatch . . . anything which their practical senses told them would be of value. Interference was useless. The scoundrels . . . were inflamed with drink, and were alarmingly demonstrative in the flourishing of deadly weapons. Sometimes women and children, and not infrequently men, would be stopped as they were bearing from their homes objects of especial worth, and the articles would be torn from their grasp by gangs of these wretches.

Besides the looting, which the authorities were unable to thwart, trouble developed from a new source. By the time the conflagration was burning itself out on the night of October 9, firebugs took to the streets trying to start new blazes, some for the thrill of it and others because they had seen how fire created opportunities for looting. Seven men were shot after being caught setting fires and another was stoned to death by an angry mob, his body left on the street as a warning to others. For the next 13 days Chicago was patrolled by 2,400 regular and special policemen, six companies of state militia and four companies of U.S. Army troops, all under Gen. Phil Sheridan, who placed the city under martial law. Perhaps the most significant comment on the aftermath of the Chicago Fire was a historian's observation that "no part of Chicago was rebuilt more quickly than the saloons, brothels, gambling-houses, and other resorts and habitations of the underworld."

Chicago Times sensationalist newspaper

If any one 19th-century newspaper can be singled out as the most devoted to the coverage of crime news, it would have to be the *Chicago Times*, which was founded in 1854 to promote the political career of Sen. Stephen A. Douglas, a role it continued to fulfill until it was sold to Cyrus H. McCormick, the reaper manufacturer, in 1860. A year later, McCormick sold the newspaper to Wilbur F. Storey of Vermont, who made it into an antiwar publication upon the issuance of the Emancipation Proclamation, which Storey regarded as a deceitful act because it switched the war's aims. To silence Storey's blasts at President Lincoln, Gen. Ambrose Burnside seized the *Times*, provoking one of the great civil liberties controversies of the Civil War. Mobs formed at the *Times* to support the army action, while Copperhead forces swarmed around the *Chicago Tribune* office and threatened to burn down that newspaper's building unless the *Times* was allowed to publish. Tempers were dampened when Lincoln revoked Gen. Burnside's order of suppression, and the *Times* appeared again.

However, it was after the war that the *Times* emerged, under Storey, as one of the great muckraking and crusading newspapers, carrying on a steady fight against crime and political corruption, exposing the growing accommodation between the underworld and politicians and identifying reputable citizens who allowed their property to be used for immoral purposes. Storey's staff reporters originated or popularized many phrases that were to become criminal vernacular. The word *racket* appears to have been born in the *Times* on October 24, 1876, when the newspaper carried a story that noted, "big thieves are boldly traversing our streets by day, planning their racket." The *Times* headline style on criminal matters was certainly colorful as well as prejudicial. When on September 10, 1872 a notorious hoodlum named Christopher Rafferty was found guilty of the murder of Patrolman Patrick O'Meara, Storey's paper turned nearly poetic with the following headline:

SHUT OFF HIS WIND

A Satisfactory Job for Jack Ketch at Last.
The Hangman's Rope Awarded to
Christopher Rafferty.
Now, Do Not Reprieve Nor Pardon Him.
Nor Give Him a New Trial.
And, in the Name of All That's Decent,
Don't Commute His Sentence.
The Jury Concludes, in Just Twenty Minutes,
To String the Ruffian Up.

Perhaps an even more colorful headline, one still quoted in journalistic circles, appeared on November 27, 1875; it read:

JERKED TO JESUS

Four Senegambian Butchers Were
Wafted to Heaven on
Yesterday from Scaffolds.
Two of Them, in Louisiana, Died with
the Sweet Confidence of
Pious People.
While Yet Two Others, in Mississippi, Expired
Exhorting the Public to Beware of
Sisters-In-Law.

Sometimes Storey's outspoken attitudes on crime and morality got him in deep trouble. When the noted burlesque actress Lydia Thompson appeared at Crosby's Opera House with her troupe of "English Blondes," the *Times* denounced the young maids for "capering lasciviously and uttering gross indecencies." The *Times* added that Miss Thompson was not much better than a common strumpet and that Chicagoans would do well to run her out of their city. When Storey

refused to retract the statements, Miss Thompson caught him in front of his home on Wabash Avenue and beat him severely with a horsewhip.

Chowchilla school bus kidnapping

The greatest kidnap for ransom plot in terms of numbers of victims in the United States took place on July 15, 1976 near the town of Chowchilla, Calif. By blocking the road with a van, three stocking-masked armed men stopped a school bus containing 19 girls and seven boys returning from a summer school session. While one of the three masked men drove the bus off and hid it in a dried-out creek bed, the 26 children and the bus driver were herded into the van used for the blockade and a second van driven up from a hiding place. The driver and the children, who ranged in age from six to 14 years, were driven around for more than 11 hours and finally brought to a rock quarry near Livermore, less than 100 miles from the kidnap site.

There they were all transferred to a large moving van that had been buried in an isolated section of the quarry. Tarpaulins were stretched from the two small vans to the roof of the buried van so that the prisoners could not see where they were. A hole had been cut in the roof of the buried van, and the children were forced to climb down a ladder into their underground prison. Before each child was transferred, his or her name and age were recorded and a personal item or bit of clothing was taken, obviously for proof later that the kidnappers indeed held them prisoner.

The bus driver was given a flashlight and ordered into the moving van, which was then sealed off with large sheets of metal, plywood, dirt and other debris. The van, 25 feet long and 8 feet wide, had been well furnished for accommodation of the prisoners, containing a portable toilet and supplies of water, bread, potato chips and breakfast cereal. There were a number of mattresses, and ventilation was provided by 4-inch rubber tubing, with air pumped in and out by two battery-driven fans.

Later that day a police air search located the abandoned school bus, but there was no trace of the children, and terror gripped the Chowchilla area. Twenty-four hours went by without a ransom demand from the kidnappers, who were apparently determined to fuel the parents' anxiety further so that the state would be forced to make payment immediately. However, the kidnappers' plans went awry when, 16 hours after their imprisonment in the large van, the driver and some of the older children managed to dig their way out. When all the children were pulled free, the group walked toward lights in the distance. They found a quarry employee, who immediately called the police. The Chowchilla children's ordeal was over.

It took the authorities 12 days to round up the three kidnappers involved. The day before the kidnapping a woman had jotted down the license number—1C91414—of a small van near what was to prove to be the site of the abduction. She had become suspicious of the van's occupants. The school bus driver underwent voluntary hypnosis and was able to recall the license number of one of the vans—1C91414—and all but one digit of the other. The numbers were eventually traced to an Oakland car dealer, and the large buried van to a Palo Alto firm, which had sold it to one Mark Hall. Employees at the Palo Alto and Oakland firms identified the purchaser from photographs as Frederick

Newhall Woods IV, the son of the owner of the rock quarry. Some of the children recalled hearing their abductors use the names Fred and James, and since Woods was known to be close friends with two brothers named James and Richard Allen Schoenfeld, sons of a prominent Atherton podiatrist, warrants were issued for them as well. Richard Allen Schoenfeld surrendered to authorities on July 23, and his older brother was captured on July 29. On the same day, Woods was arrested by Royal Canadian Mounted Police in Vancouver.

The defendants chose a court trial rather than a jury trial, feeling that jurors would be hostile because the victims had been children. Evidence indicated that the trio had worked on the details of the kidnapping for an entire year before setting it in motion. All three were convicted of 24 counts of kidnapping and three of kidnapping with bodily harm. Richard Allen Schoenfeld got life imprisonment, and brother James and Woods drew life with a stipulation barring parole.

Cicero, Illinois mob-controlled Chicago suburb

In the heyday of the Capone mob, Cicero was known as the syndicate's town. Al Capone's private guard in Cicero totaled about 800 gunmen, while the town's police force numbered about 50. Any officer who considered standing up to the Capone gang thought twice because every official from the major down to the dogcatcher was believed to follow Capone's orders without question. Once when the mayor dared to displease Capone, the mob chieftain knocked His Honor down on the steps of the town hall and kicked him unmercifully in the groin. A Cicero policeman watched the entire procedure, reportedly looking quite embarrassed.

In 1924 the Democrats dared to put up candidates opposing the Klenha slate, which with bipartisan backing had ruled the town for three terms. The Capone forces sent in hundreds of gangsters to guarantee the proper election results. On the eve of the election, William F. Pflaum, the Democratic candidate for town clerk, was roughed up in his office and the place was totally wrecked. On election day gangsters in seven-passenger black limousines patrolled the streets, terrorizing the citizenry. Persons known to favor the Democrats were beaten. Capone men walked up and down lines of voters asking people how they intended to vote. If they gave a wrong answer, their ballots would be snatched from their hands and marked properly by the mobsters. Then a Capone hood, fingering a revolver in his coat pocket, would stand beside the voter until he or she dropped the ballot into the box. Honest poll watchers and election officials were simply kidnapped and held until the polls closed. A Democratic campaign worker, Michael Gavin, was shot through both legs; policemen were blackjacked.

Terrified Cicero citizens appealed to the courts for aid. Cook County judge Edmund K. Jarecki deputized 70 Chicago patrolmen, nine squads of motorized police and five squads of detectives and sent them to the beleaguered town. That afternoon and evening pitched battles were fought between gangsters and police. Frank Capone, Al's brother, took aim at officers piling out of an unmarked black limousine and squeezed the trigger of his automatic, but it clicked on an empty chamber. Before he could pull the trigger again, two lawmen blasted him with their shotguns.

When Al buried Frank a few days later, he could at least console himself with the knowledge that his brother had not died in vain. The Klenha slate carried the election by a huge margin.

Cincinnati riots

A common public perception in 19th-century big-city America was that enforcment agencies and the courts were corrupt and that criminals could often buy their freedom or mild sentences. This view, hardly unjustified, led to the organization of many vigilance committees and to frequent and bloody riots.

One of the worst of these took place in Cincinnati, Ohio in 1884. The public had been outraged by the action of the criminal courts, which in the previous year had sentenced to death only four persons out of 50 convicted of capital crimes. On March 28, 1884 a huge mob stormed the jail where two youths who had been let off with manslaughter convictions were being held. They lynched the pair and were finally dispersed by a militia company. The following night mobs formed again to perform additional acts of "instant justice." Stores were looted of guns, the jail attacked and the courthouse set afire and almost totally destroyed. The rioters were eventually driven off after a pitched battle with troops. Violence continued the third day, a Sunday, and that night the mobs, which now contained large numbers of criminals protesting for law and order and looting stores at the same time, again battled the militia. Soldiers were rushed in from all parts of the state and streets were barricaded to isolate the mobs. Vicious fighting continued for three more days before the barricades could be removed and street-car service restored. The death toll in the rioting was at least 45 persons with 138 more badly injured. Despite the riots, Cincinnati retained its reputation as a wide-open city during the immediate ensuing years.

coffin, double-decker   Mafia body disposal method

From the time of its first appearance in America during the 19th century, the Mafia has been most inventive in the ways it disposes of the bodies of murder victims; a great many are finally listed in official records as missing, instead of dead. Some victims have been fitted with "concrete overcoats" or ground up in garbage shredders. Top New York mafioso Tony Bender is believed now to be either part of a large Manhattan skyscraper or of the recently crumbling West Side Highway (an in-joke in certain Mafia circles is that "dagos make lousy roads").

Perhaps the quaintest of all body disposal devices is the "double-decker coffin." A murder victim is taken to one of the mob's cooperative undertakers who constructs a special panel in a coffin he has ready for an about-to-be-buried corpse. The unwanted murder victim is placed in the bottom of the coffin and a panel is put over the body. Then the right corpse is placed on top. After a properly mournful funeral, the two corpses are buried together. No undertaker has ever been convicted as a result of this method because he can always claim the mob must have dug open the grave after burial and put in the extra corpse. The undertaker cooperating with the mob on such a matter is assured of the proper financial reward because the crime family will see to it that he gets a good deal of their regular business thrown his way.

College Kidnappers   Chicago gang

During the early-1930s heyday of the kidnapping gangs, one combine that operated in unique fashion was the so-called College Kidnappers of Chicago. They specialized in snatching only underworld characters, who not only could afford to pay but also were not likely to complain to the police.

The gang got its name because most of its members were college graduates; the leader, Theodore "Handsome Jack" Klutas, was an alumnus of the University of Illinois. The modus operandi of the gang was to pick up gossip in underworld circles about who had made a big "score." They would then kidnap the individual and release him only when they received a slice of the loot. Quite often, members of the Chicago mob were their victims, a pattern that earned the College Kidnappers the enmity of the Capone operation. But Klutas and his men had little fear of organized crime and continued their onslaughts, reportedly pulling in more than $500,000 dollars in ransom money between 1930 and 1933.

In 1933 a hot rumor, later proven to have some basis in fact, spread that the College Kidnappers had merged the Dillinger gang into their operations. Faced with this disturbing news, the Capone forces decided to try to buy off the kidnappers and persuaded one of the kidnappers, Julius "Babe" Jones, to approach Klutas to arrange a deal. Klutas told Jones he would consider it but, as soon as Jones left, ordered his assassination. The attempt was made by first stealing Jones' car and then faking a telephone call, allegedly from the Joliet police, to tell him that his car had been found and could be picked up at a local garage. Jones, an old hand at College Kidnapper tricks, was suspicious and drove by the garage dressed as a woman. As he expected, he spotted two gang members parked in a car opposite the garage, ready to gun him down when he appeared.

Now trapped between the College Kidnappers and the Capones, Jones could only turn to the police, informing them about a number of the gang's hideouts. One was a brick bungalow in Bellwood. When two squads of detectives stormed the bungalow, they captured two wanted criminals. One was Walter Dietrich, one of 10 convicts Dillinger had helped to break out of the Michigan City Prison. Dietrich refused to say where Klutas was or whether he alone or the rest of the Dillinger gang had joined the College Kidnappers. Meanwhile, acting on Jones' information, the police rounded up several other gang members, but not Klutas.

Later that same day a stakeout at the Bellwood bungalow paid off. A car pulled up, and Klutas boldly strode up the walkway. As Klutas pushed open the door, four police officers trained guns on him, including Sgt. Joe Healy's machine gun. Healy said: "Hands up. Police officers."

Klutas, who had always vowed never to be taken alive, reached under his overcoat for a gun. Healy loosed a burst of machine-gun bullets into the gangster's chest. Klutas was thrown clear off the bungalow porch to the sidewalk. He was dead, and the College Kidnappers were finished.

Colonel Plug (?–1820?) river pirate
With Bully Wilson, Col. Plug was one of the two most important pirates who preyed on boat traffic along the Ohio and Mississippi Rivers. A bewhiskered giant whose real name was Fluger, Col. Plug boasted he had been a colonel in the American Revolution. Plug's modus operandi was to hide aboard a flatboat that was tied up for the night. When it got going in the morning, he would dig out the caulking between the planks and bore holes in the bottom. Col. Plug would time his work so that the boat would be scuttled opposite his hideout. His gang would row out to the flatboat in skiffs, supposedly coming to the rescue. The only person to be rescued would be Col. Plug, of course, along with the cargo; the crew and passengers would be left to drown, or, if they resisted, to be shot. Col. Plug was active for many years until, according to the legend, he bored too many holes one day and the boat he was sabotaging went to the bottom before Plug could climb out of the hold. At least, so the story was told in pirate circles, presumably accurate since suddenly Col. Plug ceased to be a scourge of the rivers.

See also: CAVE-IN-ROCK PIRATES.

colonial punishment
Punishment for crime tended to be less severe in colonial America than in the countries from which most colonists had come. The New England colonies and the Quaker settlements in West Jersey and Pennsylvania had punishments that in general were less harsh than those used in New York and the South. In New England the main thrust of punishment came in the form of humiliation; thus when Mary Mandame of Plymouth became the supposed first female sex offender in 1639, she was required to wear a badge of shame on her left sleeve. Had she failed to do so, she would have been branded in the face with a hot iron, but the mere threat of this punishment brought compliance in almost all cases. Vagrancy brought punishment in the stocks, while the ducking stool was held ready for the scold. More serious crimes brought stricter penalties. Murder and witchcraft called for hanging, and burglars were branded.

The same crime called for far different punishments in various jurisdictions. Theft in New York was punishable by multiple restitution and whipping, but in numerous Southern colonies the death penalty was often exacted when the sum taken was more than 12 pence. In several New England settlements a gentleman could commit the following offenses and be fined a sum equivalent to $10: lie eight times; swear four times; beat his wife twice; or criticize a court once.

In the Massachusetts Bay Colony in the early 18th century punishment did not end with a mere flogging or confinement in the stocks. After initial punishment offenders were then required to wear on their arm or bosom for a year or many years a large letter cut from scarlet cloth. The letter identified the crime for which the offender had been punished, such as A for adultery, B for blasphemy, D for drunkenness, I for incest, P for poisoning, R for rape, T for thievery. However, it was soon decided that this punishment was too inhumane and it was abandoned.

Whippings were often carried to excess, with the result that the convicted person often was left crippled for life. In New England an attempt was made to prevent this abuse by limiting the number of lashes to 39, as called for under Mosaic law. Contrary to common belief, no one, not even a witch, was burned at the stake in New England. However, burning and quartering were practiced in New York and the South. In the great Negro Plot of 1741 in New York, many blacks were put to the stake. Quartering was generally applied for treason and to blacks. In Maryland a black who murdered an overseer was punished by having a hand cut off, then hanging and finally quartering.

Perhaps the sternest punishments were carried out in Virginia. A slave who ran away might have an ear nailed to the pillory and then cut off. Criticism of the authorities in that colony meant an offender could be pilloried with a placard, lose both ears, do a year's service for the colony or have his ears nailed to the pillory. The most common punishment for the offense was being laid "neck and hells" in irons and then heavily fined. Virginia probably decreed more castrations of blacks than did any other colony.

See also: BOOK WHIPPINGS, BRANDING.

Colt, John C. (1819–1842?) murderer

John C. Colt was the central figure in a classic murder case in 1841 that started with a solution but concluded in a mystery.

Colt was a member of one of New York's millionaire merchant families and the brother of Samuel Colt, inventor of the Colt revolver and the Colt repeating rifle. At 22 John was tall, slim and handsome, with curly blond hair and steel gray eyes. The darling of society, he fancied himself a writer of sorts and numbered among his close friends Edgar Allan Poe, Washington Irving, James Fenimore Cooper, John Howard Payne, George Palmer Putnam and Lewis Clark.

Despite his literary bent, Colt had a quick, uncertain temper, and in a nasty argument he killed Samuel Adams, a printer he had hired to produce a book of his. Colt was tried speedily and sentenced to be hanged. There were those who said Colt would never hang, that his family was too powerful. Press exposés of Colt's treatment in the city's new prison, the Tombs, informed the public that Colt lived an exceedingly happy life for a condemned man. He had flowers on his table and a pet canary. A young Charles Dana reported: "In a patent extension chair he lolls smoking an aromatic Havana. . . . He has on an elegant dress-gown, faced with cherry-colored silk, and his feet are encased in delicately worked slippers." His food was "not cooked in the Tombs, but brought in from a hotel. It consists of a variety of dishes—quail on toast, game pates, reed birds, ortolans, fowl, vegetables, coffee, cognac."

The greatest concession to Colt's grand station was the permission granted by prison authorities that he be allowed to marry his fiancée Caroline Henshaw on the morning of November 18, the day of his execution. Newspaper announcements of the bizarre nuptials-gallows ceremony brought out thousands of thrill seekers who jammed Centre (later Center) Street at dawn. Miss Henshaw was forced to come by carriage to a side street entrance to the Tombs at about 11:30. During the actual wedding ceremony, carpenters assembling the gallows in the courtyard politely suspended their hammering, a fact a guard relayed to the crowd outside. The crowd moaned at that. It moaned again when word was passed, "They're married." Other news was passed as it happened. "The guests have gone. . . . There are silk curtains across the cell door. . . . They've ordered champagne. . . . They're testing the gallows!"

Shortly after 1 P.M. the new Mrs. Colt was advised that she had to leave, and she did so "smiling bravely." Later, there would be much conjecture over whether Caroline slipped her groom a large dagger with which he could stab himself in the heart and thus escape the noose. At 3:30 P.M. the Rev. Henry Anton, who had officiated at the wedding, was ordered to offer his final services to the condemned man. At that moment the tinder-dry wooden cupola atop the adjacent Hall of Justice mysteriously caught fire. Within three minutes smoke was pouring into the interior

of the prison. Panic broke out and several guards raced out of the building. Convicts banged on their bars and begged to be let out, and some apparently were by the few remaining keepers. In the smoke-filled confusion, Rev. Anton rushed up to Sheriff Monmouth Hart and cried: "Mr. Colt is dead! He has a dagger in his heart!"

Instead of proceeding to the cell, the sheriff rushed around in search of the doctor who was there to pronounce Colt dead after his now unnecessary execution. At 7 P.M. a hurriedly convened coroner's jury officially declared Colt had committed suicide. It was a remarkable hearing, with no official identification of Colt being made. Not even Rev. Anton was called to testify. The body was released and buried that same night in the yard of St. Mark's Church. Afterward, the recently widowed Mrs. Colt disappeared.

At first, the newspapers focused on the source of the death dagger, including in the speculation every member of the wedding party. Only when it later was conceded by officials that a number of prisoners had escaped during the fire, did it suddenly occur to anyone that Colt could have escaped in the confusion—if there was a body to substitute for him.

The New York Herald commented, "We have no doubt that Governor Seward will order an investigation at once into this most unheard of, most unparalleled tragedy." No investigation was ever held, however, although even George Walling, who was appointed chief of police shortly therafter, gave considerable credence to the idea of a substitute corpse. So too did Colt's friends. In 1849 Edgar Allan Poe received an unsigned manuscript from Texas written in the unmistakable hand of John Colt. He took the manuscript to Lewis Clark, editor of *The Knickerbocker* magazine, and found Clark too had gotten a copy. They concluded it was Colt's way of letting them know he was alive and still trying for a literary career. Then in 1852 Samuel Everett, a close friend of Colt, returned from a visit to California and told others in the Colt circle of friends that he had met John Colt while horseback riding in the Santa Clara Valley. According to Everett, Colt lived in a magnificent hacienda with his wife, the former Caroline Henshaw.

Many students of crime dismiss the substitute corpse theory and regard Everett's story as apocryphal, insisting it was just an exotic fillip to an incredible tale. Others find the chain of events too mired in coincidence. That Colt should commit suicide just at the moment of a mysterious fire during which several prisoners escaped, they say, staggers the imagination. And why did the widowed Mrs. Colt disappear from New York City after her husband's death?

confessions, false

In Chicago during the 1950s a pregnant woman was viciously slain and her body dumped in a snowbank. Almost immediately a factory worker came forth and confessed. He stood a good chance of becoming a modern-day lynching victim since a spirit of vengeance dominated the woman's neighborhood. That sentiment dissipated, however, when a 19-year-old sailor at the Great Lakes Naval Station also confessed to the slaying. This second confession turned out to be the real one.

In 1961 a young widow in New York tearfully told police she had killed her husband several years earlier. His death had been attributed to natural causes. The body was

exhumed and an autopsy performed. The man had died of natural causes, and psychiatrists found the woman was merely suffering from delusions that stemmed from a guilt complex that she had failed to be a good wife to her late husband.

Both of these persons could easily have been convicted of the crimes to which they so eagerly confessed. Throughout hundreds of years of legal history, the confession has been viewed by the courts and society as the "queen of proofs" of criminal guilt. Yet, each year probably thousands of persons in this country confess to crimes that they did not, and could not, have committed. Why do they do it? Some are neurotics who will confess to any crime just for the excitement of being the center of attention; for example, more than 200 persons confessed to the Lindbergh baby kidnapping. Others are motivated by bizarre guilt feelings for some other incident, often trivial; they seek punishment, consciously or subconsciously, for a crime they did not commit.

Whenever legal experts discuss false confessions, the subject of the mutiny of the *Hermione* is raised. The *Hermione* was a British frigate captained by a harsh disciplinarian named Pigot. In September 1797 the seething anger of the crew erupted against Pigot and his officers. The men of the *Hermione* not only murdered the captain and the officers, they butchered them. The crew then sailed to an enemy port, but one young midshipman escaped and got back to England. He identified many of the offenders, and some of them were run down and hanged.

Many innocent sailors confessed to taking part in the *Hermione* mutiny. One admiralty officer later wrote:

In my own experience, I have known, on separate occasions, more than six sailors who voluntarily confessed to having struck the first blow at Captain Pigot. These men detailed all the horrid circumstances of the mutiny with extreme minuteness and perfect accuracy. Nevertheless, not one of them had even been in the ship, nor had so much as seen Captain Pigot in their lives. They had obtained from their messmates the particulars of the story. When long on a foreign station, hungering and thirsting for home, their minds became enfeebled. At length, they actually believed themselves guilty of the crime over which they had so long brooded, and submitted with a gloomy pleasure to being sent to England in irons for judgment. At the Admiralty, we were always able to detect and establish their innocence.

The last sentiment was, of course, self-serving and perhaps not shared by all. Sir Samuel Romilly related the fate of another seaman who confessed to taking part in the same incident. He was executed. Later, Sir Samuel learned that when the mutiny had taken place on the *Hermione*, the sailor was at Portsmouth aboard the *Marlborough*.

American criminal history is replete with persons confessing to crimes and indeed to noncrimes. The classic case of the latter occurred in Vermont during the 19th century, when two brothers, Stephen and Jesse Boorn, confessed in colorful detail the slaying of Russell Colvin, their brother-in-law. They were both sentenced to death, but Jesse, in recognition of the fact that he had confessed first, had his sentence commuted to life. Stephen's hanging was only postponed when Colvin fortuitously returned home after an absence of seven years, during which time he had had no idea that he had been "murdered."

Probably the great-granddaddy of all cases involving false confessions was the Los Angeles murder of Elizabeth Short in 1947. The case was to become famous as the Black Dahlia murder. The police took full written confessions from at least 38 suspects, and after more than 200 others had telephoned their admissions of guilt and offers to surrender, the police stopped keeping count of confessions.

In the Black Dahlia case the number of confessions was attributable to the sadistic nature of the crime. Such vile crimes invariably produce great numbers of confessions, as though the neurotic confessors literally beg for the spotlight of revulsion and contempt. Many, experts say, are made by persons propelled by a death wish and eager to find the most spectacular method of committing suicide, e.g., in the Black Dahlia case, going to the gas chamber. Others have different motivations. When a girl named Selma Graff was bludgeoned to death by a burglar in Brooklyn during the 1950s, the police got the usual rash of phony confessions. One of them came from a young ex-con out on probation for auto theft. He carried within him a vicious hatred for his mother, who was always so embarrassed by his criminal traits and who at the moment was threatening to notify his parole officer that he had been visiting bars. So he walked into police headquarters and gave himself up for the Graff killing. His story proved to be a hoax when he was unable to supply the murder weapon and could not describe the Graff home accurately. Finally admitting his falsehood, he said he gladly would have gotten himself convicted of the murder, even gone to the chair, in order to torment his mother.

Privately, even some former prosecutors say all confessions should be suspect, that it is illogical to expect that a police officer who has worked hard to extract a confession from a suspect will be just as diligent in his efforts to test whether the confession is true or not. More often, the police and prosecutors have clung to discredited confessions in an effort to convict someone who later proved to be an innocent man. A case in point was George Whitmore, Jr., the man who was wrongly accused of the notorious "career girl" sex slayings of Janice Wylie and Emily Hoffert in their Manhattan apartment in 1963. Whitmore-type incidents, especially repudiated confessions, were cited by the Supreme Court in the landmark Miranda decision, which led to curbs on police powers to interrogate suspects. Some attorneys, such as O. John Rogge, a former assistant attorney general of the United States and author of the book *Why Men Confess,* hold to the theory that no repudiated confession should ever be used in court. They believe that the Supreme Court is gradually moving, perhaps with some steps backward from time to time, in that direction. Quite naturally, prosecuting attorneys claim that such action will make convictions next to impossible to obtain.

See also: BLACK DAHLIA, HAROLD ISRAEL.

Connors, Babe (1856–1918) St. Louis madam

Outside of the bagnios of New Orleans, no brothel contributed more to the arts than the famous St. Louis parlor of a plump mulatto madam named Babe Connors. More than most practitioners of her trade, Babe thought of her places, especially her famous Palace, which she opened in 1898, not only as houses of sexual pleasure but also as centers of entertainment, mostly erotic of course, but musical as well. The Palace itself was a work of art, featuring magnificent crystal chandeliers, extremely expensive rugs, tapestries and objets d'art. Babe staged renowned shows in which her most lovely octoroons danced on a mirrored floor wearing elegant evening gowns and no underclothes. But the highlight of the show was always music and song. For years Babe presented the incredible old black singer Mama Lou. Mama, who wore the traditional calico dress, gingham apron and bright bandana, gave forth with famous downhome field songs and blues. Music-loving whites flocked to Babe Connors' establishment to listen to Mama Lou. Even the great Ignace Paderewski journeyed to hear Mama Lou and accompany her on the parlor piano in the early 1890s. Virtually all of Mama Lou's songs were obscene, but many provided the original melodies for such later hits as "Bully Song" and "Hot Time in the Old Town Tonight."

While Babe Connors' resorts, such as the Palace on Chestnut Street and the earlier Castle on Sixth Street, were among the most lavish in the country, racial law and custom restricted their profit level to about a third or less than what other great houses of the period netted. But even as $5 houses, Babe Connors' famed resorts produced revenues that made her among the most illustrious women of her kind and allowed her to live in fun-loving elegance. Her open carriage was one of the sights at Forest Park, where Babe, bedecked with feathered boa and parasol, rode by in regal splendor, nodding her head only at those gentlemen who acknowledged her first. In her later years Babe converted to Catholicism and, unlike most of her scarlet sisters, was permitted burial in consecrated ground.

"Cooper, D. B." (?–?) legendary airline hijacker
A hijacker who commandeered an airliner, collected a $200,000 ransom and then apparently parachuted to earth, "D. B. Cooper" achieved folk hero status in the Pacific Northwest. His daring 1971 exploit made him the perpetrator of the nation's only unsolved skyjacking. D. B. Cooper T-shirts were sold, and books about his crime were written. The community of Ariel, Wash., near the spot where Cooper was believed to have landed, has held annual daylong celebrations on the anniversary of the crime.

On Thanksgiving eve 1971, a man calling himself D. B. Cooper bought a ticket for a Northwest Orient Airlines flight from Portland, Ore. to Seattle, Wash. Once airborne, Cooper, wearing dark glasses, told a flight attendant he had a bomb in his briefcase and demanded $200,000 in $20 bills and four parachutes. After the plane, a 727 Trijet, landed in Seattle, the hijacker released the 36 passengers and all but three of the crew upon receipt of the ransom money. He then ordered the 727 be flown to Reno, Nev. When the plane landed in Reno, there was no trace of Cooper, but the rear exit door under the tail was open. The FBI theorized that Cooper, dressed only in a business suit and street shoes, jumped from the plane over southwest Washington into a howling wind and a freezing rain.

Did D. B. Cooper survive? Although the FBI never said so officially, it was known to have felt that the hijacker-extortionist had most likely perished in the plunge. However, no body has ever been found. The $200,000 in ransom had been paid in marked bills, none of which turned up until 1980, when a few thousand dollars was discovered partially buried along the north bank of the Columbia River near Vancouver, Wash. The bills had been dug up by children playing in the sand during a family picnic. It was unclear whether the money had been buried there or washed downstream years ago from a Columbia River tributary. While the find reinvigorated the investigation of the case, the true believers in D. B. Cooper refused to accept the theory that the money had been blown away when Cooper died on impact. They felt it could have been lost or, because it was a small portion of the loot, deliberately discarded by Cooper in an effort to make it appear he had not survived. Obviously, as far as the legend goes, until a body is found and identified, D. B. Cooper lives!

Corbett, Boston (1822–?) killer of John Wilkes Booth
An army sergeant named Boston Corbett, whose name has always figured prominently in logical or illogical Lincoln conspiracy plots, was one of the pursuers of John Wilkes Booth, the man who assassinated the president. When Booth was trapped in a tobacco-curing barn near Port Royal, Va., Corbett shot and killed him after the structure was set afire. Did Corbett shoot Booth because, as he claimed, God had told him to or because he was part of a conspiratorial cover-up, as some later investigators claimed? There is little doubt that Corbett suffered from serious disorders that led to further unstable behavior and criminality. He later castrated himself so that he might better "resist sin." After he fired two pistols into a crowded session of the Kansas legislature, Corbett was committed to a mental institution. He escaped and vanished from sight forever.

corpus delicti

Technically, a corpus delicti refers to "the body of the crime," which in homicide cases means first that death has occurred and second that the death was caused by a criminal agency. Typical of the laws in other states, the New York penal law demands the following in all homicide cases: "No person can be convicted of murder or manslaughter unless the death of the person alleged to have been killed and the fact of the killing by the defendant, as alleged, are each established as independent facts; the former by direct proof, and the latter beyond a reasonable doubt."

Naturally, a number of murderers have escaped prosecution because they succeeded in getting rid of the body *without anyone seeing it*. The law is not required to produce the actual body, however, if it can produce witnesses who saw the body and can thus testify that a crime had been committed. In one case neighbors heard shooting in a Bronx luncheonette and saw several men carry a body from the establishment to a car. Although the body was never found, the testimony of the witnesses was sufficient to prove that a murder had occurred. A corpus delicti can also be proved if bone or body fragments necessary to human life can be identified.

Cortez, Gregorio (1875–1916) fugitive

Mexicans in Texas still sing the "Ballad of Gregorio Cortez." In the song, the hero, pistol in hand, defiantly declares, "Ah, so many mounted Rangers just to take one Mexican!"

Cortez came to Texas with his family when he was 12. He worked as a ranch hand until he and his brother took over a farm. In 1901 the Karnes County sheriff came to arrest the brothers on charges of horse stealing. Gregorio Cortez denied the charges and refused to surrender. The sheriff opened fire and wounded his brother. Gregorio then shot and killed the sheriff. Fearing Texas justice, which was undoubtedly prejudiced in its treatment of Mexicans, Cortez fled. He was to fight off posse after posse, some with up to 300 men, that tried to take him. The chase covered more than 400 miles. During it he became a hero to his compatriots, fighting for his and their rights. A posse caught Cortez close to the Mexican border and in the ensuing gun battle he killed another sheriff.

The legal battle on Cortez's behalf lasted four years, with hundreds of Mexicans contributing to his defense fund. They looked upon Cortez's act as a protest against American injustice. He was cleared in the killing of the first sheriff but sentenced to life imprisonment for killing the second. Protests continued until in 1913, at the age of 38, he was freed. He died three years later but the "Ballad of Gregorio Cortez" preserves his memory.

Crater, Joseph Force (1889–1937?) missing judge

On August 6, 1930 a portly 41-year-old man wearing a high-collared shirt, brown pin-striped double-breasted suit and extremely polished and pointed shoes stepped into a taxi in front of a Manhattan restaurant, waved good-bye to a friend and rode off into history, to become known as America's greatest vanishing act. The man was Justice Joseph Force Crater of the New York Supreme Court. From that day forth, Crater was never seen again—alive or dead. His disappearance provided grist for the mills of jokers, playwrights, graffiti writers,

Twenty-five years after Judge Joseph Force Crater's disappearance, his wife, since remarried, calls for a renewal of the hunt for him.

cartoonists and amateur detectives over the next half century.

Crater was born in Easton, Pa., graduated from Lafayette College and earned a law degree at Columbia University. He established a successful New York practice and formed important political connections, later rising to the presidency of the Cayuga Democratic Club, an important part of the Tammany organization. In April 1930 Gov. Franklin D. Roosevelt appointed him to the New York Supreme Court.

Crater cut short a vacation in Maine to return to the city in order to take care of some business. He was seen in his court chambers on August 5 and 6 and had his aide cash two checks for him totaling $5,150. Later that day he met some friends

at a restaurant and then stepped into the taxi and oblivion.

The investigation into his disappearance eventually mushroomed into a months-long grand jury probe that quizzed hundreds of witnesses but produced no leads to explain what happened to him. One theory was developed about why he had vanished. The grand jury uncovered considerable evidence of corruption in the Cayuga Democratic Club, which brought on the much publicized Seabury probe.

Meanwhile, the tantalizing mysteries of the case continued. Under New York City law, cabbies were required to keep records of all their trips, starting points and destinations. But despite many appeals from the police, a $5,000 reward offered by the city and a $2,500 reward offered by the *New York World,* the cabbie who picked up Judge Crater never came forward nor offered any information concerning the case. If he had, Crater's movements could have been traced at least one more step.

On countless occasions in the 1930s, the case seemed to be a fraction of an inch from being solved, but each lead fizzled. There was no limit to the type of leads the police ran down over the years. The missing Crater was identified wrongly as a gold prospector in the California desert country; a human torch who died of self-inflicted burns in Leavenworth, Kan.; a skeleton at Walden, Vt.; an unidentified murder victim in Westchester County, N.Y.; a man who hanged himself from a tree less than 15 miles from the Crater summer home at Belgrade Lakes, Maine; an amnesia victim in the Missouri State Insane Asylum; a sufferer of "daytime somnambulism."

Then again he was a Hollywood race tout; a free-spending American tourist in Italy; an ill-shaven door-to-door beggar in Illinois ("I didn't pull his whiskers but I'm pretty sure they were false," one Chicago housewife bubbled to police). Perhaps the best of all was the GI who returned from overseas in 1946 with the emphatic intelligence that Crater was operating a bingo game in North Africa for a strictly Arab clientele.

Jokers, of course, got into the act. Assistant Chief John J. Sullivan was sitting at his desk one day when a call from Montreal was switched to him. A very calm voice said: "I can't tell you my name, because I don't care to get mixed up in it, but Judge Crater is now in room 761 at my hotel. I am in the hotel now, but I don't dare give you my name." In a matter of minutes Sullivan had the Montreal police breaking into the room of a honeymooning couple.

Throughout the country a number of dying bums felt compelled to make deathbed confessions, each admitting that he was the judge. One in the Midwest, who lived long enough for the police to question him, admitted finally that he was just trying to "get myself a decent burial instead of being laid in that pauper's plot all the other boys end up in."

In 1937 Judge Crater was ruled legally dead, and his widow remarried. At the time, it was estimated the hunt for Crater had expended 300,000 Depression dollars. Even by the 1950s the Judge Crater legend had not faded. Former police commissioner Edward P. Mulrooney, under whose supervision the case was first investigated, revealed he still carried a picture of Crater in his pocket at all times. "You never know but that someday you might run into him," he said. "I'd give my right arm to find him." During the following decade the police were still up to the search, digging up a Yonkers, N.Y. backyard in the hope of finding the judge's bones. Nothing came of it.

Crazy Butch gang

During the 1890s and first few years of the 20th century, the most efficient gang of young criminals in New York City was the Crazy Butch gang. Crazy Butch, the leader of the gang, had been tossed into the world at the tender age of eight. Renouncing his alcoholic parents, he never acknowledged his family name. After surviving for two years as a shoeshine boy, Crazy Butch became a pickpocket. When he was about 13, Butch stole a dog, which he named Rabbi, and trained it to steal handbags from careless women's hands. Rabbi would snatch a purse, race through the streets until it lost any pursuers and then meet Crazy Butch at Willett and Stanton Streets, tail wagging and the purse clenched in his teeth.

In his late teens Crazy Butch switched his operation from a dog to a gang of 20 to 30 youths, whom he trained to prowl the streets snatching handbags and muffs. Butch would lead his minions down a street on a bicycle, bump into a pedestrian, preferably a little old lady, and alight to help her up while at the same time berating her as a careless walker. As people pressed in to see what was happening, Crazy Butch's boys would thread through the mob rifling pockets and purses. When the crowd was completely milked or a policeman appeared, Butch would apologize to his victim and pedal away. At the gang's headquarters, his protégés would turn in their spoils, and Crazy Butch would reward each with a few pennies.

By the turn of the century, Crazy Butch and many of his followers had advanced to such adult occupations as musclemen, sluggers and, on occasion, paid murderers, often pursuing their criminal endeavors in bicycle teams. A subchief under the celebrated Monk Eastman, Crazy Butch held his followers, some 60 strong, always at the ready should they be needed to do battle with the Five Points Gang of Paul Kelly, whose ranks already included a young hoodlum named Johnny Torrio and would soon be graced by such names as Luciano, Yale and Capone. Crazy Butch demanded his men be ready for action at all times. Once, hearing the Five Pointers were preparing an onslaught, Crazy Butch decided to test his boys' preparedness. So, one night Crazy Butch and three of his men charged up the stairs and into the hall of the gang's Forsyth Street headquarters, blazing away with two revolvers each. The gang members, who were boozing or playing cards, either went out the windows or down the backstairs. Little Kishky, who had been sitting on a window sill, was so startled he fell backwards out the window and was killed. Crazy Butch was furious; he wanted his men better prepared for action than that.

Crazy Butch survived a number of gun battles with the Five Pointers and other gangsters under Humpty Jackson, but his own gang and the great Eastman gang started falling apart at the same time. In 1904 both he and Eastman disappeared from the scene. Eastman was sentenced to 10 years in prison for robbery, and Crazy Butch was killed by Harry the Soldier in a fight over a girl, an expert shoplifter called the Darby Kid.

Crazy Butch is seldom remembered today in criminal histories, but he trained many of the early 20th-century gangsters and especially the sluggers of the union wars. Big Jack Zelig had started out under Crazy Butch. In fact, that notorious bruiser had always quaked under Butch's rage.

Cunninghams' revenge

In 1855 a band of 13 Mexican bandits, Juan Navarro's band, raided the Arizona ranch of Dave Cunningham and made off with his daughter, 15-year-old Mary. Cunningham and his two sons, John and Adrian, took up the pursuit and soon discovered the sad fate of the girl. She had been raped, and then she and her pinto pony had been forced over a precipice. The trail of the bandits showed they were headed for Mexico. The older Cunningham turned back. He had a wife and ranch to take care of. The two boys went on in what a president of the United States would later call "the most audacious feat ever brought to my attention."

They tracked Navarro's band to the town of Naco and then on to Agua Prieta, where the gang had taken over a cantina. One bandit came outside to relieve himself, and the brothers stabbed him to death with their razor-sharp skinning knives. Soon, another bandit came out to call to the first one. He met the same fate. Two other bandits emerged, accompanied by a woman. John jumped on one, neatly slitting his throat. Adrian, however, missed his man, who drew a long knife and gashed Adrian's arm before John came to the rescue and stabbed the bandit. The woman began screaming and the brothers fled. The remaining nine-man Navarro band did not give chase but rode off, after shooting up the town in anger. They obviously were not sure who or how many men had done the killings.

Eventually, after a run-in with the Mexican police, who were suspicious of their reasons for being in Mexico, the brothers again caught up with Navarro's band heading toward their home base at Chihuahua. They crept close to the bandits' sleeping camp and opened fire. The brothers did not know how many they had killed until dawn, when they found five corpses and the tracks of four horses. Navarro was among the missing.

Now, however, Navarro knew he was being hunted and set a trap for the two brothers. One bandit rode ahead with the four horses while Navarro and the other two bandits waited in ambush. In the ensuing shoot-out two bandits were killed, but Adrian was badly wounded in the leg. The brothers continued their pursuit with Adrian suffering in agony. Only Navarro and one other bandit were left. The Cunninghams had no choice but to make their way to Chihuahua openly, even though they knew Navarro would be waiting for them. Gangrene had infected Adrian's leg, and when they reached the town, a doctor said there was no alternative but amputation. Meanwhile, John Cunningham went out searching for the two bandits. He found them in a cantina. On the lookout for any American, they were instantly suspicious of him and may or may not have recognized him. When John walked out of the cantina, Navarro and the other bandit followed him. Outside, John Cunningham whirled, drew two six-guns and opened fire. Both Mexicans dropped, and John stepped over them and fired several more shots into their bodies.

John Cunningham was arrested, but no charges could be pressed against Adrian. While they languished in Chihuahua, a detachment of U.S. cavalry under Maj. Ben Hunt, returning from a mission to Mexico City, passed through and heard of the affair. Maj. Hunt went to see the Cunninghams. The niceties of Mexican law did not impress Hunt; with a veiled threat of force, he secured the release of John Cunningham and returned the brothers to the United States. The Mexican government filed a protest, saying that what the brothers had done amounted to an armed incursion into Mexican sovereignty. A complete report of the affair was made to President Franklin Pierce, who decided that the Cunninghams would not be extradited to Mexico. He called their bloody ride "the most audacious feat ever brought to my attention." Eventually, Mexico let the matter drop.

Cyclone Louie (1882–1908) Coney Island strongman and murderer

Using the name Cyclone Louie, Vach Lewis was a noted professional strongman who was always available for a hit assignment, thereby earning the title of the Coney Island Killer in the early 1900s. When two men were found strangled on the beach one morning with their necks virtually wrung like chickens, all Coney Island knew Cyclone Louie had done the deed. So too did the police, but two dancing girls and six other members of their family insisted the strongman had spent the entire night under their tender ministrations after he had allegedly wrenched his back while wrapping an iron bar around his neck. There Cyclone Louie lay moaning, too weak to unwrap the cursed metal. The police were forced to drop the charge against Louie, who shortly thereafter regained his strength and unbent the iron bar.

While Cyclone Louie's murder services involved a substantial fee, he rendered similar duty without charge for Kid Twist, the last great leader of the Eastman gang before it fractionalized upon his killing. The big, hulking Cyclone Louie followed Kid Twist around like a loyal dog, marveling at his mental superiority. There were those who said that Cyclone Louie would never meet his mental equal. But although he wasn't bright, Cyclone Louie was nonetheless useful to Kid Twist. One service he performed was the elimination of "the Bottler," the partner of Kid Twist and Kid Dahl in the operation of a profitable crooked card game in a Suffolk Street house on Manhattan's Lower East Side. Twist and Dahl had simply declared themselves in on the Bottler's operation and later decided to declare the Bottler out. Thus, at the time of the Bottler's murder Kid Twist was in the Delancey Street police station arguing with the desk sergeant for the release of a fellow gangster who had purposely got himself arrested, and Kid Dahl was in a Houston Street restaurant involved in a loud argument with the proprietor. With those alibis firmly in place, Cyclone Louie walked in on the card game and shot the Bottler dead in front of 20 players, each of whom later claimed either to have been elsewhere or, if they admitted being there, to have been looking in the other direction.

Cyclone Louie died in the service of Kid Twist on May 14, 1908 while making the rounds of Coney Island dives. The pair ran into a mortal enemy of Twist's, Louie the Lump, in one dive and ordered him to jump out the window, a rather unfriendly suggestion since they were on the second floor of the building. Louie the Lump was forced to leap but survived and, being a member of the Five Points Gang, quickly put in a call to Manhattan for reinforcements. Twenty gunmen answered the summons and stationed themselves outside the dive, where Twist and Cyclone Louie were drinking themselves senseless. When the pair emerged from the joint, Louie the Lump shot Kid Twist in the brain. Cyclone Louie tried to run for it but was cut down by a Five Point volley and tumbled dead atop his beloved mentor. Later, every Five Pointer involved insisted his bullet struck Cyclone Louie. The police do not seem to have made an accurate count of the bullets that brought about Cyclone Louie's demise. The only one ever arrested for the crime was Louie the Lump. The killer's lawyer made a fervent, if somewhat tortured, plea of self-defense, which evidently had some effect since Louie the Lump was sent to prison for a mere 11 months.

Dannan, Emmanuel (1843–1851)
murder victim, folk hero

Known as the "boy who wouldn't lie," eight-year-old Emmanuel Dannan became an instant Wisconsin folk hero when he was killed by his adopted parents, Samuel Norton and his wife, in 1851. Both of Emmanuel's English-immigrant parents died before he was five years old, and he was saved from the poorhouse by an uncle, who unfortunately died a year later. The Samuel Nortons then adopted the child.

Emmanuel was eight when he happened to see his stepparents murder a peddler. The Nortons ordered the boy to lie to the police, but he said he would not. He was hanged by his wrists from the rafters of the family's log cabin deep in the woods and beaten with willow switches for two hours. During his ordeal the only thing the boy would say was, "Pa, I will not lie!" After two hours the boy's spirit was still unbroken, but his body was and he died. The facts came out in an investigation, and the Nortons were both sent to prison for seven years, while Emmanuel's tale spread throughout the area.

There was talk of erecting a monument to his memory, and a total of $1,099.94 was collected, only to be siphoned off by a fund-raiser. Over the years the story of Emmanuel Dannan's bravery became part of the state's folklore, and finally, on May 2, 1954 a monument was erected in his memory at Montello, Wis. The inscription read, "Blessed are they which are persecuted for righteousness sake, for theirs is the kingdom of Heaven." Since then, Truth Day in Montello has been celebrated every May 2.

Daybreak Boys   New York criminal gang

Although no member was much over the age of 20, the Daybreak Boys were among the most desperate New York gangs in the 1850s. It was said that no one could join the gang until he had killed at least one man, but this was an exaggeration since some members were as young as 12 or even 10 and hadn't yet advanced to homicide. However, once in the gang, such delinquents were quickly initiated in the practice. Police estimated conservatively that from 1850 to 1852 alone the gang committed at least 20 murders—and more likely over 40—and stole loot worth $200,000. What made the gang so fearsome was its habit of scuttling ships just to demonstrate its power and willingness to kill even when there was no hope for gain. The roster of leaders of the gang was a who's who of the most dangerous criminals in New York during the 1850s: Nicholas Saul, Bill Howlett, Patsy the Barber, Slobbery Jim, Cowlegged Sam McCarthy and Sow Madden.

In time, the depredations of the Daybreak Boys became so troublesome the police declared a virtual war on them and killed with an abandon that matched the tactics of the Daybreakers themselves. Three officers named Blair, Spratt and Gilbert killed 12 of the gang in various gun battles in 1858. By the end of 1859 the gang, having lost so many of its leaders, broke up, although individual members still remained dangerous criminals on their own for years afterward.

dead line   Fulton Street, New York City

Attempting to contain a growing wave of bank robberies in the financial district, Inspector Thomas F. Byrnes of the New York City police announced on March 12, 1880 the establishment of a "dead line" at Fulton Street. He said known criminals would be "dead," i.e., arrested, if they were found south of the line. The plan, like so many others by Byrnes, who was always more flamboyant than effective, proved to be a dud. But the officer is credited by some scholars with popularizing the word *deadline* in America.

dead man's eyes   superstition

An old story has it that the last thing a murder victim sees is his killer and that this image remains imprinted on the retina. Some superstitious murderers have gone to considerable trouble to shoot out a victim's eyes in order to destroy such imaginary evidence. Monk Eastman, a famed gangster and murderer at the turn of the century, supposedly heard the theory discussed once and suddenly remembered it after his next murder. He thereupon reclimbed three flights of stairs and shot out the dead man's eyes.

The origin of the superstition is unknown, but it came into renewed vogue around 1900, when criminals had become impressed with such scientific advances as fingerprinting, which was making police detection more effective. Even now, there are a few reports of murder victims found with their eyes shot out each year.

Dead Man's Tree   Chicago "murder announcement" site

During the infamous Aldermen's Wars that wracked Chicago's 19th Ward, the so-called Bloody Ward, from 1916 to 1921, a poplar tree on Loomis Street in Little Italy became famous as the Dead Man's Tree. Both sides, those supporting John "Johnny de Pow" Powers and those backing Tony D'Andrea, took to announcing the impending death of a victim by posting his name on the tree, a notice that, if it did not completely shatter his nerve, at least offered the marked man an opportunity to set his affairs in order. In a majority of the 30 deaths that occurred during the wars, the victim's name had been written on the tree; none of these deaths were ever solved.

See also: ALDERMEN'S WARS.

Dead Rabbits   early New York gang

From the 1820s until their final decline in the 1870s, the Dead Rabbits were a huge gang of criminals who controlled much of the Lower East Side, excluding the Bowery, and achieved great renown as thieves and thugs. When they went on looting forays or to do battle with other gangs, their leaders carried a dead rabbit impaled on a pike. The Dead Rabbits were also noted political sluggers, supporting pro-Irish candidates. They were given credit for controlling the voting booths in 1856 when Tammany Hall's Fernando Wood was reelected mayor during an election in which at least 10,000 fraudulent votes were cast. Wood won by a little more than 9,000 votes.

The main foes of the Dead Rabbits were the Bowery Boys, who were aligned with the anti-Irish Native American Party, and the two organizations, each with satellite supporters, fought many pitched battles. The greatest of these occurred on July 4 and 5, 1857, when the Dead Rabbits and the Plug Uglies and several other Five Points gangs marched into the Bowery to loot stores and do battle with the Bowery Boys. Armed with knives, pistols, clubs, iron bars and huge paving blocks, they attacked a Bowery Boys headquarters, putting a small contingent of the enemy to rout. When the news of the outrage spread, the Bowery Boys, in alliance with the Atlantic Guards and other gangsters determined to protect the sanctity of the Bowery, poured out of their holes onto Bayard Street to engage in the most desperate and largest free-for-all in the city's history.

The police made an early and feeble effort to control the fighting but merely took a few prisoners before wisely retreating. By this time the fighting forces had grown to an estimated strength of about 400 to 500 on each side. The *New York Times* reported:

Brick-bats, stones and clubs were flying thickly around and from the windows in all directions, and men ran wildly about brandishing firearms. Wounded men lay on the sidewalks and were trampled upon. Now the Rabbits would make a combined rush and force their antagonists up Bayard Street to the Bowery. Then the fugitives, being reinforced, would turn on their pursuers and compel a retreat to Mulberry, Elizabeth and Baxter streets.

While the rioting was going on, other gangsters used the opportunity to attack households and stores along the Bowery and several other streets, and residents and storeowners had to barricade their buildings and fight off attacks with shotguns and pistols. In the afternoon a much larger force of police moved into the area and cleared the streets, forcing the rioters into the houses and up to the roofs. One gangster who refused to surrender fell from the roof of a house onto Baxter Street. As he lay there, his head in a pool of blood, his foes stomped him to death. As soon as the police retreated with more prisoners, the fighting resumed. It continued until three regiments of troops were brought into action the next day. At that point, eight rioters were dead and more than 100 wounded, half of whom required long hospitalization. More of their dead were carried off by both sides and it was common knowledge that several new graves decorated the underground passages and cellars of the Five Points and Paradise Square.

Small bands of the rioters continued battling for another week, while the general citizenry demanded something be done to curb the criminal elements. The Dead Rabbits resented descriptions of themselves as criminals and so informed the press. The *Times* reported:

We are requested by the Dead Rabbits to state that the Dead Rabbit club members are not thieves, that they did not participate in the riot with the Bowery Boys, and that the fight in Mulberry street was between the Roach Guards of Mulberry street and the Atlantic Guards of the Bowery. The Dead Rabbits are sensitive on points of honor, we are assured, and wouldn't allow a thief to live on their beat, much less be a member of their club.

Nonetheless, several noted sluggers of the Dead Rabbits, and the Bowery Boys as well, were never seen alive again.

See also: BOWERY BOYS.

Death Corner   Chicago murder locale

During the heyday of the Black Hand, this loose society of extortionists terrorized Italian communities in America, demanding money from designated victims and promising them death if they refused. The most dangerous locale in Chicago's Little Italy at this time was the intersection of Milton and Oak Streets, nicknamed Death Corner because so many Black Hand victims were slain there. In one 15-month period, from January 1, 1910 until March 26, 1911, 38 Black Hand murders occurred there.

There never was one official Black Hand organization; rather the extortions and killings were carried out on a freelance basis by various criminals. It is likely that some so-called Black Hand murders were really private affairs and disguised as Black Hand matters to confuse the police. Whatever the case, none of the 38 murders were ever solved, and there were many residents of Little Italy who would always go blocks out of their way to avoid passing Death Corner.

See also: SHOTGUN MAN.

De Feo, Ronald, Jr.   (1951–)   mass murderer

In November 1974 Ronald De Feo, Jr., stunned Amityville, Long Island by shooting to death his mother, father, two brothers and two sisters as they slept. It marked the start of what can only be described as a "murder groupie" rage.

The type of killings De Feo perpetrated is hardly unusual on police blotters, yet his crime supposedly made the house haunted. The alleged ghostly experiences of its next owners were described in a book, *The Amityville Horror*, which became a best-seller.

As for De Feo himself, no more than a necessary prop in the ghostly tales that followed, he tried unsuccessfully to plead insanity and was sentenced in 1975 to a total of 150 years imprisonment.

de Kaplany, Dr. Geza   (1926–)   murderer

Dubbed the Acid Doctor, Dr. Geza de Kaplany committed what one expert called "the most horrendous single murder in American history" and caused a further scandal when he was paroled. Dr. de Kaplany was an anesthetist at a San Jose, Calif. hospital. He wooed and eventually married his 25-year-old fiancée, Hajna, a part-time model and leading beauty of California's Hungarian community, largely on the basis of his professional status. The marriage proved a failure. Exactly why is not absolutely clear: according to the prosecution in the subsequent murder trial, de Kaplany was unable to consummate the marriage, but the defense contended his love had been rejected. For whatever reason, de Kaplany decided in his own words, "to ruin her beauty."

He assembled an elaborate torture kit in their honeymoon apartment and, on the evening of August 27, 1962, even stopped off to get a manicure so as not to puncture the rubber gloves he would wear. Exactly what de Kaplany did early the following morning, during what he called "my one-hour crackup" is best left to the medical texts. In any event, neighbors in the building got annoyed by loud music from the de Kaplany apartment, and despite the music, they could hear some terrible wailing. The police were summoned, and they took Hajna away, her once lovely face and body now covered with third-degree, corrosive burns. Careless ambulance attendants burned their own hands moving her body.

The bedroom resembled a torture chamber, the bedclothes virtually disintegrated in acid. There were bottles of nitric, sulfuric and hydrochloric acids in a leather case. Also found were rubber gloves, a roll of adhesive tape and a note that read, "If you want to live—do not shout; do what I tell you; or else you will die."

Hajna did die but only after suffering excruciating pain for three weeks in a hospital, with her mother praying for her death and nurses unable to look at de Kaplany's handiwork.

During his trial, at which he pleaded both "not guilty" and "not guilty by reason of insanity," de Kaplany denied wanting to kill his wife, only to mar her looks. He was convicted and escaped with just one life sentence because the jury was assured by a spokesman for the state prison system that he would be classified a "special interest prisoner," that is, someone almost certain never to be paroled. To add to that precaution, the judge ordered that photographs of de Kaplany's wife's body be kept in his file. Later on, it was discovered the pictures had not remained there very long.

Many Californians were both amazed and shocked when they heard an announcement in 1976 that de Kaplany had been paroled and quietly put aboard a plane to Taiwan. Pressed for an explanation, the Adult Authority, the state parole board, said that de Kaplany had been released six months ahead of any possible scheduled parole because a missionary hospital in Taiwan urgently needed the skills of a cardiac specialist. Since de Kaplany was not a heart specialist but an anesthesiologist whose skills had wasted for 13 years and whose medical license had been revoked, the explanation seemed implausible. The uproar over the parole of a murderer many people thought would never be released from prison was tempered only by the fact that he prudently had been sent out of the country.

Dewey, Thomas E. (1902–1971) prosecutor and near assassination victim

Thomas E. Dewey was only one of several prosecutors, especially in New York State, to use his crime-fighting prowess to advance himself politically, moving on to the governorship and twice running for president, in 1944 and 1948. Dewey had started off as a Wall Street lawyer, and observers would note that as a prosecutor of industrialists, businessmen and financiers, he showed limited brilliance and effectiveness. In prosecuting gangsters, however, the Dewey zeal was limitless and telling. In various roles—U.S. attorney, special prosecutor and district attorney—he clapped in prison the likes of Waxey Gordon, Louis Lepke, Gurrah Shapiro and Lucky Luciano.

Before he got Luciano, Dewey set his sights on Dutch Schultz, the king of Harlem policy rackets and numerous other criminal enterprises. Although the Dutchman was a brilliant criminal leader, he was also a bit of a flake, fond of solving pressing problems with a gun. When Dewey's investigators closed in on his operations, Schultz went before the national board of the crime syndicate to demand that the prosecutor be assassinated as a solution to both Schultz's present problems and the future ones of others. When the crime syndicate was formed, a firm rule was agreed upon, as Luciano stated it, that "we wouldn't hit newspaper guys or cops or DAs. We don't want the kind of trouble everybody'd get."

Led by the forces of Luciano and Lansky, the crime board voted down Schultz. "I still say he ought to be hit," the mad dog underworld leader is reported to have snarled in defiance. "And if nobody else is gonna do it, I'm gonna hit him myself."

At first, the syndicate decided that Schultz was simply blowing off steam, but then it was discovered in October 1935 that Schultz was setting an assassination plot in place. He had Dewey's Fifth Avenue apartment staked out by a man who posed each morning as the father of a child pedaling a velocipede. What could be less suspicious than a devoted parent strolling with his offspring? Dewey and the two body guards always at his side passed them without suspicion on their way to a nearby drug store, where Dewey made his first phone call of the morning to his office from one of several booths. He did not use his home phone for fear it might be tapped.

Once the "caser" with the child learned this, a murder plot was worked out; a killer carrying a gun with a silencer would be inside the drug store first and shoot Dewey when he entered one of the booths. Dewey's bodyguards waiting outside would not be aware of a thing as the killer walked out past them.

Schultz's mistake was involving Albert Anastasia in the plot. Anastasia was close to Luciano, and although he also favored killing Dewey, he would never betray Luciano. He passed the word about the plot to Luciano and others in the syndicate. Luciano was horrified. So were most of the others. An immediate trial was held and the death sentence passed on the absent Schultz. According to Martin A. Gosch and Richard Hammer in *The Last Testament of Lucky Luciano*, Meyer Lansky, while not casting a dissenting vote, told Luciano: "Charlie, as your Jewish *consigliere*, I want to remind you of something. Right now, Schultz is your cover. If Dutch is eliminated, you're gonna stand out like a naked guy who just lost his clothes. The way La Guardia and the rest of them guys've been screamin' about you, it's ten to one they'll be after you next."

Luciano allowed that Lansky could be right, but the syndicate had no other choice than to eliminate Schultz. The vote taken was unanimous On October 23, 1935 Schultz was shot to death in a chop house in Newark, N.J.

Dewey did not learn of his "almost assassination" until 1940, when it was revealed to him by Murder, Inc. prosecutor Burton Turkus. Dewey listened impassively to the step-by-step details, but his eyes widened perceptibly when mention was made of the proud papa with the tot on the velocipede. After five years he apparently still remembered them.

By that time, as a result of Dewey's efforts, Lucky Luciano had been sent to prison for 30 to 50 years on a charge of compulsory prostitution, the longest sentence ever handed out for such an offense. After the end of World War II, Dewey backed a parole board's recommendation that Luciano be released, an action for which Dewey was roundly criticized by political opponents. The move was made because of Luciano's aid to the war effort, Dewey said, but it may also have been based to some degree on what had to remain an unspoken gratitude for Luciano's having saved his life. Perhaps somewhat ingraciously, Luciano to his dying day insisted there was yet another reason; the mob had contributed $90,000 in small bills to Dewey's campaign fund.

Dillinger, John Herbert—double

The death of John Dillinger in July 1934 marked the end of crime's greatest folk hero of the 20th century, and it was therefore hardly surprising that his death was not accepted by many. This has been a common behavioral reaction. For decades there were people who believed Jesse James had not been shot by Bob Ford, that a substitute corpse had been used. And for decades one "real Jesse James" after another turned up. In the cases of the Apache Kid and Butch Cassidy, the weight of opinion seems to favor the theory that they survived their alleged demises, but the identification of their corpses was far more controversial.

The disbelief about John Dillinger started instantly after his death and continued for years. In a book entitled *Dillinger: Dead or Alive?* (1970), Jay Robert Nash and Ron Offen made perhaps the most complete case that the great public enemy had not been killed by FBI agents. Their basic premise was that the FBI had been duped into thinking the dead man was Dillinger, and when the agency discovered otherwise, it could do nothing but develop a massive cover-up.

What makes this case less than totally acceptable is the number of people such a plot would have required. Certainly Anna Sage, "the woman in red," and her East Chicago police contact or contacts. And someone would have had to have planted a phony Dillinger fingerprint card days before the killing. According to this theory, "Jimmy Lawrence" was not a Dillinger alias but the name of a real minor hoodlum whose career was rather hazy.

Proponents of the fake Dillinger theory make much of glaring discrepancies found in Dillinger's autopsy report, which was allegedly lost for more than 30 years. For instance, in the report the dead man's eyes were listed as brown, Dillinger's were blue. But this was an autopsy performed in Cook County during the 1930s, a time when coroners' findings nationwide were notorious for being replete with errors. The autopsy was performed in a "looney bin" atmosphere. A reporter for the *Chicago Tribune* appeared in news photos propping up Dillinger's head and was identified as the "coroner." Even after the autopsy was performed, Dillinger's brain was actually "mislaid" for a time. If all errors made in autopsies of that period were taken seriously, probably just half the victims of violent deaths could really have been considered dead.

Another question that must be raised is how John Dillinger lived happily ever after and on what. By all accounts, he had less than $10,000 available to him for a final, permanent escape. Could he stay away from crime forever? And if he could not, would he not have been identified sooner or later? And what of Anna Sage? Despite promises made to her by the FBI, she was deported back to her native Romania. She could undoubtedly have bought a reprieve from that fate had she come forward with the true facts about a Dillinger hoax.

In sum, the "Dillinger lives" theory appears to be a case of wishful thinking, one fostered by the fact that John Dillinger was too good—or too bad—to be allowed to die.

Doane gang   Revolutionary War outlaws

The American Revolution was the first golden age for criminality in this country. The turmoil produced by the shifting fortunes of war created the ideal setting for bands of cattle rustlers, horse thieves and highway robbers. If a criminal stole from the British, he could count on the sympathies and sometimes even the active support of revolutionaries; if he preyed on known enemies of England, he was to the British a supporter of the Crown. Into this law enforcement vacuum stepped the notorious Doanes (sometimes called Doans), who left a trail of plunder through eastern Pennsylvania and parts of New Jersey.

Commanded by raw-boned Moses Doane, a fierce-looking man with long hair and a fur hat, the gang, composed of five of his brothers and as many as 10 to 15 others, became the terror of Bucks County, Pa. especially. Moses Doane declared himself a Tory so that upon the anticipated triumph of the British, he and his confederates would be labeled Loyalists and free from the threat of punishment. On that basis, the Doanes stole only from the patriot side, but at no time was any of their loot delivered to His Majesty's forces. Their most daring robbery took place on a cold, windy night in October 1781, when 16 members of the gang boldly rode into Newtown, Pa. and headed directly for the home of John Hart, Esq., the treasurer of Bucks County, who was in the habit of hid-

ing government funds in his home for fear of seizure by the British. Terrifying Hart and threatening his children, Moses Doane forced him to reveal the various hiding places of a total of about $4,500 in today's currency, then little short of a king's ransom. The robbery showed how proficient the Doane spy service was. Whenever and wherever in Bucks County a hoard of patriot money was to be found, the Doanes soon knew it. Tax collectors who changed their appointed rounds found that such intelligence was not long kept from the Doanes. Ironically, the Newtown robbery coincided with the collapse of Moses Doane's strategy of aligning himself with the British cause. Just three days previously, Cornwallis had surrendered at Yorktown, dooming the hopes of the Crown. The Doanes were now labeled outlaws by the recognized forces of law and order and were on the run. Their forays continued for several years, but they had few safe refuges other than caves, there being as many storied Doane cave hideouts in Pennsylvania as there were Jesse James caves in Missouri.

From 1783 on, wanted posters for various gang members dotted the Pennsylvania and New Jersey countryside. Before that, the Doanes had intimidated the local inhabitants by exacting vengeance on the nearest inhabitant to any wanted poster. If an individual didn't remove the poster, he faced a visit from the Doanes, one he would not forget—if he survived it. But by 1783 fear of the Doanes was fading, and additionally, some gang members, such as the fabled James "Sandy Flash" Fitzpatrick, had split off with gangs of their own. Fitzpatrick was hanged in 1787. On September 24, 1788 Abraham and Levy Doane, by then more critical to the gang than Moses, were executed on the

Philadelphia Commons. A short time thereafter, Moses Doane was also caught and hanged.

Dobbs, Johnny (?–1892) bank robber and murderer

Johnny Dobbs was one of the most successful crooks in America during the 19th century. A colorful fence, bank robber and murderer, he was credited by authorities with netting himself at least $1 million over a 20-year criminal career.

During his youth Dobbs, whose real name was Michael Kerrigan, served in the Patsy Conroy gang of river pirates and then became a bank burglar of renown, working with the likes of Worcester Sam Perris Shang Draper, Red Leary, Jimmy Hope, Jimmy Brady, Banjo Pete Emerson, Abe Coakley and the King of the Bank Robbers, George Leonidas Leslie, in whose murder Dobbs later participated. Dobbs played a key role in the celebrated $2.7 million robbery of New York's Manhattan Savings Institution in 1878. He reportedly took part in bank jobs all over the East that netted perhaps $8 million in loot.

With a portion of his revenues, Dobbs opened a saloon at 100 Mott Street, just a short distance from police headquarters, and blatantly operated there as one of the biggest fences in New York. He supposedly fenced over $2 million in hot money and securities, keeping about $650,000 as his own share. When asked once why crooks congregated right by police headquarters, he replied, "The nearer the church the closer to God."

Dobbs and his accomplices murdered Leslie because they believed the King of the Bank Robbers was informing on them in exchange for the opportunity to start a new

life elsewhere. Although he was not convicted of the murder, Dobbs was sent to prison for a number of robberies and spent most of the 1880s in various institutions. A week after he was discharged from the Massachusetts State Prison, he was found lying in a gutter in New York City and taken to Bellevue Hospital's alcoholic ward. He died there broke on May 15, 1892. To pay for his burial, one of Dobbs' former mistresses pawned an expensive brooch he had presented to her in happier days.

Doctors' Mob great New York riot

On a Sunday evening in April 1788, a strange and bloody riot developed after a young medical student, annoyed by several children peering in the window of the New York Hospital in lower Manhattan, picked up the arm of a corpse he had just dissected and pointed it at them. "This is your mother's hand," he yelled. "I just dug it up. Watch out or I'll smack you with it." Ironically, one child among those who scattered upon hearing that terrifying threat had just lost his mother. He rushed home and told his father of the event. The man rushed to the cemetery where his wife had recently been buried, and by the greatest of coincidences, the grave was open and the woman's body gone. In a rage, the man headed for the hospital, telling his friends on the way what had transpired. Within minutes he was joined by an angry mob of hundreds.

Armed with torches, bricks and ropes, the members of the mob screamed for the doctors to come out. Dressed in street clothes most of the physicians slipped out by mingling with the crowd. Frustrated, the mob stormed the hospital and wrecked tables holding valuable specimens. One doctor and three students who remained behind to try to stop them barely escaped with their lives and were put in jail by the sheriff to protect them.

The mob's fury was not spent, and the rioters spilled back into the street looking for doctors. They attacked many doctors' homes. One of the homes was that of Sir John Temple, who was not a physician, but "Sir John" sounded like "surgeon." The medical student whose jest started the riot, John Hicks, Jr., was almost cornered in a physician's house but escaped over the rooftops.

On the following morning, April 14, authorities fully expected the riot to be over, but the mob's violence increased and scores of doctors were forced to leave the city. Later in the day a huge, ugly mob moved toward Columbia College in search of more grisly specimens and the "savage experimenters" who had gathered them. Several prominent citizens tried to intervene to end the madness. Alexander Hamilton was shoved aside. John Jay was knocked unconscious with a rock.

Meanwhile, Gov. George Clinton had called out the militia and prepared to use force to put down the violence. Baron Friedrich von Steuben, a hero of the Revolution and one of the most popular men in the city, begged the governor to hold off. Standing in front of the troops, he said he would try to dissuade the rioters. For his efforts the baron got hit on the head with a brick. In a quick turnabout, Steuben got to his knees and shouted, "Fire, Clinton, fire!"

The militia cut loose and 20 rioters fell in the first volley alone. In all, eight rioters were killed and dozens more injured.

Still, the riot continued until the morning of the 15th, when the mob was at last sated and returning physicians could tend the wounded rioters. Laws were passed giving medical researchers access to the bodies of executed persons, but this hardly fulfilled the need, and grave robbing remained a serious problem for many years, although no more bloody riots such as the Doctors' Mob incident occurred.

Draft Riots

Beginning early on the morning of July 13, 1863 and continuing for three more bloody days, great riots broke out in New York City, leaving, according to the best estimates, 2,000 dead and another 8,000 wounded. The cause of the rioting was indignation over President Lincoln's draft, fanned by racial hatred, Irish resentment at occupying the lowest level of the social and economic order, and the greed of the great criminal gangs of the Bowery and the Five Points, which saw a chance to loot the city much as had been done during the earlier anti-abolitionist and anti-English Astor Place riots of the 1830s and 1840s.

There were minor disturbances of the peace in opposition to the draft in Boston, Mass., Portsmouth, N.H., Rutland, Vt. and Wooster, Ohio, but none approached the size or ferocity of the New York riots. There the city's poor, largely Irish, allied with the Democrats in opposition to the war, rioted to protest the draft, which they saw as trading rich men's money for poor men's blood through a provision in the law that allowed a potential draftee to buy out of the service for $300. Since this was a monumental sum to the Irish, it meant they had to do the fighting and dying in the conflict between the North and the South.

What had started out as violent protest against the draft turned by the second day into savage lynching of blacks—the cause of the war in the Irish poor's eyes—and whole-

Burning of the Second Avenue Armory caused many deaths.

sale looting, as rioters and criminals sought to seize armory supplies, overpowering and then torturing, mutilating and murdering defending soldiers. Some saw in the great riots a Roman Catholic insurrection, which they were not, although along with the "No Draft" signs were some that sang the praises of the pope and proclaimed, "Down with the Protestants." Considerable church properties of various Protestant faiths were among the 100 buildings burned to the ground by the rioters, but none belonging to the Catholic faith were touched. Lone Catholic priests turned back rioters bent on looting and killing, but Catholic archbishop Hughes refused to counsel the rioters to disband until the fourth day, when the violence had run its

course. On that day he addressed a pastoral letter entitled "Archbishop Hughes to the Men of New York, who are called in many of the papers rioters." Later, the archbishop was to acknowledge that he had "spak too late."

The rioters were bent on mayhem, and some of their crimes were heinous indeed. Policemen and soldiers were murdered, and the children of the rioters picked the bodies clean of every stitch of clothing, proudly wearing the bloodstained garments as badges of honor. Great throngs—estimated to be between 50,000 and 70,000 persons in all—stormed across Manhattan from the Hudson to the East Rivers, looting stores, burning buildings and beating every black they saw. At least three black men were hanged before sundown of the first day, and thereafter, the sight of bodies hanging from lampposts and trees were common throughout the city. The blacks' bodies were all viciously mutilated, slashed with knives and beaten with clubs. Often, they were mere charred skeletons, the handiwork of the most ferocious element in all early American riots—women. Trailing behind the men, they poured oil into the knife wounds of victims and set the corpses ablaze, dancing beneath the awesome human torches, singing obscene songs and telling antiblack jokes.

The black settlements were the scene of much of the violence, the target of those of the rioters more concerned with bloodletting than looting. A house of prostitution on Water Street was burned and its occupants tortured because they refused to reveal the hiding place of a black servant. In New Bowery three black men were cornered on a rooftop and the building set afire. For a time the men clung by their fingers to the gutters while the mob below chanted for them to fall. When they did, they were stomped to death.

Meanwhile, as other groups of rioters attacked armories in search of weapons and police stations in anger at the police resistance to them, a mob sought to destroy the offices of Horace Greeley's prodraft *New York Tribune*. They started several blazes that forced the staff to flee by the back stairway. Greeley was compelled to take refuge under a table in a Park Row restaurant. A police garrison of 100 men retook the newspaper's premises and extinguished the fires, and the following day 100 marines and sailors took up guard in and around the building, which bristled with Gatling guns and a howitzer posted at the main entrance.

By late evening the mobs moved further uptown, leaving the scene behind them filled with numerous fires. At 11 o'clock a great thunder and lightning storm extinguished the blazes. Had it not, many historians believe the city would have been subjected to a conflagration far worse than the Great Chicago Fire a few years hence. Complicating the firefighting was the fact that several fire units had joined the rioters and others were driven away from many of the blazes by the rampaging mobs.

Probably the greatest hero of the first day of the riots was Patrolman George Rallings, who learned of a mob's plan to attack the Negro Orphanage at 43rd Street and Fifth Avenue where 260 children of freed slaves were sheltered. He spirited the children away before the building was torched. Only one tiny black girl was killed by the ax-wielding rioters. Overlooked in the exodus, she was found hiding under a bed and axed to death.

The fighting over the ensuing three days reflected the tides of military battle, as first the rioters and then the police and various

Drawing shows the corpse of a policeman killed in the riot being abused by children and women following in the wake of the mob.

militia units took control of an area. A pitched battle that left an estimated 50 dead was fought at barricades on Ninth Avenue until the police finally gained control of the thoroughfare. Rioters captured Col. H. J. O'Brien of the Eleventh New York Volunteers, tied a rope around his ankles and dragged him back and forth over the cobblestones. A Catholic priest intervened long enough to administer the last rites and then departed. For three hours the rioters tortured O'Brien, slashing him with knives and dropping stones on his body. He was then allowed to lie suffering in the afternoon sun until sundown, when another mob descended on him and inflicted new tortures. Finally, he was dragged to his own backyard, where a group of vicious Five Points Gang women squatted around him and mutilated him with knives until at last he was dead.

On July 15 militia regiments sent toward Gettysburg were ordered back to the city, and by the end of the 16th, the rioters had

By the second day most of the rioters' fury was taken out on blacks, many of whom were lynched.

"killing the people." As a result of political influence almost all of the hundreds of prisoners taken in the last two days of the riots were released. This was especially true of the gang leaders of the Five Points and the waterfront who were caught leading looting expeditions during the fighting. In the end, only 20 men out of the thousands of rioters were brought to trial. Nineteen of them were convicted and sentenced to an average of five years in prison. No one was convicted of murder.

On August 19, the city now filled with troops, the draft drawings resumed, and those who could not pay $300 were sent off to war.

been quelled. The losses by various military units were never disclosed, but the toll of dead and wounded was believed to have been at least 350. The overall casualties in the riots, 2,000 dead and 8,000 wounded, were greater than those suffered at such famous Civil War battles as Bull Run and Shiloh; virtually every member of the police force had suffered some sort of injury. The number of blacks lynched, including bodies found and others missing, was believed to total 88. Property losses probably exceeded $5 million. Among the 100 buildings totally burned were a Protestant mission, the Negro Orphanage, an armory, three police stations, three provost marshals' offices as well as factories, stores and dwellings. Another 200 buildings were looted and partially damaged.

Even while the riots were going on and in the days following them, Democratic politicians seeking to embarrass a Republican president and a Republican mayor, demanded the police and troops be withdrawn from their districts because they were

Driscoll, Danny (?1860–1888) gang leader and murderer

The last great New York ruffian gang of the 19th century was the Whyos, captained jointly in their heyday by Danny Lyons and Danny Driscoll. In the 1880s Lyons and Driscoll reportedly mandated that a potential member of the gang had to kill at least one man. It is perhaps fitting that this brutal pair were themselves hanged within eight months each other.

Driscoll went first. In 1887 he and tough Five Points gangster Johnny McCarthy became involved in a shooting dispute over whom a young prostitute, Breezy Garrity, was working for. Breezy made the mistake of standing around to see who the winner would be, presumably to hand over to him her recent receipts. In the fusillade one of Driscoll's stray shots struck and killed her. It was clearly a case of unintentional homicide, and by most measures of justice Driscoll should have escaped with something less than the ultimate penalty. However, the authorities had been after Driscoll for years on suspicion of several murders and were not going to allow a golden opportunity such as this to slip away because of legal niceties. The prosecution hardly had to remind the jurors of the many atrocities committed by the Whyos, since everyone living in New York ventured out in constant fear of these gangsters. Driscoll, screaming outrage and frame-up, was sentenced to death, and on January 23, 1888 he was hanged in the Tombs.

See also: WHYOS.

Earle, Willie (1922–1947) lynch victim

One of the most shocking cases of a Southern jury refusing to convict whites for the lynching of a black man occurred following the 1947 killing of 25-year-old Willie Earle in South Carolina.

Earle was picked up for questioning following the fatal stabbing of a cab driver near Liberty, S.C. He was taken to the Pickens County Jail, where he was interrogated and protested his innocence. Earle was not charged with the slaying, but word spread of his arrest, and outraged cabbies gathered in Greenville to discuss the murder of a fellow driver. Soon, a large mob, armed with shotguns and knives, formed a convoy and headed for the jail. They broke into the jail and forced the jailer to open Earle's cell. Earle was dragged screaming to an automobile and taken in convoy to Saluda Dam, where he was "questioned" and "confessed." The prisoner was then driven to Bramlett Road in Greenville County and viciously put to death there. Earle was stabbed several times and one lyncher shat-tered the butt of his shotgun on the victim's skull. Others in the mob knife-gouged huge chunks of flesh from Earle's body. Only then was the pathetic prisoner finished off with several shotgun blasts. Satisfied, the lynchers drove home.

The killing shocked the nation and indeed most people in South Carolina. The FBI was called and cleared the jailer of violating Earle's civil rights, finding that he had not willingly released the prisoner. However, the agency cooperated with local authorities in identifying 28 persons among the lynch mob. Twenty-six of these confessed their part in the lynching. Gov. Strom Thurmond named a special prosecutor and pledged that justice would be done, a feeling, observers agreed, that was shared by most residents of the state.

Nevertheless, the result of the trial reflected the long-standing behavior of juries in cases where whites were accused of lynching blacks. The defense offered no testimony whatsoever, and despite the confessions, all the defendants were found "not guilty."

Egan's Rats   St. Louis gang

First organized in St. Louis about 1900 by Jellyroll Egan, the Rats became the most feared gang in the city. Egan specialized in renting out his men as "legbreakers" to anti-union businessmen. When such activities became less profitable about 1920, Dinty Colbeck, who had taken over the reins from the late founder, turned Egan's Rats in new criminal directions. Operating out of a poolhall called Buckley's, Colbeck controlled bootlegging operations in the St. Louis–Kansas City area and masterminded a number of spectacular safecracking and jewelry thefts, many with the aid of the best safecracker of the 1920s, Red Rudensky.

Dinty Colbeck cut a flamboyant figure in St. Louis and paid enormous bribes to crooked politicians and policemen to allow his enterprises to operate without harassment. Approaching an officer on the street, he was known to pull out a big wad of bills and say, "Want a bribe, officer?"

Like many of the other independent gangs that had been given a new life by Prohibition, Egan's Rats could not cope with the changing crime scene of the post-bootlegging 1930s. Colbeck was killed by rival gangsters and the surviving Rats had to find new homes in other criminal combinations.

executions, public

From the time of the first execution in this country's history in 1630, that of John Billington, one of the original pilgrims on the Mayflower, Americans followed the European custom of public executions on the dubious theory that such legal killings would serve as a warning to others.

Throughout the years such public executions were no more than circuses, drawing proportionally a far greater audience than Sunday football games. In the Old West many hangings were reserved for the weekend so that as many people as possible would be free for the festivities. When in 1824 a hatchet murderer named John Johnson was hanged in New York City at 13th Street and Second Avenue, journals of the day reported that some 50,000 spectators attended the execution. Perhaps the most spectacular hanging in New York took place on Bedloe's Island, now the home of the Statue of Liberty, where the murderer Albert E. Hicks was executed on July 13, 1860 not merely for the edification of those squeezed on the island for the event but for thousands more who jammed aboard a mass of ships, from small craft to large excursion vessels, that filled the water around the island. Hawkers paddled in rowboats between the craft selling their wares.

In due course, many communities and many sheriffs banned public executions, finding that they could run a ghoulish sort of black market selling invitations to private executions at hefty prices. However, the custom of public executions stretched into the present century, even extending to electrocutions. In some states, primarily Southern ones, a portable electric chair was brought into the courtroom and the condemned man was executed there before as many spectators as could get inside. The current was fed into the courtroom from a van-type truck equipped with the necessary generators. A journalist once asked Sen. Theodore G. Bilbo of Mississippi if he did not think such executions were little different than lynchings. "Ah," Bilbo replied, "this is pretty tame compared to a lynching."

The last public execution in the United States took place in Owensboro, Ky. in 1936, when a 22-year-old black named Rainey

Bethea was hanged for the murder of a 70-year-old white woman. Some 20,000 persons crowded into the town for the big event, and when Bethea was pronounced dead, souvenir hunters fought over the hood that covered his head, ripped off pieces of his clothing and even tried to cut chunks of flesh from his hanging body.

See also: RAINEY BETHEA, ALBERT E. HICKS.

eye gouging

Eye gouging was a common crime in pre-20th-century America, especially in the big cities, where Irish gangsters used the technique—often against Englishmen—and on the frontier, where it was a part of the so-called rough-and-tumble style of fighting and much used against the Indians. In his diary Maj. Eluries Beatty tells of witnessing one eye gouging in Louisville, Ky. In 1791: "One of these . . . gougers, a perfect bully; all the country round stood in awe of him, for he was so dextrous in these matters that he had, in his time, taken out five eyes, bit off two or three noses and ears and spit them in their faces."

So despised did this cruel practice become that vigorous laws were passed in many jurisdictions specifically to combat it. In the Northwest Territory a law was promulgated stating:

Whosoever . . . shall voluntarily, maliciously, and on purpose, pull out or put out an eye while fighting or otherwise . . . shall be sentenced to undergo confinement in jail . . . and shall also pay a fine of not less than fifty dollars and not exceeding one thousand dollars, one fourth of which shall be for the use of the Territory, and three fourths . . . to the use of the party grieved, and for want of means of payment, the offender shall be sold into service by the court . . . for any time not exceeding five years, the purchaser finding him food and raiment during the term.

Such punishment was perhaps the only reason a white man on the frontier could be sold into servitude.

Gouging was not easy to eradicate. As late as the 1870s a New York gangster named Dandy Johnny Dolan became celebrated for the invention of an improved eye gouger made of copper and worn on the thumb for instant use. Dolan was hanged in 1876, and for the next quarter century, magistrates meted out heavy penalties against eye gougers. The public became particularly exercised about the practice, and political leaders, who relied on and supported the great gangs of the city, passed the word that eye gouging was out. A criminal caught in possession of a pistol, two or three knives and a pair of brass knuckles had no great fear of the law provided he had the proper political protection, but if he was found with eye gougers, he would be abandoned by his patrons and given severe punishment. Over the years the practice of eye gouging faded away, proof perhaps that rigid enforcement of the laws could in fact eliminate a considerable amount of crime.

fence stealing

Although widely practiced, the stripping of fences is hardly considered much of a crime and is often the work of children seeking supplies for building a clubhouse. But in past years it was a serious problem, being among other things a way to obtain firewood and a method to encourage a farmer's stock to "stray."

In this sense, fence stealing was considered a serious offense that called for very severe penalties. A 1659 ordinance in New Amsterdam reveals how stern the colonial punishment for the crime was. It read, "No person shall strip the fences of posts or rails under penalty of being whipped and branded, and for the second, of punishment with the cord until death ensues."

Fields, Vina (?1865–?) madam

The concept of the madam with the "heart of gold" is, of course, more fancy than fact; yet if one woman of that calling had to be singled out for the characteristic, it would be Vina Fields, a black madam who flourished during the last two decades of the 19th century in Chicago. About her, even the antivice muckraker William T. Stead conceded, "She is probably as good as any woman can be who conducts so bad a business."

Vina Fields maintained the largest brothel of the day in Chicago, one that generally had no fewer than 40 prostitutes and as many as 70 or 80 during the World's Fair of 1893. Madame Fields employed black harlots only but allowed patronage by whites only. From 1885 until just about the end of the century, she operated a fancy house on Custom House Place, and during that time, no man ever complained to the police about being robbed there. Vina insisted she never paid a penny in protection money, which may have been the only time she told a lie. Hers was the one house in Chicago where black prostitutes could count on getting a fair shake, drawing a far larger percentage of the take than elsewhere. Because of her generosity, she could also maintain strict discipline. In a famous book on corruption and vice, *If Christ Came to Chicago*, Stead wrote, "The rules and regulations of the Fields house, which are printed and posted in every room, enforce decorum and decency with pains and penalties which could be hardly more strict if they were drawn up for the regulation of a Sunday School." Fields permitted no drunkenness, no soliciting from the windows and no overexposure in the parlors or hallways. She held a court every three days, and girls who had broken rules were fined, ordered to perform menial duties, banned from the parlor or, for major infractions, evicted from the house.

Stead further commented:

Strange though it may appear, [she] has acquired the respect of nearly all who know her. An old experienced police matron emphatically declared that 'Vina is a good woman,' and I think it will be admitted by all who know her, that she is probably as good as any woman can be who conducts so bad a business. . . . She is bringing up her daughter who knows nothing of the life of her mother in the virginal seclusion of a convent school, and she contributes of her bounty to maintain her unfortunate sisters whose husbands down south are among the hosts of unemployed. Nor is her bounty confined to her own family. Every day this whole winter [1893–94] she had fed a hungry, ragged regiment of the out-of-work. The day before I called, 201 men had had free dinners of her providing."

There are many tales, though all unsubstantiated, about what became of Vina Fields in her later years.

Fink, Isidor (c. 1899–1932) suspected murder victim

The killing of Isidor Fink on March 9, 1929 in a tiny little laundry he operated on East 132nd Street in New York City has remained one of the most perplexing in the history of American crime. Alfred Hitchcock wrote about it and undoubtedly toyed with the idea of filming it but failed to come up with a logical solution. Ben Hecht wrote *The Mystery of the Fabulous Laundryman*, but that short story hardly pleased the locked-room addicts seeking a plausible explanation.

Fink kept the doors and windows of his one-room laundry locked at all times because of fear of robberies. A woman napping next door heard three shots in rapid succession and then something heavy, like a body, thud to the floor. She called police. When Patrolman Albert Kattenborn arrived, he found the door bolted and was unable to enter. He lifted a small boy up to the transom, but the boy found it locked. He smashed the glass, climbed inside and opened the door. Fink was dead on the floor. Patrolman Kattenborn let no one else enter and made the boy wait until detectives showed up. Fink had two bullet wounds in the chest and one in the left wrist. The immediate conclusion of the detectives was that he must have committed suicide since it was evident that no one could have gotten out of the room.

The problem with that solution was the suicide gun. It was nowhere to be found, and Fink had died almost instantly. The small boy was searched to make sure he had not secreted the weapon on his person. Then the police set about searching the room. Perhaps Fink had tied the gun to some sort of elastic device that pulled it out of sight. They literally ripped the room apart. No gun. No loose boards. No hidden panels. No trap doors. A squad of specially picked sleuths was sent up from headquarters to solve the mystery. At first, they worked with vigor, then with some irritation and finally in total bewilderment. Reluctantly, the police accepted the fact that they had a case of murder, one that through the years became a favorite of the Sunday supplements. About the most profound conclusion ever to be drawn from the Fink case was the published comment of a detective after a year's work on the puzzle: "That damn two-for-a-cent mystery gives me the creeps!"

Fitzpatrick, Richie (1880–1905) gangster and murderer

One of the few non-Jews to achieve high stature in the Eastman gang, the last great Jewish outfit to dominate crime in New York City, Richie Fitzpatrick, a lethal young Irishman, won the appreciation of leader Monk Eastman because of his great cunning at killing. Once assigned by Eastman to eradicate the owner of a Chrystie Street dive, Fitzpatrick pulled a cunning ruse long before the brothers Corleone thought of it in *The Godfather*—he had a gun planted in the toilet of the dive. Immediately suspect when he walked in, Fitzpatrick permitted himself to be searched and then informed the dive operator that Eastman had ordered him assassinated. He said he was defecting from the Eastman ranks and was thus willing to aid the dive owner. Fitzpatrick's story was accepted, and he joined in a round of drinks, swearing allegiance to his new allies. His next move was to heed the call of nature. When Fitzpatrick emerged from the toilet, he shot the dive operator dead and fled before his henchman could react.

When Eastman was taken by the law for a 1904 attempted robbery, the leadership of the gang fell to an uneasy combination of Fitzpatrick and Kid Twist, so named because of his criminal cunning. It was soon obvious that the pair would have to settle the leadership problem violently, and the gang began to divide into warring factions. The Kid suggested a peace conference in a Chrystie Street

dive. Fitzpatrick accepted with alacrity, and the underworld awaited to see what deceit he would conceive to eliminate his foe. Unfortunately for Fitzpatrick the Kid too was noted for his trickery. As the talks began, the lights suddenly went out and a revolver blazed. When the police reached the scene, Fitzpatrick was alone in the back room with his arms folded across his chest and a bullet in his heart.

The underworld applauded the treachery; Kid Twist, the saying went, "had twisted first."

Five Points   New York City crime district

Every account of crime in old New York is replete with references to the Five Points and the gangs and crimes it spawned. It was the incubator of crime in the city for an entire century. Its early history was tame enough, being a relatively homey place at the junction of Cross, Anthony, Little Water, Orange and Mulberry Streets. In the center of the Five Points was Paradise Square where the poor people of the city came for their fresh air and recreation. By the 1820s the area had turned first seedy and then vile, and the Five Points became a hellhole of impoverished humanity that produced crime in awesome, if predictable, numbers. By the time of the Civil War, the Points and Paradise Square area housed no less than 270 saloons, and many times that number of dance halls, houses of prostitution and green-groceries that dispensed more liquor than vegetables or other provisions. It was already described as a slum section far more wicked than even the Whitechapel district of London.

Perhaps Charles Dickens offered the most graphic picture of the district in his *American Notes:*

The teeming Five Points in 1829.

Let us go on again, and plunge into the Five Points. This is the place; these narrow ways diverging to the right and left, and reeking everywhere with dirt and filth. Such lives as are led here, bear the same fruit here as elsewhere. The coarse and bloated faces at the doors have counterparts at home and all the whole world over. Debauchery has made the very houses prematurely old. See how the rotten beams are tumbling down, and how the patched and broken windows seem to scowl dimly, like eyes that have been hurt in drunken frays. Many of these pigs live here. Do they ever wonder why their masters walk upright instead of going on all-fours, and why they talk instead of grunting?

So far, nearly every house is a low tavern, and on the barroom walls are colored prints of Washington and Queen Victoria, and the American Eagle. Among the pigeon-holes that hold the bottles are pieces of plate glass and colored paper, for there is in some sort a taste for decoration even here. And as seamen frequent these haunts, there are maritime pictures by the dozen; of partings between sailors and their lady-loves; portraits of William of the ballad and his black-eyed Susan; of Will Watch, the bold smuggler; of Paul Jones, the pirate, and the like; on which the painted eyes of Queen Victoria, and of Washington to boot, rest in a strange companionship. . . .

From every corner, as you glance about you in these dark streets, some figure crawls half-awakened, as if the judgment hour were near at hand, and every obscure grave were giving up its dead. Where dogs would howl to lie men and women and boys slink off to sleep, forcing the dislodged rats to move away in quest of better lodgings. Here, too, are *lanes and alleys paved with mud knee-deep; underground chambers where they dance and game; the walls bedecked with rough designs of ships, of forts, and flags, and American Eagles out of number; ruined houses, open to the street, whence through wide gaps in the walls other ruins loom upon the eye, as though the world of vice and misery had nothing else to show; hideous tenements which take their names from robbery and murder; all that is loathsome, drooping and decayed is here.*

This was the Five Points that gave New York such gangs as the Dead Rabbits, Chichesters, Plug Uglies and Roach Guards and, much later, the dreaded Whyos and the Five Points Gang. From the ranks of the Five Pointers came such fledgling gangsters as Johnny Torrio, Frankie Yale, Lucky Luciano and Al Capone, an impressive result of 100 years of crime breeding.

Today, the old Five Points section takes in parts of Chinatown and Little Italy and a large portion is taken up by Columbus Park. Much of the area consists of decaying housing that the former residents of the Five Points would have considered luxury apartments.

See also: OLD BREWERY.

floaters   murder victims

Almost every waterfront city in America during the 18th and 19th centuries came to know the term *floater*, used to describe a corpse found floating in the water after meeting with foul play. It was a term imported from England to refer to such crimes, which were common along the Thames in London.

The "floater" capital of the United States was probably Buffalo, N.Y., the terminus of the Erie Canal beginning in 1825. The canal at Buffalo was probably the most crime-infested waterway in the country, and murder victims were dumped there with monotonous regularity. The primary source of this pollution was the dives of Canal Street, whose rear areas extended over the canal, supported by wooden dock pilings. Unsuspecting canalers and lakers were hustled to these places by shills to be trimmed with exorbitant prices. However, if a man had a bundle and was uncooperative about parting with it, he was fed enough knockout drops to put a team of horses to sleep.

He would be hauled into a back room, stripped of all his clothes and dumped naked down a slick wooden chute into the canal with hardly an incriminating splash. Not even the cold water would be enough to revive him, and he eventually would be discovered floating face down in the murky water. The police would know no more than that he had been killed in one of about 100 places on Canal Street and would close the file on the case by listing the victim as a "floater." In one week in 1863 no fewer than 14 floaters were fished out of the canal, five on one morning alone.

Flour Riots   New York mob action

The Great New York Fire of December 1835 was largely responsible for bringing on the Panic of 1837, as banks failed and insurance companies went bankrupt, and set the stage for the bloody Flour Riots of 1837. Because many employers in New York could not rebuild, thousands were thrown out of work and economic activities ground slowly down. There was also a falloff in the supplies of food, and by the autumn of 1836 the price of a barrel of flour had risen first to $7 a barrel and then to the unheard-of sum of $12. Actual starvation developed in the slum areas of the Five Points and the Bowery as bread, a staple of the poor's diet, disappeared. By February 1837 the flour depot at Troy, N.Y. had on hand only 4,000 barrels of flour as opposed to the usual 30,000, and it was predicted the price would rise to $20 a barrel or more. New York newspapers denounced as gougers certain merchants who allegedly were hoarding great amounts of grain and flour, waiting for bigger profits.

On February 10 an enormous mob attending a meeting in City Hall Park moved en masse on the big wheat and flour store of Eli Hart & Co. on Washington Street. Despite defenses by the watchmen, the huge mob battered down the doors and began throwing barrels of flour, sacks of wheat and watchmen out the windows. Several watchmen were seriously injured, and the flour and wheat were spilled out of their containers and scattered by the rioters. They destroyed an estimated 1,000 bushels of wheat and 500 barrels of flour before they were driven off by a large contingent of police supported by two companies of national guardsmen. The rioters scattered, carrying off their dead and wounded. However, the mob simply poured across the city and launched a new attack on the store of S. H. Herrick & Co. Once again, a large amount of flour and wheat was destroyed before the rioters were dispersed. Ironically, very few of the mob made an attempt or even thought to carry off any of the precious flour. And the following day the price of flour increased another dollar.

The Flour Riots did little to alleviate the condition of the poor, who, like their counterparts a century later, simply learned to make do on less until the country emerged from its economic woes.

Ford, Emma (c. 1870–?) female crook

Detective Clifton Wooldridge, a turn-of-the-century historian of criminality in Chicago, described a black woman named Emma Ford as the most dangerous strong-arm woman in the city. In point of fact, it would be a close call between Emma and another black woman, Flossie Moore, with whom she maintained a sometimes-friendly, sometimes-unfriendly rivalry.

Emma was a highly successful pickpocket and panel-house worker, but her first love was always violent street muggings. Operating alone or teaming up with her sister, Pearl Smith, Emma would prowl Chicago's South Side and attack men with razors, brass knuckles, knives, guns and sawed-off baseball bats. One of her favorite tactics when a victim did not prove instantly submissive was to slash his knuckles with a razor. Emma Ford had an imposing air about her, being over 6 feet tall and weighing more than 200 pounds. She had both strength and panther-like agility. According to detective Wooldridge: "She would never submit to arrest except at the point of a revolver. No two men on the police force were strong enough to handle her, and she was dreaded by all of them." While incarcerated in Denver before coming to Chicago, she once seized a prison guard by the hair, lifted him off the floor and plucked out his whiskers one by one. In the Cook County Jail she once held a guard submerged in a water trough until he almost drowned. On another occasion she badly scarred six other female convicts with a hot iron. Every time she was released from jail, the word would spread rapidly, and unhappily, throughout the Levee that "Emma Ford's loose again."

Emma terrorized the South Side area until 1903, when she vanished. Speculation had it that she had been set on by a half-dozen male toughs and sent to her reward, or had returned to Denver, or had gone to New York, or had found a "loving man" and gone off to raise a family. In any event, Chicago did not see her again.

See also: FLOSSIE MOORE.

Forty Thieves   19th-century New York gang

The first criminal gang in New York City with a disciplined membership and an acknowledged leadership was the Forty Thieves, a group of Lower East Side Irish immigrants who served as political sluggers as well as muggers and holdup men.

The gang, which was formed in the early 1820s, met regularly in a grocery speakeasy run by a colorful wench named Rosanna Peers on what is now Center Street. In that speakeasy their chieftain, Edward Coleman, would parcel out assignments and criminal beats to the stickup artists. Each man was expected to bring in a certain amount of loot and knew that if he consistently missed his quota, there was a number of younger criminals in the area eager for the opportunity to join the Thieves.

It was perhaps unrealistic to think that a gang of that size could maintain such discipline in an area as lush as early New York, and indeed, by 1850 the Forty Thieves had just about dissolved as a result of individual members striking out on their own or joining other bigger, more loosely organized gangs. Oddly, the name Forty Thieves then passed on to the Tammany Hall politicians, who by 1850 had begun their systematic looting of the city treasury. The Common Council of 1850 was given the sobriquet Forty Thieves, an affront to the remnants of the old gang of strong-arm robbers, who regarded themselves as much more honorable than politicians.

Forty-Two Gang   Chicago juvenile gang

Perhaps the worst juvenile gang ever produced by this country, the 42 Gang out of the "Patch," or Little Italy, section of Chicago became a source of recruits for the Chicago mobs in the post–Al Capone era.

Even among the wild juvenile gangs of the 1920s, the 42ers were known as crazy, willing to do anything for a quick buck. They stripped cars, knocked over cigar stores, held up nightclubs, slipped into peddlers' stables and stole from their carts or killed their horses, hacking off the hind legs to sell as horse meat. Many neighborhood Italian girls idolized the 42ers, not only becoming their sexual playthings but also going along with them on their nightly crime capers to act as lookouts or "gun girls," secreting the gangsters' weapons under their skirts until needed so that the boys would be "clean" if stopped by police.

The gang derived its name from the story of Ali Baba and the Forty Thieves, which had always fascinated the members. In 1925 they decided to go Ali Baba two better and called themselves the 42 Gang, an exaggerated figure since at their "founding" meeting there were only 24 members. But in ensuing years their numbers did grow to about 42. The violence-prone gang committed any number of murders, including stoolies and policemen among their victims, but paid a high price. In 1931 University of Chicago sociologists conducted a study of the gang and came up with some staggering statistics. More than 30 of those considered to be the original 42ers had either been killed or maimed or were doing time for such crimes as murder, rape, armed robbery or other felonies.

In 1928, when a number of 42ers were confined to the boys' reformatory at St. Charles, the institution's head, Maj. William

J. Butler, received a long-distance phone call from Chicago. "This is the 42 Gang," he was informed. "Unless you let our pals go, we'll come down there and kill everybody we see. We've got plenty of men and some machine guns." Butler was inclined to laugh off the threat until Chicago police told him the 42ers probably meant it. The state militia was called out to guard the school, and Butler armed himself with a gun. A few days later, a 42er advance guard of three punks headed by Crazy Patsy Steffanelli was picked up outside the reformatory walls. Crazy Patsy readily admitted harboring plans to machine-gun his buddies to freedom. The incident brought forth a spate of stories about the 42ers, pointing out they should not be sent to St. Charles (an institution meant primarily for wayward boys rather than hardened criminals), even those of a tender age. The *Chicago Tribune* editorialized that the 42ers were a separate criminal class and should be sent either to such higher institutions as Joliet or to the electric chair.

The great ambition of the 42ers was to receive recognition from the big bootleggers and the Caponeites, and after a successful caper they would turn up in mob hangouts, dressed to the hilt and spending money like water. While the big bootleggers occasionally used them as beer runners or drivers, they still regarded the 42ers as "those crazy boys."

But even the Capone men could eventually be convinced by enough accomplishments. It was one of the "mooniest" of the gang, Sam Giancana, who finally made it into the syndicate, winning the support of its two top men, Paul Ricca and Tony Accardo, who took Giancana on as his driver. When Giancana finally proved he could curb his temper and wild behavior and be a disciplined, cun-

ning gangster, he quickly moved up the organizational ladder, eventually becoming head of the entire outfit. And with Giancana's climb, the remnants of the 42 Gang were integrated into the mob.

Four Deuces   Capone mob gambling den

One of the most notorious "pleasure" joints run by the Capone mob was a four-story structure on Chicago's South Wabash Avenue. The first floor was given over to a bar, and gambling activities occupied the next two. The fourth floor sported a lavish bordello. It was also the scene of numerous murders.

The Four Deuces was not without competition, especially from the nearby Frolics Club, which dispensed both liquor and women at lower prices. This unfair competition was dealt with in an imagina-tive fashion. One night when a murder occurred in the Four Deuces, the boys lugged the body over to the Frolics and stuffed it into the furnace. One of the Capone men then called the police with an irate complaint that the Frolics was running an illegal crematorium. The police rushed over and found evidence of a corpse in the furnace. The Frolics was promptly padlocked, and the authorities ripped it apart in search of more corpses. None were found, but the Frolics never reopened.

Friendly Friends   Chicago madams' association

In the early 1900s a group of "better class" madams in Chicago formed a trade society "to protect our interests," which meant, among other things, controlling prices and competition and, most important, seeing they got their money's worth for the protection they bought.

The Friendly Friends specifically did not invite the most successful madams of the era, the Everleigh sisters, to join. In fact, most of their proceedings were given over to investigating ways of eliminating the fabulous Everleigh Club, the city's most renowned brothel, which took away so much of the "cream" of the business from their own fashionable establishments. The Friendly Friends were reportedly behind a number of plots to frame the Everleighs in various ways. When a young male member of a leading Chicago family accidentally shot himself in his home in 1905, a story spread that the man had really been the victim of a shooting in the Everleigh Club. The rumor was later put to rest after it was revealed that a black vice operator, Pony Moore, had offered one of the Everleigh Club's courtesans $20,000 to sign an affidavit confirming the alleged shooting. It was generally agreed that most of the money for the bribe plus whatever went to Moore had come from the Friendly Friends.

The leaders of the society were madams Zoe Millard, Georgie Spencer and Vic Shaw. Madam Millard was the most disturbed of all by the Everleigh competition and once administered a frightful battering to one of her prize bawds for speaking nicely of the Everleighs. Madam Spencer was the hell raiser of the group, ready with a complaint to the police whenever anything occurred that displeased her. Her wrath intensified greatly when police pressure increased as a result of public indignation over the vice in Chicago's Levee area. "Redolent of riches and ablaze with diamonds," according to one account, she stormed into the office of police captain Max Nootbaar, hammered on his desk with her jeweled fist and declared: "Listen to me, policeman! I'm rich. I own a hotel that's worth forty-five thousand dollars. I own a flat worth forty thousand, and these stones I'm wearing are worth another fifteen thousand. I'd like to see you interfere with my business."

Capt. Nootbaar was that rare bird, an honest Chicago police officer, and he eventually drove Madam Spencer into wealthy retirement in California.

Of all the Friendly Friends, Vic Shaw held on the longest, trying to keep the society in business even after the shuttering of the Levee district. She continued later with a lavish call house on South Michigan Avenue. As late as 1938 when she was about 70 years old, she turned up operating a similar resort on the North Side.

Frisco Sue (1853–?) stagecoach robber

Despite the Hollywood concept of the cowgirl hellion, the number of Western badwomen can be counted on one's fingers. The facts about even those who really existed have been steeped in the stuff of which legends are made. One of the real female villains was a lady known simply as Frisco Sue, a former San Francisco dance hall shill and prostitute, supposedly of breathtaking beauty.

In 1876, at the age of 23, Frisco Sue left for the Nevada gold fields, not to trim the miners, as other prostitutes did, but rather to reform herself. Sue decided she could escape her dreary profession by turning to a career of violent crime. Realizing she could not work alone, she shopped around for a suitable partner and finally settled on a minor road agent named Sims Talbot. If Talbot had any misgivings about working with a woman, Frisco Sue had, we are assured by various biographers of the day, all the necessary charms to make him forget them.

Sue's plans were to become very rich and transport herself to a new life in Europe, posing as an orphaned heiress. But that dream was to founder in the reality of her life of crime. The couple's first effort at stagecoach robbing netted them only $500—Sue had rolled society drunks for more than that in her California days. She was furious, and Talbot had a hard time calming her down. But he quickly hit upon a daring scheme that appealed to her. Now that the stage had been robbed, Talbot explained, the line would be confident it would not be robbed again right away and would therefore put on board a valuable shipment. So the couple held up the same stagecoach on its return run. Talbot's strategic thinking was less than perfect: this time the stage carried two shotgunners. Talbot had barely time to announce, "Hands up!" when he was blasted out of his saddle, shot dead. Frisco Sue was captured and sent to prison for three years. The Western press would not let her legend die, however, and there was always a story about some blade's plans to bust the lady free. It didn't happen. Frisco Sue served her time and then disappeared. According to one oft-told tale, she was seen a number of years later in San Francisco, married to a millionaire, but then the West always liked stories that ended with a happy and ironic twist.

funerals of gangsters

When Dion O'Banion, Chicago's notorious Irish gangster, went to his grave in 1924, a newspaper commented, "Presidents are buried with less to-do." His bronze and silver casket, made to order in Philadelphia and rushed to Chicago by express car, cost $10,000. Forty thousand persons passed through an undertaker's chapel to view the body as it "lay in state," as the *Chicago Tribune* put it.

To the "Dead March" from *Saul*, the pallbearers—triggermen Two Gun Alterie, Hymie Weiss, Bugs Moran, Schemer Drucci and Frank Gusenberg, and labor racketeer Maxie Eisen, president of the Kosher Meat Peddlers' Association—bore the casket to the hearse. Close behind them came Johnny Torrio, Al Capone and their henchmen. Despite the solemnity of the occasion, police plainsclothesmen were still fearful of a shoot-out and circulated among the gangsters confiscating firearms.

The funeral procession was about a mile long, with 26 cars and trucks carrying flowers, including particularly garish ones sent by Torrio, Capone and the Genna brothers, all of whom probably had been involved in planning O'Banion's murder. Some 10,000 persons followed the hearse, jamming every trolley car to the Mount Carmel area, where the cemetery was situated. At the cemetery 5,000 to 10,000 more spectators waited.

"It was one of the most nauseating things I've ever seen happen in Chicago," commented Judge John H. Lyle, an honest Chicago jurist—somewhat of a rarity in that area.

The O'Banion funeral typified the gaudy gangster funerals of the 1920s. Similar, though not quite as lavish, treatment was given to any number of the O'Banion gang, as one after another went to his reward. Before the O'Banion funeral, with its 26-vehicle flower procession, a previously deceased member of the gang, Nails Morton, had been honored with 20 cars. When Hymie Weiss departed, the flower train dropped to 18 vehicles; a patient Bugs Moran had to explain to the grieving widow that since the passing of Morton and O'Banion, 30 others in the gang had expired, obviously reducing the number of donors and, consequently, the amount of flowers. After Schemer Drucci was shot dead by a police officer, his funeral was a touch less impressive than Weiss', although he still was buried under a blanket of 3,500 flowers. His widow commented, "A cop bumped him off like a dog, but we gave him a king's funeral."

Attendance at gangster funerals by public officeholders was more or less obligatory during this period. After all, the underworld had bought them and therefore, had a right to call on them. Thus, when Big Jim Colosimo, the great whoremaster and mentor of Johnny Torrio—who with Al Capone plotted his demise—was assassinated in 1920, the honorary and active pallbearers included two congressmen, three judges, a future federal judge, a state representative, 10 aldermen and a host of other politicians and community leaders. Mayor Big Bill Thompson sent personal representatives to express his heartfelt loss. It made sense, considering the fact that Colosimo's organization had piled up huge votes for Thompson and his Republican allies. In his eulogy of Big

Jim, Alderman Bathhouse John Coughlin of the First Ward said: "Jim wasn't a bad fellow. You know what he did? He fixed up an old farmhouse for broken-down prostitutes. They rested up and got back in shape and he never charged them a cent."

Into the 1930s the big gangster funeral was considered a must. "That's what buddies are for," one mobster explained to a reporter. However, by the time Al Capone died in 1947, low key was the vogue, and it has been basically that way ever since. The only untoward events at such affairs are scuffles between mobsters and reporters and photographers.

When Frank Costello died in 1973, his widow saw to it that his unsavory friends stayed away from the funeral. The burial ceremony was over in a few minutes. The only person to approach her was a cousin of Frank. Hat in hand, he whispered what she expected to be words of condolence. "What are you going to do with Frank's clothes?" he asked. Mrs. Costello walked on without bothering to answer.

Gallatin Street   New Orleans crime area

From 1840 until 1880 Gallatin Street in New Orleans was described as having more crime per square foot than any street in America. Indeed, it had the distinction of not containing a single legitimate enterprise anywhere on its two-block length. Running from Ursuline Avenue to Barracks, it offered enough debaucheries from dusk to dawn to sate the country boys, city slickers, sailors and steamboat men seeking varied pleasures. Such visitors, one historian noted, were in turn sought out by "a horde of harlots, sneak thieves, garroters who openly carried their deadly strangling cords, and footpads with slung shots looped about their wrists." There were barrelhouses where for 5¢ a man bought no mere glass of liquor but all the booze he could drink, dance houses that were also bordellos and sailors' boarding houses from which seamen were at times shanghaied. It was often said that a miracle man in New Orleans was one who could enter Gallatin at Ursuline with money in his pocket and emerge at Barracks with his cash and skull untapped. At times, the police entered the street by day in large armed groups but were nowhere to be seen after sunset.

Much of the mayhem on Gallatin Street was the work of the Live Oak Boys, a gang formed in 1858 by one Red Bill Wilson, a vicious thug who always concealed a knife in his bushy red beard. The Live Oak Boys were not a disciplined bunch. While they collected protection from virtually every house on the street, that was no guarantee they would not smash such a place to pieces when they had a mind to, which proved a rather common occurrence. Then too, they considered any payment they received from an establishment null and void if the proprietor of a rival business offered them a bounty to shut down the competition.

Despite such depredations, any resort on Gallatin was invariably a gold mine. Typical was Archie Murphy's, which in a decade of operation left the proprietor in a state a newspaper described as one of "extreme wealth." Murphy achieved that happy status by encouraging his girls "not to allow any sucker to get away." One of his more skillful harpies was Lizzie Collins. A foolhardy farmer once bragged to Lizzie that he had $110 in gold tied in a handkerchief around his leg. He shrewdly refused all drinks but jumped at Lizzie's invitation to go upstairs. As the couple entered Lizzie's room, three other harlots jumped on the man and held him while Lizzie poured whiskey down his throat. When the farmer was helpless, Lizzie retrieved the handkerchief with the gold and then called on the Murphy bouncers to toss the farmer into the alley. The farmer pressed charges and Lizzie was arrested, but the case was dismissed when the farmer could produce no evidence other than his word.

Lizzie Collins went on to suffer a bizarre fate. Years of drink addled her brain and she developed a mania for stealing items that Archie Murphy found little use for. Instead of taking a man's money, she would drug or knock him out and then cut all the buttons off his pants. Archie Murphy tried to get Lizzie to mend her ways, but he finally kicked her out. For some years thereafter, Lizzie stalked Gallatin Street practicing her strange pastime, becoming one additional peril for visitors to the street.

See also: MARY JANE "BRICKTOP" JACKSON, LIVE OAK BOYS.

Gallus Mag (c. 1860s) female thug

Described by New York police as the most savage female ruffian of the period from just before to just after the Civil War, Gallus Mag was a towering six-footer known as the Queen of the Waterfront. Her antecedents were English, but little else was known about her. At times, she would refuse to give any information and, on other occasions, would provide varying and contradictory stories. Once when a saloon habitué asked Gallus

Mag her age, she punished him for his nosiness by smashing his skull with a mallet, chewing off his ear and throwing him into the street.

Gallus Mag, who earned her nickname by wearing galluses, or suspenders, to hold her skirt up, held sway in the legendary Hole-In-The-Wall Saloon on New York City's Water Street, where she was a partner with One-Armed Charley Monell and acted as bouncer. The saloon was a "bucket of blood" where more men were said to have been robbed or killed than in any other watering hole of that era. Despite her duty to keep the peace, Gallus Mag was a prime cause of the violence. She would stalk the dive looking for trouble and was well prepared for it, with a pistol always tucked into her skirt and a bludgeon strapped to her wrist. Whenever she found a man violating the rules of the place, such as robbing a stranger without a permit from the management, she would immediately crack him over the head. Her custom was to then seize the offender's ear between her teeth and drag him out the door. If her victim dared to struggle, she would bite his ear off. Gallus Mag became infamous for this act and kept all such severed ears in a huge jar of alcohol behind the bar, a trophy collection that was one of the more gory sights on the crime-ridden waterfront.

Gallus Mag's only real female competition was the notorious Sadie the Goat, so named because when she spotted a likely victim for a mugging she would lower her head and butt him in the stomach. A blow to the head would end the victim's resistance, and Sadie would rifle his pockets at leisure. One day Sadie attempted to butt her way to a victory over Gallus Mag, but a mallet proved more than a match for Sadie the Goat's skull. Gallus Mag chewed off her rival's ear, and Sadie

GARDNER, Roy

fled the East Side waterfront in disgrace. The vanquished warrior later achieved great fame as the leader of the Charlton Street pirates on the West Side, who terrorized the Hudson River for many miles north of the city. When the Charlton Streeters were finally broken up, Sadie the Goat returned to the East Side and made her peace with Gallus Mag, accepting Mag's primacy as the queen of the area. This total surrender so impressed Gallus Mag that she magnanimously fished around in her alcohol jar of ears and returned Sadie's severed member to her.

Gallus Mag's reign on the East Side waterfront ran from the late 1850s to 1871, when the Hole-In-The-Wall was closed because of the numerous murders and other crimes committed there. Many tales circulated about Gallus Mag's subsequent fate: one that she found true love with a poor young man and another that she found true love with a rich old man. Whatever her fate, the waterfront was never the same after her reign.

See also: HOLE-IN-THE-WALL SALOON.

Gardner, Roy (1888–1940) escape artist

As a criminal, Roy Gardner was less than a master, getting himself caught frequently. The problem for the law was not catching him but holding him. One of the leading columnists of the early 1920s, S. Jay Kaufman, wrote in the *New York World:* "There is no end of fascinating questions in the career of this extraordinary man. How often do we find a criminal who has taught Emerson and Thoreau, fought for liberty across the border, knocked down the great Jim Jeffries, written a book of scholarship that is a classic in its field? Roy Gardner is Renaissance man born too late in a world he never

made. He is a man of whom they make legends, and we are in need of legends to brighten this dreary world."

Roy Gardner was America's greatest escape artist during the Roaring Twenties, and as he slipped in and out of the hands of the law, he produced one fantastic newspaper headline after another. Born in 1888, the son of a well-to-do Detroit businessman, Gardner appeared to have a brilliant future when he graduated from college with honors. He showed a strong literary bent and at a very early age became a faculty member of a Midwestern college. His record in the English department was outstanding, and a work he published on 17th-century literature was very well received.

By all rights, Roy Gardner should have become a fixture in the academic world and lived out a useful educational career, but youthful enthusiasm and a craving for adventure caused him to drop out. He went to Mexico to live with the revolutionaries. In 1908 Gardner was caught bringing ammunition to the Carranza army and was sentenced to death after a summary government trial. He escaped from the military prison at Hermosillo before the execution could be carried out. Three other Americans escaped with him. Later, two were wounded and recaptured, but Gardner and the other American made it away clean.

Having no desire to return to the university life, Roy headed to the West Coast and took a fling at prizefighting, becoming a sparring partner for James J. Jeffries. It was through his acquaintances in the boxing world that Gardner turned to crime. With two others, he pulled a $19,000 van robbery. Afterward, one of his accomplices was caught and he implicated Gardner, who spent two years in San Quentin as a result.

102

When he got out, he went straight and got married. Gardner opened his own welding shop in Oakland, Calif. and prospered until the shop burned to the ground. He had no insurance. Thereafter, Gardner went to Los Angeles and took a job as a welder. He also started to do some serious writing, but after a while, honest work ceased to interest him. He robbed a mail truck in San Diego, netting only a small sum of money, and was soon caught.

Gardner played the role of the flippant criminal, answering the judge with Shake-spearean quotes and constantly showing off his literary knowledge. The judge was unimpressed and sentenced him to 25 years at the federal penitentiary on McNeil Island, Wash. Gardner was stunned at the sentence. Then he regained his composure. "You'll never get me there," he shouted as he was being led away. No one paid him any mind.

But Roy Gardner was right. He overpowered his train guards, seized their weapons and hopped off the train as it neared Portland, Ore. While a vast manhunt for him was launched in the Pacific Northwest, he went east through Canada, holed up in Minneapolis and eventually moved to Davenport, Iowa, where he took a job as a welding instructor. Soon, the old restlessness surfaced, and he returned to Napa, Calif., where his wife lived under constant surveillance. He slipped past the stakeout to see her and sneaked away again. A neighbor spotted him and called the police, but despite an intensive hunt, with his picture splashed across the newspapers, Gardner escaped.

In May 1921 he robbed a Southern Pacific mail car of $200,000 in cash and securities. By not fleeing the area, however, he again proved to be a poor thief. Six days later, he was caught in a Roseville gambling room, betting big and bragging about how smart he was. When apprehended, Gardner had only a small amount of his loot and refused to say where the rest was.

Another 25 years was added to his sentence, and the law put him on a train for McNeil Island once more and once more failed to get him there. Already the newspapers had dubbed him the Escaping Professor and printed his boast that he would not be taken as far as Tacoma, Wash.

On the train Gardner asked his two guards for permission to go to the toilet. The officers, being cautious, accompanied him and kept another prisoner handcuffed to him. The four trooped to the men's room, one of the large types of the 1920s. Nothing untoward happened until they moved to the sink. Suddenly, using his free hand, Gardner pulled a gun from under the sink. He and the other prisoner, Norris Pryor, handcuffed the officers and taped their mouths shut with the tape that had been used to secure the gun in its hiding place. How it got there Gardner never revealed. As the train slowed in the Vancouver yards, Gardner and Pryor jumped off, disappearing in the misty rain.

Gardner's escape made headlines across the country, and he became one of the nation's most glorified criminals. Unfortunately for him, he became so recognizable that he was readily recaptured. The newspapers speculated about how far the law would succeed in transporting Gardner this time, but the authorities took no chances. He was shackled to two unarmed officers and guarded at a distance by two others. When he entered the prison, one journalist mourned "the end of a legend."

It wasn't. On Labor Day 1921 Gardner was watching a baseball game from the bleachers of the prison ball field. As all eyes were focused on the field, he and two other convicts dropped through the bleacher seats to the ground. They cut through the barbed wire fence with wire cutters Gardner had stolen from the machine shop and raced for undergrowth 50 yards from the fence. If they made that, they would have a chance. The tower guards didn't see them until they were halfway there. In the fusillade of bullets that followed, Gardner's two companions went down. Gardner was wounded in the left leg but made the bushes. He hid out there until dark while guards searched for him and police craft circled the island. What they didn't know was that Gardner had retraced his escape route and was hiding out in the prison barn. He treated his wound, which was not too serious, and milked a cow whenever he got hungry.

Gardner stayed hidden for 48 hours, by which time it was decided he had reached the mainland. Only then did he move to the water's edge, drift $2^1/_2$ miles to Fox Island and from there swim to the mainland. He vanished for a few weeks and then was back in the headlines. Audaciously, he had addressed a letter to President Warren Harding offering a deal. He wanted his sentences suspended so that he could return to his wife and young children "to start life anew." In return, he promised to pay back to the government some $250,000 in loot, which he said he had salted away.

It made good newspaper copy but had no results. The president naturally ignored the offer.

Gardner was now 33 years old. Somewhere between his escape from the prison in September and November 15, all the fight went out of him. He tried to hold up a mail clerk on a train in Arizona but was easily overpowered. This time he was sent to Leav-

enworth, his sentence now having reached 75 years. He never escaped custody again. Gardner's reputation earned him a transfer to the new maximum security federal prison at Alcatraz in 1934, but he was sent back to Leavenworth two years later because of his good behavior. Two years after that, he was freed. The newspapers speculated investigators wanted him to lead them to his stolen money hoard, but the real reason for his release was his poor health. Thereafter, Gardner lived alone in a rundown hotel in San Francisco, his wife having died years before. In January 1940, at the age of 52, the Escaping Professor made his final break to freedom. He turned on the gas.

Gem Saloon, gunfight at the

While the O.K. Corral is the most famous shoot-out site in America, far more deadly gun duels and killings took place at the infamous Gem Saloon in El Paso, Tex. It was here in January 1877 that Pink Higgins outdrew Merritt Horrell, chalking up another death in the Horrell-Higgins feud. But just as there was *the* gunfight at the O.K. Corral, so too was there *the* gunfight at the Gem, one that probably had more stock elements than any of a score of famous duels: right against wrong, a man bucking incredible odds, mistaken identity, black Western humor and a prime example of the art of gunfighting.

The duel or more correctly, duels were fought on April 14, 1884. On that day a gambler and dandy named Bill Raynor, who had gained his reputation as a gunfighter by planting eight foes in the ground, turned "mean" and walked through town looking for a fight. Given his reputation, he found no takers. After challenging every man in a barbershop, he moved on to the Gem. He sauntered into the saloon's gambling room and finally provoked one faro player, Bob Rennick, into demanding Raynor stop leaning on him. Raynor told him he was stepping out to the bar to have a drink and was then coming back in to kill him. The other players advised Rennick to move away from the table so they could continue their game in peace. Rennick checked his six-gun, moved to the wall and began watching the doorway. A minute or so later, Raynor burst into the room, his guns blazing. Four shots splintered the chair Rennick had vacated; Rennick stepped out from the wall and answered with two shots that caught Raynor in the stomach and chest. Raynor staggered out to the street and collapsed in the arms of a noted visitor in town, Wyatt Earp, asking Earp to inform his mother that he had "died game."

Raynor was taken to the doctor's office, where his friend Buck Linn rushed to him, inquiring about who had shot him. Raynor gave a garbled answer that indicated the man who had gunned him down was Bob Cahill. Linn vowed to take vengeance on his friend's alleged assailant. When this news got back to the Gem, Cahill, an inoffensive gambler who had never shot a gun, became petrified. A friend named Dan Tipton handed Cahill a loaded .45, and Wyatt Earp gave him a fast lesson in gunfighting, to wit: stay calm, take plenty of time aiming and shoot for the belly button. This was standard advice, but observers could not tell how much of it the frightened Cahill had absorbed. Five minutes later, Buck Linn entered the saloon. After spotting the little gambler, he pulled his gun and fired four fast shots from a distance of 12 to 15 feet. All missed. Cahill aimed his .45 and sighted in on Linn's belt buckle when he was about 8 feet away. His aim was high, and he shot Linn right through the heart.

Thus ended the Gem's most famous shoot-out, although Raynor did not expire for 48 hours. On the chance that he might recover, both Rennick and Cahill, who had pushed their luck to the limit, rode hard for Mexico. The two victors had popular support, one drunk at the bar proclaiming: "I'm damned glad Bill got it. He should have been killed years ago." From the silence that greeted his comment, the drunk realized there was still the chance that Raynor might recover. He added quickly, "If Bill gets well, what I said don't go." But Raynor, fortunately for the drunk, didn't make it.

The *El Paso Herald* stated: "The victims had no one to blame but themselves. Their train of life collided with loaded revolvers and they have gone down forever in the smash-up. Thus endeth the first chapter of our spring fights."

Ging, Katherine "Kitty" (1867–1894) victim of hypnotic murder

Criminologists have often cited the killing of 27-year-old Kitty Ging in Minneapolis, Minn. in 1894 as an authentic case of hypnosis being used to cause a murder. The facts are hazy at best and certainly subject to various interpretations.

Early that year Harry T. Hayward, a smooth-talking local wastrel, had completed a course in hypnotism and tried out his techniques both on Kitty Ging and on Claus Blixt, a dim-witted building engineer and handyman. Eventually, Haywood induced Kitty to give him several thousand dollars, all her ready cash, so that he could "invest" it for her. How much of this was due to "hypnotic powers" and how much to the sheer weight of his personality cannot be measured. In any event, he also was able in time to get Kitty to make him the beneficiary of two $5,000 life insurance policies.

Meanwhile, Hayward was spending long sessions with Blixt too. "He always made me look into his eyes," the simple-minded Blixt later said. "He said that unless I looked into his eyes, I couldn't understand what he was saying." What Hayward was usually saying was that crime paid and was easy. Blixt insisted Hayward "induced" him to set fire to a vacant factory building on which Kitty Ging held a mortgage. She collected $1,500 in insurance and the money eventually found its way into Hayward's pockets. Since Hayward gave some of the money to Blixt, it was unclear how much of Blixt's acts had been due to his own greed and how much to Hayward's hypnotic powers.

Hayward now began to plot Kitty Ging's murder so that he could collect her life insurance. Apparently, he had less than total confidence in his power to induce Blixt to carry out the crime because he first approached his own brother, Adry Hayward, to commit the murder while he established an iron-clad alibi. The astounded Adry rejected the proposition. He later said: "I don't know why I listened when Harry talked to me of this dreadful thing. He kept looking at me as he talked, and sometimes I felt as if I was being hypnotized. When I refused, he talked about getting Blixt to help him. He said Blixt was so simple-minded that he could easily be influenced."

Adry related his conversation with his brother to a lawyer friend of the family, who simply ignored the story as too preposterous until Kitty Ging's body, her head crushed in and a bullet wound behind her ear, was found on the evening of December 3, 1894. The lawyer then took his information to the Hennepin County district attorney's office,

and Blixt and Adry and Harry Hayward were brought in for questioning. Hayward proved to be a tough man to crack, possessing a perfect alibi for the time of the murder: attendance at the Grand Opera House.

For a while, Adry attempted to shield his brother, and Blixt insisted he was not involved in any way. Finally, Blixt broke and admitted murdering Kitty Ging, arranging to do so at a time when Harry Howard had an alibi. He said that before his act he had spent several long sessions with Hayward during which he was told over and over again that murder was an easy crime to commit and get away with. After Blixt's admission, Adry talked, and finally, Harry Hayward confessed to masterminding Kitty's murder, saying his mistake "was in not killing Blixt, as I had originally intended."

Claus Blixt was sentenced to life imprisonment and Harry Hayward, "the hypnotic plotter," was condemned to die on December 11, 1895. His execution proved as bizarre as his crime. He promised to cause no trouble if the scaffold was painted bright red and the rope dipped in red dye. The authorities agreed to these requests but refused to allow him to wear red clothing or to use a red hood in place of the traditional black. On the scaffold Hayward recited a prayer and asked God's forgiveness for his sins. Then he shouted: "Don't pay any attention to that! I just said it to oblige one of my lawyers. I didn't mean a word of it! I stand pat. . . ."

At that moment the outraged executioner, without waiting for his signal, sprang the trap.

Gophers   New York gang

One of the last of the all-Irish gangs of New York, the Gophers were the kings of Hell's

Kitchen until they disintegrated in the changing society of the pre–World War era. The Gophers controlled the territory between Seventh and Eleventh Avenues from 42nd Street to 14th Street. Brawlers, muggers and thieves, they gained their name because they liked to hide out in basements and cellars. With an ability to summon 500 gangsters to their banner, they were not a force to be dismissed lightly by the police or other gangsters.

They were such hell raisers and so fickle in their allegiance that no one could emerge as the single leader of the gang. Thus, the Gophers never produced a gangster with the stature of Monk Eastman, the greatest villain of the period. Among the most prominent Gophers, however, there were numerous subleaders, such a Newburg Gallagher, Stumpy Malarkey, Happy Jack Mulraney and Marty Brennan.

Another celebrated Gopher was One-Lung Curran, who in due course expired due to this deficiency. Once when his girlfriend wailed that she was without a coat for the chilly fall weather, Curran strode up to the first policeman he saw and blackjacked him to the ground. He stripped off the officer's uniform coat and presented it to his mistress, who, being an adept seamstress, converted it into a military-style lady's jacket. This event caused such a fashion sensation in Gopher society that thugs by the dozen soon were out on the streets clubbing and stripping policemen.

In brute power and violence, the police could seldom match the Gophers. To do so would have accomplished little anyway, since the gang enjoyed a measure of protection from the ward's politicians, who found the Gophers of immense assistance during elections. They however, were too anarchistic to

exploit this advantage to the fullest, feeling that with raw power they could achieve anything they wanted.

The Gophers had no reason to fear the police when they looted the New York Central Railroad freight cars along Eleventh Avenue. But while they might enjoy a measure of tolerance from public officials, they failed to grasp the extent of corporate power and the railroad's ability to field a virtual army against them. The New York Central's special force was staffed with many former policemen who had suffered insults and injuries from the gangsters and who were anxious for the opportunity to retaliate. Railroad property became a no-man's land, and the company detectives began to venture further afield to devastate Hell's Kitchen itself. The Gophers were smashed, their prestige savaged and their unity crushed. Gallagher and Brennan went to Sing Sing, and many others were killed or maimed. Factions of the Gophers joined other criminal combines, but these were organizations that specialized in purely criminal ventures and wasted neither time nor strength on unprofitable street bashings. An era of American criminality was ending.

See also: LADY GOPHERS.

grabbers 19th-century New York procurer gangs
Grabbers was the popular name given in the 1860s and 1870s to the procurer gangs operating in New York. The two most important gangs were those headed by Red Light Lizzie, perhaps the most noted procurer of the time, and her principal rival, the brazen Hester Jane Haskins, also known as Jane the Grabber. Both gangs operated out of business offices and each month sent a circular out to clients advertising their newest wares.

Procuring was generally tolerated by the police so long as the grabbers followed the usual procedure of sending out "talent scouts" to outlying villages upstate and surrounding states to lure young girls to the metropolis with promises of high-paying jobs. The girls were then "broken into the life."

A "grabber scandal" of sorts erupted in 1875 when the Haskins woman began specializing in recruiting girls from good families, the better-paying brothel clients being much enticed by having the company of females of refinement. Too many girls disappeared, however, which created quite a stir. Jane the Grabber was arrested with a number of her minions and sent to prison. Upon their release they were "rousted" out of New York by the police apparently because of intolerance for procurers who could not understand certain class distinctions.

Grady gang 19th-century sneak thief gang
During the 1860s the art of sneak thievery achieved new heights thanks to a New York gang of thieves masterminded by John D. Grady, better known as Travelling Mike.

Travelling Mike, perhaps the number two fence of the era, after the infamous Marm Mandelbaum, was a stooped, dour-faced little man who padded the streets winter and summer wearing a heavy overcoat and carrying a peddler's box on his shoulder. Mike's box did not contain the standard peddler's stock of needles and other small articles, but rather pearls, diamonds and bonds, all stolen property. He never ventured out with less than $10,000 with which to make his daily purchases from various criminals. Mike was frequently to be seen at the notorious Thieves' Exchange, near Broadway and Houston Street, where fences and criminals

met each night and dickered openly in the buying and selling of stolen goods.

To drum up more business, Travelling Mike organized his own gang and planned their jobs. His most famous underling was "Billy the Kid" Burke, a brilliant sneak thief who was arrested 100 times before his 26th birthday but was still able to retire, according to legend, a wealthy man. Mike engineered a raid on the money hoard of Rufus L. Lord, a grasping and penurious financier of the day. Worth $4 million, Lord spent his time clipping coupons and counting his hoard of money in a dingy office at 38 Exchange Place. He was so miserly that he wore tattered and patched clothing and would not light his office with more than one candle at a time. Yet in business he was extremely cunning and was supposedly able to milk the last penny out of any adversary.

In March 1866 Travelling Mike approached Lord about securing a loan for an alleged business venture, and long discussions were held about terms. Finally, on March 7 the fence returned to Lord's office accompanied by his minions, Greedy Jake Rand, Eddie Pettengill, Hod Ennis and Boston Pet Anderson. When Travelling Mike offered to put up high-class security for the loan and suggested an interest rate of 20 percent, Lord bounded from his chair and seized him by the lapels, imploring him to close the deal immediately. While the anxious Lord was thus distracted, Boston Pet and Pettengill slipped in the darkness to the huge safe the financier often absentmindedly left open and made off with two tin boxes. Travelling Mike then agreed to close the deal and said he would return in an hour to sign the necessary papers.

When the gang opened the tin boxes, they counted loot totaling $1.9 million in cash and negotiable securities. Rand, Pettengill, Ennis and Boston Pet instantly joined Billy the Kid Burke in wealthy retirement, while only Travelling Mike continued in the rackets.

Mike did not consider the Lord caper his crowning achievement. He learned that his archrival, Marm Mandelbaum, had trailblazed a new business method in crime by forming a gang whose members were paid strictly on salary, with all the loot going to her. Travelling Mike, with devious acumen, approached her criminals and purchased much of their loot at extremely low prices. Since the gangsters would have netted nothing extra otherwise, both they and Travelling Mike profited. Only Marm was victimized. When she learned of the plot against her, she dissolved her gang and railed about the lack of honor among thieves, with Travelling Mike specifically in mind.

Grant, Ulysses S. (1822–1885) traffic offender
Both before and after he entered the White House, Ulysses S. Grant was a notorious speedster with horse and rig. On at least two occasions, Grant, while in command of the Union armies, was fined $5 in precinct court. Such an offense was not so readily handled during Grant's first presidential term. President Grant was apprehended in the nation's capital for racing his horse and buggy at breakneck speed on M Street between 11th and 12th. The arresting constable, a man named William H. West, was dragged some 50 feet after seizing the horse's bridle. When Constable West recognized Grant, he started to apologize, but the president said, "Officer, do your duty." The horse and rig were impounded for a time but finally returned to Grant when no charges were pressed. A constitutional dilemma developed, much as it would a century later in the Watergate scandal, about whether it was possible to indict a president without first impeaching him.

Green Chair Curse Chicago underworld superstition
One of the most colorful legends in crime is that of the Green Chair Curse, also sometimes referred to by the chroniclers of Chicago crime as the Undertaker's Friend. The curse was named after a green leather chair in the office of William "Shoes" Schoemaker, who became Chicago's chief of detectives in 1924. Several of Chicago's top gangsters were hauled into Schoemaker's office for grilling and ordered to sit in the green chair. Several of them died violent deaths shortly thereafter. This could hardly be considered a startling coincidence in view of the death rate in Chicago's gang wars during Prohibition.

The newspapers, however, quickly seized on a great story and belief in the curse of the green chair began to grow. In time, Schoemaker started keeping a record of the criminals who sat in the chair and later died violently. When the "inevitable" event occurred, Shoes put an X by the gangster's name. There were the bloody brothers Genna (Angelo, Tony and Mike), Porky Lavenuto, Mop Head Russo, Samoots Amatuna, Antonio "the Scourge" Lombardo, John Scalise, Albert Anselmi, Schemer Drucci, Zippy Zion, Pickle Puss DePro, Antonio "the Cavalier" Spano. Undoubtedly aprocryphal tales had it that other gangsters, including Al Capone, absolutely refused to sit down in the chair.

When Shoes retired in 1934, there were 35 names in his notebook and 34 had Xs after them. Only one criminal, Red Holden, was still alive and he was doing time in Alcatraz for train robbery. "My prediction still stands," Shoes informed reporters. "He'll die a violent death. Maybe it'll happen in prison. Maybe we'll have to wait until he gets out. But, mark my words, it'll happen."

Holden, however, outlived Shoes, who died four years later. The chair passed to Capt. John Warren, Shoes' aide, and he continued to seat an occasional hoodlum in it. By the time Warren died in September 1953, the green chair death rate was said to stand at 56 out of 57. Only Red Holden was still alive. He had been released from Alcatraz in 1948 and thereafter was involved in several shoot-outs, which he survived. Then he was convicted of murder and sent to prison for 25 years. On December 18, 1953, he died in the infirmary of Illinois' Statesville Penitentiary. The newspapers reported he was "smiling" because he had "beaten the chair"—the green one rather than the electric one.

Holden's passing set off a newspaper search for the illustrious green chair that had so cursed the underworld, but alas, it was no more. The chair was traced to the Chicago Avenue police station, where it had been confined to the cellar after Capt. Warren's death. When it was found to be infested with cockroaches, it was chopped up and consigned to the furnace before Holden died in his hospital bed. Otherwise, some claimed, Holden would never have escaped its curse.

Green Parrot murder

The murder at the Green Parrot Restaurant and Bar on Third Avenue near 100th Street on July 12, 1942 was a run-of-the-mill crime, the slaying of the proprietor during an apparent holdup; yet it is remembered today by New York police as a case with a most un-

usual solution. Although there had been 20 patrons in the bar at the time of the shooting, none would admit seeing anything, insisting they had been at the far end of the bar or in booths lining the wall.

It was not unusual in this tough section of East Harlem to find such a group of uncommunicative witnesses. A few acknowledged that they had seen a man with a gun, heard a shot and ducked. When they lifted their heads, the patrons said, the man with the gun was gone, and owner Max Geller was lying on the floor behind the bar in a pool of blood. Had the man simply walked in, drawn a gun and shot the bar owner? Or had it been an attempted robbery? None of the witnesses was certain. Only one of them had yelled "Robber, robber, robber!" And that was the establishment's green parrot, kept on a perch behind the bar.

The Green Parrot Bar was actually a community landmark because of the bird. It was a reason to bring guests and tourists to the place, for this was no ordinary talking pet with a few limited phrases but a crotchety old creature with the vocabulary of a longshoreman. An unsuspecting visitor might be told to offer the parrot a cracker. If he did so and expected a grateful reaction, he was sadly disillusioned. Such acts of friendship only provoked outrage from the bird, who would cut loose with a torrent of sulfurous language. But the creature was clearly the keen sort. Evidently, Geller had cried out "robber" during the attack on him, and the parrot had picked up the cry.

Knowing that a robbery had been attempted and finding a solution to the case were two separate matters, however. For almost two years the case remained unsolved, forgotten by almost everyone except Detective John J. Morrisey, who occasionally would return to the neighborhood in an attempt to dredge a forgotten fact from the memories of the witnesses. Finally, he learned that in addition to cursing the bird had been taught to greet several patrons by name. It was a long, tedious process but after a number of weeks the bird would pick up a patron's name and repeat it, appealing to the vanity of the customer.

The detective returned to the Green Parrot and tried to teach the bird his name and some other expressions. If the bird was smart, it was also stubborn and took weeks to pick up what the police officer taught it. Suddenly, Morrisey realized it was impossible for the parrot to have picked up the word *robber* after just hearing it once. No, the bird hadn't been saying "robber" but something else.

A short time later, Morrisey arrested Robert Butler, a former resident of the area, in Baltimore, Md., where he was working as a lathe operator. He had vanished from New York right after the Geller murder. As the case turned out, the bird had not been shrieking "robber" but had actually been repeating a name he had learned earlier: "Robert, Robert, Robert!" Butler was the only bar patron greeted by that name, and it was he whom the parrot had identified as the murderer. Indeed, he had not tried to commit a robbery but had shot Geller in a drunken rage because the bar owner had refused to serve him, claiming he was intoxicated when he entered.

On February 10, 1944 the only killer ever convicted because of a parrot was sentenced to seven to 15 years in Sing Sing.

Green Tree dance house

The dime-a-dance halls of the 20th century trace back to the much more bawdy dance houses of the 19th century. All such dance houses featured three attractions: liquor, women and, least important, dancing. Most dance houses would have at least 20 to 30 girls who not only were unsalaried but indeed had to pay rent for rooms or cubicles on the upper floors of the building. They made their living from the customers they could lure to their room to engage in paid sex or to be robbed. When business was especially good, harlots would be imported from a nearby brothel. The general rule was that the nearer the dance house was to the waterfront, the rougher and meaner it was. The Green Tree on Gallatin Street in New Orleans was a good example of one of the more depraved dancehall establishments.

The Green Tree opened its doors in 1850. An old woman ran the place with a firm hand. The first floor of the establishment was divided into two rooms. The first room, much bigger than the second, sported a long bar, which could accommodate as many as 250 patrons elbow to elbow. A smaller room in back was for dancing and featured a piano and a fiddle, occasionally supplemented by a few brass instruments. At times, the bouncers would have to enforce a minimum of decorum on the dance floor, where some of the girls would try to stimulate business by suddenly whipping off their dresses and dancing in the nude. The clients would sometimes follow suit, and the bouncers would have to clear the floor of couples doing everything else but dancing.

The bouncers, as many as six at a time, were always armed at least with clubs and brass knuckles. Besides maintaining order in the back room, they were needed to handle trouble at the bar. They were not too concerned with ordinary fights or an occasional knifing, provided the culprit showed the decency to clean up afterward by dumping his victim or victims outside the premises. The bouncers' main concern was to prevent physical damage to the house, and they would move in quickly and viciously the second any furnishings were splintered.

The history of violence at the Green Tree can be traced through the fate of its various owners. The first owner, the old woman, disappeared from the scene in the mid-1850s. Her place was filled by Harry Rice, who lasted until 1864, when he was almost stoned to death by a group of Union soldiers objecting to the high water content of the liquor served. It took a detachment of U.S. cavalrymen to save him, and Rice, maimed for life, closed shop. The resort was reopened the following year by Mary Rich, better known as One-Legged Duffy because of her wooden leg. She failed to last a year, being murdered on the premises by her lover, Charley Duffy, who not only knifed her to death but also smashed her skull in with her own wooden leg. Paddy Welsh, a veteran saloon keeper, took over but got in trouble with one of the worst criminal gangs of the district, the Live Oak Boys, who wrecked the dive, admonishing Welsh not to open up again. Welsh paid no heed to their warning, however, and a few days later, his body was found floating in the Mississippi.

William Lee, a former drum major in the U.S. Army, remained in New Orleans after the Civil War and eventually took charge of the Green Tree. He was stabbed to death by a gangster in an argument over a woman. The last owner of the Green Tree was Tom Pickett, who saw the place torn apart by Live Oak bullies in 1876. After brooding about the fact that it would take a fortune to try to refurbish the establishment, Pickett went out hunting with a revolver. He found several Live Oak men in a saloon and shot two of them dead. He was sent to the state penitentiary for life but escaped in 1885 when it caught fire. Pickett was later identified in New York, but the authorities apparently made no effort to return him to justice. As for the Green Tree, it became regarded as a jinx. When the premises next opened, it was a bakery.

See also: LIVE OAK BOYS.

Hairtrigger Block   Chicago "shoot-out" area

During the Civil War, Chicago gambling thrived as it probably did in no other city, North or South. In the gamblers' vernacular, the city was a "sucker's paradise," teeming with army officers and, more important, paymasters, soldiers from the front with many months pay, speculators rich with war contracts and so on, all ready and eager to lose their money at cards. The center of the gambling industry, which was illegal but well protected through heavy payments to the police, was on Randolph and Clark Streets, which contained palatial "skinning houses" for trimming the suckers. Naturally, with fortunes won and lost so easily, shootings and killings were common and probably far more frequent than could be found in any town of the Wild West. In fact, Randolph Street between Clark and State was commonly referred to as Hairtrigger Block because of the many shootings that took place there.

Some of the shootings were between professional gamblers themselves over matters such as possession of a "mark" or out of just plain nastiness. The most famous feud on

Hairtrigger Block was between two big gamblers, George Trussell, the dandy of Gambler's Row, and Cap Hyman, described as "an insufferable egotist, an excitable, emotional jack-in-the-box." They could barely tolerate each other when sober, but when drunk they would immediately start shooting at each other; each probably shot at and was shot at by the other at least 50 times. Both, especially when intoxicated, were incredibly bad marksmen, and the usual damage was to windows, bar mirrors and street signs. So long as the shooting was confined to Hairtrigger Block, the police did not intervene; unfortunately, the two gamblers often staggered off to other areas in search of each other and continued their shooting sprees, leading the *Chicago Tribune* to declare that "the practice is becoming altogether too prevalent in this city."

In 1862 Hyman once staggered into the lobby of the Tremont House hunting for Trussell, fired several shots and allowed no one to leave or enter the hotel for an hour. Hyman was frequently arrested and fined for his forays, and after paying the penalty, he would meticulously deduct the amount from his usual police payoffs. Whenever a Trussell-Hyman duel started, the inhabitants and habitués of Hairtrigger Block immediately wagered on which one would be killed. As it turned out, neither of the two ever prevailed over the other. Trussell was shot to death by his mistress in 1866; Hyman went insane and died in 1876.

Harrison, Carter (1825–1893) corrupt Chicago mayor

In a city where crooked politicians were the rule, Chicago mayor Harrison Carter, who served five separate terms in the 19th century, was perhaps the most audacious of the lot. While newspapers were constantly exposing Harrison's involvement in the ownership of many vice properties and connected him with known criminals and corrupters, Chicago voters kept right on electing him to office.

Born in Kentucky in 1825 and a graduate of Yale, Harrison came to Chicago in 1850 and quickly made a fortune in real estate, becoming a financial and political power. Elected mayor, he soon realized he could rent out a number of his properties for three or four times their former rental values by giving them over to saloon, gambling and prostitution enterprises. In 1877 the *Chicago Times* pointed out that an entire block occupied by buildings housing every sort of vice activity was owned by "Our Carter." Despite this intelligence, the voters of Chicago promptly reelected Harrison on his next try for the mayorality.

Harrison's close connections with the underworld started in the 1880s, when he formed a working relationship with Mike McDonald, the crime king of Chicago.

McDonald handled the "fix," charging most criminals a percentage of their take in exchange for a guarantee of immunity from official persecution. Gamblers, vice operators, swindlers, pickpockets and other crooks were allowed to keep from 40 to 65 percent of their take, with the rest going to McDonald, who in turn paid off the police, judges, aldermen and other city officials and supplied bribe money to fix juries. Describing this arrangement, the famed muckraker William T. Steed wrote: "Many people had a finger in the pie before the residue reached Mr. Harrison. But however many there were who fingered the profit en route, there was enough left to make it well worth the Mayor's while."

As part of the agreement between Harrison and McDonald, the latter retained an important say in the police department, replacing an honest police chief, Simon O'Donnell, with the more compliant William J. McGarigle. In 1882 McGarigle was shifted to the wardenship of the Cook County Hospital, where he then hired McDonald's contracting firm to paint a public building for $128,500. A number of bribes were given to aldermen to approve the deal and the paint job was done—with a mixture of chalk and water. When the scandal broke, McGarigle left town without packing a bag, and a number of aldermen were sent to jail. McDonald and Harrison were unscathed, however.

Harrison was elected to his fifth term in office by promising Chicagoans an open town for the Columbian Exposition of 1893. And he certainly kept his promise, simultaneously insuring that the public was fleeced as expeditiously as possible by the underworld with, above all, no scandal to taint the good name of the fair and the city. Typical of these arrangements was the one made with the pickpockets via McDonald. Under an agreement reached by the politicians and the pickpockets, whose negotiations were handled by Eddie Jackson, the dean of the dips, no fair visitor was to be robbed at the entrance gates, since if they were, they would have no money to spend inside. The terms of the agreement required that a pickpocket seized at the gate return the loot to the victim if he could be found; if not, the money went to the police. Regardless of what finally happened to the loot, the pickpocket would be required to pay the arresting officer $10 for his release. This was a harsh measure, but as a sop to the pickpockets, they were promised that any thief arrested in the downtown area between 8 A.M. and 4 P.M. would be released when brought to the Central Station House.

With such arrangements the fair was a bonanza for the underworld as well as the business interests of Chicago. On American Cities Day, October 28, 1893, three days before the fair closed, Harrison delivered a speech at the fairgrounds and then returned home ahead of his family and servants. When he went to answer his door bell, Harrison was shot dead by a disgruntled office seeker named Prendergast. The public display of grief was overwhelming, and Harrison was given a funeral that rivaled anything since the grand passage of Abraham Lincoln's body. Over the next two decades the late mayor's son, Carter Harrison II, held sway in Chicago, much of the time as mayor, while McDonald and his successors in the underworld noticed little change in their relationship with City Hall.

Hastings, Mary (1863–?) madam

A young prostitute from Brussels, Belgium with previous experience in Paris, Toronto, British Columbia, San Francisco, Portland and Denver, Mary Hastings arrived in Chicago at the age of 25 and immediately set about earning her reputation as the worst madam in the city's history. She boasted that her first bordello at 144 Custom House Place contained only harlots who were thrown out of "decent houses." To satisfy some customers' desires, however, she hired procurers to kidnap girls as young as 13 from other cities. Frequently, she would go on such forays herself, returning with girls between 13 and 17, whom she had lured to Chicago with the promise of jobs. Once the girls were safely confined in one of her houses, they would be subjected to a process of brutalization and rape to introduce them to "the life." In one typical case, three young girls were locked in a room overnight with six men. Those girls Madam Hastings had no need for in her own houses she would sell to other establishments for sums varying from $50 to $300, depending on their age and beauty.

Madam Hastings bought police protection by paying cops on the beat $2.50 a week plus free drinks, meals and girls whenever they desired. Naturally, the payoffs to ward politicians and the higher brass at the Harrison Street police station were much higher. When she once complained that the charges were excessive, a police captain stormed back, "Why, damn you, what are you made for but to be plundered?"

While virtually all the police accepted bribes for overlooking mere prostitution, many refused to be bought when the offense involved was the forceful procuring of young girls. In 1895 hard evidence against her was finally supplied by four girls from Cleveland who had escaped a Hastings house by climbing down a rope made of sheets and reached a police station. A raiding party crashed into the house and freed five other girls. After bail was posted by her "solid man," Tom Gaynor, Madam Hastings was indicted. She promptly fled to Canada, and the bail was forfeited. When she returned, however, strings were pulled, and the funds were returned to Gaynor. Then Madam Hastings decamped again for Canada, this time signing over all her property to Gaynor so that it could not be seized by the courts. By mid-1897 she was able to return once more because the witnesses against her had scattered. However, when she tried to reclaim her brothels, Gaynor threw her out on the street, to the cheers of the inmates. Finally, he let her have $200, and Mary Hastings left the city for good.

Hatfields and McCoys   mountaineer feud

America's classic mountain feud between the Hatfields in West Virginia and the McCoys in Kentucky was in many respects an extension of the Civil War. The Hatfields, under the leadership of young Anderson "Devil Anse" Hatfield, had sided with the South, while the family of Randolph McCoy took up the Union cause. Both families rode with border guerrilla bands and built up a hatred that would long outlive the war.

After the war, although relations were strained, there was no important confrontation until 1873, when Randolph McCoy accused Floyd Hatfield of stealing a hog. The case finally came for adjudication before Parson Anse, a Baptist minister who dispensed justice in the backcountry. Mountaineers streamed to the trial, all armed with long knives, or "toothpicks," and long-barreled rifles. Supporting the Hatfields were the Mahons, Vances, Ferrels, Statons and Chafins. On the McCoy side were the Sowards, Stuarts, Gateses, Colemans, Normans and Rutherfords. Six supporters of each side were placed on a jury, and it appeared matters would be deadlocked. However, one of the jurors, Selkirk McCoy, who was married to a Hatfield, voted in favor of the Hatfields, breaking the tie. He pointed out that both men had presented sound arguments, but in the final analysis possession was what counted and there did not seem to be enough grounds to take the hog away from Floyd Hatfield.

The decision ended the legal battle but ill feelings festered. It was only a matter of time before violence erupted. The first to die was Bill Staton, a Hatfield supporter who had vowed to kill McCoys. How many died after that was never accurately counted; both clans were close-mouthed on such matters, but the bloodbath escalated. When Ellison Hatfield, a brother of Devil Anse, was shot by McCoys in an election day dispute in 1882, the Hatfields took three McCoy brothers hostage and warned them they would die if Ellison died. Two days later, Ellison died and the three McCoy brothers were tied to papaw bushes along a stream and shot to death.

Word about the various murders seeped out to the cities of Kentucky, and the governor of the state finally posted rewards for the capture of any Hatfields. Since the majority of the Hatfields and their supporters lived in West Virginia, and the McCoys and their followers mostly resided in Kentucky, the matter soon flared into a dispute between the two states. In 1888 the Hatfields, who resented the fact that the McCoys kept trying to bring in the law, decided a major drive was necessary to eliminate their foe. A large Hatfield contingent attacked the home of Randolph McCoy. Wearing masks, they yelled out, "Come out, you McCoys, and surrender as prisoners of war!" When the call went unanswered (Randolph McCoy was not present), they shot in the windows and set fire to the house. Randolph's young daughter ran out and was slain. Then his son Calvin emerged and went down in a fusillade. Old Mrs. McCoy tried to run to her daughter and was clubbed over the head and left for dead. This would be the last great reprisal in the feud.

Newspapers all over the country reported the atrocity. Kentucky law officers made several raids into West Virginia, and at least two Hatfield clansmen were killed and nine others captured. West Virginia appealed to the Supreme Court to have the captives returned. The High Court handed down a quick decision stating the law provided no method of compelling one state to return parties wrongfully abducted from another state. Of the nine, two were executed and the others sent to state prison.

By 1890 the feud was about over. A year later, Cap Hatfield wrote a letter to a local newspaper stating the Hatfields were declaring a general amnesty and that "the war spirit in me has abated." Shortly thereafter, Devil Anse came out of hiding, finally sure no Kentucky lawmen would be waiting to apprehend him.

By the time Devil Anse died in 1921 at about 100 years of age, the two clans had intermarried frequently. In the younger generations the feud was nothing more than ancient history, like the Civil War itself.

Heitler, Mike "de Pike" (?–1931)
brothel keeper and murder victim

A wizened, ageless brothel keeper who looked something like a Surinam toad, Mike "de Pike" Heitler could be described as Chicago's "grand old man" of merchandised vice, with a career that spanned about half a century.

Heitler got his nickname de Pike, from the fact that he ran the cheapest fancy house in Illinois and hence was a piker. But Mike actually prided himself on being the first to introduce modern assembly line methods in the world's oldest profession. He operated a 50¢ house at Peoria and West Madison. The customers stood in line at the foot of the stairs and handed Mike half a dollar, which he rang up on a cash register. When a girl came downstairs with a satisfied customer, Mike gave her a brass check that she could redeem for two bits, and then the man at the head of the line took her back upstairs.

Helping de Pike keep the traffic moving was another quaint character, Charlie "Monkey Face" Genker. Monkey Face would scurry up the doors of Heitler's houses and poke his homely face through the transom to urge the prostitute and her customer to hurry up. The sudden appearance of that monkey face proved disconcerting to many customers, and the more knowledgeable regulars would go through their paces quickly in hope of beating Genker to the punch.

Heitler operated with certain peacefulness for many years, aside from an occasional arrest and conviction for white slavery, but he lost much of his personal clout when Al Capone tightened his hold on the entire prostitution racket in Chicago and the surrounding area. Heitler's choice was either to come in as a paid employee or simply be declared "out." Through the 1920s his position continued to deteriorate as Capone turned more to Harry Guzik to look after prostitution operations. Smarting over this lack of respect, which he considered his due, Heitler took to informing on other Capone activities.

He told Judge John H. Lyle about the mob's part-time headquarters in a resort called the Four Deuces. As recounted in *The*

Dry and Lawless Years, Heitler told the judge:

> They snatch guys they want information from and take them to the cellar. They're tortured until they talk. Then they're rubbed out. The bodies are hauled through a tunnel into a trap door opening in the back of the building. Capone and his boys put the bodies in cars and then they're dumped out on a country road, or maybe in a clay hole or rock quarry.

Heitler made the mistake of passing on information to others who evidently were not as hostile toward Capone as he assumed. He wrote an anonymous letter to the state attorney's office revealing many secrets about the Capone brothel empire. Not long afterward, the letter turned up on Capone's desk. Heitler was summoned to appear before the mob leader at his office in the Lexington Hotel. Capone insisted only Heitler could have imparted the specific information and told him, "You're through."

Still, Heitler continued to write letters. In one, which he gave to his daughter, he named eight Capone figures as being responsible for the murder of *Chicago Tribune* reporter Jake Lingle. Unfortunately for Heitler, he apparently gave another copy of the letter to the wrong people and on April 30, 1931 his charred remains were found in the smoldering wreckage of a suburban house.

Hell's Kitchen   New York crime area

Hell's Kitchen, known for a time as New York City's most crime-ridden area, was originally a notorious pre–Civil War dive, but after that conflict the name was applied to a large area to the north and south of 34th Street west of Eighth Avenue. The dominant gang of the area was the original Hell's Kitchen Gang, bossed by one of the true ruffians of the late 1860s and 1870s, Dutch Heinrichs. According to one contemporary account, Heinrichs and his toughs exacted tribute from every merchant and factory owner in the district. The gang thought nothing of breaking into private houses in broad daylight and beating and robbing pedestrians at will. About 1870 Heinrichs absorbed the Tenth Avenue Gang led by Ike Marsh, the mastermind of New York City's first train robbery, and quickly grasped the wisdom of raiding the railroads. Thereafter, much of the gang's activities focused on looting the Hudson River Railroad yards and depot on 30th Street.

The railroad hired its own detectives to try to curb the gang's activities. When that action proved insufficient, it began to pay bounties to police officers for each arrest of a Hell's Kitchen gangster. Under this steady harassment, Heinrichs was finally sent to prison for five years. Even though the power of the original Hell's Kitchen Gang eventually waned, the area remained a stronghold of other gangs well into the 20th century. Only the advent of Prohibition caused these gangs to lose their distinctive neighborhood character, as they spread their activities over more of the city.

Hickok, James Butler "Wild Bill"
(1837–1876) gunfighter and lawman

In some respects James Butler "Wild Bill" Hickok was a genuine Western hero despite the fact that he was a master of the art of back-shooting as he demonstrated in his great gun battle with the "McCanles Gang" in 1861. However, most of his so-called great accomplishments, except for those during his tour as an army scout, were probably false.

Sifting out the truth from Hickok's tall tales could occupy a lifetime. As a scout in 1868, he saved 34 men in an Indian siege in the Colorado Territory by riding through the attackers' ranks to get help. But he did not, as he boasted to the Eastern press, knock off 50 Confederate soldiers with 50 bullets fired from a new-fangled rifle.

Born in Troy Grove, Ill. in 1837, Hickok was originally called "Duck Bill" because of a long nose and protruding lip. Once he had demonstrated his great ability with a gun, however, the other young blades thought it wiser to call him Wild Bill.

The Hickok legend began in 1861, when, as was described later in a ridiculous profile in *Harpers Monthly,* he wiped out the so-called McCanles Gang of nine "desperadoes, horse-thieves, murderers and regular cutthroats" in "the greatest one-man gunfight in history." In fact, there was no McCanles gang. Dave McCanles was a rancher who was owed money by a freighting company for which Hickok was working. With his 12-year-old son in tow, McCanles, probably unarmed, came to the branch office at Rock Creek Station, Neb. for his money. Two of his ranch hands, most certainly unarmed, waited outside. An argument ensued inside the building between the manager and McCanles; Hickok, hiding behind a calico curtain, shot the rancher dead. The two ranch hands outside the building were then killed by other members of the depot crew; one possibly was shot by the depot manager's wife. McCanles' 12-year-old son survived only by running away. Hickok was charged with murder, but the boy was not permitted to testify and the charge got lost in the shuffle.

A few years later, Hickok demonstrated he did have great shooting ability by gunning

Wild Bill Hickok's reputation as a fearless lawman was built on the numerous ridiculous stories told of him by dime novel writers who overlooked his many less laudable traits.

down Dave Tutt in a face-to-face duel at a distance of 75 yards. As his fame in that exploit spread, the Hickok legend grew and was expanded on with every retelling. Tutt, like McCanles, became a savage outlaw, when in fact he and Hickok had been friends since youth and their quarrel was over a girl.

In 1869 Hickok was elected sheriff of Ellis County and promptly killed two men in Hays City, the county seat. One of these killings was a remarkable performance. He had his back turned on a troublemaker named Sam Strawan when the latter started to draw. Hickok whirled, drew and shot first, killing Strawan. That November, in spite of these accomplishments, Hickok was voted out of office, apparently for taking more graft from brothels and gaming saloons than the average sheriff.

Hickok left town but returned in July 1880 and promptly got into a drunken brawl with five cavalry troopers. He shot two, one fatally; the others backed off. Hickok fled town again.

In April 1871 he was hired as city marshal of Abilene, Kan. with orders from the city fathers to clean up the town. Wild Bill did some shooting, but basically, he found it more gratifying to take protection money from gamblers and pimps rather than to interfere with their business. He spent his afternoons at the card table and almost every night in the town's red-light district.

In October 1871 Wild Bill got into a gunfight with a gambler named Phil Coe and mortally wounded him. As Coe fell, Hickok's deputy, Mike Williams, came rushing through the crowd, guns drawn, to help Hickok. Hearing Williams' footsteps, the marshal whirled and fired off two quick shots before he saw who it was. Williams died instantly of two bullets in the head. That was all the citizens of Abilene could take, and within a few weeks Wild Bill was fired and forced to leave town. Although his record in Abilene actually was a sorry one, it is still sighted today as one of the greatest reigns by a lawman in the history of the West.

The remaining five years of Hickok's life were pretty much downhill. He joined Buffalo Bill Cody's Wild West Show for a time but found the work both tiresome and degrading. He quit and tried his hand at prospecting and gambling, not having too much success in either. He was arrested several times in the Wyoming Territory, said a

newspaper report, "as a vagrant, having no visible means of support."

In June 1876 Hickok turned up in Deadwood, Dakota Territory with Calamity Jane, an amazon whore. Hickok, who had accumulated a spot of cash, ensconced himself at Mann's Saloon Number 10 along the main street. On August 2, 1876 Wild Bill was playing poker and mulling over what to do with his hand—two pairs, aces and eights—when a saddlebum named Jack McCall slipped up behind him and shot him through the brain. Thereafter, the hand of aces and eights became known as a "dead man's hand." McCall claimed he was avenging his brother, whom he said Hickok had killed. Asked why he hadn't met Hickok face to face, McCall shrugged. "I didn't want to commit suicide," he said.

Hicks, Albert E. (?–1860) gangster and murderer

One of New York's most legendary thugs in the 1850s was Albert Hicks, a freelance gangster who eschewed working with any of the great gangs of the period because he felt he could fare better as a lone wolf criminal. The record bears out his judgment; he lived a carefree existence and never appeared to worry about money. The police suspected Hicksie, as he was called, of a number of robberies and possibly a dozen murders but, as he often said, "suspecting it and proving it are two different things." His reputation was such that when he was working a certain street along the waterfront, gangs of footpads knew they would be wise to move elsewhere.

Remarkably, Hicksie's downfall came about simply because he was not recognized by a Cherry Street shanghaier in whose establishment he had wandered dead drunk. The crimp operator put laudanum in his rum, and when Hicksie awakened the next morning, he was aboard the sloop *E. A. Johnson*, headed for Deep Creek, Va. on an oyster run. After ascertaining that the captain, named Burr, had a money bag along to pay for his cargo, the unwilling sailor resolved to murder the skipper and the other crewmen, two brothers named Smith and Oliver Watts. He did so in particularly bloody fashion, decapitating two of them and dazing the other and then chopping off that victim's fingers and hands as he clutched the rail in a futile attempt to avoid being thrown overboard.

After looting the sloop and letting it drift off, Hicksie returned to Manhattan with quite a substantial booty. Soon, he fled the city for Providence, R.I. with his wife and child. But he left a trail. Having flashed large sums of money, he came under suspicion when the bloodstained *Johnson* was discovered and put under tow five days after the murders. Hicksie was located in Providence and found in possession of the personal belongings of the captain and one of the Watts brothers.

He was tried for piracy and murder on the high seas and sentenced to be hanged on July 13, 1860. About a week before his scheduled execution, he made a full confession to the warden of the Tombs. Hicks was certainly one of the most celebrated villains of the day and his confession made him all the more infamous. There was a steady stream of visitors to the Tombs to see the noted blackguard shackled to the floor of his cell. For a small fee paid to the jailers, a visitor was permitted to speak a few words with the murderer.

Among those calling on Hicksie was Phineas T. Barnum, the great showman, whose American Museum enjoyed enormous

"Hicksie" was a freelance killer whom even the organized waterfront gangs steered clear of.

popularity. Barnum told the flattered villain that he wished to obtain a plaster cast of his head and bust for display in the museum. After haggling the entire day, Hicksie agreed to pose for $25 and two boxes of 5¢ cigars. After the cast was made, the magnanimous Barnum returned with a new suit of clothes, which he traded to Hicks for his old suit, with which he wished to adorn a display dummy. Later, Hicks complained to the warden that Barnum had cheated him, that the new suit was shoddy and inferior to his old one.

Hicks was to be hanged on Bedloe's Island. He was ushered from the Tombs to the mainland dock by a fife and drum corps and a procession of carriages full of dignitaries. Thousands lined the procession route and cheered Hicksie, who graciously waved back to them. His only protest was that his suit did not fit, for which he cursed Barnum, but the warden informed him there was no time for alterations.

It was estimated that at least 10,000 persons witnessed the execution on Bedloe's Island. The scaffold was positioned only 30 feet from the water and hundreds of boats, from small craft to large excursion vessels, formed a solid line offshore. Hicksie's body was left suspended for half an hour and then cut down and transported back to Manhattan. His corpse was buried in Calvary Cemetery, but within a matter of days it was stolen by ghouls, who sold it to medical students more than willing to pay a premium for the chance to study the brain of such a notorious and bloodthirsty criminal.

Hole-In-The-Wall Saloon 19th-century New York dive

One of the toughest saloons in New York City between the 1850s and the 1870s was the legendary Hole-In-The-Wall, located at Dover and Water Streets in the heart of the crime-ridden Fourth Ward. A stranger happening into the Hole-In-The-Wall, operated by One-Armed Charley Monell, could be mugged while standing at the bar. If he survived, he was tossed out into the street; if he was wise, he dusted himself off and left without further protest. When such an assault proved fatal, the mugger was expected to bring a cart to the side door after dark and carry the corpse away.

The dive was famous for its two women bouncers, Gallus Mag and Kate Flannery. Gallus Mag would have been enough on her own. A 6-foot Englishwoman of indeterminate age, she earned her nickname because she wore galluses, or suspenders, to hold her skirt up. She always carried a pistol in her belt and a bludgeon strapped to her wrist. While she was expert with either weapon, Gallus Mag's routine method for maintaining order in the dive was to beat a troublesome customer to the floor, grab his ear with her teeth and drag him to the door. If the man still resisted, Gallus Mag would bite his ear off. She kept these trophies in a jar of alcohol behind the bar.

It was at the Hole-In-The-Wall that one of the underworld's most infamous duels was fought in 1855 by Slobbery Jim and Patsy the Barber, two vicious members of the violent Daybreak Boys. The pair had mugged a portly immigrant by the seawall at the Battery, knocking him unconscious and relieving him of all his wealth, 12¢. Then Slobbery Jim lifted the unconscious victim over the wall and deposited him in the harbor, where he drowned. The two killers adjourned to the Hole-In-The-Wall to divide their loot, such as it was. Since he had done the heavy labor of lifting the victim over the wall, Jim insisted he should get 8¢. Certainly, he would not settle for less than 7¢. Patsy the Barber was furious, pointing out that he had done the original clubbing of the victim and was thus entitled to an equal share.

The dispute turned violent when Slobbery Jim bit down and chewed on Patsy the Barber's nose. Patsy promptly drew a knife and stuck it in Jim's ribs. The blow had no effect on Jim, however, and the pair wrestled on the floor. The fight went on, incredibly, for some 30 minutes without interference from Monell or Gallus Mag or anyone else, since this, after all, was no drunken brawl but a professional dispute. The battle finally ended in Slobbery Jim's favor when he got hold of the knife and slashed his opponent's throat. As the blood gushed from the wound, Jim proceeded to kick the Barber to death. It was the last seen of Slobbery Jim, who fled the city and was not heard of again until the Civil War, when some New York soldiers insisted they'd seen him in the uniform of a Confederate Army captain.

The Hole-In-The-Wall was too deadly a place even for the Fourth Ward and it was finally shut down by the police in 1871 after the occurrence of seven murders in two months; no one knew how many other unreported slayings had happened there.

See also: GALLUS MAG.

Honeymoon Gang   19th-century New York gang

One of the most brutal New York gangs in the mid-1800s was the Honeymoon Gang, whose members were considered so beyond the pale that they were denied protection by the politicians who took care of most other organized gangsters because of their value as electoral enforcers.

By 1853 the Honeymooners had so terrorized the East Side's 18th Ward that it became literally unsafe to walk there. Every evening the gang would place their men at each corner of Madison Avenue and 29th Street and attack every well-dressed citizen who came along. At midnight the Honeymooners' "basher patrol" would adjourn to a drinking establishment to spend a portion of the night's ill-gotten gains.

The Honeymooners were not molested by police until George W. Walling was appointed captain of the district in late 1853. Organizing the city's first Strong Arm Squad, he picked out his six burliest men, put them in plain clothes and sent them into the Honeymooners' turf armed with locust clubs. The beefy officers simply walked right up to the gangsters and battered them senseless before they could bring their own bludgeons and brass knuckles into play. A few nights of this treatment convinced the Honeymooners to evacuate their ambush posts. But this did not satisfy Walling, who then provided every policeman on his roster with the identifications of all the Honeymooners. Whenever one was sighted, he was attacked and beaten mercilessly. Within two weeks the Honeymoon Gang vanished, its members scattering to other wards where police tactics were not so rough.

Hook Gang   19th-century New York waterfront gang

The Hook Gang was composed of thugs who worked the East River area around the Corlears' Hook section of New York from the late 1860s to the late 1870s.

Known as the daffiest of all river pirates, the Hookers were captained by Terry Le Strange, James Coffee, Tommy Shay and Suds Merrick. Neither the gang nor its individual members thought any job was too big for them. Coffee and Shay once rowed up to the boat of an eight-man rowing club and, with guns leveled, ordered them to head for the Brooklyn shore. When they got within 50 yards of shore, they forced the rowers to jump and swim for it and headed back to Manhattan with their prize boat. Long before the rowers got back to sound the alarm, the pair had transported the outsized craft to the Hudson docks and sold it to the skipper of a canal boat.

Another gang member, the redoubtable Slipsey Ward, finally overstepped himself when he mounted the deck of a schooner at Pike Street and attempted single-handedly to overpower the crew of six. He had downed three before he was stopped; he ended up with a long sentence at Auburn Prison for this crime. On more than one occasion, the Hookers would pull a number of wagons up to a likely boat in dock and, after simply cor-

The Hook Gang, 19th-century river pirates, fought pitched battles with police for more than a decade before finally being driven from the East River.

doning off the street, loot it at their leisure. Once, an officer a few blocks away saw their barricades and, thinking there was some authorized work going on, helpfully diverted traffic onto a side street.

In a manner of speaking, the Hookers had no one to blame but themselves for their eventual demise. It all started when one of their number, Nigger Wallace, tried to rob three men in a rowboat. They turned out to be three detectives taking the sun on their day off, and Wallace ended up dunked and towed off to jail. This started the police thinking that if they had some decoy craft on the river, they could catch the pirates in their act. Thus, in 1876 the Steamboat Squad was organized. By the end of the decade, the police had cleared the Corlears' Hook area. Many of the Hookers were imprisoned, others scattered and the rest shifted their activities to safer, onshore thefts and burglaries.

See also: SUDS MERRICK.

Horrell-Higgins feud

One of Texas' bloodiest feuds, the Horrell-Higgins conflict broke out in central Texas in 1873 over charges of cattle rustling around the frontier town of Lampasas, northwest of Austin. Suspicion centered on the men of the Horrell spread. When the sheriff attempted to arrest one of the Horrell men, he was promptly killed. A squad of state officers were dispatched to Lampasas to take care of the Horrells, once again with fatal consequences for the law officers. A group of Horrells were found in the Gem Saloon and ordered to give up their guns and surrender. Shooting broke out immediately. When the gunsmoke cleared, four officers lay dead or dying. Only Mart Horrell, who was wounded, was arrested. However, when he was placed in the jail at Georgetown, his friends and brothers broke in and freed him. The Horrells then moved their herds into New Mexico to avoid further problems with the Texas authorities.

Finding themselves ensnarled in similar rustling disputes in New Mexico, the Horrells returned to Texas, where two of them were tried and acquitted in the killing of the four law officers. Meanwhile, new suspicions about the Horrells rustling cattle were voiced, especially by the Higgins clan, which had lost a considerable amount of stock. Pink Higgins led his family in a war against the Horrells. Higgins, a fiery gunfighter, threatened to wipe out every Horrell. In January 1877 Pink killed Merritt Horrell at the Gem.

With all sorts of legal charges against both clans, someone broke into the courthouse one night in July 1877 and removed the records of all pending criminal cases. The families then prepared to settle the matter between themselves. Later that same month the two factions fought a bitter gun battle for several hours in the streets of Lampasas. At least one innocent bystander was among those killed.

horse poisoners

Common during the early decades of this century in New York, horse poisoning was one of the most detested of all crimes, viewed with horror by the public, the police and even much of the underworld. The horse was the lifeline of many businesses, such as the produce, ice cream, beer and seltzer trades. Businessmen faced with stiff competition would often hire gangsters to destroy the competition's trade. The simplest way to do this was to poison a rival's horses, thus destroying his distribution system. It was a common sight on the Lower East Side to see a produce seller with two dead horses desperately trying to sell his stock at half price to clamoring housewives before it was all ruined.

By 1913 three gangs of horse poisoners under the leaderships of Yoske Nigger, whose real name was Joseph Toplinsky, Charley the Cripple, whose real name was Charles Vitoffsky, and Johnny Levinsky dominated the field. They would steal or poison horses to order. Unlike their clients, these three did not engage in cutthroat competition among themselves. Instead they divided the field into separate monopolies, with Yoske Nigger handling the produce markets, truckmen and livery stables; Charley the Cripple the seltzer and soda water dealers and manufacturers; and Levinsky the ice cream trade. Whenever an order came in from some area not covered by this jurisdictional agreement, the three handled the matter jointly.

A defecting member of one of the gangs finally revealed to the police the trio's scale of fees:

Shooting, fatal	$500
Shooting, not fatal	$100
Poisoning a team	$50
Poisoning one horse	$35
Stealing a horse and rig	$25

The first two items, of course, referred to human victims and were much higher than the rates a client could find elsewhere. Since many gangsters at the time hired out to do a murder for as little as $10 to $20, it was not surprising that most of the trio's business was limited to horses. Yet the horse poisoners were hated by other gangsters who had no qualms about shooting humans but found the poisoning of dumb beasts despicable.

Eventually, the three poisoners felt the full wrath of the law when a chicken dealer named Barnett Baff was shot to death in 1914. According to the police theory, Baff's competitors had paid the staggering sum of $4,200 for his violent demise. This money, was supposedly given to Levinsky, Yoske Nigger and Charley the Cripple, who divided it up after paying a mere $50 to the actual hit man. Under close surveillance and harassment by the police, the trio abandoned their poisoning practices and retired to reputable business lives in the wilds of Brooklyn, remaining honest, it was said, until the bootlegging era beckoned them back to criminality.

Hotsy Totsy Club   New York speakeasy

Among all the notorious New York speakeasies that thrived during Prohibition, none had a worse reputation than the Hotsy Totsy Club, a second-floor joint on Broadway between 54th and 55th Streets. Although Hymie Cohen fronted as the proprietor, a big chunk of the place was owned by gangster Legs Diamond. Diamond utilized the club to hold court and directed several rackets from there. He also used it as an execution site. Many crime figures whom Diamond wished to prevail upon would be invited there for some revelry and a business discussion. If they failed to go along with Diamond's view of things, they were murdered in a back room and later carried out "drunk."

The Hotsy Totsy's bloodiest claim to fame came in 1929, when Diamond and sidekick Charles Entratta gunned down a hoodlum named Red Cassidy. Also killed in the wild shoot-out at the bar was an innocent bystander, Simon Walker, who nonetheless happened to be wearing two loaded revolvers in his belt. Unlike the pair's other murders in the club, a great number of witnesses were present during the shooting causing Diamond and Entratta to flee.

From hiding, Diamond directed a reign of killings to clear his name. That meant the bartender had to be rubbed out, along with three customers who had seen what had happened. The cashier, a waiter, the hat check girl and another club hanger-on disappeared, although their fate was not entirely a mystery to police or the newspapers. But suspicions meant little. Diamond and Entratta surrendered and were charged with the killings at the club. But they were soon freed because the authorities had no witnesses to present evidence against them.

Hounds   19th-century San Francisco anti-foreigner gang

Officially bearing the high-sounding title of the San Francisco Society of Regulators, the Hounds, as they were more commonly called, were a collection of young thugs organized to contain the peril to Anglo-Americans presented by Spanish Americans in San Francisco in 1849.

Under the pretense of a fiery patriotism, flamed by the influence of the Know Nothings, the Hounds set about driving the for-

Using a patriotic pretense, the Hounds first attacked Hispanics in San Francisco and then turned their violence on whites as well.

eigners out of the gold fields, a goal that had a good deal of public support. They beat, stabbed and shot helpless Mexicans and Chileans whenever they had the chance and extorted money and gold from those few who had managed to accumulate any wealth. Officials made no effort to stop these outrages until the Hounds got the idea that the good people of San Francisco should pay them for their protection of the community. Then no man's property or life—be he Spanish or Anglo-American— was safe. The Hounds roamed the streets in bands, robbing stores and pedestrians in broad daylight. Merchants trying to stop them were stabbed. The gang victimized saloons, gorging themselves on the best of food and drink and telling the proprietor to collect from the city as they walked out. If there were objections, the building was set on fire. The Hounds increased their atrocities against the "greasers" and blacks. They cut off the ears of a black man who had accidentally brushed a Hound in passing. A Mexican who talked back to a Hound had his tongue ripped out by the roots.

In the summer of 1849 the Hounds, in full battle array—almost all were veterans of the Mexican War—made their most violent onslaught against the Mexican tents and shanties. The authors of a contemporary account wrote:

These they violently tore down, plundering them of money and valuables, which they carried away, and totally destroying on the spot such articles as they did not think it worth while to seize. Without provocation, and in cold blood, they barbarously beat with sticks and stones, and cuffed and kicked the offending foreigners. Not content with that, they repeatedly and wantonly fired among the injured people, and amid the shrieks of terrified women and the groans of wounded men, recklessly continued their terrible course in different quarters, wherever in fact malice or thirst for plunder led them. . . . There were no individuals brave or foolhardy enough to resist the progress of such a savage mob, whose exact force was unknown, but who were believed to be both numerous and desperate.

This outrage at last galvanized the whole town. Money was collected for the relief of the destitute Spanish-Americans and 230 volunteers were deputized to round up the Hounds. Many of the gang immediately fled the city, but 20-odd Hounds, including one of their leaders, Sam Roberts, were taken. Several witnesses, including a number of injured Spanish-Americans who later died, testified against the prisoners. Roberts and a man named Saunders were sentenced to 10 years at hard labor, while others drew shorter

punishments. But within a few days political supporters of the gang won their release and none of the sentences were ever carried out. However, the Hounds were too frightened ever to reorganize and within a short time virtually all of them left the area.

House of All Nations   celebrated brothel

While the Everleigh Club was undoubtedly Chicago's, America's and perhaps the world's most famous brothel, another much more reasonably priced contemporary at the turn of the century was almost as well known in the Windy City. It was the celebrated House of All Nations, a bordello on Armour Avenue that was considered a must-stop for on-the-town sports.

The House of All Nations was famed for two qualities: its employees allegedly came from all parts of the globe (or at least could affect the proper accents) and they came in different price ranges. There was both a $2 and a $5 entrance, and in typical whoredom flimflammery, the ladies of the house all worked both entrances, dispensing the same services for either price tag. One commonly held belief in Chicago was that Asian prostitutes working in the house plied their profession during the winter months clad in long underwear because they were unable to take the chilly Chicago climate. The practice gave the Oriental harlots an added "exotic" quality that made them even more popular, but it should be noted that for a small additional fee they would strip down to the skin and brave the elements.

The House of All Nations was shuttered prior to the start of World War I, a victim of the great vice cleanup of the notorious Levee section on Chicago's South Side.

Howe and Hummel   shyster lawyers

Howe and Hummel were easily the grandest shysters ever to seek out a loophole, suborn a witness or free a guilty man. Practicing in New York from 1869 to 1906, they made a mockery of the law. Rotund, walrus-mustached William F. Howe was a great courtroom pleader who could bring sobs to any jury. Young Abe Hummel was a little man who was marvelously adept at ferreting out loopholes in the law, to the extent that once he almost succeeded in making murder legal.

At the age of 32, Howe came to America from England, where his career as a medical practitioner had terminated in a prison term for performing an illegal operation on a woman patient. He studied law and within three years he opened up shop on New York's Centre (later called Center) Street. Howe was an instant success because of his resonant voice and a face that could turn on and off any emotion he wished to display for a jury. Years later, David Belasco, the theatrical producer, watched Howe's tearful performance winning an acquittal for a woman who had shot her lover full of holes. "That man," he said, "would make a Broadway star."

In the late 1860s Howe hired young Abe Hummel as his law clerk and in almost no time promoted him to partner. Anyone so adept at finding holes in the law was too good to lose. One case that illustrated Hummel's ability involved a professional arsonist named Owen Reilly. Hummel suggested they save the prosecution the trouble of a trial by pleading Reilly guilty to attempted arson. Only after the plea was accepted did anyone notice that there was no penalty for the crime of attempted arson. However, the statutes did say that the sentence for any crime attempted but not actually committed was to be one-half of the maximum allowable for the actual commission of the crime. Since the penalty for arson at the time was life imprisonment, obviously the defendant's sentence had to be half a life. Howe made nonsense of that standard.

"Scripture tells us that we knoweth not the day nor the hour of our departure," he told the judge. "Can this court sentence the prisoner at the bar to half of his natural life? Will it, then, sentence him to half a minute or to half the days of Methuselah?" The judge gave up and set Reilly free; the state legislature rushed to revise the arson statutes shortly thereafter.

On another occasion the pair almost managed to make murder legal in New York State. It happened in November 1888, when a client named Handsome Harry Carlton was convicted of having killed a cop. Since the jury failed to recommend mercy, the death penalty was mandatory. Little Abe studied the statutes very carefully and pointed out to Howe that in the month of November there was no death penalty for murder on the books, the state having abolished hanging the previous June, with the provision that it be replaced by the electric chair. The new death-dealing apparatus was to start functioning on the following January 1, and as Hummel noted, the law specifically said that electrocution should apply to all convictions punishable by death on and after January 1.

When Carlton came up for sentencing, early in December, Howe objected as the judge prepared to pronounce the death penalty. In fact, he objected to any sentence being passed on Carlton. If the jury had recommended mercy, Carlton could be sentenced to life imprisonment, the lawyer noted. "However, my client has been convicted of first-degree murder with no recommendation of mercy and there is no law on the books covering such a crime.

He then read the precise language in the new law and concluded that all the judge could do was turn his client free. Nonplussed, the judge delayed sentencing while the case moved to the state supreme court. Quite naturally, Howe and Hummel's contention made headlines across the country. In New York the public reaction was one of utter shock. According to the lawyers' contention, anyone committing murder between June and the new year could not be executed. Other murderers confined in death cells clamored to be released on the ground that they were being wrongfully held and could not be executed.

The district attorney's office vowed to fight the matter, and Inspector Thomas Byrnes of the New York Police Department's Detective Bureau pledged to the public that his men would continue to clap murderers behind bars, law or no law.

In the end, Howe and Hummel lost out on their interpretation; the high court ruled that no slip in syntax could be used as an excuse to legalize murder. Harry Carlton swung from the gallows two days after Christmas, a nick-of-time execution. However, if Carlton had lost out, Howe and Hummel did not; their crafty efforts brought many felons and murderers to their office door.

Buoyed by the publicity, the two shysters coauthored a book entitled *In Danger, or Life in New York: A True History of the Great City's Wiles and Temptations*. They explained in the preface that it was published in the interest of justice and to protect the innocent from the guilty, but what they actually turned out was a primer on every type of crime—blackmail, house burglary,

card sharping, safecracking, shoplifting, jewel thievery and, of course, murder.

It became an immediate best-seller, with bookstore owners noticing a lot of traffic in their shops by persons who did not appear to be frequent book buyers. The book became required reading for every professional or would-be lawbreaker, from streetwalkers to killers. More and more when Howe and Hummel asked a new client, "Who sent you?" the stock reply was, "I read about you in the book."

No one ever computed exactly what percentage of murderers Howe and Hummel got off scot-free, but a prosecutor once estimated it was at least 70 percent, and "90 percent of them were guilty."

Whenever they had a client who was obviously as guilty as could be, the pair went into their bandage routine, having the defendant appear swathed in yards of white bandage, as though to suggest so frail a mind that his brains might fall out at any moment. One contemporary account tells of a Howe and Hummel client who simulated a village idiot's tic by "twitching the right corner of the mouth and simultaneously blinking the left eye." As soon as he was cleared, the defendant's face "resumed its normal composure, except for the large grin that covered it as he lightly removed the cloths from about his forehead." Another client, whose supposedly blithering insanity was accompanied by muteness and an ability to communicate only by sign language, seized Howe's hand gratefully when the verdict was announced in his favor and boomed, "Silence is golden."

The pair did not always resort to such trickery. When it was more convenient, they simply bribed witnesses and appropriate officials to get records changed, yet somehow they never ran into deep trouble until after

Howe died in 1906. The following year Hummel was caught paying $1,000 to facilitate a divorce action. He was sentenced to two years in prison. Released at the age of 60, Hummel retired to Europe and died in London in January 1926, a regular to the end in the visitors' section during trials at the Old Bailey.

See also: HANDSOME HARRY CARLTON, *IN DANGER*, FREDERICKA "MARM" MANDELBAUM.

hypnotism and crime

Can a person under hypnosis be made to commit murder or another crime? For years the possible use of hypnotism in murders and other crimes has been a subject of debate in scientific circles, with the weight of opinion apparently slowly shifting to the side of those who think it possible. Even legal authorities have admitted the need to deal with the problem. In the 1950s a New York prosecutor, Assistant District Attorney Sheldon S. Levy, raised the possibility of law-abiding citizens being hypnotized against their will and made, by various means, to commit acts they would not do if they had their usual control over themselves. Writing in the *Journal of Criminal Law,* he quoted findings of some psychologists that "a hypnotist who really wished a murder could almost certainly get it."

Of course, it has never been proven that a hypnotist can actually get another person to commit a murder for him, since such a test, obviously, cannot be carried out. Yet numerous stage hypnotists have demonstrated the ability to get people to commit other crimes against their conscience. In a well-publicized demonstration at New York City's Carnegie Hall, one hypnotist called several people to the stage and induced them to rob members of the audience when they returned to their seats. He did so by hypnotizing them and giving them cards that read: "You must raise money for a charity that will save hundreds of children from starvation. The people from whom you are taking things are wicked and do not deserve their ill-gotten gains. You cannot possibly be caught."

The hypnotized persons returned to their seats without the audience being informed about what they had been instructed to do. When they were told to return to the stage, they had with them a number of wallets and a woman's handbag, all stolen without the victims' knowledge.

The note, according to student of hypnotism, had broken down all mental resistance by the subjects. While no one can be forced to perform an act that he knows is wrong, they say, he can be induced to commit an illegal act if he is convinced it is right. The note had the added value of assuring the subjects they would not be caught, thus overcoming any fear factor. Similarly, in tests at various universities hypnotized subjects threw sulfuric acid into a person's face, which unknown to them, was protected by an invisible sheet of glass. Some subjects threw the acid with an obvious pleasurable display of violence, while others shuddered and only threw it after considerable hesitation.

Disbelievers say such experiments prove nothing because the subject, although in a trance, is still aware that the experiments are being conducted in a laboratory or entertainment atmosphere and thus knows he will not be permitted to do anything wrong. Since a hypnotized person "knows" he won't be called upon to commit murder, he will pick up a gun and fire it, reasoning the weapon will be loaded with blanks. Assistant District Attorney Levy countered this view by pointing out that all a hypnotist bent on homicide would have to do was convince a person that he was merely undergoing a psychological test and that the gun contained blanks and then substitute real bullets.

Occasionally newspaper stories report a person's claim that he or she was hypnotized into committing a crime, but there is no recent record of any such story being accepted. Indeed, the California Supreme Court once said that "the law of the United States does not recognize hypnotism."

One classic murder case that seems to come closest to proving the murder by hypnosis theory occurred in Minnesota in 1894. Harry Hayward was a young blade about Minneapolis who was known as a lady's man as well as a hard-drinking, heavy-gambling, all-around sport. He was also a student of hypnotism, having taken a course on the subject. Some students of crime are convinced that he used this power to win the favors and money of Katherine Ging and to get her to assign her insurance—$10,000 worth—over to him.

Hayward was also practicing his power of hypnosis on a local handyman named Claus Blixt, whom he convinced to carry out relatively minor crimes, such as burning down a small factory on which Kitty Ging held a mortgage. Kitty collected the insurance money, and Hayward collected from her. Soon, the lady was down to no assets but her life insurance. For days Hayward talked to the handyman, always making him look into his eyes as he spoke. Hayward later confessed, "I would repeat over a few times how easy it was to kill someone, and pretty soon he would be saying right after me, 'Sure, that's easy; nothing to that.'"

Whether the handyman was actually under hypnosis at the time he murdered Katherine Ging or whether his will to resist the idea

had simply been broken by suggestions made during earlier trances was never made clear. But either way, Blixt committed the murder while Hayward was miles away establishing an alibi. Hayward was later hanged for the killing, but the handyman, a relatively pathetic character, was allowed to plead guilty and drew a lesser sentence.

Another supposed hypnotic murderer, convicted in 1894, was Dr. Henry Meyer, who left a string of corpses from New York to Chicago. Before setting himself up as a doctor in the Midwest, Meyer had studied hypnotism in Leipzig, Germany under Professor Herbert Flint, one of the celebrated mesmerists of the era.

Meyer murdered several persons to collect on their insurance polices. He killed his first wife and then the husband of another woman so that he could marry her. When he saw a chance to kill his second wife for $75,000, he conceived a murder plan involving hypnosis. Meyer chose as the tool of his plot a plumber named Peter Bretz, an ideal hypnotic subject who soon fell under his spell. He convinced the plumber that he was in love with Mrs. Meyer, who apparently was ready herself for an affair of the heart, and should run away with her. Bretz was to take the second Mrs. Meyer to Arizona, offer to show her the Grand Canyon and, when nobody was around, shove her over the canyon lip. The plumber and the intended victim had actually reached the Grand Canyon when he broke out of the spell. The couple then returned to Chicago and revealed the plot to authorities. But since the authorities at that time could not possibly get a grand jury to swallow such a tale, Meyer went free to commit another murder before being brought to justice. Students of hypnotic crime insist the Meyer case deserves closer study. Basically, despite the claims of some believers in the feasibility of hypnotic murder, the justice system continues to ignore the question.

hypnotism and detection

Experts agree that hypnotism, if properly used, can play an important role in fighting crime, far greater than the potential danger that it may be when employed in the commission of crimes. In the 1976 kidnapping of 26 children in a school bus in Chowchilla, Calif. hypnosis helped the bus driver remember part of the license plate number of a van used in the kidnapping so that the police were able to trace the vehicle to the criminals. New York police made an arrest in the murder of a young female cellist at the Metropolitan Opera House after a ballerina who had seen a man with the musician was enabled by hypnosis to give a description for a police sketch. Part of what convinced police that Albert DeSalvo was the Boston Strangler was his description under hypnosis of gory details concerning the sex murders and the tortured thoughts that made him commit his terrible crimes.

Similarly, hypnotic examination of a young man, Allen Curtis Lewis, who had admitted to pushing a young woman, Renee Katz, onto the New York City subway tracks in 1979, as well as of a Connecticut teenager, Peter Reilly, who had confessed murdering his mother, helped clear them, revealing, among other things, how their confessions had been produced by subtle coercion.

There are, however, a number of obstacles to widespread police use of hypnosis. One is that attempts have been made to interrogate suspects under hypnosis against their will. The second objection is that hypnotized persons do not necessarily give reliable infor-

mation. In the $2.7 million Brink's robbery during the 1950s, police traced a license plate number furnished under hypnosis only to find it belonged to a college president who had an iron-clad alibi not only for himself but for his car as well. In another case a man charged with the murder of a child supplied "hypnotized" evidence that indicated his wife, rather than he, was the guilty party. However, discrepancies turned up indicating that the suspect had used the opportunity to try to shift the guilt away from himself.

A classic example of the perils of accepting as legal evidence a confession obtained by hypnosis is the case of Camilo W. Leyra, Jr., who was convicted and sentenced to death for the 1950 hammer slaying of his 74-year-old father and 80-year-old mother. He was released from the death house in 1956 after an appeals court overturned his conviction for a third time because the only evidence against him was his original confession obtained through hypnosis. Stated the New York Court of Appeals:

> The prosecution has produced not a single trustworthy bit of affirmative, independent evidence connecting the defendant with the crime. Under the circumstances, a regard for the fundamental concept of justice and fairness, if not due process, imposes upon the court the duty to write finis to further prosecution against the defendant. . . . It seems quite probable that the police and the District Attorney, relying too heavily on the confessions that they had obtained . . . failed to do the essential careful and intensive investigation that should be done before a defendant is charged with a crime, certainly one as serious as murder.

Despite the dangers of misuse, there is little doubt that the practice of hypnosis will continue to grow. The New York Police Department has firm rules against using the method on any person even slightly suspected of being guilty of the crime. At one time Los Angeles police had 11 officers trained in hypnosis and have used the method in 600 cases. In 90 percent of the cases the hypnotic probes were said to have provided information that led to an arrest.

ice pick kill murder technique

Long a favorite rubout method of Mafia hit men, the so-called ice pick kill is employed to make a murder victim's death appear to be the result of natural causes. Generally, the victim is forced into a men's room or some isolated place, and while two or three of the hit men hold him still, the killer wielding the ice pick jams the weapon through his eardrum into the brain. The pick produces only a tiny hole in the ear and only a small amount of bleeding, which is carefully wiped clean, but massive bleeding occurs in the brain, causing death. Examination of the victim by a doctor generally results in a finding that the person has died of a cerebral hemorrhage. Only expert medical examiners are capable of uncovering murder. When a gangland murder victim is found with numerous ice pick wounds, police generally theorize the victim struggled so much that the normally meticulous execution proved impossible and the victim was simply ice-picked to death.

Ida the Goose War New York underworld feud

If Homeric Greece had its Helen of Troy, the New York underworld had its Ida the Goose. Despite her rather unromantic name, the only one that has come down through posterity, Ida the Goose was a noted beauty, a maiden whose favors were traditionally reserved for the leaders of the notorious Gopher Gang of Hell's Kitchen. Ida was the last woman, so far as is known, to have caused a full-scale gang war over an affair of the heart.

In the early 1900s the Gophers were one of the most prominent gangs of the city, especially following the fractionalization of the powerful and bloody Eastman gang as a result of the imprisonment of their leader, Monk Eastman. One group of Eastmans, perhaps 400 to 500 strong, rallied to the banner of Chick Tricker, who maintained his headquarters at his own Cafe Maryland on West 28th Street. The Tricker gangsters engaged in all sorts of criminality from robbery to homicide. Their main battles generally were fought against other former members of the Eastman gang who had joined up with Big Jack Zelig or Jack Sirocco. Tricker hardly wanted an additional war with the Gophers, but he proved powerless against the momentum of events that bore down on him.

It started when a tough Tricker gangster, Irish Tom Riley, who, despite his name, was probably a Spanish Jew, won the heart of Ida the Goose and lured her from the bosom of the Gophers to the Cafe Maryland. The enraged Gophers sent a delegation to retrieve their lost princess, but both she and her new lover refused to agree to her return to Hell's Kitchen. Tricker merely shrugged. He would not order the surrender of Ida, since that would represent a loss of face. Over the next several weeks the Gophers and the Trickers had numerous hand-to-hand confrontations, including a few nonfatal stabbings, but after a while finally it appeared the Gophers had lost interest in launching a total war to regain Ida the Goose.

Thus, it was a surprise when on a snowy night in October 1909 four Gophers brazenly strolled into the Maryland and ordered beer at the bar. About a half-dozen Trickers, their noted leader absent, sat at tables eyeing the intrusion with both shock and disbelief. Had Tricker himself been present, he probably would have ordered an immediate attack on the hated intruders. As it was, only Ida the Goose spoke up with indignation. "Say! Youse guys got a nerve!"

The Gophers silently drained their mugs and then one said, "Well, let's get at it!"

They whirled around, each man holding two revolvers, and opened fire. Five of the surprised Trickers went down, several mortally wounded. Only Ida's lover was unscathed, and he scrambled across the floor and dove under his lady's voluminous skirts.

The Gophers made no move to shoot him, instead watching Ida the Goose to see what she would do.

The lady surveyed the scene a moment, shrugged and contemptuously raised her skirts. "Say, youse!" she said. "Come out and take it!"

Trembling on his hands and knees, her lover crawled out to the middle of the floor. Four revolvers barked, and he fell dead with four slugs in him. One of the Gophers strode forward and put another bullet in his brain. The four assassins then turned and walked out to the street, followed at a respectful distance by Ida the Goose. She fully understood the honor bestowed on her by having been the cause of such a great battle, and it was said that she nevermore strayed from her place of adornment in Hell's Kitchen.

In Danger primer for criminals

Probably no book ever published in America was more blatantly an instruction guide to criminality than *In Danger, or Life in New York: A True History of a Great City's Wiles and Temptations*, which appeared in 1888. The book was signed, "Howe and Hummel, the Celebrated Criminal Lawyers." Howe and Hummel indeed were celebrated attorneys and probably the most corrupt New York has ever seen. As they declared in a moral-toned preface, the two wrote the book after being moved by a clergyman's sermon in which he had declared, "It had been well for many an honest lad and unsuspecting country girl that they had never turned their steps cityward nor turned them from the simplicity of their country home toward the snares and pitfalls of crime and vice that await the unwary in New York." That was the last piece of high-minded drivel to appear in the book, the rest of which was given over to a detailed guide on what to steal and how.

By way of invitation, Howe and Hummell wrote of "elegant storehouses, crowded with the choicest and most costly goods, great banks whose vaults and safes contain more bullion than could be transported by the largest ships, colossal establishments teeming with diamonds, jewelry, and precious stones gathered from all the known and uncivilized portions of the globe—all this countless wealth, in some cases so insecurely guarded."

Having thus whetted the appetites of novice and would-be criminals, they hastened to add that "all the latest developments in science and skill are being successfully pressed into the service of the modern criminal." The ever-helpful authors went into detailed technical descriptions of various devices used by jewel thieves and shoplifters, such as "the traveling bag with false, quick-opening sides . . . the shoplifter's muff . . . the lady thieves' corsets." There were instructions for making one's own burglar tools and descriptions of the methods used in various skin games and the mathematical formulas used for rigging cards. And did crime pay? Howe and Hummel never said so in so many words, but, e.g., of shoplifting they stated, "In no particular can the female shoplifter be distinguished from other members of her sex except perhaps that in most cases she is rather more richly and attractively dressed."

The great shysters also touted certain legal services available at "what we may be pardoned for designating the best-known criminal law offices in America."

In Danger was severely criticized by the police and denounced from the pulpits, but each fresh denunciation merely produced more sales of the book.

See also: HOWE AND HUMMEL.

insurance frauds—faked deaths

Cases of "dead men" turning up alive are common in insurance company fraud files, although the industry has never seen the virtue of publishing any statistics on the subject. There is, of course, even less information on those who have gotten away with such fraud. One of the most publicized disappearance frauds of all was perpetrated in the 1930s by John H. Smith, who had once run for governor of Iowa. Smith made it look as if he had been burned to death in an auto accident, substituting an embalmed body in his fire-gutted car. Mrs. Smith later confessed her husband had faked his own death to fleece an insurance firm out of $60,000 stating, "Under our plan, I was to collect the insurance or accept it when the insurance company paid it to me, and then meet John when he got in communication with me, which might be from one to two years."

Smith might have gotten away with his plot had he not developed a roving eye. He committed bigamy during his disappearance by marrying an 18-year-old Kansas farm girl. That was something Mrs. Smith hadn't agreed to, and since her wounded pride meant more to her than $60,000, she screamed for the law as soon as she learned what her husband had done.

Probably the longest successful insurance disappearance was pulled off by socially prominent Thomas C. Buntin of Nashville, Tenn. who vanished in 1931. Shortly thereafter, Buntin's 22-year-old secretary also disappeared. Buntin had $50,000 in insurance, and after waiting the customary seven years, the insurance company paid off the claim. However, the firm, New York Life, did not close the case. It kept up a search for Buntin, and in 1953—some 22 years after he vanished—the company found him living in

Orange, Tex. with his ex-secretary under the name Thomas D. Palmer. For 22 years the couple had posed as Mr. and Mrs. Palmer and had even raised a family.

A trust fund had been established with the money from Buntin's insurance policy, and there was still $31,000 left when he turned up alive. The insurance company immediately launched legal action to get the money. As for Buntin, he obviously had not benefitted personally from the fraud. What was the reason? Very often a husband wishing to leave his wife and knowing he cannot expect a divorce will use a disappearing act to get out from under. Along with acquiring his freedom, the man can feel he has discharged all his duties as a husband and father by defrauding an insurance company into providing for his family. In the end, Buntin and his former secretary suffered no penalties from the law. In fact, after they were exposed, their neighbors sent them flowers.

Of course, producing a dead body will make a faked death even more convincing, but this often entails murder. In the 1930s Philadelphia's notorious Bolber-Petrillo murder ring specialized in killing off husbands so their wives could claim the insurance. Occasionally, they worked with a loving couple who wanted to enjoy the fruits of the husband's life insurance policy while he was still alive. In such cases the ring would kill an itinerant stranger and use him as a stand-in corpse for the husband.

Another famous insurance fraud murderer was Charles Henry Schwartz, a sort of mad scientist. When Schwartz ran his business into the ground in the 1920s, he looked for someone to use as a substitute corpse so that he could collect $200,000 in insurance. He settled on a traveling evangelist, Warren Gilbert Barbe, and murdered him in his

Berkeley, Calif. laboratory. Since Barbe didn't look much like him, Schwartz worked hard on his substitute. Because Schwartz had a scar on his own chest, he burned away a section of Barbe's chest. He pulled out two teeth from the murdered man's upper jaw to match his own missing teeth. To take care of the difference in eye color between the two, Schwartz punctured his victim's eyeballs, and then for added protection, he blew up the laboratory. Despite all this, the corpse was soon identified as someone other than Schwartz and the latter was exposed. To avoid imprisonment he committed suicide.

Beyond doubt the prize victim of all insurance swindles was a beautiful but gullible model named Marie Defenbach. She was persuaded by a Dr. August M. Unger to join him and two accomplices in a fraud in which she was to take out $70,000 worth of life insurance and then fake her own death. The men were to be her beneficiaries and were to give her half the money. Dr. Unger assured Marie he would personally handle her "demise." He would give her a special medicine of his own that would induce a deathlike sleep. Later, the doctor convinced her, she would be revived in the back room of an undertaking establishment and spirited away, with an unclaimed body left in her place for cremation. If Marie had had any sense, she would have realized that it would save the man a lot of bother and money if they just fed her some old-fashioned poison. But Marie was already mentally counting her loot.

On the evening of August 25, 1900, Marie blithely informed her Chicago landlady she was feeling ill, and she sent a messenger to get her some medicine. Fifteen minutes after taking it, she died in terrible agony. In due course, the true nature of Marie's death was uncovered by a suspicious uncle, whose investigation finally led to the arrest and conviction of the culprits.

In a curious sidelight to insurance frauds, the man responsible for the fact that few insurance company investigators carry weapons while on the job was a New Jersey man named J. R. Barlow, who had a wife and a $200,000 life insurance policy. One day he swam out from a beach and never swam back. His wife reported him as missing and applied for the insurance. The insurance company was suspicious, however, and after an intensive investigation traced Barlow to Mexico. When he was confronted by an insurance agent, Barlow turned violent, and in the ensuing struggle the investigator was forced to shoot him. Ironically, the insurance company was then compelled to pay off on his death. Soon after, the company issued a rule forbidding investigators to carry weapons.

See also: WARREN GILBERT BARBE.

Israel, Harold (1901–?) wrong man

One of America's most famous "wrong man" murder cases wrecked the elective political career of a prosecutor named Homer S. Cummings in the 1920s. The case was the murder of a popular minister in Bridgeport, Conn.

In 1924 an unidentified person shot Father Hubert Dahme, pastor of St. Joseph's Episcopal Church, in the back of the head, throwing the city into an uproar. Both the city government and a local newspaper offered rewards, and the public demanded the police come up with a solution to the crime. This they appeared to do by arresting an itinerant young man, 23-year-old Harold Israel. After many hours of questioning, Israel made a confession. He later tried to

retract it, but there was no denying that when apprehended, he had been carrying a gun of the same caliber as the murder weapon. In addition, police had the testimony of a ballistic expert that Israel's gun had been the murder weapon.

Since Father Dahme was one of Bridgeport's most popular citizens, the pressure on prosecutor Cummings was enormous. There was press speculation that a conviction in the case would earn the state's attorney a sure nomination for governor. Cummings was a former chairman of the Democratic National Committee, keynote speaker at the 1920 national convention in San Francisco and, indeed, Connecticut's favorite son for the presidential nomination. Under the circumstances, it would have been quite logical for Cummings to have accepted the sure conviction handed him. Amazingly, he did not.

Even though the public defender announced that Israel would plead guilty by reason of insanity, Cummings had strong misgivings about the case. The prosecution regarded some of the witnesses who had sworn Israel was the priest's killer as less than reliable. When he checked the area where the murder had occurred and where the witnesses said they had been standing, he determined it would have been too dark for them to recognize anyone. Cummings also had his doubts about the ballistics expert, who struck him as overly anxious to help the police solve the crime. He asked six other experts in the field to make their own findings without telling any of them that others were doing the same work. All six agreed that Israel's gun had not fired the fatal bullet.

When Israel's case came to trial, Cummings made an opening presentation outlining the findings that had weakened the prosecution's case. He then calmly proceeded to load the so-called murder gun. He aimed it downward at a 45° angle—the position the murder gun had been in—and pulled the trigger. Nothing happened. The gun, Cummings explained, had a defective firing pin and would not fire when held in that particular position.

On Cummings' motion, Israel was released. The prosecutor personally escorted the happy youth to the train station and saw him off to his home in Pennsylvania. It's possible that Cummings felt his presence was necessary to keep the police from rearresting Israel.

Years later, the Israel case was made into a movie called *Boomerang*. While Cummings won considerable praise in many circles for his work in the case, he did not get quite as much as he deserved in his native state. When Israel was cleared, Cummings' chance for the governorship fizzled. In 1933, however, he was named by President Franklin D. Roosevelt to be attorney general. As for Israel himself, he faded into obscurity, to which Cummings felt he was entitled. Still, Cummings wondered if his clearing of the young man had paid off and in the late 1930s he ordered the FBI to make a secret check on him. The agency reported that Israel was a respectable miner in Pennsylvania, a married man, the father of two children and a pillar of the Methodist Church.

Izzy and Moe revenue agents

Prohibition brought many things to the American scene: speakeasies, rot-gut liquor, gangsters, hijacking and "the ride." But Prohibition had its comic side as well, as demonstrated by the merry antics of those dry clowns Izzy and Moe. They were the greatest and wackiest Prohibition agents of all time and they fit right into the Roaring Twenties. The newspapers gave front-page coverage to their capers, one joyously announcing, "IZZY IS BIZZY AND SO IS MOE." Hundreds of hilarious newspaper stories were written about the pair, and a great many of them were no doubt true.

In 1920 Isadore Einstein was a short, smiling cherub of 225 pounds who worked as a clerk for the New York Post Office. Previously, he had been a dry goods salesman. One day Izzy showed up at the Federal Prohibition Bureau headquarters and announced his availability. That got a laugh. "Izzy," one official said, "you don't even look like a Prohibition agent." On reflection, it was decided that Izzy might thus be handy to have around, and he got the job. A product of the polyglot Lower East Side, he could speak fluent Yiddish, Hungarian, Polish, German and Italian.

Bureau officials figured the worst that could happen was that a few tough assignments would send Izzy in hasty retreat back to the post office. They decided to send him out to hit a 52nd Street speakeasy. A dozen agents had previously tried and failed to bust the place. A few had gotten past the front door, but they were served nothing stronger than beer because they couldn't produce a regular customer as a sponsor.

Izzy talked his way into the speakeasy, waddled up to the bar, plunked down his newly acquired badge and said to the bartender, "How about a good stiff drink for a thirsty revenue agent?"

The bartender nearly doubled up with laughter. "Get a load of this funny fat man!" he called to his customers. Then, fingering Izzy's badge, he asked, "Where did you buy this?"

"Give me a drink and I'll take you to the place sometime," Izzy replied.

The bartender obliged. So did Izzy. He took the man down to the Revenue Office.

Izzy's superiors were stunned . . . and immediately assigned him to another tough case. Izzy made that pinch as well.

After a few weeks on the job, Izzy started to miss his old coffeehouse buddy, Moe Smith. He asked if they had a job for Moe as well. The only trouble was, Izzy noted, that Moe didn't look like an agent either; he was fat like Izzy. Moe got the job, and the pair worked as a team, a sort of Laurel and Hardy of the Revenuers—except both were Hardy. They were so effective that some speakeasies posted pictures of the two, but that proved futile. The pair disguised themselves with false whiskers and noses. On occasion they wore blackface. Once, they donned football uniforms to bust a joint serving the thirsty athletes playing in Van Cortlandt Park in the Bronx. To crack a Coney Island speakeasy in midwinter, Izzy went swimming with a polar bear cub and was then carried quivering into the establishment by a solicitous Moe. "Quick," Moe cried, "some liquor before he freezes to death." A tenderhearted bartender complied and was arrested.

Another time, the pair marched into a speakeasy arguing loudly about the name of a particular revenue sleuth. Was it Einstein or Epstein? The bartender agreed it was Einstein. Nonsense, said Izzy, and bet the bartender double the price for two drinks. The bartender won the bet and got pinched.

Because they needed to produce liquor served them as proof of a crime, Izzy and Moe designed special funnels to be strapped inside their vests. One time, they started out at 5 A.M. and made 24 arrests by 9 A.M., just working up an appetite for breakfast. The

Bizzy Izzy and Moe, as the newspapers dubbed them, were the clown princes of Prohibition enforcement, using many disguises to make their busts.

pair's all-time record was 65 raids in one day. Their standard line when making a pinch was "Dere's sad news here." Over a five-year period their combined score was 5 million bottles of liquor confiscated, 4,392 persons arrested and convictions achieved in 95 percent of their cases, which was 20 percent of all the successful illegal liquor prosecutions in the New York district. Everybody loved Izzy-and-Moe stories. Stanley Walker once said, "Izzy and Moe almost made prohibition popular."

Once Izzy met his namesake—Albert Einstein. He asked him what he did for a living. "I discover stars in the sky," the scientist replied. "I'm a discoverer too," Izzy said, "only I discover in the basements."

Izzy and Moe became so famous that other bureaus began asking for the pair's help in busting some problem spots in their cities. In Pittsburgh they made a pinch within 11 minutes of leaving the train depot. In Atlanta it took 17 minutes, and Chicago and St. Louis, 21. They set their record in New Orleans: 35 seconds.

Unfortunately, Izzy and Moe were called on the carpet often because of their penchant for publicity. They were warned that the service had to be dignified in its procedures.

Finally, in November 1925 the boys turned in their badges. Izzy explained, "I fired myself," because they were to be transferred away from their beloved New York to the wilds of Chicago. Bureau officials insisted they had been dismissed "for the good of the service."

Both men went into the insurance business and soon numbered among their clients many of the people they had arrested for liquor violations. Izzy even published an autobiography, *Prohibition Agent Number 1*, which didn't sell very well. It seemed the public had had enough of Prohibition.

Jackson, Humpty (?–1914) New York gang leader and murderer

One of New York's most feared gang leaders at the turn of the century, Humpty Jackson was an odd combination of cold-blooded murderer and bibliophile. A man with a superior education, although a hazy past, he bossed some 50 gangsters, many of whom later became notorious in their own right. Among them were Spanish Louie, Nigger Ruhl, the Grabber and the Lobster Kid.

Humpty was never without a book on his person. His favorite writers were Voltaire, Darwin, Huxley and Spencer, and he often read various tomes in Greek and Latin. His scholarly pursuits, however, did not carry over into his professional life, which was thoroughly dedicated to crime. He always carried three revolvers on his person—one in his pocket, another slung under his hunchback, which is why he was called Humpty, and the third in a special holder in his derby hat.

Jackson's headquarters was an old graveyard between First and Second Avenues bound by 12th and 13th Streets. Sitting on a tombstone, he would dispense criminal assignments to his thugs. If a customer wanted someone blackjacked or otherwise assaulted, he or she simply approached Humpty, and for $100, in the case of blackjacking, he would see the job was done. Naturally, Jackson never soiled his own hands on such chores but merely handed them out to one of his men. Similarly, he would plan burglaries or warehouse lootings but seldom lead the forays himself. Nevertheless, Jackson was a man with a volatile temper who committed many acts of violence, which earned him more than 20 arrests and convictions. In 1909 he was sentenced to 20 years for ordering the execution of a man he'd never met. He died behind bars in 1914.

Jackson, Mary Jane "Bricktop" (1836–?) female ruffian and murderess

Nicknamed Bricktop because of her flaming red hair, Mary Jane Jackson was reputedly the most vicious street criminal, male or female, New Orleans has ever produced. Any number of the Live Oak gangsters, the city's toughest gang, backed off from confrontations with her. In about a decade of battling, Bricktop Jackson never lost a fight, killed four men and sent at least two dozen more to the hospital, from which many emerged permanently maimed. When she took up living with a notorious criminal named John Miller, the pair became known as New Orleans' toughest couple.

Born on Girod Street in 1836, Bricktop, a husky, well-endowed girl, became a prostitute at age 13. The next year she attained a measure of security when a saloon keeper took her as his mistress. When he tired of her after three years and threw her out, she charged into his saloon and gave him a fearsome beating, sending him to the hospital minus an ear and most of his nose. Bricktop then entered a Dauphine Street whorehouse, where, while she gained a following with the customers, she terrified the other girls. She was turned out of the Dauphine Street establishment and subsequently, several other brothels. Bricktop was headed for the dance halls of New Orleans' toughest thoroughfare, Gallatin Street, and got a job with the redoubtable Archie Murphy in his notorious Dance-House. Nothing was considered too rough for Murphy's place, but Bricktop Jackson proved the exception to the rule. She had to be forcibly evicted from there as well as many other tough dance houses, whose owners had foolishly thought they could control her. Bricktop finally became a freelance prostitute and street mugger. In 1856 she killed her first man and in 1857 her second; one had called her a "whore" and gotten clubbed to death for the insult, and the other, Long Charley, had been cut down with Bricktop's made-to-order knife following an argument over which way he would fall if stabbed (the nearly 7-foot-tall Charley was reported to

have fallen forward when Bricktop tested her hypothesis).

One of Bricktop's more famous murders occurred on November 7, 1859, when she visited a beer garden with two other vicious vixens, America Williams and Ellen Collins. A man at the next table, Laurent Fleury, objected to Bricktop's language and told her to shut up. Bricktop cursed even more and threatened to cut Fleury's heart out. Fleury, who had not recognized the scourge of Gallatin Street, slapped her. In a second the three women were all over him, and the luckless Fleury disappeared in a mass of flailing hands, swirling skirts and flashing knives. Joe Seidensahl, the owner of the beer garden, tried to come to his rescue but was driven back, severely cut up. A Seidensahl employee shot at the women from a second-floor window, but they drove him off with a barrage of bricks. By the time the police arrived, they found Fleury dead and his pants pocket cut out. The pocket, with money still inside, was found tucked under Bricktop's skirt. She was locked up in Parish Prison but eventually freed when an autopsy failed to show the victim's cause of death. Bricktop's lawyer contended he had died of heart disease.

It was in Parish Prison that Bricktop Jackson met a man who was, for the time, the love of her life, a jailer and ex-criminal named John Miller. The pair became a colorful item, even by Gallatin Street standards. Miller had lost an arm in a previous escapade and now walked about with a chain and iron ball attached to his stump, which made an awesome weapon. The couple supported themselves by close teamwork based on their respective skills. Bricktop would start up a romance with a stranger in a French Quarter dive and repair to the back streets with him. The man would end up with a very sore skull, no recollection of what happened and empty pockets.

The romance between Bricktop and Miller was marred by a dispute over who was the master of their nest. One day in 1861 Miller came home and decided to bullwhip Bricktop into subservience. She snatched the whip away from him, however, and gave him a bloody beating. He lashed out with his iron ball but she seized the chain in midair and began dragging him around the room. Miller pulled out a knife and slashed at Bricktop, who bit the knife free, grabbed it and then stabbed her lover five times. It was a fatal end to their relationship and one that caused Bricktop to be sent to prison for 10 years. She was released after only nine months when Gen. George F. Shepley, the military governor of the state, practically emptied the penitentiary with blanket pardons. Upon her release, Bricktop Jackson disappeared from New Orleans, a loss that went totally unlamented by honest and dishonest citizens alike.

Johnson County War   range conflict

In 1892, under the guise of driving out "rustlers," the great cattle barons of Johnson County, Wyo. waged a war of extermination against small ranchers and homesteaders. There is no question that the big stockmen, mostly absentee owners residing in Cheyenne and members of the Wyoming Stock Growers' Association, had been losing cattle and that some had been taken by the "long rope," which was the traditional way most ranchers got started, picking up mavericks on the open range, and, indeed, the way most of the big stockmen themselves had gotten started. However, there were other reasons for the losses, including poor management and overstocking of the ranges, prairie fires, grass-destroying grasshoppers and bad wea-

ther. Traditionally too, many foremen on absentee-owner ranches built up small herds of their own and blamed the shortages on outside rustlers.

The stockmen followed the usual procedure of sending in "range detectives" to kill a few rustlers but found the results in Johnson County unsatisfactory. Whenever a small rancher or homesteader was arrested on rustling charges, a friendly jury of homesteaders invariably released him. The stockmen soon discovered, however, they could control not only the state administration, which they already owned, but the press as well. Their newfound power came about after a posse of cattlemen lynched a prostitute named Cattle Kate because she apparently had accepted beef from cowboys in payment for services rendered, and the beef the stockmen alleged, was stolen. To avoid any legal repercussions as a result of the lynching, they claimed Cattle Kate was a "bandit queen" who had masterminded a vast rustling operation. The press eagerly accepted the story and printed ridiculous accounts about the depredations of Cattle Kate. Encouraged by the public relations coup, the cattle barons decided to launch a full-scale war of extermination by going into the county in force with an army of gunmen to wipe out their arch enemies, one or two at a time.

For a period of a few months, members of the Wyoming Stock Growers' Association were invited to forward the names of deserving victims to the secretary of the organization. The executive committee then selected who would go on the death list (it was later estimated that a total of 70 victims were chosen), and sent 46 "regulators" under command of Col. Frank Wolcott and Frank H. Canton, a wanted murderer, into the county on a brutal murder mission.

Their first victims were two small ranchers, Nick Ray and Nate Champion who were killed in cold blood. Sickened by the murders, a doctor and one of the reporters accompanying the invaders left the expedition. But the shootings delayed the murder army and word spread of their presence. They soon found themselves besieged by a possee of 200 county residents.

The stockmen's army was forced to seek refuge in a ranch 13 miles south of Buffalo. They faced certain extinction until the U.S. Cavalry rode to their rescue. The killers then laid down their arms, surrendered to the army and were escorted back to Cheyenne. The local sheriff, Red Angus, unsuccessfully requested that the invaders be turned over to his custody. Had they been, there undoubtedly would have been 40-odd lynchings that evening.

The Johnson County "war" ended in a total disaster for the stockmen, who spent the next few years attempting to conceal their culpability. When a muckraker of the period, Asa Mercer published *The Banditti of the Plains* the following year, the cattle barons used their power to have the book suppressed; its plates were destroyed and Mercer was even jailed for a time for sending "obscene matter" through the mails. Copies of the book were torn up and burned and even the Library of Congress copy vanished.

While the stockmen had failed to exterminate the homesteaders of Johnson County, none were ever prosecuted for their offenses.

See also: *THE BANDITTI OF THE PLAINS*, CATTLE KATE.

Johnstown flood looting

The flood that struck Johnstown, Pa., in 1889 was easily the worst disaster to occur in the United States during the late 19th cen-

"DEATH TO THE FIENDS!" A contemporary sketch revealed the swift justice meted out to looters and mutilators of the dead at Johnstown in the aftermath of the great flood there.

tury. When a 100-foot-high earthen dam broke, the resulting cataclysm killed at least 2,000 people—an average of about one out of every 10 persons living in the way of the flood—and bodies were still being found as late as 1906. However, much as the public was upset by the tragedy and the almost certain criminal negligence in the construction and supervision of the dam, it became more outraged by the looting, especially of the bodies of dead victims, that took place in the aftermath of the disaster.

As soon as the waters started to settle, hordes of looters descended on the scene to pillage business establishments and to strip the dead of cash, watches, wedding rings and the like. Dozens of looters were arrested, but they were the lucky ones. Outraged citizens killed others on the spot.

A Miss Wayne from Altoona, Pa. reported she was swept off a ferryboat by the rampaging waters and ended up on a beach, where she awakened to find herself stripped naked by looters. She feigned death and watched bands of thieves "slice off with wicked knives" the fingers of women to get their rings.

So outraged was the citizenry over this story that many persons lost interest in rescue work and set out in vigilante style to hunt for looters. One looter captured with a ring-bearing severed finger in his pocket was summarily drowned. Others were shot. Even the police, overburdened with rescue work, were caught up in the frenzy of catching looters. A publication of the period reported:

A trap was laid for a crook undertaker, who was robbing the bodies in the Fourth Ward morgue. A female was brought in, and before it was dressed for burial a diamond ring was placed upon one of her fingers, and the pseudo undertaker was assigned to take charge of the body. He was detected in the act of stealing the jewelry, and was promptly arrested by the chief of police.

Juanita (1828–1851) first woman hanged in California

The hanging of a Mexican woman named Juanita, who comes down through history by that name alone, in the town of Downieville, Calif. in 1851 brought denunciations of American border justice from as far away as England.

Downieville was at the time a mining camp full of violent miners and harlots of all ages and hues, but Juanita was unquestionably the prize beauty. One account testifies: "Her dusky hair, long and glossy, was pulled low over delicate olive features and knotted loosely at the nape of her graceful neck. It gave her a Madonna-like expression. No doubt, many a rough miner stood in awe of her beauty and bared his head in reverence mingled with a certain human admiration." But she also had some faults, being described as, among other things, "a live volcano, an enraged lioness, a fighting wildcat."

In mid-1851 Juanita found true love with a young Mexican miner and set up housekeeping. She was henceforth not available as in the past. On the Fourth of July a celebrating miner named Jack Cannon came knocking on Juanita's door, brandishing a bag of gold dust. Juanita screamed at him in Spanish to let her alone. Cannon ignored her protestations and forced his way into the cabin, actually smashing the cabin door from its hinges. A knife flashed in the Mexican girl's hand, and Cannon fell bleeding to death on the floor.

Cannon was known in the camp as a rowdy, but he was a popular one, and an angry crowd soon gathered and began talk of lynching. Juanita was dragged to Craycroft's saloon for what was supposed to be a trial, but in the meantime some of her clothing had been dipped in Cannon's blood so that her crime would be more evident. A "prosecutor" was appointed to present the case, and a young unidentified lawyer who had journeyed over the mountains from Nevada to hear the Fourth of July speeches in Downieville was permitted to defend Juanita. While the "trial" proceeded, a number of miners argued over whose rope should be used for the girl's execution. When the young attorney started making a strong case of self-defense, he was knocked off the barrel he was standing on and flung out to the street. The jury then was ready to bring in a verdict, which, of course, turned out to be guilty.

Then a Dr. C. D. Aikin, who had come to the camp only weeks before, interrupted the proceedings to declare he was treating Juanita for pregnancy. An angry murmur arose in the crowd, which numbered in the hundreds. Three other local medical men were charged with examining the girl and came back to announce the claim was a hoax. Dr. Aiken quickly was held in contempt for his humane effort to save the girl and was given 24 hours to get out of town or be hanged himself.

Juanita was dragged back to her cabin and given an hour to prepare for her fate, while a crowd gathered outside the cabin and started shouting curses at her and stoning the flimsy structure. A priest was not allowed to go to her. After the hour was up, Juanita was marched to Durgan Bridge, from which a noose hung out over the wide Yuba. Extending from the bridge was a 6-foot plank, on which the condemned woman was to stand. As she took her position, Juanita was silent, unlike during her courtroom appearance when she volubly had attacked the kangaroo proceedings in Spanish. Now she merely observed the crowd and smiled in contempt. When she spotted a friendly face, she called out, "Adiós, amigo, adiós." Then the plank was kicked out from under her.

When news of the execution reached the outside world, the press from one end of the country to the other condemned the blood-thirsty affair. Even the *Times of London* printed severe and caustic criticism of the manner in which border justice had been dispensed. Juanita was described as the first and only woman ever hanged in California, which was not true. Many Mexican and Indian women had been hanged, but hers was the first to follow a "trial."

Julian Street   Cripple Creek, Colorado vice center
Cripple Creek, the last of the Colorado gold towns, was as wicked as any of its predecessors and perhaps even a bit more open about it. Train travelers passing through the town were treated to a full view of Myers Avenue and its "line," replete with such signs as "MEN TAKEN IN AND DONE FOR." A leading turn-of-the-century journalist, Julian Street, exposed the shame of Myers Avenue to a national audience in a searing article in *Colliers* magazine, calling the thoroughfare a disgrace to the entire country. The outraged city fathers of Cripple Creek fought back by bestowing a special honor on the journalist: they renamed Myers Avenue "Julian Street."

Kelly, Honest John (1856–1926) gambler

For a quarter century beginning in the late 1890s, John Kelly was known as the most honest gambling house operator in the country, an attribute that did not stand him well with the police, since he was famous for refusing to pay for protection.

Honest John earned his sobriquet when he was a baseball umpire. In 1888 he refused a $10,000 bribe to favor Boston in an important game with Providence. Thereafter, he became the darling of the big gamblers and was trusted to be the dealer in games where tens of thousands of dollars were riding on a turn of a card. In the late 1890s Honest John opened his own gambling house in New York City and became so prosperous that he soon had operations at several locations, all renowned for being totally honest. His best-known house was a brownstone at 156 West 44th Street, where he fought many battles with the police, boasting he constantly had to buy new doors and windows to replace those smashed by indignant detectives. The worst raid occurred in 1912, when the police descended on the gambling house with crow bars and fire axes and smashed doors, windows, gambling equipment and furniture. The raid succeeded only in making Kelly a hero to the public, and when he opened the Vendome Club on West 141st Street, his business boomed. After Kelly closed the West 44th Street brownstone, the police remained convinced he was still operating it for gambling purposes and stationed an officer at the front door. Sightseeing buses took visitors past the brownstone, and guides pointed out the gambling house that wouldn't pay off the police. The guides insisted patrons entered it through trapdoors from other buildings, but further police raids never uncovered any gambling. In the early 1920s Honest John sold the building to a Republican Party organization and relocated to Palm Beach, Fla. where he operated a place with only limited success because of his refusal to pay protection. He died on March 28, 1926.

Kelly, Joseph "Bunco" (1838–1934) shanghaier and murderer

Oddly, the two greatest shanghaiers in America were named Kelly—Shanghai Kelly and

Joseph "Bunco" Kelly. At age 26, Joseph Kelly of Liverpool, England set up in Portland, Ore. in 1859 and for the next 35 years made thousands of men into unwilling seamen, filling orders from crew-short sea captains. Totally without conscience, he hesitated at sending no one to sea, recruiting his victims from anywhere along the waterfront. He often used two doxies, Liverpool Liz and Esmeralda, as sex lures to coax drunks from Erickson's Saloon, where it took 15 men to tend the block-long bar, or from the Paris House, the city's biggest brothel, or from Mark Cook's Saloon. If such tactics failed, he simply bludgeoned hapless passersby and carted them off to a ship ready to sail.

Kelly sometimes had trouble acquiring accomplices, and for good reason. After once receiving an order for 10 men, he and two assistants deposited eight drunks into a ship's hold. "Here," said the skipper, "I need ten men, I told you."

Kelly nodded, battered his two aides senseless and collected for a full consignment. The profitability of the procedure was unassailable: in addition to collecting a fee for his assistants—as well as the other shanghai victims—he also saved the money he would otherwise have had to pay them.

Kelly picked up his nickname Bunco for another of his double-dealing deeds. He would bring an apparent victim wrapped in a blanket aboardship and deposit him directly in a bunk, telling the captain, "drunkenest sailor I ever seen." Kelly would collect his $50 stipend as the ship set sail. Not until the next morning would the angered captain discover Kelly had slipped him a cigar store Indian instead of a drunken sailor.

Bunco's biggest coup occurred when he came across 24 waterfront bums either dead or dying in the basement of an undertaking establishment, where they had partaken of barrels filled with embalming fluid under the illusion they were inside the next building, which was a saloon. At the time Bunco found them, he had an order outstanding for 22 shanghai victims at $30 a head. The master of the craft was extremely pleased when Kelly oversupplied the order by two, and gratefully handed him $720 for the bunch. The next day the redfaced captain had to dock in order to unload 14 corpses and another 10 men whose lives could be saved only by energetic stomach pumping. The captain vowed never again to do business with Bunco Kelly, but he probably broke his resolutions, since in Portland a ship's master almost had to deal with Kelly, even if wisdom required a close inspection of any goods purchased from him.

Despite actions by the police, which varied from largely indifferent to modestly determined, Kelly continued his nefarious trade until 1894, when he was apprehended for murdering a retired saloon keeper, 73-year-old George Washington Sayres. Kelly denied the charge, claiming it was a frame-up by competitors who wanted to take over his business. "I am being tried not as the person who killed poor old George Sayres," Bunco said in a statement. "I am being tried for all the crimes ever committed in the North End. I am on trial because I am operating a successful sailor's boardinghouse—the finest on this coast. I am being tried because I have no influence with the city's politicians. I had nothing against George Sayres."

That last statement, at least, was accurate. The jury concluded Kelly had committed the murder for $2,000 given him by Sayres' enemies.

Kelly did 13 years in the Oregon State Penitentiary and was released in 1907. He got a newspaperman named John Kelly, no relation, to help him write a book, *Thirteen Years in the Oregon Pen*, in which he continued to proclaim his innocence. Kelly left Portland in 1909 and eventually was said to have ended up in South America, where, as proof of the adage that only the good die young, he lived until the ripe old age of 96.

See also: SHANGHAIING, SHANGHAI KELLY.

Kelly, Shanghai (1835–?) shanghaier

Without doubt the most-feared name wherever Pacific sailors gathered in the 19th century was that of Shanghai Kelly, a stubby, red-bearded Irishman who became the most prodigious shanghaier on San Francisco's Barbary Coast.

Kelly maintained a saloon and boardinghouse at 33 Pacific Street. There is no way to precisely estimate how many men passed through his notorious shanghai pipelines but it was at least 10,000. He got the best deal from shipmasters because he generally provided bona fide sailors rather than unsuspecting landlubbers who happened to stumble along. Not that Kelly didn't turn a dishonest dollar in his shanghai operations whenever he could. Occasionally, among a boatload of drugged victims, Kelly would toss in a corpse or two. Since the usual transaction only allowed time for a head count of men in various degrees of stupor, it is easy to see how a captain might not discover he had been "stiffed with a stiff," as the saying went, until he was well out into the Pacific. Police could only wonder how many murder victims were turned over to Kelly to be disposed of for a price, thus providing him with a double fee. The master shanghaier knew that such a corpse would receive a quick and unrecorded burial far out at sea.

Feared as he was, Kelly still had no trouble keeping his boardinghouse stocked with sailors, many of whom knew the fate that lay in store for them. The popularity of Kelly's place rested on his reputation of providing free women to go along with his free liquor. To many a sailor the price of their next voyage was little enough to pay. Once, in the 1870s, though Kelly received an order for 90 sailors at a time when he was understocked. Chartering a paddle-wheel steamer, he announced he would celebrate his birthday with a picnic at which there would be all the liquor a celebrant could drink. Naturally, there was an admission charge, since Kelly firmly believed in getting all he could out of any deal. He kept a close count of the willing celebrants clamoring aboard and as soon as the number reached 90 the gangplank was pulled up and the steamer paddled off. Barrels of beer and whiskey were opened and the happy picnickers toasted Kelly's health. Of course, all the drink was heavily drugged and within a couple of hours everyone aboard except Kelly and his men was sound asleep. The paddle steamer pulled up to the two ships that had ordered crews, and Kelly handed over the agreed-on number to each and collected his pay. On his way back, he rescued survivors from the *Yankee Blade* which had sunk off Santa Barbara. Luckily for Kelly, the landing of the rescued men caused great stir and nobody noticed that his picnic guests were missing. Of course, he would have felt even luckier if he had been able to sell the rescued seamen as well.

Kelly was active in his trade till near the end of the 19th century, when he faded from sight.

See also: JOSEPH "BUNCO" KELLY, SHANGHAIING.

Kid Dropper (1891–1923) New York
gangster chief

For a time in the early 1920s, the premier gangster in New York City was Kid Dropper, born Nathan Kaplan, who literally murdered his way into the position of top labor slugger-extortionist during the post-World War I period. He had come a long way from his lowly position as a minor ally of the last great New York criminal gang before the advent of Prohibition, the Five Pointers.

In his youth he earned the sobriquet Kid Dropper from his scam of dropping a wallet filled with counterfeit money on the street. He would then pick it up in front of a potential victim, pretend it was an accidental discovery and, claiming to be in a great hurry, offer to sell it to the mark, who in turn would be able to return it to its rightful owner for a reward to keep it.

As late as 1911, when he was sentenced to seven years in prison for robbery, Kid Dropper was not considered a major criminal. When he came out, however, there was a void in the labor slugging field left by the passage from the scene of Dopey Benny Fein and Joe the Greaser Rosensweig. Kid Dropper organized a gang with another Five Pointers alumnus, young Johnny Spanish, a vicious killer with perhaps more nerve than the Dropper. Previously, they had had a falling out over a woman and Spanish had done seven years for shooting her. That rift indicated the two could not work together for long, especially since each obviously intended to become "top dog."

Soon, a war broke out between the two rivals, and both fielded platoons of killers. Bullet-ridden corpses became commonplace, particularly in the garment district. The war was concluded on July 29, 1919, when three men, one always presumed to have been the Dropper, walked up behind Johnny Spanish as he left a Second Avenue restaurant and emptied their revolvers into his body.

Thereafter, the Kid headed all the important labor slugging rackets in the city, working either for the unions or the employers or both. Between 1920 and 1923 the Dropper was responsible for at least an estimated 20 murders. He became a notorious sight along Broadway in his belted check suit of extreme cut, narrow pointed shoes, and stylish derby or straw hat slanted rakishly over one eye, and at all times he was surrounded by a bevy of gunmen.

By 1923 the Dropper was beset by new and even tougher opponents than the late unlamented Johnny Spanish. They were headed by Jacob "Little Augie" Orgen, a bloodthirsty gangster with such supporters and "comers" as Jack "Legs" Diamond, Louis "Lepke" Buchalter and Gurrah Shapiro. The Dropper's men and Little Augie's followers began open warfare over control of the wet wash laundry workers and were soon involved in wholesale shoot-outs all around the town.

Finally, in August 1923 Kid Dropper was picked up on a charge of carrying a concealed weapon and hauled into Essex Market Court. The arrest of the great gang leader attracted a large number of newsmen and onlookers. When the Kid's arraignment was transferred to another court, he was led to the street by a phalanx of policemen. As he was entering the car, a minor and particularly lamebrained hoodlum named Louis Kushner jumped forward and shot him through the windshield. Kushner had been properly "stroked" by the Little Augies gang into believing that such a daring act would make him an important gangster and member of their outfit.

The Dropper crumpled up inside the car, while his wife fought her way through the police guards wrestling with Kushner. "Nate! Nate!" she cried. "Tell me that you were not what they say you were!" Instead, the Kid managed only to moan, "They got me!" and died.

Kushner in the meantime announced triumphantly: "I got him. I'd like a cigarette."

In due course, Kushner got 20 years and Little Augie absorbed the Dropper's illicit enterprises. He held them only until 1927, when he too was violently removed from power, apparently by Lepke and Shapiro, who then took over the union rackets.

See also: JACOB "LITTLE AUGIE" ORGEN.

kidnapping of free blacks

Throughout the decades preceding the Civil War, kidnapping of free blacks in the North and shipping them to the South to be sold as slaves was a thriving criminal enterprise. Kidnapping rings operated with impunity despite laws in Southern states prohibiting the practice. Such laws were mere shams since blacks were disqualified as witnesses and thus could not incriminate their captors. Entire families were abducted but many kidnap rings preferred dealing only in children and young women because such captives could be more easily contained. Some enterprising kidnappers used the ruse of marrying mulatto women and then selling them off as slaves at the first opportunity. Unscrupulous federal magistrates cooperated in schemes to seize blacks and transport them to the South under the pretext of enforcing the fugitive slave laws.

kiss of death girls   underworld jinxes

A traditional underworld archetype is the kiss of death girl, a sobriquet newspapers apply to women whose lovers seem to die at a much more frequent rate than the mortality tables and laws of chance would allow.

The origin of the term "kiss of death" girl is not clear. There is some indication that the first such female was Ida the Goose, an inamorata of the New York City underworld in the early part of this century who provoked the 1909 Ida the Goose War between the Gophers and the equally murderous Chick Tricker gang. Ida the Goose, a noted beauty despite her rather unromantic name, was the plaything of one Gopher Gang captain after another, generally upon the demise of a prior lover. Her crowning kiss of death caper occurred when, after defecting to the Tricker ranks, she was reclaimed by the Gophers after they assassinated her Tricker gang lover along with several of his fellow gang members in a celebrated cafe shoot-out.

Another famous lady who jinxed her lovers was Mary Margaret Collings, dubbed Kiss of Death Maggie by an appreciative Chicago press during the Capone era. The lady had the misfortune of losing no less than six husbands, underworld characters all, either in gang battles or confrontations with the police. It got so that guests at her weddings made wagers on how long her newest spouse would last. One reporter calculated that "six months was about par for the course."

The most famous of the breed was Evelyn Mittleman, who was labeled the Kiss of Death Girl of Murder, Inc. because of her love affair with Pittsburgh Phil Strauss, the organization's most-dedicated killer. Actually, Evelyn just seemed to be a luscious blonde who attracted men who were equally attracted by violence. At an early age, Evelyn, who came from the Williamsburg section of Brooklyn, New York City, attracted the attention of newsmen covering the breeding spots of criminality. When the Murder, Inc. investigation broke in 1940, Eddie Zeltner, a columnist for the *New York Daily Mirror*, wrote: "I knew Evelyn ten years ago, when she was barely sixteen, a gorgeous blonde who used to come from Williamsburg to Coney Island to swim, and dance in the cellar clubs which are grammar schools for gangsters."

When she was 18, Evelyn was in California with a fellow named Hy Miller, who was enamored of her. One night at a dance another man was struck by her looks. A violent disagreement ensued between him and Miller, who lost Evelyn and his life that very night. The same sort of thing happened a couple of years later back in Brooklyn. She was then dating one Robert Feurer when she caught the eye of Jack Goldstein, a Brownsville gangster involved in the wholesale fish market racket. Goldstein promptly killed Feurer when the latter objected to his attention to Evelyn. Thereafter, Goldstein proudly paraded around with Evelyn in tow until one day they happened to pass a Brownsville poolhall and were seen by Pittsburgh Phil. Phil liked what he saw and said so. Goldstein took exception to the remark and complained about his behavior. Phil quickly went back inside the pool hall and emerged with a billiard cue. He gave Goldstein a vicious going over, completely altering his features and his romantic notions about Evelyn.

Goldstein did not come around much after that, but it was not until four years later that he succumbed to the kiss of death curse. He was murdered by Pittsburgh Phil, but it was not over Evelyn's affections. A contract was put out on him because of his racket activities, and a number of killers headed by Phil,

were assigned to the hit. The hit men were ordered to hammer Goldstein into unconsciousness, but not to kill him, and to bring him directly to Phil, who insisted on drowning Goldstein personally.

Pittsburgh Phil proved to be Kiss of Death Evelyn's last victim. She was the final visitor in his death cell before he was executed in 1941. Thereafter, Evelyn, the greatest of the kiss of death girls, faded into obscurity.

See also: IDA THE GOOSE WAR.

Kitty and Jennie Gang   Chicago
two-woman gang

From 1886 until the turn of the century, Chicago men were menaced by what the police called the Kitty and Jennie Gang. Actually, the "gang" consisted of only two members, Kitty Adams and Jennie Clark, but their depredations befitted a criminal combine much larger in size. Kitty Adams first appeared in Chicago around 1880. She was the wife of a noted pickpocket, George Shine, but soon tossed him over and won a reputation of her own as the Terror of State Street. Although white, she did a short stint in a black brothel and there mastered the use of the razor, a weapon she always hid in the bosom of her dress and used when the need arose. Once when a lover of hers became overbearing, she whipped out her razor and sliced off both his ears.

About 1886 she set up a streetwalker's crib in the Levee, Chicago's segregated vice area, but really supported herself as a footpad. She started working with a very attractive young woman named Jennie Clark, who would pick up men on the streets and lead them into alleys. Here, Kitty Adams would seize the victim and put a razor to his throat while Jennie took his valuables. Between

1886 and 1893, Kitty and Jennie staged, at a minimum, 100 such robberies a year. Finally, in 1893 a victim was able to shake off enough of his fright to testify against Kitty Adams and she was sent to Joliet Prison.

Jennie Clark instantly petitioned Gov. John P. Altgeld for a pardon on the ground that Kitty was dying of tuberculosis. Altgeld ordered an investigation, and when Kitty appeared before the Board of Pardons, she had cut her gums with a toothpick so badly that she spat and coughed blood at a rate that convinced the board's members she would soon die. The pardon was forthcoming and Kitty returned to Jennie. The pair were soon back in action.

In 1896 they were both arrested for robbing a man. Kitty jumped bail, but Jennie appeared for trial before Judge James Goggin, a jurist noted for making astounding decisions. In the Jennie Clark case, Judge Goggin made his celebrated ruling that a man who went to the Levee deserved to get himself robbed. Jennie was released and the fugitive warrant against Kitty was withdrawn. Two years later, Kitty was caught again and this time a more tradition-bound jurist sent her back to Joliet, where ironically, she died of tuberculosis. Without Kitty Adams as a confederate, Jennie Clark faded from the crime records.

labor sluggers war   thug rivalry

About 1911, as unionization efforts in New York intensified, especially in the needle and allied garment industry trades, both labor and management started utilizing thugs to achieve their goals, providing the underworld with a lucrative source of income. This produced a strange underworld conflict rooted as much in class loyalties and political philosophy as in the desire for illicit revenues. Union leaders hired thugs to blackjack and murder strikebreakers and to convince recalcitrant workers to join the unions. Employers hired the gangsters to guard strikebreakers, slug union pickets and raid union meetings.

A number of gangs vied for the labor slugging business, but all clearly preferred working for the unions rather than the employers. In some cases this was undoubtedly because the unions often paid better than the employers, but it was also due to the fact that most of these labor sluggers were Jews and Italians, just as were the workers of the area. There was an inclination to help your own as long as it wasn't too unprofitable.

By about 1912–13 the labor slugging trade was dominated by an alliance of gangs headed by Dopey Benny Fein and Joe the Greaser Rosensweig. So feared was Dopey Benny that some employers once offered him $15,000 to remain neutral in a strike. Deeply offended, he replied he would accept no offer from them and stood ready to provide his gangsters to the union because his heart was always with the workingman. In fact, this was not always the case. Dopey Benny and Joe the Greaser divided up lower Manhattan into districts and assigned a vassal gang to each, and it was possible to see their men in one district supporting the union while those in another engaged in antilabor skull bashing.

In the process of establishing their monopoly, Dopey Benny and Joe the Greaser froze several rival gangs out of working for the unions. Finally, the leaders of these gangs, including Billy Lustig, Pinchey Paul, Little Rhody, Punk Madden, Moe Jewbach, and others, banded together to declare war and establish their right to support unionism. In late 1913 the two sides staged a running gun battle at Grand and Forsyth streets. Surprisingly, no one was killed, although many store windows were shot to pieces and business was generally brought to a halt.

Later battles resulted in fatalities and, more commonly, maimings. Eventually, one of the dissident leaders, Pinchey Paul, was murdered and Nigger Benny Snyder, a Fein-Rosensweig henchman, was accused of the killing. While in jail Nigger Benny concluded that he was being abandoned by the Fein-Rosensweig forces and confessed to the murder, saying it had been assigned to him by Joe the Greaser, who had tipped him $5 upon its successful completion.

In time, the dissidents were wiped out in a series of gunfights outside of various factories, but the victors had their own problems. Dopey Benny was arrested on a murder charge, and Joe the Greaser got sent away for 10 years. Benny recognized his predicament and decided to make a pitch for leniency by informing on his labor connections and fellow sluggers. On the basis of Dopey Benny's statements, 11 gangsters and 23 union officers were indicted, but in the end, none were convicted. Under his deal with the law, Benny was tried on only one murder charge and was released when the jury failed to reach a verdict.

However, Dopey Benny's power was broken, as was that of his rivals. Because of the disclosures, a number of unions thereafter refused to hire sluggers. As a result, the New York labor scene was relatively peaceful through the war years until about 1920, when the notorious Kid Dropper, formerly Nathan Kaplan, reorganized the slugger trade with those unions still willing to use such methods. In 1923 the Kid's power was disrupted by a challenge from forces aligned with Jacob "Little Augie" Orgen.

Little Augie won this second sluggers war by arranging the assassination of Kid Drop-per while he himself was under police guard, thereby becoming the new king of the labor sluggers. Two other men allied with Little Augie at this time were Louis "Lepke" Buchalter and Gurrah Shapiro, both would rise high in the ranks of the national crime syndicate established in the 1930s. Lepke, in fact, became head of that organization's enforcement arm, Murder, Inc.

Little Augie milked the labor slugging racket as well as he could, although fewer unions were willing to resort to his organizing tactics, until he began shifting his operations into bootlegging. He rejected a suggestion from Lepke that if the unions would not use sluggers, then the gangsters should move and physically take over union locals, milk the members with heavy dues and extort tribute from employers to insure against strikes. Little Augie, faced with tightened police surveillance, looked upon this as a high-risk operation. Besides, he saw he could earn enough from bootlegging to retire a rich man in a few years. So he ordered Lepke to cease such activities.

In 1927 Little Augie was machine-gunned to death either by Lepke and Shapiro or by bootlegging rivals whose customers he had stolen. Lepke soon became the king of the labor extortion racket in New York.

See also: KID DROPPER, NOBLES, JACOB "LIT-TLE AUGIE" ORGEN.

Lady Gophers New York female gang

Often referred to by the press as the ladies auxiliary of the Gophers, an early 20th century gang that controlled Hell's Kitchen in New York City, the Lady Gophers were officially known as the Battle Row Ladies' Social and Athletic Club. Its members were the first organized gang of women to engage in what may be called the "social crimes" of the 20th century.

The Lady Gophers fought side by side with the Gophers in many battles against the police. Their leader, Battle Annie, was said to have been the sweetheart of practically the entire Gopher Gang, 500 strong. In many respects, she was much smarter than her male counterparts. Known as the Queen of Hell's Kitchen, Battle Annie soon saw the special uses for an army of gangster women. She approached both labor unions and employers who had started to hire gangsters and explained the value of utilizing women sluggers. Thereafter, for a number of years Battle Annie enjoyed a handsome living supplying female warriors to either side in local industrial disputes. Her women might appear on the scene posing as either the enraged wives of the strikers or as the wives of the strikebreakers—sometimes even playing both roles—and end up scratching, biting and clawing the picketers, the strikebreakers or both.

The Lady Gophers failed to survive, however, when the male Gopher Gang disintegrated between 1910 and 1912.

See also: GOPHERS.

Lager Beer Riot

The so-called Lager Beer Riot, also known as the German Riot, in Chicago in 1855 was that city's first great mob disturbance. The cause of the riot was the city's attempt to enforce the Sunday closing law for saloons and increase their license fees from $50 to $300 a year, exacerbated by an antiforeign attitude, which in Chicago at the time meant anti-German. The Germans, clannishly isolated on the North Side, stuck to their own language, maintained their own schools and

newspapers and, of course, had hundreds of their own beer gardens. The Sunday closings and fee increases were but a prelude to a vote that summer on a drastic prohibition law. The German populace, especially the saloon keepers, saw the moves as an effort to destroy their rights. "The excitement throughout the city ran high," a contemporary historian wrote, "but the *Nord Seite* was in a perfect ferment. Meetings were held, speeches made, resolutions adopted, and pledges registered that the Germans of Chicago would die, if need be, rather than submit to this outrage upon their rights." Because they were likewise affected, the Scandinavians and Irish residents joined the German protest. The first Sunday the closing law was enforced, the German beer gardens and saloons were shut down tight by the police but American-owned bars on the South Side were allowed to carry on business via their side and back doors. The following Sunday the German saloon keepers opened for business and refused to shut down; 200 of them were immediately arrested. Later, they were freed on bail and representatives of the city and the German district agreed to a single test case that would be binding on both sides. The trial opened on the morning of April 21, 1855. As the contemporary account continues:

The liberated saloon-keepers had collected their friends on the North Side, and, preceded by a fife and drum, the mob, about five hundred strong, had marched in solid phalanx upon the justice shop, as many as could entering the sacred precincts. After making themselves understood that the decision of the court must be in their favor if the town didn't want a taste of war, they retired and formed at the intersection of Clark and Randolph Streets, and held possession of these thorough-

fares to the exclusion of all traffic. Crowds gathered from all sections of the city, friends and enemies, and the uproar was deafening.

The mob retreated after a brief but bloody fight with a score of police that left nine prisoners in custody. By 3 o'clock the protesting mob had reached 1,000 men, armed with rifles, shotguns, knives and clubs, and they advanced again, this time to be met by 200 police, who had formed a solid line across Clark Street. Amidst cries of "Shoot the police!" the mob attacked, firing guns, and the police returned the fire. Officially, only one German was killed, a police officer had his arm blown off by a shotgun and perhaps 20 others were seriously wounded. The mob carried off many of their own injured and the *Chicago Times* reported, "A few days later there were several mysterious funerals on the North Side, and it was generally believed that the rioters gave certain victims secret burial."

In all, 60 prisoners were taken by the police in what came to be called the Lager Beer Riot. Of these, 14 were brought to trial. Eventually, two Irishmen named Halleman and Farrell were convicted of rioting. A 19th century historian summed up the public reaction: "It seemed little less than a travesty on justice that in a sedition notoriously German, the only victims should be two Irishmen." The two men were granted new trials but they were never held. By then the powerful prohibition forces no longer cared. The temperance movement was gaining around the country, and an easy victory was expected in the Chicago balloting. Instead, the vote went antiprohibition by a huge margin. Many voters said they had been fearful of lawless German reaction to a "yes" vote, but Chicago was apparently thoroughly "wet" in sympathy. In any event, the Lager Beer rioters had won.

Lawes, Kathryn (1885–1937) Angel of Sing Sing

No fiction writer would ever dare to invent a character like Kathryn Lawes, the so-called Angel of Sing Sing and pass off as plausible the tear-jerking story of her death. It simply would not be believed.

The first wife of Sing Sing Warden Lewis E. Lawes, Kathryn was the mistress of the prison on the Hudson for 17 years after Lawes took over. She was known to the prisoners as a kind, understanding woman who wrote letters for them, helped many of their families and cared for them in the prison hospital. Her deeds became so legendary that she was considered an angel of mercy.

In 1937 Kathryn Lawes was killed in an automobile accident. The prisoners of Sing Sing were stunned, and their grief was real. There was genuine anguish among them when it was announced her funeral would take place in a church outside the prison walls. A committee of prisoners went to Warden Lawes to protest and insist on the convicts' right to pay their last respects.

Lawes was willing to gamble on his men. He had in the past allowed many prisoners to go home on emergency visits without escorts, a practice that had left him open to possibly ruinous criticism if anything had gone wrong. The warden took a much greater risk now by declaring he would comply with the prisoners' request.

The night before the funeral, the south gate of Sing Sing swung open and out trudged a silent procession of murderers, swindlers, thieves and crooks of all kinds—marching out of the prison to the warden's house, a quarter of a mile away. There were no guns trained on them and not a single guard accompanied them; yet not one man strayed from line, nor looked for the chance to escape. When the men entered the house, they silently passed the bier, many uttering a short word of prayer, and then walked outside, reformed their ranks and marched silently back to their prison.

Leslie, George Leonidas (1838–1884)
king of the bank robbers

Unquestionably, the greatest bank robber (although, strictly speaking, most of his capers were burglaries) of the 19th century, notwithstanding the likes of Mark Shinburn, George Bliss and other notables, was George Leonidas Leslie, who New York Superintendent of Police George W. Walling held to be the mastermind of 80 percent of all bank thefts in America from 1865 until his violent death in 1884. Leslie's gang, according to Walling, stole somewhere between $7 and $12 million. In addition, this criminal genius was called in as a consultant on bank jobs by underworld gangs all over the country. His consultation fees ranged from $5,000 to $20,000, payable in advance regardless of the take.

Leslie was contemptuous of most criminals, regarding them as too stupid to make crime pay to its full potential. Typical was the Ace Marvin gang in San Francisco. In late 1880 they gave him $20,000 to help plan a bank job. The plan was to rob a bank over the weekend so that the theft would not be discovered until Monday; that was the only part of the caper Leslie liked. All the rest was awful. Ace Marvin was not a bank man but rather a jack of all crimes who thought a bank job would be a great way to make a big score. Leslie shook his head at such amateurism. Then too, Ace's "pete" man if allowed to follow his blasting technique, probably would blow half the town into the Bay. And Marvin didn't even have a fix in

with the law. Leslie generally preferred to have a police license before he staged a heist. It made things simpler for everybody, and besides, the law came rather cheap. Finally, Marvin had not adequately planned the getaway. Leslie liked things laid out so that the escape route went down a narrow street where a carriage could be pulled out at just the right time and left in the way of any pursuers.

After listening to Ace's exposition of the robbery, Leslie junked the whole thing. He conceived a plan that called for the thieves to enter the bank not once but twice.

One night Leslie, Ace and six henchmen, including a skilled locksmith, forced the lock on the bank's side door and entered. The locksmith immediately set about replacing the lock on the door with a duplicate so that there would be no evidence of any forced entry. Meanwhile, Leslie carefully pried the dial off the safe lock with a small file. It was difficult work because he had to avoid leaving any marks or scratches. At last, the dial popped off. Then Leslie drew out a weird-looking instrument made of thin steel wire, arranged it inside the surface of the dial and then replaced the knob securely on the safe.

Even Ace Marvin understood. "Well, I'll be," he said. "That wire is going to cut out grooves under the dial every time the combination is worked!"

Leslie nodded pridefully. He explained the device was called the little joker. If Leslie had not invented it, he certainly refined it and used it to perfection. "The deepest cuts will indicate the numbers of the combination. You just won't know which order the numbers are in and will have to try all the various possibilities, but there can only be a few dozen, so you'll have the right combination in a matter of minutes."

The next morning Leslie hopped a train back to New York. When he got home, he read in the newspapers about a $173,000 burglary of a bank in San Francisco. Leslie shook his head in disgust. Everyone had estimated the loot would be well over $200,000. If he had run the job, he would have counted the money on the spot and finding it short, he would have left it in the safe and returned another time, especially since it was only a few weeks until Christmas. If Marvin had waited a while bank deposits by businessmen would have soared. In fact, Leslie might have broken in three or four times before making the haul. But Ace Marvin was not George Leslie; he just wasn't in the same class.

That year, 1880, Leslie was at the height of his fabulous career. He had come a long way since graduating from the University of Cincinnati with high honors. Everyone knew he would go far but they assumed it would be in architecture, the field in which he had earned his degree. He was born in 1838, the son of a well-to-do Toledo brewer who put him through college and set him up in an office in Cincinnati. In 1865 both Leslie's mother and father died, and he closed his office in Cincinnati, perhaps because of the resentment there by people who considered him a war slacker, and went to New York.

With his experience and background, Leslie could have walked into almost any architect's office and secured a good position. Instead, in almost no time at all, he was knee-deep in crime. Demonstrating a remarkable knack for pulling bank capers, he soon gathered around him such desperate and cunning criminals as Gilbert Yost, Jimmy Brady, Abe Coakley, Red Leary, Shang Draper, Johnny Dobbs, Worcester Sam Perris, Banjo Pete Emerson and Jimmy Hope. He pulled off bank jobs of an unprecedented

magnitude, among them the theft of $786,879 from the Ocean National Bank at Greenwich and Fulton streets and $2,747,000 from the Manhattan Savings Institution at Bleecker Street and Broadway. The take in the Ocean Bank robbery would have been even higher had not his men left almost $2 million in cash and securities on the floor beside the vault. The gang also wandered afield to pull off such lucrative capers as the burglaries of the South Kensington National Bank in Philadelphia, the Third National Bank of Baltimore, the Wellsbro Bank of Philadelphia and the Saratoga County Bank of Waterford, N.Y.

Despite all his jobs, Leslie never spent a day behind bars. When in trouble, he was represented by Howe and Hummel, the notorious criminal lawyers, to whom he once paid $90,000 to square a charge. His fame spread, both in police circles and in the underworld, and he sat in the place of honor at the dinner parties given by Marm Mandelbaum, America's most notorious fence, through whom Leslie laundered great sums of cash and securities. At the same time, Leslie led a double life, posing as a man of inherited means who, with his family background and education, was readily accepted in New York society. He held memberships in prestigious clubs and was known as a bon vivant and man about town. He could be seen at openings of art exhibits and theater first nights and gained quite a reputation as a bibliophile, possessing an excellent collection of first editions and being frequently consulted by other collectors.

Leslie seldom associated with fellow criminals except when planning jobs or visiting the Mandelbaum mansion, but he did have a way with their women. With his wife ensconced in Philadelphia, he carried on numerous affairs in New York with women belonging, in one way or another, to other criminals, most notably Babe Irving, the sister of Johnny Irving, and Shang Draper's wife, and lavished much time and money on them.

It was probably his amatory activities that proved to be the death of him, although some of Leslie's capers started going awry about a year before he was killed. He was known to have become quite rattled after J. W. Barron, cashier of the Dexter Savings Bank of Dexter, Maine, was killed in one of his ill-fated schemes. When several criminals were arrested for the Manhattan Bank job and police gained knowledge about the Dexter matter, many felt Leslie had arranged the leaks to protect himself.

Early in May 1884 Leslie returned to Philadelphia and told his wife he planned to get out of crime and that they would move elsewhere to start a new life. He admitted he was worried about being assassinated. Against his wife's protests, however, he returned to New York City. She would never again see him alive.

During the last week of his life, Leslie was seen on a number of occasions in different locations. He seemed to make a point of never sleeping two nights at the same place.

On May 29 Leslie stopped in Murphy's Saloon on Grand Street and was given a letter addressed in a woman's handwriting. He read it and said something about doing an errand "over the water," meaning Brooklyn. On June 4 his decomposing body was found at the base of Tramps' Rock, near the dividing line between Westchester and New York counties. He had been shot in the head.

The murder was never officially solved, although the accepted theory is that he was killed by Shang Draper, Johnny Dobbs, Worcester Sam Perris and Billy Porter, all residents of the Williamsburg section. Furthermore, it seems probable that Draper's woman was forced to write the letter that lured Leslie to his death. Clearly Leslie had gone off in expectations of a pleasant tryst. There were no bloodstains on his clothing when his body was found, and he had apparently been dressed after his death. The King of the Bank Robbers, the man who had stolen millions, was buried in a $10 plot in Cypress Hill Cemetery, a fate little better than that of the city's paupers.

See also: FREDERICKA "MARM" MANDELBAUM.

Lincoln, Abraham   target of body snatchers

After Abraham Lincoln was buried in 1865, authorities found it necessary to move his casket 17 times, mainly to prevent it from being stolen and held for ransom. That feat was almost achieved in 1876 by Big Jim Kenealy and his gang of counterfeiters. They concocted a weird plot to steal the body, rebury it elsewhere and then return it in exchange for money and the release of the outfit's master engraver, Ben Boyd, then doing 10 years in prison. Their plot was foiled when an informer working on counterfeiting matters infiltrated the gang and tipped off the Secret Service.

The would-be body snatchers were thwarted just as they were moving the casket, then kept in a mausoleum in a lonely section of forest two miles outside of Springfield, Ill. Nevertheless, the gang succeeded in eluding the Secret Service agents who swooped down on them. After 10 days all were rounded up, but Kenealy suddenly had a surprise for the authorities. He had previously determined that there was no law on the books making it illegal to steal a dead body, not even that of a martyred president. However, all the gang members were convicted and given the maximum sentence, one year in prison, for attempting to steal a coffin.

For the next two years the casket remained hidden under a pile of scrap lumber until it was moved again. Finally in 1901, it was locked in a steel cage and buried 10 feet below the floor of a national shrine in Springfield.

Lincoln, Warren (1870–1941) murderer

When Chicago defense lawyer Warren Lincoln retired to the pleasant surroundings of Aurora, Ill. just after reaching 50, he was anticipating a happy existence. But the faults of his wife, Lena, which Lincoln had ignored as long as he had the hustle and bustle of criminal court life to distract him, now became his obsession in the solitude of Aurora. She opposed, not necessarily in order, liquor, tobacco and sex. In short, she was a bore. Adding to his misery was Byron Shoup, his brother-in-law, who moved in as something of a permanent guest. Since Lincoln was used to the workings of a criminal mind, it was perhaps inevitable that he should come to think of murdering the two of them. No doubt, he felt he could get away with it. In Chicago he had once won acquittals for five very guilty murderers in a row. One day both Lena and Shoup were missing. Lincoln sadly told friends that his wife had left a letter saying she was running off with another man. That being the case, Lincoln said, he had ordered Shoup out of the house. Lincoln then went back to tending his garden. He used lots of fertilizer much of which he mixed himself. His special mixture contained a great deal of ashes, including those of Lena and Shoup.

In time, suspicions were voiced and Lincoln was caught in a number of lies concerning his missing wife and brother-in-law. Police dug up his garden searching for their bodies but found nothing.

The only parts of Lincoln's victims that he hadn't burned were their heads, which he'd planted in flower boxes on his porch and later covered with cement. But Lincoln wasn't worried about any trace of the heads, since he had covered them with quicklime. Eventually, the police dug up the flower boxes and found two perfectly preserved heads. Unfortunately for Lincoln, he once had employed a rather dimwitted greenhouse helper who had mistakenly transposed a barrel of quicklime with a barrel of slaked lime. Instead of covering the heads with quicklime, which would have disintegrated them quickly, Lincoln had covered them with slaked lime, which acted as a preservative. He was sentenced to life in Joliet Prison and died there in 1941.

Little Pete (1864–1897) tong warrior

With the possible exception of Mock Duck, the resourceful tong warrior who dominated the West Coast, Fung Jing Toy, or Little Pete, as the English-language press dubbed him, may have been the greatest fighter in America's Tong wars. Coming to the United States at the age of five, he was raised in the tong way of life and death. From the balcony of his San Francisco home at Washington Street and Waverly Place, he watched the great fight between the Suey Sings and the Kwong Docks in 1875. He is said to have plotted then how the tide of battle could have gone differently; at the time he was 10.

By 1885 Fung Jing Toy was Little Pete, a man of considerable wealth accumulated by peddling opium, dealing in female slaves, running gambling enterprises and filling murder contracts. He soon became the owner of a shoe factory on Washington Street, which gave him honest cover in the eyes of the law. Meanwhile, he had become a legend in San Francisco's Chinatown. On contract, he once chopped down a high-ranking member of the Suey On Tong. Immediately, the Suey Ons sent three warriors after him to avenge the killing. They cornered him in an alley and one swung a hatchet down on his skullcap, but instead of Little Pete collapsing, there was just a metallic clang. His assailants then swung at his chest and again drew clangs rather than blood. The attackers' puzzlement didn't last long, for Little Pete drew his own hatchet and quickly dispatched two of them. The last one fled. Following the attempted assassination, word quickly spread that Little Pete was indestructible. In fact, he wore a coat of chain mail and inside his hat was a curved sheet of steel fitted around his head.

By the time he was 25, Little Pete controlled the Sum Yop Tong, bringing it immense wealth, much at the expense of the Sue Yop Tong, which had previously been the major power in Chinatown. This brought about one of San Francisco's bloodiest tong wars, in which Little Pete directed his forces with the genius of a Napoleon. He is believed to have been responsible for the death of at least 50 rival hatchet men.

Little Pete slept in a windowless room, and on each side of his bolted door was chained a vicious dog. In addition, a minimum of six heavily armed hatchet men were nearby at all times. When he went out, he wore his suit of chain mail and employed a bodyguard of three white men, one in front, one beside him and one bringing up the rear.

Some of the hatchet men taken into custody for the murder of Little Pete. Even Little Pete's coat of mail (center) failed to prevent his assassination.

The whites were symbols Little Pete found useful. It implied to his enemies that he had great influence with white law authorities, which indeed he had. His payoffs to the political leaders of San Francisco, especially to Christopher A. Buckley, the blind political boss of the city, were said to be enormous.

Little Pete's end came in a moment of carelessness. On the evening of January 23, 1897, he went to a barber shop. He had left his home hurriedly with only one bodyguard and then sent this man to buy him a newspaper. Two hired killers, Lem Jung and Chew Tin Gop, entered the shop as Little Pete was bending his head under a faucet so the barber could wet his hair properly for plaiting. Lem Jung shoved the barber aside, grabbed Little Pete by the hair and jammed the muzzle of his revolver down the back of the tong leader's neck, inside the coat of mail. He pulled the trigger five times, and Little Pete hit the floor dead, with five bullets in his spine. His murderers fled to Portland, Ore., where they were greeted as great warriors, and then went back to China to live out their lives in luxury on the blood money they had received.

See also: TONG WARS.

Live Oak Boys New Orleans gang

Probably the outstanding example of the mindlessly brutal criminal organizations that plagued America's big cities during the mid-19th century was the Live Oak Boys of New Orleans. Lasting about a generation, most of them met a bitter fate.

Formed about 1858 by Red Bill Wilson, a vicious thug who always concealed a knife in his bushy red beard, the Live Oakers were not a gang in the usual sense of the word. There was no recognized leader, no regular organization and no division of loot. They often committed crimes on the spur of the moment, allying themselves with whatever other Live Oakers happened to be handy, and each kept what he stole. Sometimes they even stole from one another. In 1867 this unwholesome trait cost the gang two of its most-noted brutes.

Live Oaker Henry Thompson had been asleep at the shipyard the gang utilized as a rendezvous (the shipyard owner had long since desisted from trying to evict them because of their threat to burn the place down) when he awoke to find fellow Live Oaker Jimmy O'Brien, with whom he had tied on a drunk the night before, searching his pockets. Thompson started struggling, whereupon O'Brien jammed a knife into his heart and continued the search, being rewarded with a few coins. Unfortunately for the latter, a black and a small boy had witnessed the murder, and O'Brien was sent to the penitentiary, where he later died.

The Live Oakers devoted their nights to robbing and killing. They were feared throughout the city for their vicious forays, but most of their activities were confined to Gallatin Street and the surrounding area; in its dives they loafed, slept and planned their crimes. They were particularly the bane of dance house proprietors, raiding at least one such establishment almost nightly, either out of sheer deviltry or because they had been hired to do so by a business rival. When the Live Oakers stormed a place brandishing the oaken clubs that gave them their name, bartenders, customers, musicians and bouncers quickly repaired out the rear exit and harlots fled upstairs. They then would take apart the establishment at their leisure, smashing furniture, gouging up the dance floor, destroying the musical instruments and, quite naturally, emptying the till and carting off all the liquor they desired.

The only place safe from their depredations was Bill Swan's Fireproof Coffee-House on Levee Street. Swan was a former member of the gang who had acquired enough money to go into business. His resort enjoyed the protection of the Live Oakers, partly for old time's sake but also because Swan always provided the gang with free drinks.

Among the more notable members of the Live Oak Boys, in addition to Red Bill Wilson, Bill Swan, Henry Thompson and Jimmy O'Brien, were Jimmy's brother Hugh and his two sons, Matt and Hugh, Jr.; Crazy Bill Anderson; Jack Lyons; the three Petrie brothers, Redhead, Henry and Whitehead; Yorker Duffy; Barry Lynch; Jack Lowe; Tommy Lewis; Charley Lockerby and his son Albert; and Billy Emerson. Most of these were either killed, sent to prison or became drunken derelicts.

The most ferocious of all was Charley Lockerby, a short, powerful man who was credited with several murders. He was mortally wounded in a gun duel with a saloon keeper named Keppler, whom he killed. Doctors at Charity Hospital marveled over how long Lockerby lasted despite his fatal head wound. Hugh O'Brien was killed after robbing a fisherman of a rowboat and setting out on the Mississippi with the whiskey-besotted idea of becoming a pirate.

In a way, the lucky ones were those of the gang who were killed or imprisoned. With the passage of years the others turned into derelicts. While in earlier days there was no record of the New Orleans police standing up in combat to the Live Oakers, that changed as the gang members aged and turned helpless. In 1886 the *New Orleans Picayune* made the following comment about Crazy Bill Anderson, who generally was arrested for drunkenness 10 or 12 times a month:

> *Now he is handled without gloves by the police, and is kicked and cuffed about like any other common drunkard. Yet, there was a day . . . when the police really feared to approach him with hostile intentions, and it usually occupied all the time, strength and attention of four able-bodied policemen.*

By the late 1880s it was common for the young toughs of the city to seek out old Live Oakers to beat and torture. In time, only Bill Swan, the entrepreneur of the bunch, remained of a gang known as the terror of New Orleans for almost three decades.

See also: GALLATIN STREET, GREEN TREE DANCE HOUSE.

Loving, Cockeyed Frank (1854–1882)
gambler and gunfighter

A cockeyed gambler who worked the Colorado circuit, Frank Loving went down in history as the victor in one of the West's most famous gun duels, one that went far to establish the myth that triumph belonged to the man who fired slowly and last.

The gunfight was the culmination of a long-standing feud over a woman between the gambler and Levi Richardson, a hard case reputed to have killed three men. On April 5, 1879 words turned to lead at Dodge City's Long Branch Saloon. Richardson, being the much faster draw, started firing first, fanning his pistol as the pair waltzed around a gaming table and a stove. With the men so close together that their pistols almost touched—Richardson got off some five shots but, except for one shot that scratched his opponent's hand, did no more than hit the wall.

There is some confusion about Loving's shooting, but apparently, his first three shots also hit nothing but wall. Finally, at a distance of no more than a couple of feet, he found the mark with three shots, and Richardson dropped, fatally wounded. Loving hung around Colorado bars for the next three years, telling of his exploit and expounding his theory that a "cool head" will always prevail in a gunfight. In April 1882 in Trinidad, Colo. he met up with a former lawman named Jack Allen. In one duel the pair exchanged 16 shots and every one missed. When they met again the next day Allen shot first and more accurately and Cockeyed Frank fell dead, although he lives on today as the epitome of the great Western duelists.

lynching

The extent of lynching in the United States had never been accurately measured. Before 1882 there were no reliable figures at all. Since then the records have been reasonably accurate. Statistics compiled at Tuskegee Institute indicate that from 1882 to 1936 at least 4,672 persons were lynched in this country; of this total, almost three quarters,

LYNCHING

A contemporary drawing of the lynching of two black men and three black women for the killing of a white man in Greenville, Ala. in 1895. One account assured readers that the 100 men in the lynching party were "all cool and brave."

or 3,383, were blacks, and 1,289 were whites. Between 1886 and 1916 lynch mobs killed a minimum of 2,605 blacks, and in 1892 alone the figure was 160.

By the 1890s the frontier was being tamed and lynchings in the West started to decline, but in the South they started to increase. In that decade 87 percent of all lynchings occurred in the South; from 1930 to 1937 the South had 95 percent of all lynchings. While the standard assertion in the region was that lynchings were necessary to protect white womanhood, less than 30 percent of black lynch victims during the seven-year period were accused, let alone proved guilty, of rape or attempted rape.

Obviously, these figures give an incomplete picture of the extent of lynching. Omitted entirely is any reference to Chinese or to Indians, probably the most common victims of lynchings in the West. While the literature

and history of the West describe the lynching of murderers, claim jumpers, rustlers and thieves, it has always been members of minority groups who have most felt the lynch mob's wrath. The early German settlers seem to have had a particularly strong bent for lynching Indians. In 1763 German settlers, fired up by the passions of the French and Indian War, butchered 20 peaceful Conestoga Indians, many women and children, near Lancaster, Pa.

This lynching, hardly the first to occur in the colonies, preceded the activities of two Virginians, Colonel Charles Lynch and Captain William Lynch, both of whom are credited in various texts as being the first lyncher and the one who lent his name to the practice. The evidence appears to favor William Lynch.

Whoever deserves the credit, lynching became a widespread practice in America, employed for whatever reasons the lynchers thought just. The Vicksburg Volunteers in the 1830s used it to get rid of the gamblers who were driving the residents of that Mississippi port city to poverty with their crooked games. The Vigilantes of San Francisco did much to clean up San Francisco, ridding the city of a number of cutthroats and crooked politicians. Probably the greatest lynching rampage in the West occurred in the 1860s, when the Vigilantes of Montana wiped out the Innocents, a massive outlaw gang run by a sheriff, the notorious Henry Plummer. During six weeks in late 1863 the vigilantes hanged an estimated 26 Innocents as well as the sheriff himself. Many lynchings were probably stage-managed by private detectives, railroad detectives and range detectives, who would take suspects into custody and make a point of jailing them in an area where the feeling of the community ran high against the detainees. Their apparent strategy was to fan the public's ire and then stand to one side as a lynch mob took over.

The various Ku Klux Klans that were established starting in 1866 aimed to keep the South under the control of white Protestants. Naturally, blacks were the most frequent victims of the Klan, but others who felt the whip and the hangman's rope included Jews, Catholics, bootleggers, pacifists, "Bolshevists," internationalists and evolutionists. While hangings and shootings were the most common methods of lynching in the South, methods of shocking cruelty were often used. In 1899 thousands of whites took special excursion trains to Palmetto, Ga. to watch a black man being roasted alive.

Two of the most outrageous lynchings of this century involved white victims. One was Leo Frank, a pencil company executive in Georgia who was lynched in 1915. Frank was taken from a prison where he was serving a life sentence for the murder and rape of a young girl, a crime of which he was almost certainly innocent. What he was not innocent of was being Jewish and rich. Frank was hanged by vigilantes calling themselves the Knights of Mary Phagan, the name of the girl whom Frank had been convicted of murdering. Shortly thereafter, most of the Knights were initiated into a "reincarnated" Invisible Empire of the Knights of the Ku Klux Klan.

The other shocking case occurred in the aftermath of the 1933 kidnap-murder of California department store heir Brooke Hart in 1933. A huge mob broke into the jail in San Jose where Hart's two confessed murderers, John Maurice Holmes and Thomas Harold Thurmond, were being held, and hanged the pair after brutally mistreating them. The tenor of the times was best articulated by Gov. James "Sunny Jim" Rolfe, who announced the lynch mob provided "the best lesson ever given the country. I would pardon those fellows if they were charged. I would like to parole all kidnappers in San Quentin and Folsom to the fine patriotic citizens of San Jose."

But despite such publicized mob executions of whites, the vast majority of lynching victims in the 20th century have been blacks. From its inception in 1909, the National Association for the Advancement of Colored People fought mob violence and campaigned for a federal antilynching law, but congressional action was always frustrated by filibusters in the Senate. About 1935 the number of lynchings started to decrease, and by 1952–54 there was, for the first time in the nation's history, a three-year period without a reported lynching. Since then there have been some lynchings, but by and large, they have become a thing of the past. While no antilynching statute has ever been adopted, the 1968 Civil Rights Act, which makes it a federal offense for two or more persons to join in a conspiracy to violate a citizen's constitutional rights whether or not death occurs, has been considered effective in preventing lynchings.

McGlue, Luke   fictitious thief

During the boom years of Dodge City, Kan., from about 1877 to 1887, the nefarious Luke McGlue committed more crimes in the "wickedest little city in America" than anyone else. If a man had his hotel room looted, it was most likely the work of Luke McGlue. If a man's luggage disappeared, it was that damnable Luke McGlue again. If a man's trousers disappeared while he was visiting a harlot in a crib, she would tell him—with a straight face—it was the work of Luke McGlue. Luke McGlue specialized in robbing greenhorns or constantly playing practical jokes on them, and they would leave town happy to have seen the last of him. Well, not literally, since they had never seen Luke McGlue. Nor could they have. Luke McGlue didn't exist. He was invented by the denizens of Dodge City as an explanation for the many practical jokes and petty thefts greenhorns were subjected to. Even Wyatt Earp assured such victims he was on the lookout for Luke McGlue and would deal with him severely when he caught him.

McGuirk's Suicide Hall   New York
underworld dive

Few dives on New York's Bowery ever descended to the depths of McGuirk's Suicide Hall, the favorite haunt of the lowest female criminals and prostitutes around the turn of the 19th century.

Men were permitted in Suicide Hall, and if they were fortunate enough not to be drugged and robbed, they could very likely find sexual companionship for as little as a nickel. Gangsters low on their finances, however, were always welcomed as patrons and fawned over by women desperate to obtain a sponsor or protector. The place teemed with "lush workers" (women who robbed drunks), pickpockets, purse snatchers, burglars, panhandlers, beggars, drug addicts and female thieves of all descriptions.

The only real competition Suicide Hall faced for the patronage of these dregs of female humanity was Mother Woods' on Water Street. The two establishments often engaged in price wars and sought additional business by permitting almost any unwholesome activity on their premises. Suicide Hall won out, allowing McGuirk to make his famous boast that more women had killed themselves in his place than in any other house in the world. After seven years of existence, the establishment passed from the scene in 1902, a victim of constant police raids and better economic conditions, which reduced female criminality and generally destroyed the low Bowery dives. The Suicide Hall building later housed the Hadley Rescue Mission.

Magruder, Lloyd (1823–1863) murder victim

The motive for the killing of Lloyd Magruder was a common one, greed. But the murder case was to become famed in the literature of psychic happenings, since the crime could be said to have been solved as the result of a dream.

Magruder was a mule train operator who traveled the Montana-Idaho gold camps in the early 1860s. His closest friend was Hill Beachy, a lifelong acquaintance who ran a hotel, the Luna House, in Lewiston, Idaho Territory. In October 1863 Magruder set out back through the Bitterroot Mountains to pick up a new load of gold. His party consisted of five muleteers, including a man named Bill Page; three guards, David Howard, Chris Lowery and James Romaine; and two prospectors. As the party crawled into their sleeping bags one night, the three guards killed Magruder, the two prospectors and four of the teamsters—all except Bill Page. Page was not part of the murder plot, but the three killers decided they needed someone to lead them through the snow-driven passes.

Bad weather forced them, against their plan, to come into Lewiston. There, they ran into Hill Beachy, who looked at them with amazement. Several nights earlier, Beachy had had a horrifying dream that some men

had killed Magruder out on the trail. The men who had just come into town looked like the killers in the dream. Of course, Beachy felt silly; he had no proof that Magruder was even dead and could hardly go to the law with a demand that the men be held. So, he watched them leave Lewiston.

A few days later, someone found a few of Magruder's pack animals shot to death. They also discovered Magruder's six-gun and some other personal effects. Beachy was now convinced the men he'd seen were Magruder's killers, since they had ridden into town from the same direction Magruder would have been traveling. Even if they had not seen Magruder, they should have at least noticed the dead pack animals. Getting himself deputized, Beachy swore out warrants for the arrest of the four men and tracked them through Washington Territory, Oregon and into California, where he finally caught up with them and brought them back to Idaho. He coaxed Page into testifying against the other three. Page was given his freedom, but on March 4, 1864 the rest were hanged in a ravine outside Lewiston before a crowd of 10,000, most of whom wanted to see the outcome of the "dream murder."

Much was made of the psychic import of Hill Beachy's dream. Yet the area around where the killings had occurred was violent country, rife with murders; e.g., one band of holdup men committed over 100 murders there in less than a year. Given those grim circumstances, nightmares like Hill Beachy's must have been common enough occurrences.

Mahaney, Jack (1844–?) thief and great escape artist

One of the most colorful and famous American criminals in the 19th century, Jack

Mahaney was called the American Jack Sheppard because of his constant and daring escapes from captivity. Twice he was locked up in Sing Sing and twice he escaped. He also escaped from New York City's Tombs Prison on two occasions and broke out of several other Eastern prisons. Several times he leaped from speeding trains and somehow avoided what seemed certain death without even suffering serious injury. His numerous exploits made him one of the regulars to grace the illustrated covers of the *National Police Gazette*.

Born to a wealthy family in New York in 1844, he was sent to boarding school at the age of 10, where he was an "undisciplined terror" despite numerous floggings. Jack ran away from the boarding school and joined up with a gang of notorious young dock rats. Caught by the police, he was sent to the House of Refuge and promptly made his first escape from incarceration, taking a dozen youths with him.

Eventually, Mahaney came in contact with Italian Dave, an infamous Five Points Fagin who gave him a liberal education in crime. In a rickety tenement on Paradise Square, Italian Dave ran his own boarding school for some 40 youths, instructing them in the art of sneak thievery. The boys, aged nine to 15, learned how to pick pockets with the aid of fully dressed dummies. Italian Dave quickly came to regard young Mahaney as his prime pupil and allowed him privileges extended to no other youth. Mahaney was permitted to accompany Italian Dave on his more important jobs. On other occasions they would walk the streets together and young Jack was given the opportunity to pick out a logical mugging victim. If the master approved, they would fall on the unfortunate pedestrian, rob him and adjourn back to Paradise Square.

Young Jack soon tired of working with Italian Dave because of the latter's unwillingness to share the loot, and he severed connections with the Fagin. Italian Dave was supposedly shattered by the loss of his protege and tried to win Mahaney back by offering him 10 percent of all future earnings, a truly magnanimous gesture, at least by Dave's standards. However, Jack Mahaney was ready for bigger and better things, first organizing his own gang of butcher cart thieves and then becoming an accomplished burglar and all-around crook. It was in this period that he achieved his fame as a great escaper, becoming a hero to the urchins of the New York slums. In later years, Mahaney joined a group of confidence men and appears to have adopted a number of aliases, so that his subsequent exploits are shrouded in mystery.

Maison Coquet   "legal" bordello

Around 1800 the Maison Coquet, a lavish gambling den and brothel, opened on Royal Street in the center of New Orleans, advertising itself on street corner placards as operating with "the express permission of the Honorable Civil Governor of the city." In point of fact, the so-called legal status of the establishment was accomplished more by daring than decree. At the time, New Orleans was in the process of being transferred from Spanish to French rule, creating a power vacuum. The Spanish owned but no longer reigned, and the French were doubtful of their status. It may well be that bribes were paid to someone, but in any case, the resort opened and operated with impunity.

When the American flag was raised over New Orleans in December 1803 following the Louisiana Purchase, the Maison Coquet was an established reality, as were a number of other fancy brothels. By their simple, though dubious, assertion of official recognition, the Maison Coquet and its imitators established a quasi-legal existence that gave New Orleans the nearest thing to legalized prostitution anywhere in America. So firmly rooted was this tradition that it did not disappear until World War I.

Malloy, Indestructible Mike (1872–1933)
murder victim

Perhaps the most durable American murder victim, Indestructible Mike Malloy was an unheralded barfly who achieved fame and earned his nickname posthumously. He was selected to be murdered in 1932 by a Bronx, New York insurance murder ring headed by a speakeasy operator named Tony Marino. Marino was assisted by his barkeep, Joe Murphy, and two others, Frank Pasqua and Dan Kriesberg. They had killed their first victim the previous year, a young blonde named Betty Carlsen. Marino had befriended Betty, who was down on her luck. He brought her into the speak, gave her drinks on the house and even set her up in a room nearby. Betty had never been treated so well. She couldn't do enough to thank Marino, even signing some papers so he could run for public office. Actually, what she signed was an insurance policy naming her newly found benefactor her beneficiary. One frigid night Betty passed out in the speakeasy and the boys carried her back to her room, laid her out on the bed naked, poured cold water over her and left the window wide open. When she was found dead the next morning, the coroner declared her death the result of pneumonia compounded by alcoholism. The boys collected $800, not an inconsiderable sum in that Depression year.

Then the murder ring started glad-handing Mike Malloy, a derelict more accustomed to getting the bum's rush whenever he entered the speakeasy. Now, he was greeted like an old buddy. They gave him a back room to sleep in so that he would not have to freeze in some drafty hallway. By the way, did Mike think it was a good idea for Marino to run for office? Absolutely, Mike's life was soon insured for a total of $3,500 under a double-indemnity clause. The boys shrewdly figured they would not avail themselves of that provision but settle for $1,750, thus allaying suspicions.

At first, the four tried to get Malloy to drink himself to death, but the more he drank the more he seemed to thrive. Since that method appeared to offer only bankruptcy for Marino, they switched to giving Malloy some "new stuff" that had come in, actually automobile antifreeze, which of course was poisonous. After consuming some of the new stuff, Malloy commented that it was quite smooth. A couple of hours later, Mike collapsed on the speakeasy floor and they dragged him out back to let him expire in privacy. An hour later, a beaming—and thirsty—Malloy was back at the bar. Over the succeeding days the boys kept lacing his drinks with ever stronger doses of antifreeze and finally, in desperation, with turpentine. Malloy downed shot after shot and lived. Even when the four took to using diluted horse liniment laced with rat poison, nothing happened. They had to wonder what Malloy had been drinking all his life.

The boys decided nothing liquid would kill Malloy. They switched to food and started giving him raw oysters, tainted and soaked in wood alcohol. Malloy downed two dozen at once and gave the treat his approval. "Tony," he told Marino, "you oughta open up a restaurant, you know first-class food."

After several days of tainted oysters followed by rotten sardines, with which Malloy always requested some of that "new booze," the plotters were ready to throw caution to the wind. They got him drunk and then lugged him to Claremont Park, where they stripped off his coat, opened his shirt, poured a five-gallon can of water on him and dumped him in a snowbank.

The next day the boys scanned the newspapers for a report of a corpse being found in the park, but there was nothing. Pasqua, sneezing fiercely as a result of his battle with the elements while carrying Malloy to the park, was most upset. Finally, that evening Malloy appeared wearing a new suit. He explained he had really tied one on the previous night and wound up practically clothesless in the park. But it had all turned out well. The police had found him and had a welfare organization outfit him with new clothes before he was released to the world.

Truly desperate, the would-be murderers hired a criminal who was working as a cab driver to kill their seemingly indestructible victim. Once again, they got Malloy into a drunken stupor and then took him at 3 A.M. to the deserted intersection of Gun Hill Road and Baychester Avenue. They held him upright as the cab driver backed his taxi up and then roared forward at 45 miles per hour. At the last instant they jumped back leaving the weaving Malloy standing in the path of the oncoming cab. When struck by the vehicle, Mike catapulted into the air. To make absolutely sure that he had done the job right, the cabbie backed his taxi over Malloy's prone body.

This time their victim was surely dead. But nothing appeared in the newspapers. They visited the morgue looking for his body. No Malloy. They contacted the hospitals. No Malloy. In fact, Malloy didn't show up again for three weeks. When he did, he said he had been in the hospital after having a car accident. The hospital had listed him under the wrong name. Seeing how downcast his friends were, Mike assured them he was all right, that he had suffered a concussion of the brain and had a fractured shoulder. "But I'm all right," he said, "and I sure could use a drink."

At this point, the boys were beyond desperation. They even contacted a professional hit man about machine-gunning Malloy on the street. The explanation would be that he was a poor unfortunate caught in the crossfire of a gangland battle. Unfortunately, the hit man wanted $500 for the job and the boys were getting close to having a losing proposition on their hands as it was. The plan was abandoned. The four decided that only straightforward murder would work. They rented a furnished room for Malloy and, on February 22, 1933, ran a hose from a gas jet to his mouth and held it there until he stopped breathing.

Unfortunately for the killers, they had to get a corrupt doctor to sign a phony death certificate citing lobar pneumonia as the cause of death.

By now there were just too many people involved in the plot. A cab driver was complaining to friends that he had been hired to run down a guy and had been paid so little it failed to cover the cost of fixing the dents in his cab. A gunman told of losing out on a hit contract with some pikers. The police got wind of an insurance ring killing people in the Bronx and started checking around. They learned of an Irishman being buried within four hours of his death. And without a wake? That was unusual. They exhumed the body and started asking questions. Everybody started talking—the doctor, the cab driver, the hit man, even the undertaker. When accused, each of the four murderers tried to shift the blame to the remaining three. On various dates in June and July 1934, the four—Marino, Pasqua, Kriesberg and Murphy—died in the electric chair at Sing Sing, none of them nearly as well remembered as Indestructible Mike Malloy.

Mandame, Mary (c. 1639) Pilgrim sex offender
Mary Mandame of the Plymouth colony was the first American woman to be forced to wear a mark on her clothing for a sex offense. Specifically, she was charged in 1639 with "dallyance diverse tymes with Tinsin, an Indian" and "committing the act of uncleanse with him." Her punishment was to be whipped through the streets of Plymouth and thereafter to always wear a badge of shame on her left sleeve. Since Mary Mandame's name does not appear again in historical records, it would seem that she obeyed the terms of her punishment. Had she not, she would have been branded in the face with a hot iron. In 1658 the punishment given to Mary was extended to wives found guilty of committing adultery. This cruel punishment became the basis for Nathaniel Hawthorne's *The Scarlet Letter* (1850).

See also: COLONIAL PUNISHMENTS.

Mandelbaum, Fredericka "Marm" (1818–1894) fence
The most notorious fence, or receiver of stolen goods, in the 19th century was Fredericka Mandelbaum, better known to the underworld as Marm because of her often maternalistic attitude toward criminals. Indeed, the sobriquet Ma Crime, as she was called by the press, was well justified since,

unlike the fences of today who insulate themselves from the actual commission of crimes, she was an active plotter and bankroller of many of the great capers of the period.

It would be difficult to put a dollar value on the loot Marm handled in her three decades of activity, from 1854 to 1884, but it certainly was in the tens of millions. In fact, it could be said that Marm Mandelbaum, rather than the later-arriving Lucky Luciano and Meyer Lansky, first put crime in America on a syndicated basis. She angeled, or bossed, the operations of several gangs of bank robbers, blackmailers and confidence men, gave advanced courses in burglary and safe blowing and outdid Dickens' Fagin with a special school for teaching little boys and girls to be expert pickpockets and sneak thieves.

Fredericka came to America from her native Prussia in 1849 with her rather meek husband, Wolfe, whom she supposedly had induced to embezzle funds from his employer. Arriving in New York City, they bought a home and dry goods store at 79 Clinton Street in the teeming Kleine Deutschland section of Manhattan's East Side. Wolfe Mandelbaum would have been content to be an honest businessman, but Fredericka soon began dabbling in stolen goods, and by 1854 the store was nothing more than a front for her illegal operations. Soon, she required several warehouses in Manhattan and Brooklyn in which to keep her stolen articles and remove their labels, trademarks and other means of identification. She retained the famous criminal law firm of Howe and Hummel to keep herself and her growing legion of thieves out of serious trouble. Other flunkies handled her direct payments to the police.

Upon her arrival in New York, Fredericka weighed 150 pounds, a weight she was to double as she grew in stature, literally and figuratively, in the underworld. She had a sharply curved mouth, unusually fat cheeks, small, beady black eyes, bushy brows and a high, sloping forehead. She generally wore a tiny black bonnet with feathers over her mass of tightly rolled hair. Although far from a raving beauty, she was lovingly regarded by the underworld. One leading thief, Banjo Pete Emerson, was quoted as saying, "She was scheming and dishonest as the day is long, but she could be like an angel to the worst devil as long as he played square with her."

While she was undoubtedly the leading criminal in America during the latter part of the 19th century, Marm was—by her own standards—a lady. She was treated with respect by the ruffians with whom she dealt on a daily basis. Vile language was definitely not permissible. A party at the Widow Mandelbaum's—Wolfe died in 1874—was definitely the highlight of the underworld social season, and Marm was not above, or below, playing gracious hostess to the better half of town, whose homes and purses her thugs robbed regularly. Her parties were also attended by judges, police officials, politicians and the like. Marm, ever on the lookout for ways of improving the social life and mores of the underworld, judiciously mixed into these gatherings the best of the criminal lot. Thus, at the dinner table the wives of a judge and an important City Hall figure might well find themselves flanking someone like Mark Shinburn, a burglar of distinction and one of Marm's favorites. Shinburn, insisted that he was an aristocrat at heart and detested associating with crooks even for business reasons.

Marm took an intense interest in all her flock, constantly trying to improve them in mind and manners. When it came to

A dinner party at Marm Mandelbaum's was always a high point in the New York underworld's social life.

finances, however, she dropped any pretensions of being a lady and was as tightfisted as they came, seldom if ever granting a thief more than 10 percent of the value of any stolen article he sold her. Yet, after completion of a deal, Marm might turn right around and hand that same individual several hundred or thousand dollars for a needed operation or as a retirement kitty. It was Marm who counseled Shinburn to save his money, go back to Europe and live out his life in luxury. Buying himself a title with a portion of his loot, Shinburn became Baron Shindell of Monaco and lived aristocratically ever after.

Following the Civil War Draft Riots in New York, Marm was the biggest receiver of the goods looted, much of which she disposed of as far away as Chicago; fittingly enough, a good portion of the loot taken during the Chicago Fire a few years later ended up in Marm's New York warehouses.

Besides Shinburn and Emerson, some of the top criminals who worked at her beckon were George Leonidas Leslie, the King of the Bank Robbers; Sheeny Mike Kurtz, burglar extraordinary; Shang Draper, master of the panel game rackets; Ned Lyons; Johnny Dobbs; Jimmy Irving; and Bill Mosher and Joe Douglas, these last two the confessed kidnappers of little Charley Ross. There was no loot Marm could not handle, including stolen horses shipped in by the Loomis gang from upstate New York.

Marm became the queen mother of the leading lady crooks. There were Queen Liz and Big Mary, the top shoplifters of the day and instructors in one of Marm's schools for the underworld juniors; Black Lena Kleinschmidt, blackmailer, pickpocket and sneak thief; Sophie Lyons, wife of bank robber Ned Lyons and a renowned con lady; Old Mother Hubbard; Kid Glove Rose; Little Annie; and Ellen Clegg. Marm liked all these ladies because they shared her desire for respectability and because, above all, they recognized her as their social queen. Only Black Lena ever challenged Marm's position. It happened when Marm started courting the rich. Black Lena moved to Hackensack, N.J., posed as the wealthy widow of a South American mining engineer and began giving elaborate functions that rivaled Marm's.

Although the social columns of the day referred to Black Lena as the Queen of Hackensack, she continued to spend two days a week in New York working her illegal trade to replenish her coffers. She was finally dethroned when she wore an emerald ring that one of her dinner guests recognized as having been stolen from a friend's handbag. Marm read the news of Black Lena's arrest and exposure with pure delight. "It just goes to prove," Marm told the tittering ladies of her court, "that it takes brains to be a real lady."

Marm's own fall from grace came in 1884, a seemingly unlikely event considering the amount of protection money she paid the police. Her problem came in the form of one

Peter B. Olney—a sort of oddity for his day—a district attorney without a price. Convinced the police would never catch Marm, Olney turned to the Pinkertons. After four months of inten-sive work, one of the agents gained her confidence by posing as a thief. Soon after, thieves working with Marm stole a supply of silk from the store of James A. Hearn and Sons on 14th Street, but the bolts had been secretly marked by detectives. Later the same night a task force of Pinkertons smashed through the doors of Marm's house and found the stolen silk. But that was nothing compared to what else they found. As one reporter put it:

It did not seem possible that so much wealth could be assembled in one spot. There seemed to be enough clothes to supply an army. There were trunks filled with precious gems and silverware. Antique furniture was stacked against a wall and bars of gold from melted jewelry settings were stacked under the newspapers. There were scales of every description to weigh diamonds.

Marm, her son Julius and her clerk Herman Stroude were clapped behind bars. It was the first and only night Marm spent in jail. The following day she posted $21,000 bail and got her lawyer Bill Howe working on a fix so that she could continue operations. However, Tammany Hall was having problems with reformers and Marm was advised her day was over. She shrugged, gathered up what was believed to be $1 million in cash and fled. When she didn't show up for her trial, the newspapers berated the police for not keeping her under constant surveillance.

The Pinkertons were put back on the job and within a month they located her in Toronto, Canada, but under existing extradition laws, she could not be forced to return to the United States. She did come back twice, however. In disguise and weeping profusely, she turned up in 1890 for the funeral of her daughter in Kleine Deutschland. The local papers learned of it, but the police professed to be skeptical—until Marm was safely across the border again.

In 1894 Marm came back to New York for burial, dead at the age of 76. The newspapers reported that several of the mourners at the cemetery had their pockets picked.

See also: HOWE AND HUMMEL, GEORGE LEONIDAS LESLIE.

mattress girls   prostitutes

Almost from its founding, New Orleans became the sex capital of America and the mecca for countless traveling prostitutes seeking to make a living in the world's oldest profession. Competition was so intense and the houses so crowded that many prostitutes could not find lodgings and took to carrying a mattress on their heads, ready to set up for business in an alley or open field. Some of them branched out from New Orleans, trekking up the Mississippi or westward with their trusty mattresses on their heads. The call "Mattress girl a-comin'" often caused considerable excitement. In time, reform elements in various communities, including New Orleans, either drove such prostitutes away or into houses where it was felt they belonged, and a quaint, if demeaning, custom vanished from the scene.

Maxwell Street police station   Chicago's most corrupt precinct

When in the early 1920s Charles C. Fitzmorris, Chicago's chief of police, publicly stated,

"Sixty percent of my police are in the bootleg business," he was not referring to the Maxwell Street police precinct in the heart of Little Italy. There, the percentage was placed, according to a popular saying, at 110 percent, which was not a mathematical impossibility. Chicago's Little Italy at the time was the heart of the city's bootleg alcohol production and was for thousands of immigrant families a sort of cottage industry that earned them a rather fine living. This racket was controlled by the notorious Gennas, a family of five ruthless brothers. The Gennas induced Italian families to set up portable copper stills in their kitchens or the back rooms of their stores for extracting alcohol from corn sugar. In return, they received a set fee of $15 a day, far more than immigrants could make as simple laborers. Those families that refused usually changed their minds quickly when they received Black Hand threats. So pervasive was the "alky cooking" that all of Little Italy was enveloped in the stink of fermenting mash.

It was an activity that could hardly be kept secret from the police of the Maxwell Street precinct, a matter the Gennas easily handled with bribes. There was plenty of money available for police graft, since a home still could produce 350 gallons of raw alcohol a week for considerably less than $1 a gallon and the Gennas, after processing the alcohol further in their plant at 1022 Taylor Street, sold the product wholesale for $6 a gallon.

The Maxwell Street cops got their cut out of this huge gross, being paid $10 to $125 a month depending on their importance and length of service. There were regular payoffs to some 400 officers plus larger stipends for plainclothesmen, detectives attached to the state attorney's office and five police captains. All day on the monthly payday, police officers would troop in and out of the Taylor Street plant, many openly counting their graft on the street. The Gennas found they had to contend with a particularly venal form of police dishonesty, officers from other precincts showing up and pretending to be from the Maxwell Street station, hence the 110 percent figure. The local police brass solved this dilemma by furnishing the gang with a list of badge numbers to check all claims against. Because an occasional Genna truck would be seized by police in other parts of the city while making deliveries, the Maxwell Street precinct also supplied police escorts through such dangerous zones. The police tried to shut down those alky cookers not working for the Gennas but were generally put off when the independents insisted they were operating Genna stills. To solve that problem, the Gennas supplied the police with a complete list of their stills. Whenever a private operation was unearthed, the police would move in with axes and destroy it, often alerting the newspapers in advance so that the precinct's aggressive fight against crime would be publicized.

"Merrick, pulling a Dick"   saying for a lucky survival

In Missouri the saying "pulling a Dick Merrick" was more popular in the 1860s and 1870s than the expression "a Frank Merriwell finish" was in the 1920s and connoted an even more miraculous conclusion to a tight situation.

In 1864 Dick Merrick and Jebb Sharp were convicted and sentenced to hang in Jackson County for the robbery and murder of a horse trader named John Bascum. It was a period of no-nonsense treatment of murderers, and the execution was scheduled

to be held the day after the jury's verdict. Early that morning the condemned pair were rousted out of their jail beds and duly dispatched. On returning to the jail, Deputy Sheriff Clifford Stewart was stunned to find Merrick and Sharp sitting in their cell. It took a few hours for the sad truth to be uncovered. During the night two drunks had been heaved into a cell to sleep off their inebriation, and it was they who had been taken to the scaffold. Since the pair were still so boozed up, they were in no condition to protest, indeed to comprehend, what was being done to them. Quickly, the matter was rushed to the sentencing judge, who ruled that since the men had not been hanged at the prescribed time, they had to be released. Merrick and Sharp wasted no time raising dust on the trail, leaving behind only the folklore about "pulling a Dick Merrick."

Merrick, Suds (?–1884)   burglar and river pirate

For most of the 1860s and into the 1870s, Suds Merrick was one of the most-renowned river pirates in New York City. He was one of the coleaders of the Hook Gang, which plundered the East River docks and cargo boats moored there. The Hookers were at least 100 strong, and many of their crimes were masterminded by Merrick.

In 1874 Merrick, Sam McCracken, Johnny Gallagher and Tommy Bonner boarded the canal boat *Thomas H. Brick,* tied up the captain and set about looting the cargo at their leisure until they were surprised by police. Merrick escaped by diving overboard, but his three accomplices were captured and sentenced to long terms at Auburn Prison.

After the incident, Merrick fell into disfavor with the Hookers, who were suspicious about the affair. Some thought Merrick must have been in trouble with the law and set up the trio in exchange for his own freedom. Since there was no proof of this, he was simply allowed to resign from the gang. For the next 10 years Merrick operated as a lone wolf, carrying out numerous burglaries and muggings. He was ignored by the rest of the Hookers, and there is no record of other criminals attacking him, which indeed would have been a foolhardy enterprise since Merrick was virtually unbeatable in a fight at anything near even odds. He never ventured abroad without a knife and gun and generally wore brass knuckles or carried a blackjack up his sleeve. In 1884 he was found murdered in the Bowery. There were no clues as to who might have done the killing, and the police seemed singularly unconcerned about solving the case, considering the murder a definite civic improvement.

See also: HOOK GANG.

Metesky, George Peter (1903–1994)
New York's "Mad Bomber"

Starting in 1950, New York's mysterious Mad Bomber terrorized New York City for eight years, planting 32 homemade bombs in train stations and movie theaters, including Radio City Music Hall. The bombings injured 15 people and created a period of anxiety that was said to have hurt Manhattan's theater business as much as television did.

Actually, the Mad Bomber had gone through an earlier period of maniacal bombings in 1940–41, virtually all of them duds. Then a decade later, the Bomber started up again, this time more efficient in his production of explosives. The bombings were followed by notes that ranted about the local utility company, Consolidated Edison. He often signed these notes "Fair Play." Metesky set off bombs in Radio City Music Hall, Grand Central Station, Penn Station and several theaters. A train porter at Penn Station was permanently crippled by one of the bombs and seven persons suffered serious injuries from a blast in a theater.

The hunt for the Mad Bomber got nowhere for years until he wrote a letter to a newspaper in which he once more castigated Consolidated Edison and charged the company had caused him to contract tuberculosis. Finally, a close study of the firm's records turned up a former employee, George Peter Metesky, who in 1931 had had an accident working for the company and had previously made a claim of having developed tuberculosis on the job.

Metesky was taken into custody at his home in Waterbury, Conn. and accused of attempted murder. The assortment of charges against Metesky made him liable to a total of 1,235 years imprisonment, but he was found criminally insane and incarcerated in a mental hospital in New York state. Pronounced cured some 15 years later, Metesky was set free in 1973 and had the charges against him dropped. A bachelor in his seventies, Metesky went home to take care of his ailing sister and later rejected a marriage proposal from a pen pal.

Mickey Finn   knockout drink

Named after a Chicago barkeep, a Mickey Finn is a drink used to put a victim into a state of collapse so that he can be robbed. Mickey Finn did not originate the drink but bought the recipe of a secret voodoo mixture that could be added to alcohol and water.

Finn, who operated the Lone Star Saloon and Palm Garden on Chicago's notorious Whisky Row during the Gay Nineties, ordered his employees to give the drink to any lone customer. Two of the employees, Isabelle Ffyffe and Gold Tooth Mary Thornton, eventually testified before a special crime commission. Gold Tooth Mary, so named because her single tooth was crowned with the precious metal, explained the potency of the drink: "When the victims drink this dopey stuff, they get talkative, walk around in a restless manner, and then fall into a deep sleep, and you can't arouse them until the effect of the drug wears off." While so incapacitated, the victim would be lugged into the back room, where Finn, in an odd ritual, would be waiting in a derby hat and a clean white apron to "operate." The victim would be searched to the skin for valuables, and if articles of clothing were deemed to have any worth, they too would be taken. The victim would then be dressed in old rags and dumped in an alley. When he awoke, he seldom had any recollections of what had happened. Eventually, Finn lost his license and was put out of business. He thereupon sold his secret recipe to several other eager saloon keepers and use of Mickey Finns soon spread throughout the country.

Midnight Terrors   Gay Nineties New York gang

One of the most mindless, vicious street gangs in New York in the 1890s was the Midnight Terrors, named for their nocturnal muggings. Overflowing with self-esteem, the Terrors decided to form a baseball team. They raised money for uniforms and equipment in their home territory, the First Ward, by robbing and beating anyone who seemed likely to have money; as one of the Terrors said, "Dat's de way we was to get the uniforms for de ball club."

The Terrors enjoyed considerable freedom from a police department not eager for confrontations as long as they confined their depredations to their own area and to their "own kind." The Terrors, however, carried their actions to the public parks and even to their baseball games. Watching them was not the safest activity for a baseball fan, as some of the bench warmers would circulate in the crowd looking for potential mugging victims. The Terrors disappeared around the late 1890s, victims of their own crude operating methods, which resulted in their repression.

Miller, John (1829–1861) New Orleans criminal and jailer

One of the most colorful, if deadly, scourges of antebellum New Orleans was John Miller, a one-armed brute with a chain and iron ball attached to the stump that was left of his other arm. It proved to be a most effective weapon in his criminal endeavors.

Miller was born in Gretna, across the river from New Orleans, and became that community's principal ruffian. So far as can be determined, he never did an honest day's work in his life, making enough by venturing over into the French Quarter two or three times a week to fall on some unsuspecting visitor and make off with his purse.

In 1854 Miller branched into fight managing, taking under his wing a heavyweight named Charley Keys, who soon became the champion of the Gretna side of the Mississippi. He arranged a bout between Keys and Tom Murray, the so-called bruiser of Gallatin Street. Miller wagered a considerable sum on his man, who was soon being belted mercilessly by Murray. It became apparent that if the fight continued, Murray would surely win. Realizing this, Miller stuck a knife into Murray's chief backer. A general riot ensued, enabling Miller to keep his money but resulting in the loss of his left arm. After the riot he attached a chain and iron ball to the remaining stump of his left arm, and with a knife in his right hand, he was as fearsome an opponent as one could meet in the back alleys of the city. He proved this in 1857, when he killed a man in a fight. Since Miller was "disabled," he got only two years for this offense. If that struck the citizenry as unusual, it didn't compare to the stir caused by what happened to him when he completed his term in the parish prison. In an ironic turnabout arranged by the parish politicians of the day, Miller was kept on as a prison guard. While some claimed that there had been a genuine "reformation of his character," Miller's case was widely credited as a prime cause of the creation of the New Orleans Vigilance Committee for the purpose of "freeing the city of thugs, outlaws, assassins and murderers."

Miller left his position more or less voluntarily, having discovered there his true love, a prisoner named Mary Jane Jackson, better known in the vicious slums and dives of the city as Bricktop Jackson, who was also doing a stint for murder. When she was released, the couple repaired to a love nest in Freetown. A mean street fighter, Bricktop gave away nothing in a match with any of the tough bullies of Gallatin Street. While there is no absolute proof that she was the toughest female in the city, there is no doubt that as a couple Bricktop and Miller were unequaled in viciousness by any other husband-wife team in the city. A half-dozen Live Oak gangsters were known

to have backed off from a battle with Bricktop Jackson and Miller, swinging his iron ball.

In keeping with Miller's past history, there is no record of the couple ever supporting themselves honestly. They would strut through the French Quarter arm in arm, with many a man staring at Bricktop, who was a most attractive woman. Finally, Miller would leave her alone, and it was usually just a matter of moments before she would attract a male admirer. She and her new friend would then be seen departing for a destination unknown but reasonably deduced. When next seen, if ever, the gentleman involved would be sporting a very bruised head, not surprising considering the bruising potential of an iron ball.

The love of Bricktop Jackson and John Miller ended on December 5, 1861, when Miller came home with a cowhide whip and announced to the entire neighborhood that Bricktop was in need of a thorough thrashing. It soon became clear which of the pair was the toughest. Bricktop took the whip away from him and beat him unmercifully. Miller tried to brain her with his iron-ball, but she grabbed the chain in midair and pulled him around their living quarters. In desperation, Miller drew a knife and tried to slash her. Bricktop wrestled the knife free and, shoving him against the wall, stabbed her lover five times. Miller was dead when his body hit the floor.

The *New Orleans Picayune* commented, "Both were degraded beings, regular penitentiary birds, habitual drunkards, and unworthy of any further notice from honest people." Bricktop Jackson served nine months for the killing.

See also: MARY JANE "BRICKTOP" JACKSON.

Miner, Bill (1847–1913) stagecoach and train robber

Although he had one of the longest careers of any stagecoach and train robber, running from the 1860s until 1911, colorful Old Bill Miner seldom gets the recognition he deserves in histories of American crime. He was, so far as can be determined, the man who invented the phrase "Hands up!"—an Americanism as distinctive as the English road agent's order "Stand and deliver!"

At the age of 13 young Bill ran away from his Kentucky family, which his footloose father had abandoned a few years earlier, and went West to become a cowboy. He ended up in the California gold fields, but the only place he ever searched for gold was in the pokes he stole from sleeping miners. In 1863 he did a stint as an army dispatch rider and then set up his own business as a mail rider. Bill made good money carrying the mail but invariably spent more than he earned. By 1869 he had hit the outlaw trail (although he may have been at it as early as 1866), robbing a stagecoach near Sonora, Calif. of a few hundred dollars. Pursued by a posse, Bill was captured when his horse dropped dead in his tracks. He probably avoided being lynched only because he looked so young; prudently, he announced his age as 16.

Bill was sentenced to 15 years in San Quentin. Behind bars he became an avowed religionist and in 1879 the authorities released him early for good behavior. But instead of leading a saintly existence thereafter, Miner headed for Colorado and became a train robber. He and a hard case named Bill Leroy made a daring duo, notching up a long string of train and stagecoach holdups until Leroy was captured in a gun battle with vigilantes and strung up. Bill fought his way free in the same gunfight,

leaving three bullet-ridden possemen behind him. That brush with death had a sobering effect on Miner, who promptly made for San Francisco and from there to Europe, where he became a free-spending tourist on the proceeds of his Colorado crimes.

Miner actually plotted out some train robberies in England but wisely decided his American style would stand out too much and assure his apprehension. He bounced around the continent for a while and finally wound up in Turkey, where he joined up with desert bandits in the slave trade. When the law started looking for a light-haired American, Bill hightailed it for Africa, finding his way to South Africa. In Capetown he considered the idea of holding up a diamond train, a thought he abandoned, as he said in his memoirs, "when I saw they [the guards] would be too much for me."

The next stop was South America and a stint at gunrunning, but Miner hankered for the Western outlaw trail and by November 1881 he was back in business in California as a road agent, holding up the Sonora stage for $3,000. Pretty soon, Bill had posses on his trail again and fled to Colorado, where he pulled another holdup before returning to California to rob the Sonora stage once more, this time with a partner named Jimmy Crum. They were caught shortly thereafter and Miner was sent back to San Quentin under a 25-year sentence. He emerged from prison in 1901, again a reformed man determined to follow the Good Book. By 1903 he and two others were holding up trains in Oregon and Washington. With the law hot on his trail, Old Bill moved into Canada to continue his unlawful activities. He was finally arrested there after a train robbery and, at the age of 60, was put away for life. When he heard the sentence, Bill just smirked at the judge, declaring, "No jail can hold me, sir." He was right. A year later, in August 1907, Miller tunneled under the prison fence and escaped.

For the next four years Old Bill, now stoop-shouldered and white-haired, pulled off several bank and train jobs in Washington and Oregon. The Pinkertons sent out an alert for his apprehension, figuring he would be easy to catch since there weren't too many stoop-shouldered, white-haired old codgers robbing trains and banks. By February 1911 Bill had worked his way to White Sulphur, Ga., where he led a gang of four others in the holdup of the Southern Railroad Express. Even though he had put some 3,000 miles between that robbery and his previous job, Old Bill was identified and eventually run down in a Georgia swamp by a Pinkerton-led posse.

Once more, he received a life sentence, this time at the state penitentiary at Milledgeville, Ga. On three occasions in 1911–12, Old Bill escaped, but he was soon recaptured each time. When caught the last time, he was up to his waist in swamp water with bloodhounds baying at him, Bill confided to his captors, "Boys, I guess I'm getting too old for this sort of thing."

He returned to the prison and spent his final year and a half tending a flower garden and dictating his adventures to a detective who had come to admire the incorrigible old crook. One day he told a fellow prisoner he had a plan for getting out, but he died peacefully while asleep in his cell in late 1913.

Mock Duck (1878–1942) tong leader

Recognized as the greatest tong warrior ever to appear in any American Chinatown, Mock Duck became the top Chinese gangster

Although the meaning was lost on the white man, the flag of truce atop the On Leong Tong House on Mott Street signaled peace between the On Leongs and Mock Duck's Hip Sings.

in the nation, exerting power from New York to Boston and all the way to San Francisco. He led the upstart and relatively small Hip Sing Tong in their great battles against the On Leong Tong, the rich and powerful society that dominated Chinese rackets, especially opium, gambling and prostitution, until Mock Duck's appearance in New York City in 1900.

To wrest control of the rackets, the rotund, 22-year-old Mock Duck had to topple the near-legendary Tom Lee, who had cultivated a reputation as the unofficial mayor of Chinatown. Tom Lee was celebrated in the white press because of his massive payoffs not only to the police but to newspapermen as well. With no more than a handful of supporters, Mock Duck approached Tom Lee and blandly informed him that he desired half the revenues from all gambling and singsong girl (prostitute) operations, adding, "If this is not agreeable with your honorable self and that of your wonderous tong, we shall have to fight."

Tom Lee stared at Mock Duck for a long time, then laughed and walked on without saying a word to this upstart. By that evening all Chinatown was laughing over Mock Duck's impudence.

Mock Duck waited only 48 hours before demonstrating he was very serious about his demands. A fire started in an On Leong boardinghouse on Pell Street, killing two tong members. Tom Lee could not be absolutely sure this was the work of Mock Duck and his Hip Sings, but he could be certain of who was responsible for the next attack. An On Leong member walking on Doyers Street was set upon by a pair of Hip Sing *boo how doys,* or hatchet men. The next day his head was found in the gutter.

Tom Lee countered with orders to kill all Hip Sings, especially Mock Duck. What followed was an incredible series of survivals by Mock Duck that was to win him the nickname Clay Pigeon of Chinatown and to convince many Chinese that he was truly unkillable. Two On Leongs waylaid him late one night, jabbing daggers into his shoulders. Mock Duck lunged free, shot them both and ran back to the Hip Sing battle headquarters on Pell Street with the two knives still embedded in him.

In the next assault the On Leongs used guns. Mock Duck was walking out of Hip Sing headquarters when an On Leong gunman grazed his coat with one shot and hit him square in the midsection with another. Remarkably, Mock Duck escaped injury, as the bullet struck his belt buckle.

After these two attacks Mock Duck took to wearing a bulletproof vest made of chain mail. Now, he was a match for the *boo how doys.* Whenever he met three or four enemy hatchet men, he would go into a squat, clamp his eyes shut and start blazing away with two pistols. As a terror tactic, the routine was unbeatable. Mock Duck was not a very accurate shot, but that was the beauty of his tactic. If he had taken careful aim and fired, the *boo how doys* might have moved in on him without fear, figuring that with his poor marksmanship, he never would hit them. But with his eyes shut and both guns singing in mad tattoo, their fate was in the hands of luck. Invariably, they broke ranks before the unorthodox assault and fled. Indeed, the gods seemed to be on the side of Mock Duck. Despite his wild shooting—high, low and to the side—he almost always drew blood from his foes.

In desperation, Tom Lee placed a $1,000 bounty on Mock Duck's head and lesser sums, all the way down to $25, on the heads of lesser Hip Sings. This action set off a war among the Chinese the likes of which had never been waged in America. Mock Duck proved to be the better strategist. He formed an alliance with the Four Brothers, one of the oldest and most-respected family guilds in China. In America the family guilds had been undermined by the tong organizations, a fact that annoyed many members of the Four Brothers. After Mock Duck promised them renewed cultural power once the On Leongs were eliminated, the Four Brothers joined the battle.

Mock Duck added to his fighting power by importing two incredible *boo how doys* from San Francisco. One was Sing Dock, among the most fiendish killers the tong wars ever produced. The other was Yee Toy, a pasty-faced little executioner often called "the girl face." Many a hatchet man met his end because he did not regard the one with the effeminate features as much of a threat. It was estimated that Sing Dock and Yee Toy murdered close to 100 men in the tong wars. They followed Mock Duck unquestioningly. Yee Toy later killed Sing Dock in a private quarrel, only to be stabbed to death himself a year later by his best friend, who had been bribed by the On Leongs.

Mock Duck had other weapons in his arsenal. While Tom Lee had the police on his side, Mock Duck keenly realized that with New York in a spasm of reform, the crusading Rev. Charles Parkhurst made a better ally. He went to see Parkhurst and told him that as a decent Chinese trying to make an honest living, he was being persecuted by the gangsters of Chinatown. He described the terrible gambling dens and singsong girl houses. Parkhurst was enraged and forced the authorities to raid every address furnished by Mock Duck. One On Leong establishment after another on Pell and Doyers streets was hit. Mock Duck cunningly outmaneuvered Tom Lee by not giving Parkhurst information on the locations of On Leong establishments on Mott Street. Thus, Tom Lee realized he could not loose the police on Hip Sing places, for Mock Duck would then turn the white crusader on his Mott Street dens, which at the time were the On Leongs' prime source of income.

Tom Lee was totally outfoxed and finally solved his problems by going on an extended vacation. In 1906 a truce was arranged but it lasted only about a year, giving Mock Duck the opportunity to consolidate his power. Then he struck again. Tom Lee returned to try to rally the On Leongs but lost what remained of his influence after their decisive defeat during the great war of 1909–10.

Mock Duck was now the supreme power in Chinatown. However, occasional bad luck dogged him. In 1912 an On Leong hatchet man invaded a Hip Sing gambling house on Pell Street while Mock Duck was conducting tong business in the basement. Two plain-clothes police detectives walking by a short while later heard the sounds of shooting.

Rushing into the basement, the officers found Mock Duck sitting at a table reading a Chinese pamphlet on the origins of feudalism. Another Chinese stood nearby with his hands up his sleeves. A third sat at the table opposite Mock Duck with his head slightly bowed, as if in deep thought. Mock Duck allowed he had heard some shots but said he had just entered the place by the back door. The second Chinaman was equally evasive. The officers turned to the third man but he wouldn't talk either—he couldn't, having expired with a bullet in his heart.

The police couldn't prove that Mock Duck had killed the On Leong warrior but they were able to pin something on him. In his pockets they found a mass of slips of paper with Chinese characters on them and proved in court that these were policy slips.

Mock Duck was convicted and served two years in Sing Sing. When he came out, the invigorated On Leongs struck with full fury. Numerous attacks on Mock Duck failed. The police arrested him on several occasions and he was accused of murder a dozen times, but the charges were always dropped for lack of evidence. In 1918 Mock Duck disappeared, leading to conflicting reports that he had retired from the rackets or that he had been murdered. Both stories were proved erroneous when he reappeared in 1921, announcing a new peace in Chinatown. He did the same thing in 1924 and 1928.

It was clear that Mock Duck's enemies, within Chinatown and without, could not depose him. Finally, however, in 1932, U.S. officials, together with representatives of the Chinese government, prevailed upon him to make peace. By that time Mock Duck was ready to retire, satisfied that the affairs of Chinatown had become so institutionalized that his followers could no longer be overthrown.

Mock Duck left Chinatown, taking up residence in a lavish home in a remote section of Brooklyn. Until his death in 1942, he returned to Chinatown once a week to visit a relative who ran an importing firm on Pell Street. He arrived in a chauffeured limousine, which waited with motor running while Mock Duck joined his kin in partaking of tea and dried octopus flakes. Always, about 10 young Hip Sing stalwarts stood guard outside until he left. The protection was not necessary, however, for even the On Leongs had long realized that Mock Duck was indestructible.

See also: BLOODY ANGLE, TONG WARS.

Molasses Gang 19th-century New York hoodlums

The Molasses Gang, composed of relatively small-time thugs, operated in New York City for a half-dozen years starting in 1871 and are best remembered for their comic behavior. Captained by Jimmy Dunnigan, they never rose beyond the level of sneak thieves and till-tappers who victimized small store owners. After several members of the gang entered a store, one would remove his soft hat and ask for it to be filled with sorghum molasses. The explanation would be that it was a bet on how much the hat would hold. When the hat was filled, the thugs would clap it on the proprietor's head and pull it down over his eyes, practically blinding him. While the proprietor wrestled with that sticky problem, the gang would leisurely loot the establishment.

Other gangs regarded the Molasses Gang as flaky and undependable men, who might just walk away in the middle of an important caper if they thought of something more entertaining to do. By 1877 the law had had enough of the gang's outrageous behavior and clapped the last of them in jail.

Monk, Maria (1817–1849) anti-Catholic hoaxer

One of the most infamous impostors of her time, a young girl named Maria Monk became a rallying point in the 1830s for American Protestants against what was regarded as the evils of popery, fanning emotions that were later exploited fully by the Know-Nothings. Maria arrived in New York in January 1836 in the company of a Canadian clergyman, the Rev. W. K. Hoyt, who told all who cared to listen that he had saved her from a life of sin in the famous Hotel Dieu nunnery in Montreal. More likely, Rev. Hoyt had, as Maria was to admit in moments of candor, met her following a street corner solicitation.

The pair had with them the first draft of what they claimed was Maria's memoirs of her years as a novice and nun at the Hotel Dieu. When published under the title of *The Awful Disclosures of Maria Monk*, it was to say the least most shocking in its charges. According to Maria, the remote cellars of the nunnery were strewn with the bones of nuns who had resisted the advances of amorous priests. She said the sisters were called upon nightly by priests from a nearby monastery, who ventured through subterranean passages to conduct their amorous and abusive exercises. Maria had a tiny tot with her whose origin she traced to these nocturnal visits from the neighboring clergyman. A later investigation by Canadian authorities turned up rather convincing evidence that the gentleman who had fathered the child—though not in the nunnery—was a Montreal policeman.

Maria and Hoyt found as sponsors for the book the Society for the Diffusion of Christian Knowledge, especially its president, Dr. W. C. Brownlee, pastor of the Collegiate Dutch Reformed Church and himself the author of a militant anti-Catholic best-seller, *Popery*. Dr. Brownlee thought so highly of this supposed refugee from a nunnery that he took her into his own house under the care of his wife, leading in time to complaints by the Rev. Mr. Hoyt that Maria was a "damned jilting jade."

By that time Maria was worth fighting over; her book sold an astonishing 20,000 copies almost immediately. Anti-Papists could delight in a variety of chilling charges; for example, one nun's punishment for some minor infraction was to be stretched out on a mattress

with her face upwards, and then bound with cords so that she could not move. In an instant, another bed [mattress] was thrown upon her. One of the priests, named Bonin, sprang like a fury first upon it with all his force. He was speedily followed by the nuns until there were as many on the bed as could

find room, and all did what they could do, not only to smother, but to bruise her. Some stood and jumped upon the poor girl with their feet: and others, in different ways, seemed to seek how they might beat the breath out of her body. After the lapse of fifteen or twenty minutes, Father Bonin and the nuns ceased to trample on her and stepped from the bed. They then began to laugh. . . .

Maria assured her readers "speedy death can be no great clamity to those who lead the lives of nuns," and she offered to visit the Hotel Dieu "with some impartial ladies and gentlemen, that they may compare my account with the interior parts of the building, and if they do not find my description true, then discard me as an impostor."

Her challenge was not taken up, but in time even firm believers in Maria developed doubts. Maria's mother in Montreal denied that her wastrel daughter had ever entered a nunnery. Moreover, she insisted that she had been visited in 1835 by the Rev. Mr. Hoyt, who offered her $500 to say such were the facts. Eventually, Dr. Brownlee concluded he had been hoodwinked; not only did the girl's story appear contradictory but she had also run off in the meantime with his young clergyman protege, John J. L. Slocum. In 1836 Slocum brought suit against the publishers of the book for Maria' share of the royalties, all of which had been appropriated by the Society for the Diffusion of Christian Knowledge. The resulting trial clearly demonstrated Maria's story to be a hoax.

This, however, did not stop Maria. In August 1837 she turned up at the house of a Dr. Sleigh, a Philadelphia clergyman, and told a tale of being kidnapped by a group of priests and held captive in a nearby convent. She had escaped, she said, by promising one of the priests that she would marry him. The result of all this was, of course, a sequel to her first book, *Further Disclosures of Maria Monk*.

The second publication also did rather well, but Maria evidently saw little of the financial rewards. Slocum persuaded her to sign over to him a number of rights to both publications and he then decamped for London to arrange for their foreign publication.

Maria's life plunged downward. She became a habitue of the dives of the Bowery, a drunken hag before she was 30. She was confined in jail for picking a man's pocket in 1849 and died that year at the age of 32, although her true identity went unnoticed for some time. But *The Awful Disclosures of Maria Monk* has outlived her. To date, well over 300,000 copies have been sold.

Monsieur New York (c. 1822–?) hangman

The most famous American executioner of the mid-19th century was "Monsieur New York," that state's official hangman, whose true identity was a closely guarded secret. For years newspapers referred to him by that nickname or a more prosaic one, George. He was considered a master of his craft, and one of the few executioners of the era who could dispatch a condemned person with a minimum of disconcerting suffering, prolonged strangling or, the most embarrassing of circumstances, unwarranted decapitation.

Monsieur New York got his start in the profession in the early 1850s, when he approached the sheriff of New York and offered to carry out the hanging of a black convicted of murder. At the time, he was about 30 years old and a butcher's assistant at the Washington Market. He had read about and sought to emulate Jack Ketch, the renowned high executioner of Great Britain. Because the previous hangman had abruptly walked away from the job, a not uncommon occurrence, since few could cope with the public attitudes and comments once they were identified, George's offer was accepted. The job was his, subject of course to a demonstration of his efficiency.

Observers described the execution as a "beautiful job" and George was named a deputy sheriff, although only a handful of officials knew his real identity. As he performed further commendable jobs, his fame spread and Monsieur New York was soon in demand in many parts of the country. His standard fee was $100 per execution plus all expenses, which often included a carpenter's charge for constructing the proper gallows and the price of a sound rope. Newspapers in communities he visited somberly informed their readers that "his daily visits to the slaughter-house had made him familiar with the use of the windlass to the perfection of an application for the humane accommodation of the law-breaking community."

Even the army made use of Monsieur New York's unsurpassed abilities, calling on him in 1861 to execute one Capt. Beale, a Confederate officer charged with nefarious activities, and a Capt. Kennedy, a Union officer who had burned down a hotel in New York. Like many artists, Monsieur New York had a temperament and in 1869, in a moment of pique, refused to do any hangings for the current sheriff. As a result, the *Police Gazette* reported, "the departure of John Real was sadly bungled." Needless to say, the sheriff placated his star hangman shortly thereafter.

Possibly because of rivalry, neighboring New Jersey for a time refused to avail themselves of Monsieur New York's services. During this period one Bridget O'Brien was scheduled to die in New Brunswick for the murder of her mistress. While the master hangman was professionally ignored, he was extended the courtesy of an invitation to the hanging.

"Boys, that Jerseyman will make a mess of the job," was his immediate comment when he viewed the gallows; disaster loomed, he warned.

"What are you trying to do, you damned fool!" he cried out in dismay when he saw how the Jersey hangman was handling the rope. "Then," one account of the event stated, "unable to restrain himself, the scientific strangler pushed his way through the crowd and saw to it that Bridget was sent out of this vale of tears in as laudable style as conditions would permit and the hand of an artist could assure."

In the 1880s, Monsieur New York's last decade of service, a newspaper revealed he lived with his family in a house near the East River in the vicinity of 125th Street and that he was a member of the Methodist Church. The neighborhood was rife with speculation about his identity and many a family man, determined to lay to rest any suspicions about himself, made it a point to be seen on a street in his neighborhood whenever an execution was taking place downtown. To the end, the identity of Monsieur New York remained a secret.

Mooners   moon-affected criminals
An official publication of the New York City Police Department reads: "Mooner. A mentally disturbed person who is activated during a full moon."

It is neither a novel nor a new belief. Sir William Blackstone, the great British jurist,

was the first to define the mooner theory in legal terms.

A man who is a lunatic or non compos mentis is one who hath understanding, but by disease, grief or other accident, hath lost the use of his reason. A lunatic is indeed properly one that hath lucid intervals, sometimes enjoying his senses and sometimes not, and that frequently depending upon the change of the moon.

And backing up these two authoritative views is the experience of numerous cops on the beat who believe that a full moon spells trouble for them. At the time of the full moon, it invariably seems that more screwballs and more drunks are abroad, more family quarrels erupt and more false fire alarms are sounded. Veteran newspapermen claim that during the full moon a higher percentage of crackpots turns up in city rooms with tips of zany stories. A survey made in Connecticut showed that during the period of the full moon some types of crimes increased by as much as 200 percent. Violent robberies rose about 100 percent and breaking and entering went up some 78 percent. Drunk cases doubled and fatal accidents quintupled.

Arsonists are notoriously affected by the full moon. Some years ago investigators for the National Board of Fire Underwriters solved a mysterious string of fires in a Pennsylvania town by tracking the cycle of the moon. Explaining the firebug's capture, the investigators remarked, "The majority of the fires set by this man falls within the full-moon cycle, and his apprehension was brought about by surveillance based on the theory that the person responsible for the fires would set another during the next full moon."

This country's classic moon murderer was DeWitt Clinton Cook, who by the age of

20 had committed 300 burglaries and numerous attacks on women in California. During Cook's crime rampage a leading expert on abnormal behavior, police psychiatrist Dr. J. Paul de River, warned the authorities they were dealing with a mooner whose "attacks on women will continue every month until he is caught." On February 24, 1939, the night of a full moon, Cook killed Anya Soseyeva, a pretty young drama student at Los Angeles City College. He was not captured until a moon burglary in August. When Cook was caught, Dr. de River diagnosed him as "a nocturnal prowler who likes to wander in lonely places at night."

While more and more evidence accummulates indicating that "moon madness" may be a genuine affliction, jurors are not prepared to hand down insanity verdicts on such ground. Cook went to the gas chamber, and the Pennsylvania arsonist, a 24-year-old fireman, was sentenced to 30 to 60 years.

Moore, Flossie (1866–?) female mugger

Described by a police biographer as "the most notorious female bandit and footpad that ever operated in Chicago," Flossie Moore, a black woman, appeared in the Levee and other vice districts in Chicago in the late 1880s and soon was making much more money than any of her male counterparts. She openly declared that a holdup woman in Chicago had to make at least $20,000 a year or be a disgrace to the profession. Flossie did considerably better than that, earning $125,000 from late 1889 to mid-March 1893, when she was sent to Joliet Prison for five years for a particularly vicious mugging of an elderly farmer who had been visiting the city.

Flossie considered herself the black queen of crime in Chicago and got extremely jealous when her rival for that crown, a strong-arm woman named Emma Ford, made a bigger score. Often, the next man down the street had to pay for that. As befitting a crime queen, Flossie always carried a huge roll of bills in the bosom of her dress and another in a stocking, sported a white lover named Handsome Harry Gray, to whom she gave an allowance of $25 a day, an astonishing figure for the era, and appeared at balls staged by brothel keepers in gowns costing $500 and more. To handle her legal problems, she paid a lawyer $125 a month, but the man had to work for his money. Flossie was arrested as often as 10 times in a single day, and in one year alone she was scheduled for trial in criminal court three dozen times. Once when fined $100, she laughed at the judge and said: "Make it two hundred. I got money to burn!"

When she was sent to Joliet in 1893, Flossie quickly proved to be the most uncontrollable woman ever imprisoned there, twice almost killing a matron and serving a good portion of her sentence in solitary confinement. Flossie Moore returned to Chicago after serving her sentence but soon complained she was a marked woman, constantly watched by the police. About 1900 she left Chicago for New York; thereafter, no more is known of her.

Moore, Lester (?–?) mystery subject of epitaph

Lester is a real question mark. Did he ever live? More importantly, did he ever die? No devotee of graveyard humor is unfamiliar with the inscription on Lester's tombstone in the Boot Hill Cemetery at Tombstone, Ariz. It reads:

Here lies
Lester Moore
Four slugs
From a forty-four
No Les
No More

According to one story, a Wells Fargo guard was responsible for sending Lester to his poetic reward, but there seems to be no written record of that fact. Western historian Denis McLoughlin destroys a humorous, if morbid, bit of Americana by suggesting that no one is buried there, pointing out, "The aroma of the prankster emanates from this plot of ground; no date of death accompanies the verse, and had the latter originated during Tombstone's lead-swapping period, '*four* balls *from a .44*' would have been apt for the time."

Morton, Samuel J. "Nails" (?–1924) Chicago mob gunman

Nails Morton was a top gun in the Dion O'Banion gang, which from 1920 to 1924, the year of O'Banion's death, fought the Italian mobsters even. Morton was held in awe by other Chicago mobsters because in World War I he had won the Croix de Guerre in France and received a battlefield promotion to first lieutenant.

Morton was an inventive sort of killer, but he was to become more noteworthy because of the way he died and the act of revenge that followed. Nails was fond of horseback riding in Lincoln Park, "where the society swells ride." One day, in what the mob considered vicious treachery, a horse threw him and kicked him to death. The O'Banion gang took the required vengeance. Four of them, Bugs Moran, Schemer Drucci, Little Hymie Weiss and Two Gun Alterie, went to the riding stable and, with drawn guns, snatched

the animal. After leading it to the spot where Morton had been killed, the animal was dispatched, in proper underworld style, with four slugs in the head, the incident later forming the basis for an episode in Mario Puzo's *The Godfather.*

Municipal Brothel San Francisco bordello

The nearest thing to a governmental whorehouse in America was San Francisco's infamous Municipal Brothel in the early part of the 20th century. Because it soon became common knowledge that virtually all of the profits of the establishment flowed into the pockets of city officials and their political sponsors, the famous house, officially known just as 620 Jackson Street, soon won its more recognizable name. Saloon keepers and other businessmen who sought political favor advertised the brothel to customers. When strangers in town asked policemen where women could be found, they were obligingly directed to it; an officer who failed in that assigned task could count on being transferred to a less favorable beat. The house was a regular stop for Jackson Street trolleys, and if no ladies were aboard, the conductors shouted, "All out for the whorehouse!"

The brothel was first opened in 1904 as a three-story affair with some 90 cubicles. Recruitment of women was the duty of Billy Finnegan, a veteran character in San Francisco vice. He rented out space at a daily rate ranging from $2 to $5 per crib with a guarantee of immunity from arrest. After the place was destroyed by the earthquake and fire of 1906, a four-story and basement structure containing 133 cribs and a saloon was erected in its place. The prices varied according to floor and the beauty of the individual women. The basement was given over to

Mexican harlots, who charged 25¢. The first, second and third floors were occupied mostly by American and French women, with the prices rising from 50¢ to 75¢ and up, to $1 on the third floor, which was populated exclusively by what customers were assured were "genuine Frenchies." The fourth floor was given over to black prostitutes at 50¢.

Not only were the inmates protected from arrest under the political rule of Boss Abe Ruef and his puppet mayor, Eugene Schmitz, but most other brothels in the immediate area were shuttered to guarantee a good return for the political figures. Testimony before a grand jury in December 1906 established that Herbert Schmitz, the mayor's brother, owned a one-quarter interest in the brothel and that, despite their denials, both the mayor and Ruef took a cut of the profits, in Ruef's case $250 a week. The indictment of Mayor Schmitz, Boss Ruef and several members of the Board of Supervisors, whom Ruef himself described as "being so greedy for plunder that they'd eat the paint off a house," led to the fall of the administration in 1907. None of the indictments in the case was acted upon, although Ruef eventually went to prison for bribery.

Despite the wave of reform that hit San Francisco, the brothel continued to operate for a time, but from early 1907 it was subjected to many police raids, under pressure from a grand jury and the newspapers. The pervasiveness of the bribery involved was indicated by the fact that at first the harlots were simply driven off rather than arrested. When they finally were arrested, they were permitted to post small bonds, which they promptly forfeited. In September 1907 Chief of Police William J. Biggy visited the resort personally and ordered it closed when he found it swarming with boys as young as 14

years of age. The following year Chief Biggy crossed San Francisco Bay in a police launch to attend a conference. Later, he reembarked and was never seen alive again. His body was found floating in the bay a week later.

With Biggy's death, efforts were made to reopen the brothel but they were soon abandoned because of the opposition of a crusading priest, Father Terence Caraher, the *San Francisco Globe* and the new chief of police, Jesse B. Cook, formerly an acrobat and tumbler with the troupe of Renaldo, Cook and Orr.

Murder Stable early Mafia burial site

The accidental discovery of the infamous Murder Stable in New York City in 1901 drove home to Americans that there was a "Mafia" or a "Black Hand," or at least some kind of organized gang of Italian criminals.

In the spring of 1901 the U.S. Secret Service began investigating rumors of an anarchist plot to kill President William McKinley. Among those asked to aid in the investigation was a New York police detective named Joseph Petrosino, who would become legendary for his battles with the Mafia and with various Black Handers. Petrosino reported there was no organized conspiracy but there was much talk among anarchists of an individual possibly attempting such an assassination. McKinley was killed by such an "independent," Leon Czolgosz, in Buffalo, N.Y. some three months later. During the course of the investigation, Petrosino and the Secret Service had stumbled onto the so-called Murder Stable, a property located in Italian Harlem at 323 East 107th Street. Digging up the premises, they found the remains of approximately 60 murder victims. The property was owned by one Ignazio Saietta, better known in Italian crime circles as Lupo the Wolf. When it became apparent the victims had been killed as part of an effort to consolidate Italian control of the waterfront, the Secret Service dropped out of the investigation. It was left to local officials to contain Lupo and the notorious Morello gang he worked with. Lupo successfully insisted he was just the landlord and knew nothing, and he remained an awesome figure in the New York crime scene for another two decades.

Murieta, Joaquin (c. 1830–1853 or 1878)
bandit

The greatest desperado of the early gold rush days in California may have been the Mexican-born Joaquin Murieta, or Murrieta or Muriati. There is considerable confusion about his last name and indeed even over whether such a person existed, notwithstanding the fact that his pickled head was later brought in by California Rangers.

The Murieta legend seems to be a mixture of fact and folklore. The most likely version is that Murieta was born about 1830 of Spanish parents near Alamos, Mexico and studied in the Jesuit school there. He took up arms in a revolt against the Mexican government by many of his native Sonorans as well as Mayo and Yaqui Indians. In 1848 Murieta, now married, joined thousands of Sonorans on a trek to California to escape their war-ravaged province.

Murieta apparently turned to crime after seeing the way the Americans, who had won California in the Mexican War, treated his countrymen. After supposedly being run off a number of gold claims, he vowed

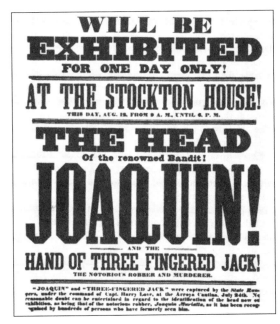

Joaquin Murieta was a major attraction both in life and after his apparent death.

vengeance, organized a gang of cutthroats and outlaws and cut a swatch of terror through California. In 1853 the state legislature established the California Rangers and commissioned them to bring in not one but five "Joaquins": Joaquin Ocomorenia, Joaquin Valenzuela, Joacquin Botellier, Joaquin Carrillo and Joaquin Murieta. The Rangers, under Capt. Harry Love, set forth on their mission, inspired by the $1,000 reward posted for Murieta's capture. Love and his men did have an encounter with Manuel "Three-Fingered Jack" Garcia and killed him and another unidentified Mexican. The more Love contemplated this second man the more he reckoned he was the notorious Joaquin. Garcia's mutilated hand and "Joaquin's" decapitated head were placed in jars of preserving fluid and transported to San Francisco.

Although newspapermen were skeptical of the claim, the governor was impressed and paid out the reward. After that, the head of Joaquin and the hand of Garcia went on tour around the country. Murieta's head was on display until it was destroyed in the San Francisco earthquake of 1906.

Of course, the Mexicans of California never acknowledged that the head was that of the celebrated Joaquin. They said he escaped his pursuers and eventually settled down to a life of farming in Sonora, where he died in 1878. To the Mexicans his looting and killing of Americans were not acts of banditry but of active warfare against a foreign invader. In the barrios of California, Murieta is still referred to as *el Patrio,* or the Patriot, perhaps on the assumption that if he had not existed, he should have.

Natchez-under-the-Hill Mississippi
vice center

One of the most crime-ridden river ports of 19th century America, Natchez-under-the-Hill was separated from the tamer part of the city, which was located on a high bluff. Because of this separation, the under-the-hill district was not subject to the same type of reform movements that had swept the better part of town in previous years. Simply stated, there was "no reason for decent folks to go down to that hell." Providing the coarse rivermen with whatever they wanted and could pay for, lower Natchez shocked the few decent visitors who ventured into it. One John Bradbury said in 1810, "For the size of it there is not perhaps in the world a more profligate place." Another described it as "the safest place in America to kill another human being with no threat of retribution." Gamblers and prostitutes always did a thriving business, with as many as 150 flatboats and keelboats tying up there on an average day in 1808. Baby girls were said to have been born in certain whorehouses and grown up there to become working prostitutes by the age of 12.

Some of these unfortunate girls reportedly never even saw upper Natchez, knowing no more of the world than the rough rivermen who stormed ashore each day.

Among the most famous citizens of Natchez-under-the-Hill were a tavern owner named Jim Girty and his paramour, Marie Dufour, the leading madam of the town. Girty was regarded by rivermen as unkillable, having survived a number of gun and knife fights. Legend had it that Girty's chest was not ribbed but solid bone that deflected pistol ball or blade. Marie Dufour was also known for her prowess in battle. She invariably won wrestling contests with rivermen, the loser taking a traditional dunking in the Mississippi. Despite her ruggedness, Marie was also known for her womanly charms and ran *the* high-class house of prostitution in Natchez. The couple came to a tragic end when Girty proved not completely unkillable, being shot down from ambush after a gambling dispute. Marie Dufour rushed to his side and, finding him dead, committed suicide by shooting herself in the mouth.

In 1835 vigilantes tried to clean up lower Natchez, driving off and killing a number of gamblers, while many of the prostitutes escaped with the rivermen aboard their flatboats. However, immediately after each raid the gamblers and the harlots set up business again. Such occasional forays by the outraged citizens were not likely to drive out criminal elements when vice could make its organizers rich in just a year or two. Some prostitutes who knew how to save money soon had enough to buy themselves a flatboat and sail down to New Orleans in comfort, where they would set up a floating bordello and, perhaps in due course, open a lavish house in the French Quarter.

Natchez-under-the-Hill continued in its violent ways until the Civil War, but the decline of the steamboat cut off its lifeblood, and it gradually became just another prosaic and dreary river port with no more than legends to remind visitors of its tawdry past.

Nelson Tombstone   libelous epitaph

When H. Lawrence Nelson of Raleigh, N.C. was killed in 1906, his friends and relatives had inscribed on his tombstone: "H. LAWRENCE NELSON, born Dec. 16, 1880. Murdered and robbed by Hamp Kendall, Sept. 25, 1906."

Indeed, a farmer named Hamp Kendall had been convicted of the crime and sentenced to life imprisonment. However, 11 years later, in 1917, Kendall was pardoned; the real murderer had confessed. Then began the great Battle of Nelson's Tombstone. Kendall petitioned the courts to have the offending tombstone altered, but the courts said they had no jurisdiction. County officials declined to take action, pointing to a state law that made it a felony to tamper

with a tombstone. The Board of Deacons of the church that owned the graveyard property also insisted they had no power to act. Kendall then appealed to the governor, stating, "No man can stand under the scandal of this tombstone in the town where he is making an honest living." He was informed that it was not a state matter and had to be handled by county or city authorities. After years of trying, Kendall finally succeeded in convincing the legislature to pass a law declaring illegal "any tombstone which charges anyone with a crime." In 1950 the accusing inscription was removed, clearing Kendall's name 33 years after he was pardoned for the crime.

New Orleans procuresses

Even in cities that openly allowed prostitution in the 19th century, the crime of procuring was frowned upon even by the corrupt police who took bribes from brothel owners. Many officers in such wide-open cities as Cincinnati and Chicago never thought twice about breaking up a procuring ring preying on young innocents. The exception to this rule was post–Civil War New Orleans, where the procuring trade was largely in the hands of women who seemed to have little or no trouble with the law despite the particularly unsavory character of their profession, giving rise to the term "New Orleans procuresses."

The activities of the procuresses went back a long time in the city's history, but they received little public attention until 1845, when it was revealed that Mary Thompson was doing a thriving business selling virgins out of a cigar store blind on Royal Street. She sold these inexperienced girls for sums of $200 to $400, depending on their looks. In March 1845 she became friendly with 15-year-old Mary Fozatte and gave her presents of clothes, toy jewelry and candy. Then she sold the girl to an elderly gentleman for $350. As she was taking her merchandise to a house on Burgundy Street, young Mary broke away and ran home. Most indignant, the procuress charged the girl with stealing. The case against her was dropped, however, and in turn, she was awarded $50 damages. The police, as one writer put it, "told Mary Thompson that if she tried to sell another girl she might be punished."

In the post–Civil War era the procuresses were kept busy supplying girls for houses of prostitution in several cities besides New Orleans: Atlanta, Memphis, Galveston and a number of other southern cities. They took orders for "stock" and "fresh stock," which meant inexperienced children worth very high fees. In the late 1860s a schoolteacher-procuress, Louisa Murphy, had a set price of $800 for a young girl.

By the 1880s the procuresses operated with increasing boldness. Such notables as Miss Carol, Mother Mansfield, Spanish Agnes, Emma Johnson and Nellie Haley, called the Queen of the Procuresses, sent out mail circulars of their stock. By that time the competition was so fierce that the price for virgins sometimes dropped as low as $50.

Spanish Agnes got into only minor difficulties when in 1890 police discovered she had sold the owners of a Galveston brothel two girls who had been reported missing by their parents. In a newspaper interview, Agnes said:

> I frequently receive orders from the keepers of fashionable places. These ladies ask me to send them girls, or women for that matter. I always prefer to have experienced women than virtuous girls, because there is less fear of trouble. I am in correspondence with women like Molly Waters and Abbie Allen of Galve-ston; these people write to me for girls. Some time ago I received an order from Miss Abbie Allen to send her some girls, and soon after Miss Lena Smith informed me that she could secure two nice young girls. . . . I do not like to have anything to do with innocent girls . . . . Not a very long time ago a mother brought her three daughters to me and offered them for sale. Two, she said, were bad, and the youngest still unacquainted with vice and the wickedness of the world. She demanded $25 for the girls, and expressed her belief that she ought to get more for the guileless maiden.

The procuress added she bought all three girls and realized a substantial profit.

In 1892 a newspaper reporter doing an exposé on the work of procuresses approached Emma Johnson about buying a 15-year-old girl, then demurred at making the actual purchase. The Johnson woman was incensed: "You're a fool! The girl's a virgin! You'll never get another chance like this in New Orleans!"

There was no record of Emma Johnson coming to grief because of the revelations, and in fact, the New Orleans procuresses continued to prosper until 1917, when Storyville and much of the brothel operations in New Orleans were shut down by the military as a wartime health measure.

New York fire of 1835   looting spree

The New York Fire of December 16–17, 1835 produced an orgy of looting as well as the saying, "I'm a firefighter and well-to-do, thank you."

The fire started in a five-story building on Merchant Street in the fledgling financial district. By the time the alarm was sounded at 9 A.M. on the morning of December 16, it had already spread to surrounding buildings. Most of the city's 49 engines and six hook-

and-ladder units responded, but because of the weather they faced a brutal task. The temperature was 17° below zero, and hydrants had frozen solid, while the engine pumps froze over with ice unless constantly heated. The ice covering the river was broken through and bucket brigades formed, but these efforts were unavailing. By 11 P.M. the fire had swept into Water and Pearl streets and Exchange Place, the home of the stock exchange at the time. Within another hour 13 acres of Manhattan were ablaze, and the glow could be seen as far away as Philadelphia.

By the early morning hours of December 17, the tenement dwellers and criminals of the Bowery and the Five Points had descended on the scene and engaged in incredible looting. While Marines from the Navy Yard dynamited buildings to form firebreaks around the financial district, many of the firefighters joined the looters and were seen carrying goods out of burning shops and disappearing. Looters made off with hoards of clothing, jewelry and furniture, which had been heaped in the street without adequate guards. Thugs set afire those buildings that weren't already burning to cover their criminal activities. A group of irate citizens caught one thug as he was firing a store on Broad Street and hanged him from a tree. It was three days before harried police got around to cutting down the frozen body.

The fire was finally contained at the end of the second day, but by that time much of New York was in ruins. Almost 700 buildings were gutted and losses, estimated at $22 million, bankrupted most insurance companies and were credited with bringing on the Panic of 1837.

During the week following the blaze, the police staged numerous raids on the hovels of the poor and criminal classes of the Bowery and Five Points districts, repossessing huge amounts of loot. Moving vans were required to handle the booty in several individual buildings. No raids, however, were made on the homes of firefighters, although Fire Chief Handsome Jim Gulick was dismissed for failing to curb the spreading of the fire or the illegal activities of many of his men. However, when the firefighters threatened to go on strike, the fire-panicked city reinstated him. In the Bowery and Five Points a bitter greeting came into vogue: "I'm a firefighter and well-to-do, thank you."

Nineteenth Street Gang   pro-Catholic
New York gang

In the 1870s a pack of juvenile criminals, whose members continued in the gang until they reached their mid-twenties, terrorized New York City's Poverty Lane, the area from 19th to 34th Streets around Second Avenue. The leader of this band, called the 19th Street Gang, was an incredibly mean punk named Little Mike. What made this gang of pickpockets, sneak thieves and muggers unique was its unswerving religious affiliation. Violently pro-Catholic, it often attacked Protestant missions and schools. But the gang's main purpose was stealing and its members victimized cripples, blind men and children as well as storekeepers. The only defense against these attacks was for a potential victim to prove he was Catholic. Thus, a man being waylaid might be asked to give his baptismal name, recite his catechism, name his parish priest or reveal his Easter duty. Even this was not always a complete defense. As Little Mike is quoted as having said to one victim: "You're a good Catholic all right, but we haven't made a score in a long time. We're taking half your money." Happily for the public, the gang faded away by the mid-1880s.

nobles   labor musclemen

During the heyday of union organizing, especially in the needle and allied garment industry trades, it became common for both fledgling unions and employers to hire thugs to win their battles. Employers used goons to guard strikebreakers, slug union pickets and raid union meetings; the labor unions used them to blackjack and murder strikebreakers and pressure those workers who did not wish to join the union. Yet even these thugs had some loyalty, and although they seldom let their feelings interfere with business, they basically considered themselves in sympathy with the workers.

During this period a group of workers in New York haunted the employment agencies of the Bowery and Sixth Avenue looking for work as strikebreakers, since the pay for such efforts was much higher than normal wages. Ironically, the thugs assigned to protect these strikebreakers held them in such ill repute that they referred to them as "finks." They, on the other hand, considered themselves so superior, despite their evil work, that they called themselves "nobles."

These nobles so preferred practicing their art on behalf of the unions, which generally paid better than the employers, many of whom were penny pinchers, that from 1913 to 1915 they engaged in open warfare among themselves for the right. This conflict came to be known as the Labor Sluggers War.

See also: LABOR SLUGGERS WAR.

O'Connor, "Terrible Tommy" (1886–?)
escaped murderer

Although the electric chair became the mode of execution in Illinois in 1928, the scaffold it replaced remains stored in a basement room of the Chicago Criminal Courts Building, available for a final hanging should an escaped murderer ever be caught. His name is Terrible Tommy O'Connor, a convicted murderer who in 1921 escaped custody just four days before his scheduled execution by feigning illness and, while being taken to the prison medical office, pulling a gun that apparently had been smuggled to him. Since then the authorities have been required by a court order to retain the gallows until the gangster's fate has been definitely determined.

For a time after his escape Terrible Tommy probably received more newspaper coverage than any other gangster except Al Capone. Speeches bemoaning his escape were made in the U.S. Senate and there were serious proposals that the army be used to hunt him down, but despite the uproar, Tommy was never caught. Through the years newspapers have run feature stories on the manhunt and on the rope that still awaits O'Connor. If he is still alive and if he is ever caught, Terrible Tommy's advanced age (he would be over 100) and the Supreme Court's ban on executions ordered before 1972 make his hanging rather unlikely.

According to a stipulation made by the Illinois legislature at the time the electric chair was adopted, the gallows will one day be removed from its storage room and set up in the galleries of the Chicago Historical Society. But before it could become an exhibit of grim things long past, the death of Terrible Tommy had to be a certainty. The law remained bound to enforce the court's sentence: "You shall hang by the neck until you are dead." Finally it was decided that the exhibit no longer needed to be put on hold.

Old Brewery   tenement of death

No other building in America, perhaps the world, had as many murders committed within its walls—a police estimated average of one killing a day for 15 years, or well over

Probably more murders were committed within the walls of the Old Brewery, a five-story tenement that had windows on only three floors, than in any other building in the United States.

5,000—as a 19th-century New York tenement called the Old Brewery. Built in 1792 as Coulter's Brewery in the old Five Points section of lower Manhattan, it produced a beer famous throughout the eastern states. Condemned for use as a brewery in 1837, it was transformed into a filthy tenement of 100 rooms, housing at least 1,000 persons. The building was five stories in height but only three floors had windows; many rooms had no windows and received neither sunlight nor fresh air. Some children born there literally did not see the outside world until their early teens.

In this nightmare existence, men, women and children committed murder and were, in turn, murdered, their bodies often left to rot or buried under the floors or in the walls. The occupants were divided about equally between blacks and immigrant Irish. All the basement rooms were occupied by blacks, many of whom had white wives, while the Irish tended to populate the upper floors. On the first floor was a large room called the

Den of Thieves, where more than 75 men, women and children, black and white, lived without furnishings of any kind or any conveniences. Many of the women were prostitutes who entertained their customers there, at least the brave ones who risked entry.

Throughout the upper floors ran a long corridor, aptly called Murderers Alley, that led off to the individual rooms. In the 1850s, 26 people dwelled in one room no more than 15 feet square. In this room a little girl was once foolish enough to show a penny she had begged and was promptly stabbed to death, her body shoved in a corner for five days until her mother dug a shallow grave in which to bury her. In 1850 an investigator discovered not one of the occupants had been outside the room for a week, although some had stood in the doorway waiting to attack a more fortunate dweller passing through the alley with food.

Throughout the Old Brewery every imaginable criminal roamed—thieves, pickpockets, whores, murderers. Twenty-four hours a day there were fierce fistfights and drunken orgies; screams of luckless victims and cries of starving children; and men, women and even children writhing on the floor with delirium tremens.

While the police knew murder was common and that many wanted criminals hid out in the Old Brewery, they seldom entered its vile confines; when they did, they went in groups of 40 or 50. If only five or six policemen entered together, they knew they might never emerge alive. More than likely, they would be murdered and every stitch of clothing stripped from their bodies.

Just as the police could not enter safely in small groups, the building's residents could not leave safely in daylight hours, unless they took some underground tunnels that snaked out through the Five Points. So greatly were these residents hated and feared that a denizen leaving the Old Brewery in daylight would be pelted with brickbats thrown by pedestrians determined to drive him or her back inside. Many of the inhabitants of the Old Brewery had previously been persons of some importance. It was said that the last of the Blennerhassetts, the second son of Harman Blennerhassett, who had joined Aaron Burr in the great conspiracy to establish a Western dictatorship, vanished into the Old Brewery never to be seen again. He and other persons of some consequence soon sank to the level of the rest of the residents, living and dying amidst the violence, insanity and sexual promiscuity that were accepted facts of life within the Old Brewery.

Occasionally, missionaries tried to alter conditions in the Old Brewery, but being mostly Protestant, they were driven away by the Irish inhabitants who considered them heathens. Finally, the Missionary Society, with money from a fund drive headed by Daniel Drew, succeeded in buying the building for $16,000; the city contributed $1,000 toward the purchase. In December 1852 the society asked the police to drive the inhabitants out so that the building could be razed in preparation for the construction of a mission house. The police had to fight many battles at close quarters to clear out the residents and gangsters, and at least 20 wanted murderers fell into their net. Children, never having seen the light of day, blinked in terror when brought outside. As the building was ripped down, laborers carried out several sacks filled with human bones that they had found inside the walls, beneath the floorboards and in the cellars.

Although the destruction of such buildings was hardly a solution to the problem of city slums, the Old Brewery was beyond redemption.

See also: FIVE POINTS.

O'Leary, Big Jim (c. 1860–1926)
Chicago gambler

Jim O'Leary, the son of the Mrs. O'Leary of cow and Chicago Fire fame, grew up to be one of the city's most prominent gamblers and a millionaire. He started out as a handyman for the bookmaking syndicates, quickly learned the ropes and soon made a try at operating a gambling resort of his own. Its blueprints called for stockades, barbed-wire fences, alarm boxes, lookout posts for armed sentries, cages for ferocious watchdogs and a whole network of tunnels. Situated in Long Beach, Ind., 23 miles from the center of Chicago, the ambitious resort failed to draw the crowds O'Leary hoped for and it folded.

O'Leary moved back to the Windy City and opened a gambling house on South Halsted Street near the stockyards. He then set up a string of bookie operations and poolrooms. Big Jim, as he became known because of his stature in the business, fostered the idea of a floating gaming resort. He outfitted the steamboat *City of Traverse* as the first vessel in American history strictly devoted to gambling. Each afternoon about 1,000 horse players came aboard for a leisurely sail on Lake Michigan and remained out on the lake until all the day's races were run. Results were flashed to the boat by wireless. The police finally grounded the *City of Traverse* by arresting passengers as they disembarked and by scrambling the wireless messages giving the odds and results of the races.

O'Leary returned to his South Halsted Street house determined to make it the premier gambling resort in the country. It certainly became one of the most lavish, complete with a restaurant, a Turkish bath, bowling alleys and a billiard room. But its main attraction was the horse parlor, outfitted with plush couches and chairs, servants to provide refreshments and charts showing the odds and results of every race in the United States and Canada. Action was also taken on every other kind of sporting event as well as on elections and even the weather. Big Jim once won a $10,000 bet that there would be 18 days of rain during the month of May.

What was amazing about O'Leary was that he prospered without the usual payoffs to the police. He once was quoted by a newspaper reporter as saying: "I could have had all kinds of it, [protection] but let me tell you something. Protection that you purchase ain't worth an honest man's dime. The police is for sale, but I don't want none of them." His South Halsted Street resort boasted massive iron-bound oaken doors layered over with zinc and were, as Big Jim put it, "fireproof, bombproof and police-proof." During the gamblers' war of 1907, the doors held against bombs from rival operators. At times the police did breech the doors with sledgehammers and axes and even arrested some of O'Leary's bookies and customers, but usually the reward for their efforts was hilariously anticlimactic. Once they found the grand betting parlor devoid of furniture save for a kitchen table at which an old man was sitting reading a prayer book. When the police took to axing through his inner walls looking for hidden rooms and exits, Big Jim countered by loading the walls with red pepper. When the police axes penetrated the wall's zinc covering, they were so blinded by the pepper that several required long hospital treatment for inflamed eyes. When Big Jim O'Leary died in 1926, he was a millionaire

several times over and perhaps as famous in Chicago as the family cow.

Orgen, Jacob "Little Augie" (1894–1927)
gang leader and killer

Jacob "Little Augie" Orgen was one of the last big-time independent gangsters to fall victim to the national crime syndicate. When Little Augie was assassinated in 1927, his union racketeering in New York's garment district was taken over by the notorious Louis Lepke. Lepke refined the racket into a smoother and more professional operation and gave it syndicate support, cutting in such Italian gangsters as Tommy Lucchese, Lucky Luciano, Joe Adonis and Albert Anastasia and such non-Italians as Meyer Lansky and Bugsy Siegel. Little Augie had failed to appreciate such grandiose schemes, a shortsightedness that may well have proved to be the death of him.

Jacob Orgen was the son of highly religious Jewish parents, whom he shamed by becoming a labor slugger for Dopey Benny Fein shortly before the outbreak of World War I. Dopey Benny, the top labor racketeer of his day, carried out sluggings and murders both for unions seeking to recruit new members and terrorize strikebreakers and for employers attempting to intimidate workers and introduce strikebreakers. By 1915 effective police action had put Dopey Benny out of business, and for about four years thereafter, the labor slugging racket almost ceased. During that period of tranquility Little Augie returned to the bosom of his family and was accepted as a reformed sinner.

In 1919 Orgen, tired of leading an honest life, organized a gang called the Little Augies. At that time, labor slugging, which had recently resurfaced, and extortion of employers were controlled by the premier New York gangster of the day, Kid Dropper, who had attained his success after a savage war that culminated in the assassination of another leading mobster and killer, Johnny Spanish. Kid Dropper was notorious for not sharing any of his income and for leaving only scraps for the Little Augies of his entourage.

Augie learned the virtue of patience, slowly gathering around him some of the future big-name criminals of the era. Among those who flocked to his banner were Jack "Legs" Diamond, Gurrah Shapiro and Louis Lepke. By 1923 the Little Augies initiated open warfare with the Droppers, fighting vicious gun battles with them to control the wet wash laundry workers and, later, other groups of employees. In strength, firepower and reputation, Kid Dropper seemed invincible, but Orgen finally emerged victorious after convincing an unimportant and gullible hood named Louis Kushner that he could become a leading member of the gang by killing the Dropper. Kid Dropper, then in police custody for a minor charge, was being transferred by car from one court to another when Kushner walked up to the vehicle and shot Dropper through the windshield.

Little Augie and his lieutenants were arrested for the murder, but Kushner insisted he had done the whole thing on his own and proudly went off to prison for 20 years. Augie immediately took over the union slugging racket. However, after assuming power, he was constantly harassed by the police. Moreover, the racket was becoming less lucrative, as more sophisticated union leaders moved away from using such brash violence to achieve their goals. Lepke, who had gauged this decline, strongly urged Little Augie to move from working for unions and employers to seizing control of locals, milk-

ing their treasuries and exacting tribute from employers who wished to avoid strikes or operate nonunion shops.

Lepke saw the potential for untold riches in this method of operation, but Little Augie was moving more into bootlegging and was even thinking of retiring within a few years, with the hope that he could again win favor with his parents and family. He gave Lepke strict orders to stay away from union rackets and stick to bootlegging. Augie probably saw little reason to fear Lepke as long as he had the murderous Legs Diamond as a trusted bodyguard, but in October 1927 he was murdered as he was walking on Norfolk Street with Diamond at his side. It is to this day unclear whether Lepke was behind the murder or whether it was the work of bootlegging rivals.

Little Augie was buried in a satin-lined red coffin bearing a silver plate that read:

JACOB ORGEN
Age 25 Years

Actually, the gangster was 33 years old, but his father had considered him dead since 1919, the year he organized the Little Augies.

See also: KID DROPPER, LABOR SLUGGERS WAR.

Oriental Saloon and Gambling House

Tombstone, Arizona Territory was long known as the nastiest mining town the frontier ever saw, and in Tombstone the place to go for drinking, fighting and shooting was the Oriental Saloon Gambling House. One Western chronicler estimated that "200 men held their last drink, poker hand or conversation in and around the Oriental's precincts before being carted off to a resting place in

Tombstone's Boot Hill, their corpses filled with various bullet and buckshot holes." While it might be difficult to verify such an estimate, there is no doubt that the Oriental was the site of some of the West's most memorable, if pointless, gun duels. A case in point was the time Johnny Ringo invited Louis Hancock to have a drink with him. "All right," Hancock said, "I'll have a beer." Whereupon Ringo replied: "No man drinks beer with me. I don't like beer." It was teeth-gritting time. "Well," Hancock said, "I like beer." And Ringo responded, "I don't." Hancock faced Ringo menacingly. "Barman," he said, "I'll have a beer." The two went for their guns and Hancock lost. They buried the loser holding a bottle of beer. Some historians have questioned that last touch, but Westerners liked their anecdotes tidy and the ending provided a nice conversation piece for the Oriental.

The Oriental's history began when Jim Vizina set up for business in a canvas tent with two wagonloads of whiskey. He later erected a building, which he eventually rented to Mike Joyce, who gave the Oriental a lavishness seldom found in Western saloons. The main gambling hall and bar were decorated sumptuously and a piano was hauled all the way from Denver through blazing heat, storms, flash floods and Apache country.

After being shot in the arm by Doc Holliday, Joyce sold out to a sharp operator named Lou Rickabaugh, who then gave Wyatt Earp a one-quarter interest in the Oriental. This was not as unselfish an act as it seemed. Once the deal was struck, Rickabaugh did not have to worry about getting shot up by Earp's friend Holliday or about providing security for the Oriental, which came under Earp's protection. The barman

was a skilled gunslinger named Buckskin Frank Leslie. Two other proficient gunmen, Bat Masterson and Luke Short, ran gambling tables, and the Earp brothers and Holliday were often on the scene.

Clara Brown, a famous reporter of the era, visited Tombstone in 1880 to describe it from a woman's point of view. She called the town a hellhole but she was ecstatic about the Oriental. She wrote: "The Oriental is simply gorgeous. The mahogany bar is a marvel of beauty, the gaming rooms carpeted with Brussels, brilliantly lighted and furnished with the latest reading matter and fine writing materials for its patrons. Every evening there is the music of a violin and a piano, and the scene is most gay." Clearly, she was happy to find one haven amidst the wretchedness of Tombstone. The very day after Miss Brown left, the entertainment at the Oriental picked up. Rog King called Johnny Wilson a liar, as they stood at the bar, and emphasized his point by putting a .45 slug through Wilson's forehead.

The Oriental was such a prize money-maker it required firepower to keep it. In an attempt to seize control of the establishment, Johnny Tyler sent one of his ace gunslingers, Charlie Storms, to the Oriental for the express purpose of getting into a shoot-out. Storms picked on Luke Short, a little man but one of the West's deadliest duelists. They stopped outside where Storms announced, "I'll give you the first shot." That was just what Short had in mind, having already emptied his holster as Storms was uttering his offer. He fired three shots and then stepped over Storms' body on his way back into the Oriental to resume dealing faro. Shortly thereafter, Tyler learned of Earp's interest in the Oriental and backed off from further efforts to take over.

The Earps and Doc Holliday left Tombstone shortly after the gunfight at the O.K. Corral. Contrary to common belief today, it was not a voluntary departure, especially since it meant giving up the Oriental, but they were given strong hints to "git" and they got. The day of the vigilantes had not yet passed.

When the silver ran out, the Oriental died along with the town. The population of Tombstone dropped from 15,000 to a few hundred and the deserted saloon was stripped clean.

Outlaw Exterminators, Inc. western bounty hunters

Five hard-riding, fast-shooting bounty hunters, dubbed Outlaw Exterminators, Inc. by the press because they never brought 'em back alive, contributed greatly to clearing the Arizona Territory of badmen in the 1870s and 1880s.

Clay Calhoun and Floyd Davis were deputy sheriffs, but the other three members of the group were part-timers—Ben Slack and Dick Hunter, cattlemen, and Fred Beeber, a bartender—who laid aside their mundane jobs whenever the prospects of a nice reward thundered across the mesa. Since rewards at the time were paid on a "dead or alive" basis, the Exterminators decided "dead" was easier and just as profitable.

The band's prize catch was probably bad John Allman, so-called Cavalry Killer who went on an orgy of murder in the Arizona Territory in 1877. When Clay Calhoun brought in Allman, the body contained four bullet holes: one in the groin, stomach, chest and mouth. The holes were in such a perfect line that Calhoun's story about a shoot-out was almost certainly a fabrication. More likely, the bounty hunter had killed Allman while the outlaw was asleep. But like the dozen-odd other victims of the Exterminators, Allman was not exactly popular and nobody worried much about such details. Despite numerous gunfights and the fact that they made a lot of enemies, the Exterminators lived out full lives, the last survivor, Clay Calhoun, dying on November 21, 1948, at the age of 97.

Parks, Robert F. (1910–1950) alleged murder victim

Police files are filled with examples of attempts to make murders seem like accidents, but there also have been cases in which accidents have appeared to be murders, resulting in the near conviction of innocent persons. The death of Robert F. Parks in 1950 is often cited by criminologists as a case in point. On the night of February 13 police in Luray, Va. were summoned to the Parks home, where they found Parks, a former army captain, dead in a bedroom, an open door of which led to the dining room. He had been shot, and because of the absence of powder burns and the direction in which the bullet had entered his body, it appeared that Parks couldn't have shot himself. A bullet had gone through his right arm, passed through his heart and halted in his right side. In the dining room the police found an automatic pistol lying against the far wall from the bedroom door. A cartridge case had jammed in the gun.

Given the circumstantial evidence, the tale Mrs. Parks told was not very convincing. "I was in the kitchen," she said, "when I heard the shot. I ran to the bedroom and Bob was standing there. He looked at me and said, 'Honey, the gun backfired.' And then he fell."

Because the statement didn't square with deductions the police had made about the shooting and because evidence was found that the couple had had violent arguments on a number of occasions, Mrs. Parks was charged with murdering her husband. In all likelihood, the case would have been handled as a typical domestic quarrel leading to homicide had not a sharpeyed policeman noticed a fresh dent on a metal grille over a hot-air duct in the doorway between the two rooms. The brown paint on the grille had been chipped, and there was brown paint on the rear of the gun slide.

The police sent everything—gun, bullet, cartridge case and grille—to the FBI laboratory. There, experiments showed that the gun would go off if it was dropped on the rear part of the slide and hammer if that part of the gun hit against something. The brown paint on the grille and the gun slide proved to be identical, and the indentations in the grille could have been made by the rear sight and knurling of the hammer. When scientists fitted the rear sight and hammer into the markings on the grille, it was obvious that in the Parks home the gun would be pointing in the direction of the bedroom where Parks had been standing.

The truth was now apparent. Parks had managed to kill himself accidentally. In an apparent fit of temper, he had thrown the gun against the grille and it had fired, hitting Parks. The gun had then dropped to the floor and slid across the dining room, coming to rest against the far wall from the bedroom.

The murder charge against Mrs. Parks was dismissed.

Parrot pimp

For some 25 years around the end of the 19th century, Carrie Watson's brothel at 441 South Clark in Chicago was famed for its beautiful inmates, its luxurious trappings and its high prices. So renowned was the resort that Carrie Watson never had a need to advertise. There were no red curtains on the windows and certainly no red light over the doorway. However, Miss Watson did feel a need to add a touch of homey distinction to her premises, so she placed an expensive trained parrot in a cage outside the door. This hustler, who soon was dubbed the Parrot Pimp, would beckon: "Carrie Watson. Come in, gentlemen."

parsley racket   underworld extortion method

One of the underworld's fastest growing, if little-known, rackets is the parsley shakedown. For years in New York many Manhattan restaurants have been forced to buy mob parsley to use as a garnish for their meals. In addition to serving it with meats and salads, they have been under considerable pressure to put it in some mixed drinks as well.

As the price was jacked up from 5¢ to 40¢ a bunch, some restaurateurs found their parsley tab amounting to $150 a month. In the early 1980s a number of restaurant owners hit on a money-saving tactic. Since most diners simply shoved aside the greenery, they ordered busboys to put the parsley aside, and then it was washed for reuse.

This affront to good health and the Mafia caused considerable anguish to a 75-year-old mafioso known to New York restaurateurs as *Un Occhio,* or One Eye, a name given him because of an injury suffered back in 1934 in the bombing of an East Side bakery. *Un Occhio,* who handled both parsley and murders for the mob out of his East Harlem headquarters, walked into a few restaurants and expressed outrage at this disgraceful recycling of parsley. On the spot one steak house owner ordered 150 new bunches. *New York Daily News* columnist Jimmy Breslin commented, "That night, as they will forever, the steak house and all other midtown restaurants served meals that appeared to be growing lawns."

There has never been much doubt that New York's fondness for parsley will eventually spread around the country. At the same time the mob squashed the parsley rebellion in Manhattan, the Montana State Crime Control Commission was investigating the bombings of two restaurants in Butte. The commission reported it had intelligence that a New York "parsley king" was involved in the bombings.

Un Occhio is reported to control vast acres of parsley in Ventura County, Calif.

that can be cut five times a year, enough to feed not only New York but a green-hungry nation.

Patterson, Nan (1882–?) accused murderer

The 1904 case, one the New York newspapers dubbed The Girl in the Hansom Cab, had everything the readers of the new yellow journalism could want: a Floradora Girl, at the time the most dazzling of Broadway figures; a big-spending gambler and race horse owner; a jealous wife, and a murder mystery.

Gorgeous Nan Patterson was a Floradora Girl, not a member of the original sextette but a replacement for one who had married a millionaire. All Floradora Girls, the public believed, were destined to marry millionaires. Nan, a doll-faced, stagestruck young thing, had made it to the Great White Way after eloping in her teens. She later fell for, instead of a millionaire, a married gambler, Francis Thomas Young, known to his friends as Caesar. Young, who was what might be called a cad, and Nan were constantly seen together at the races, at gambling spas and at all the top hotels and restaurants. However, Young also had a wife, whom he wouldn't or couldn't give up. He kept his wife in one New York hotel and Nan in another on the same block. It made the gambler's life a hectic one. He paid for Nan's divorce, and in 1904 he finally decided to divorce his wife and run off with Nan. But his wife talked him out of that plan and the couple reconciled. Feeling she could win back her husband from Nan by separating them, she convinced Young to sail to Europe with her on June 4.

The day before his departure, Young spent his time with Nan Patterson. The pair drank heavily and quarreled, Nan still trying to get him to change his mind. Early the following morning, they had a make-up breakfast and entered a hansom cab for a ride down Broadway. Suddenly, there was the sound of an explosion inside the cab. Nan was heard to cry out: "Look at me, Frank. Why did you do it?"

What Nan Patterson claimed Young had done was shoot himself in the chest, out of anguish over having to leave her. It was a peculiar story in that, as newspaper sketches would explain to their eager readers, Young would have had to have been a contortionist to have inflicted the wound that had killed him. In addition, somehow the dying man had managed to put the gun back in his pocket.

Nan was arrested for murder. The state's version was that she had pulled out a gun, and when Young grabbed it, she had pulled the trigger. During two sensational trials Nan took the stand and stuck to her story despite vigorous cross-examination. In neither case could the prosecution get better than a hung jury, and speculation arose that the state simply would never be able to get a jury of 12 men to visualize a smoking pistol in such a lovely woman's hand. The district attorney's office tried a third time, with the same predictable result. In her prison cell Nan was deluged with messages of sympathy and not a few offers of marriage. It was all too much for the authorities. Ten days after the third trial, the judge granted a motion that she be discharged, and a crowd of 2,000 persons cheered her as she was released. Children sang in the streets:

Nan is free, Nan is free,
She escaped the electric chair,
Now that she's out in the open air.

That night Nan Patterson got gloriously drunk at one plush Broadway spot after another. She soon was offered starring roles in top musicals, but her career collapsed when theatergoers discovered she had no acting or other talent. Nan then reconciled with her ex-husband and they remarried. However, the union again soon ended in divorce, and The Girl in the Hansom Cab just faded away.

Perry, Oliver Curtis (1864–1930) train robber
Train robbery was often thought of as a western crime, but probably the greatest train robber of all practiced his art in the East. His name was Oliver Curtis Perry and he was described by the *New York World* as "one of the most spectacular train robbers the country has ever known." The accolade was well-deserved. Perry was a former Wyoming cowboy who had come east to make his dishonest fortune. In a series of incredible one-man capers, he displayed a daring never equaled by any other train robber.

Perry, who claimed to be a descendant of Oliver Hazard Perry, the hero of the Battle of Lake Erie in 1812, committed his first train robbery on September 29, 1891. With a small saw, he cut out a square in the wooden end of the express car of the New York Central's Fast Flyer No. 31 out of Albany and crawled through a pile of packages to overpower the messenger inside. After tying up the messenger, he broke open the safe and took $5,000 in cash and $3,000 in jewelry. Then, hanging by one hand, sawed through the air hose between the express car and the adjoining car, bringing the crack train to a halt. Perry jumped down and fled into the nearby woods, making good his escape.

Pinkerton detectives learned the identity of the robber when he turned up in Rochester spending too much money in saloons and whorehouses and dropping boastful hints. Knowing Perry's identity and catching him, however, were two different matters. The Pinkertons just missed catching him after each of two more robberies he pulled.

Perry's wildest train robbery took place near Lyons, N.Y. in 1892, a spectacular attempt that even Hollywood would have rejected as too far-fetched. Having learned that a New York Central train departing Syracuse on September 20 would contain $100,000, he somehow got on top of the icy roof of the train's express car during the height of a hailstorm, slid down a rope and kicked in a side window. Firing a shot over the head of the messenger in the car, he jumped through the window. In a savage fight Perry pistol-whipped the messenger into unconsciousness, but not before his victim managed to pull the bell rope. The bandit worked feverishly at cracking open the safe until he was interrupted by an investigating conductor. Perry fired a shot at the conductor and fled, stopping just long enough to rifle the unconscious messenger's pockets and empty the petty cash box.

Flinging open the door, he jumped out of the train, which had ground to a stop near Jordan, N.Y. He intimidated the crew and passengers with several more shots and ordered the train to move, warning that otherwise he would shoot to kill. The train picked up speed and headed for Lyons, N.Y. When it got there, a 50-man posse was formed to return to Jordan and hunt for the train robber. Just as the posse was about to leave on a special train, the conductor who had interrupted Perry in the express car spotted him moving briskly through the station.

A newspaper sketch illustrates one of Oliver
Curtis Perry's most spectacular train robberies

After he had ordered the train to pull out in
Jordan, Perry had hopped aboard the last car
and pretended to be a passenger. But for the
conductor noticing him, he would have made
good his escape in Lyons.

Perry wasn't through yet. He raced
through the train yards, with the posse after
him, and jumped aboard a freight engine
already moving out under a full head of
steam. He forced the engineer and fireman to
jump and took off with the throttle wide
open. His pursuers mounted a faster engine
on a parallel set of tracks and gave chase,
quickly closing ground on him. As they

neared several members of the posse opened
up with pistols and shotguns. Perry threw his
engine in reverse and headed in the opposite
direction. As the two engines passed each
other, Perry exchanged shots with the posse
men, who then put their engine in reverse.
Again the two cars met, with more shots
exchanged. Perry's engine and that of his pursuers flew back and forth through the train
yards, bullets filling the air. Finally, the steam
supply in Perry's locomotive dropped and he
was forced to make a run for the woods.

The posse chased Perry into the swamps.
He probably still would have escaped had
not another posse under Wayne County
Deputy Sheriff Jeremiah Collins cut him off.
Interviewed by a reporter after his capture,
Perry said, "I had to take a bold stroke with
big chances and I guess I lost."

He was sentenced to 49 years in Auburn
Prison. Even following his confinement the
press continued to fawn over him, quoting
Pinkertons Superintendent George Bangs'
description of the Lyons caper as "the most
daring train robbery attempt in criminal history. I would call Perry the nerviest outlaw I
ever heard of. There are few western badmen
who possessed his courage."

In prison, Perry was deluged by mail from
women, including many proposals of marriage. One even sent him a saw hidden inside
a Bible. After causing a number of disturbances, he was removed to the State Hospital
for the Criminally Insane at Matteawan. In
1895 Perry received another saw hidden in a
Bible from the young lady who had sent him
the same type of gift while he was in Auburn.
He sawed through the bars of his cell and,
after releasing a number of other prisoners,
slid down 80 feet of drainpipe to freedom.

With no money and a huge posse tracking
him, Perry made his way to New York City

and then slipped aboard a ferry to Wee-hawken, N.J. The town policeman there caught him as he huddled sick and hungry over a small fire.

Perry was sent to the maximum-security prison at Dannemora, but he still dreamed of making another escape. After several futile efforts he was put in solitary confinement, where he was to remain for a quarter of a century. In 1920, having long since given up hope of escaping, Perry constructed a device consisting of a block of wood and two nails and used it to pierce both of his eyes. Permanently blinded, he dictated a letter to his lawyer: "I was born in the light of day, against my will of course. I now assert my right to shut out that light. In plain words I wanted to tear out my eyes."

Perry tried to starve himself to death during his last six years but was kept alive by forced feedings until he passed away in 1930. In those final years he refused to say a word to his guards. It was a gruesome end for a man who, according to the *New York World,* had "electrified the nation with his daring exploits."

Peters, Philip (1868–1941) murder victim of Denver's Spiderman
On the evening of October 17, 1941, a Denver, Colo. couple became worried about an elderly neighbor, Philip Peters. They broke into his home and found him murdered. It turned out to be one of the most bizarre cases in that city's history, with the killer to become famous as the Spiderman of Moncrieff Place. What the police couldn't figure out was how the murderer had escaped. All the doors and windows had been locked from the inside, but no one was found hiding in the house.

About a month earlier, 59-year-old Theodore Coneys, a tramp who had known Peters years before, approached the house to beg for food. Just then Peters came out and entered a car to visit his sick wife in the hospital. Coneys slipped into the house to steal money and food but made an opportune discovery: a trapdoor, only about 2 1/2 times the size of a cigarbox lid, which led to a narrow attic cubbyhole. Rounding up a pile of rags, some food and an old crystal radio, Coneys settled into his newly found hiding place.

He planned to become a permanent uninvited boarder. Whenever Peters left the house, Coneys would descend from his attic hideout and eat, bathe and shave, using Peters' razor. On October 17 Coneys was in the kitchen eating. He thought Peters had gone out, but the old man was just taking a nap. Suddenly, the kitchen door popped open, and Peters stood there gaping. Coneys panicked. He grabbed an iron stove shaker and attacked Peters, who was screaming and had obviously not recognized him. Peters collapsed on the floor dead.

Coneys did not flee the house, feeling he had nowhere to go. He climbed back up into his hiding place and was there when the murder was discovered and the police searched the house. The officers had noticed the trapdoor but decided a man could not fit through it. They were partially right: an average-sized man couldn't but a thin man—like Coneys—could.

When Mrs. Peters returned from the hospital, she and her housekeeper kept hearing strange sounds in the house, and the tale soon spread in the area that the house was haunted. One night the housekeeper caught a glimpse of a shadowy figure creeping around. She convinced herself that it was Mr.

Peters' ghost and talked Mrs. Peters into moving.

Even with the house vacant, Coneys did not leave. The electricity was left on and he had stored up some food and could get water by scraping snow from the gutters. Often, a passerby would notice an eerie light coming from the top of the house, but whenever the police investigated, they found nothing, as Coneys, hearing them arrive, would flip off the tiny light he maintained in his lair. The police were sure children were playing in the house and deliberately attempting to frighten passersby. Still they made periodic checks on the house and on July 30, 1942 two detectives heard a lock click on the second floor. They charged upstairs just in time to see the legs of the Spiderman slip through the trapdoor.

The most bizarre case in Denver's history was solved, and Coneys was sent to the penitentiary for life.

Pineapple Primary   1928 Chicago election

A rash of political violence marred the 1928 Republican primary in Chicago, one that the press dubbed the "Pineapple Primary" because of the wholesale use of "pineapples," or bombs, to intimidate voters and office seekers alike. Professional terrorists were employed by both sides, with the Capone gang supplying many or most of the tossers. The homes of candidates were bombed and several campaign workers killed.

In the primary, Sen. Charles S. Deneen's wing of the party opposed the faction headed by Mayor Big Bill Thompson and State's Attorney Robert E. Crowe. The latter forces, combined with those of Gov. Len Small, who was known as a friend of mobsters, con-

trolled much of the patronage jobs in the state. On March 21, 1928 cafe owner and racketeer Diamond Joe Esposito was killed by a bomb. Esposito, the power behind the Genna bootlegging gang, was also close to Sen. Deneen. On the day of Esposito's funeral, bombs were placed at the homes of Sen. Deneen and Judge A. Swanson, Deneen's candidate for state's attorney.

In addition to attracting worldwide attention, the violence of the Pineapple Primary roused Chicago voters the way no other of the city's recent disruptive elections had, and the Deneen forces won easily despite Al Capone's backing of the Thompson-Crowe machine. It was a stunning upset and one that sobered Capone. In the autumn of that year, crusader Frank J. Loesch, the 75-year-old president of the Chicago Crime Commission, called on Capone in an effort to ensure peaceful elections. He asked the gangster if the Pineapple Primary indicated what would happen in the general election.

Capone's response was flamboyant and arrogant. "I'll give you a square deal if you don't ask too much of me."

"Now look here, Capone," Loesch said. "Will you help me by keeping your damned cutthroats and hoodlums from interfering with the polling booths?"

"Sure," Capone responded. "I'll give them the word because they're all dagos up there, but what about the Saltis gang of micks on the West Side? They'll have to be handled different. Do you want me to give them the works, too?"

If Capone was trying to shock Loesch, he failed. The crusader said that would make him very happy.

"All right," Capone said. "I'll have the cops send over squad cars the night before the election and jug all the hoodlums and keep them in the cooler until the polls close."

Capone, who had often bragged, "I own the police," kept his word. On election day, police squad cars toured the polling places, and there was not a single irregularity. Actually, there was little need for Loesch to make the appeal, which only gave Capone a chance to grandstand, since the candidates were all anti-Thompson and thus anti-Capone. The mobster was merely making the best of a bad situation. Besides, he knew his position would not be significantly altered by the election; he would remain top man in Chicago until federal agents nailed him for income tax evasion.

Poker Alice (1851–1930) gambler and madam

One of the few great female gamblers of the West, Poker Alice Ivers was also one of the few gamblers who was an accomplished gunfighter.

Born in England the daughter of a schoolmaster, Alice came to America with her family at the age of 12 and married an engineer named Frank Duffield in Colorado Territory when she was 19. Her husband died in a mining accident the following year, and Alice began supporting herself by teaching school. She also took up poker and was soon dealing cards in a saloon on a percentage basis. Any traces of schoolmarm decorum soon vanished completely as she began toting a gun and smoking big black cigars. She became famous for two sayings "I'll shoot you in your puss, you cheating bastard!" and "I never gamble on Sundays."

Poker Alice, as she was by then known, worked the railroad gambling circuit, beating fellow travelers in high-stake card games. She later settled in Creede, Colorado and

dealt cards in a saloon belonging to Bob Ford, the man who killed Jesse James. From there Poker Alice moved on to Deadwood, S.D., where she demonstrated her shooting prowess one night when a drunken miner accused another dealer, William Tubbs, of cheating and went at him with a bowie knife. Poker Alice drew her gun and fired, shooting the miner in his arm and knocking the knife from his hand.

Alice and Tubbs were married in 1899 and retired from gambling to run a chicken farm until 1910, when Tubbs died of pneumonia. Poker Alice then took up her gun, cigars and cards and headed back for the gaming tables, opening her own place near Fort Meade, S.D. Realizing that men do not live by gambling alone, she stocked the second floor with ladies who offered other diversions. Poker Alice's place was a gold mine, relying on a clientele of soldiers from the fort. But Alice held to her old-fashioned ways. On Sundays drinks were served but there was no gambling and the ladies upstairs did no entertaining. It was this reluctance to be completely accommodating that got Poker Alice in trouble. One night in 1920 a bunch of drunken soldiers tried to break into her place after closing time. Alice fired through a door and a soldier fell dead. She was tried and found guilty of killing the soldier, but the judge let her go, saying, "I cannot find it in my heart to send a white-haired lady to the penitentiary." Once outside the court and beyond the judge's view, Poker Alice lit up a victory cigar.

The army was not so compassionate, however, and declared Alice's place off limits. That and Prohibition drove Poker Alice out of business and she retired to a ranch to smoke cigars and recall the good old days. She died in 1930.

Police Riots of 1857, New York
warring police forces

The Police Riots of 1857 in New York between two rival forces of law officers climaxed several months of terror in New York City during which policemen battled policemen while criminals attacked citizens with impunity. Even when apprehended, a criminal could escape if a member of the rival police force happened on the scene and got into an altercation with his counterpart.

The Municipal Police was formed by the state legislature in 1853, but within four years, during the second term of Mayor Fernando Wood, it was considered so chaotic and corrupt that the legislature intervened to abolish the force it had created. In its place the state lawmakers installed the Metropolitan Police, with the governor appointing a board of five commissioners, who in turn named a superintendent, Frederick Talmadge. The new Metropolitan Police Board then called on the mayor to disband the Municipals. Mayor Wood refused, however, even after the Supreme Court ruled in May 1857 that the law creating the new force was constitutional. Superintendent George W. Matsell of the Municipals stood by the mayor, as did 15 captains and 800 patrolmen.

Things came to a head when Capt. George W. Walling, who had pledged his loyalty to the new force, was sent to place Mayor Wood under arrest. When Wood refused to submit, Walling tried to take him in by force, but with 300 Municipals inside City Hall, he had no chance and was tossed into the street. Immediately thereafter, a troop of 50 Metropolitans marched on City Hall, a striking image in their plug hats and frock coats. The Municipals swarmed out of the building and attacked them and the battle was on, eventu-

The Metropolitan Police battled the Municipal Police in several bloody confrontations in New York City during 1857.

ally extending to the corridors of the City Hall. Finally, the Metropolitans were routed. In all 52 policemen were injured, one Metropolitan was so badly beaten he was invalided for life.

The mayor and his police supporters held out until the members of the Metropolitan Police Board used the power granted them to call out the National Guard. The Seventh Regiment surrounded City Hall. Only when a platoon of infantry with fixed bayonets marched into the building and surrounded Mayor Wood in his office did he submit to arrest. He was released on nominal bail on a charge of inciting to riot and returned to his office.

Confrontations continued the entire summer, with each of the two forces attempting to carry out its functions. The public itself was to bear the heavy brunt of the dispute. When a Municipal arrested a criminal, a Metropolitan would come along and release him and vice versa, as the feud became more important than the protection of the citizenry. While the police argued the criminals simply went about their business. Pedestrians were held up on Broadway in the middle of the day, while rival officers attacked each other with clubs to determine who had the right to interfere. Soon, large gangs of thieves plundered stores and other places of business and robbed passengers on stagecoaches in the city's midst. The gangs turned on each other, fighting for the robbing rights in certain areas, and a great battle between rival gangs broke out in the Bowery. A handful of Metropolitans tried to stop the fighting but were severely beaten. The Municipals simply said the battle was none of their business, leaving it to the Metropolitans.

Whenever a Metropolitan arrested a criminal and succeeded in bringing his charge to the police station, he would find an alderman and magistrate who supported the mayor waiting there to hold an immediate hearing and release the prisoner on his own recognizance. Officials who favored the Metropolitans did the same thing in Municipal station houses.

Such was the public outcry over this breakdown in police protection that an appeal of the Supreme Court decision was rushed into court. When the original decision was upheld, Mayor Wood abolished the Municipals. Several months later, about 50 of the officers, both Municipal and Metropolitan, who had been injured in the City Hall riot filed suit against the mayor. Each received a judgment of $250 but Mayor Woods never paid. Finally, the city paid the claims, together with the legal costs involved.

procuring

A double standard toward vice held by much of society views prostitution itself tolerantly but regards procuring, the recruitment of

girls and women to serve as prostitutes, a vital part of the overall business, as far more unwholesome. In almost every major city in the United States during the 19th century, vice operators had no trouble paying off crooked police officers, and, indeed, entire police units and departments for permission to run houses of prostitution, but the enforcers of the law were less accommodating when it came to allowing procurers to supply young girls for these establishments. Some corrupt officers who accepted payoffs for almost anything else rebelled when happening upon "break-in" houses, where male specialists indoctrinated, by repeated rapes, young victims lured to the big city by the promise of well-paying jobs.

In New York's so-called Grabber Scandal in 1875, the notorious Hester Jane Haskins, better known as Jane the Grabber, was arrested by enraged police because she was recruiting girls from the better portion of society to satisfy the demands of higher-priced bordello patrons for young ladies of refinement and education. Jane the Grabber had been allowed to operate for years, recruiting gullible girls right off the boat or from upstate farm country and publishing a monthly circular that advertised her wares to whorehouse clients. But when she started kidnapping the daughters of the well-to-do, she was carted off to prison.

Procurers emerged in America shortly after the arrival of the white man. Their first victims were Indian maidens, who were bought or stolen from their tribes to be used as prostitutes. Soon, they flourished in every port city, attracting an endless stream of young girls and women, including those who spoke not a word of English. Other procurers, operating sometimes in gangs, worked the Ohio and Mississippi rivers, again either kidnapping or buying young females from their impoverished parents and selling them down river at the infamous flatboat auctions in Natchez and New Orleans. Perhaps the most famous of the procurer gangs was the one led by white slaver Sam Purdy, whose heyday was around the start of the 19th century. By 1805, however, the gang was wiped out as a result of assassinations carried out or instigated by a colorful reformer named Carlos White, the scourge of fleshpots from St. Louis to New Orleans.

In the 19th century New Orleans was probably the most tolerant of procurers with several of that city's famed procuresses being allowed practically a free hand in recruiting and despoiling young virgins, some barely in their teens. The New Orleans procuresses supplied not only houses of prostitution in the French Quarter and elsewhere in the city but also bordellos in Atlanta, Memphis, Galveston and a number of other southern cities. In their lavish brochures "fresh stock" indicated inexperienced girls, who thus commanded the highest prices. In time, fierce competition drove the prices of a virgin down as low as $50, but by the late 1860s Louisa Murphy, a schoolteacher-procuress, was commanding $800 for a young girl. Murphy had little trouble with the police whom she paid off regularly. Similarly, Nellie Haley, considered the Queen of the Procuresses in the 1880s, was never arrested in New Orleans; later in her career Nellie did run afoul of the law when she attempted to ply her trade in Chicago.

Chicago gave a mixed welcome to procurers; many operated without interference but others were harrassed whenever certain policemen experienced a sudden infusion of righteousness. Still, Chicago's vice trade required so many women that procurers operated there with or without approval, and the city became the supply point for many other cities in the Midwest.

Some procurer gangs dealt solely in foreign women, among them the band headed by French Em Duval and her husband. The Duvals ran their own brothel in Chicago on Armour Avenue but maintained a stockade outside the city on Dearborn Street, where women shipped in from New York were kept awaiting sale to buyers. The stockade had barred windows and the inmates were not permitted any street wear until they were being transported to the brothel which had purchased them. The Duval operation was broken up in 1908 by federal authorities utilizing immigration statutes, the only legal weapon available for use against vice operations prior to the Mann Act.

Another important procurer mob of the era was the Dewey Hotel Gang, considered the most efficient operation in the city. The gang, comprised of Russian Jews, specialized in providing, not surprisingly, Russian Jewesses, a prize attraction in American bordellos. The gang maintained break-in rooms and a stockade on the top floor of a hotel on Washington Boulevard. They held regular auctions, at which women were stripped and inspected by brothel keepers and sold to the highest bidders. At an auction in 1906, 25 women were sold for sums ranging from $25 to $100 apiece. This sale did not constitute the gang's total profits, however, since for a considerable time thereafter each woman had to turn over her share of the money she earned to the procurers.

No account of procuring in this country would be complete without mentioning Harry "Greasy Thumb" Guzik and his wife Alma, perhaps the most proficient procurer couple in America. One of five brothers who

as youngsters earned nickels running er–
rands and hustling for Chicago prostitutes in
the Levee district, Harry was a full-time
pimp before he reached his teens. After getting busted early in his career, he started
paying off virtually every politician and
policeman who came into view. A ward
politician once said, "Harry's fingers are
always greasy from the money he counts out
for protection." Thus, he won the nickname
Greasy Thumb.

Harry eventually accumulated a string of
whores in the Levee and married one of
them, Alma. Thereafter, the couple became
the chief procurers for all the important
brothel operators in the city, men like Big Jim
Colosimo and women like Victoria Moresco.

Harry and Alma combed the rural areas of
Illinois, Indiana and Wisconsin in search of
new girls, particularly those who dressed
"city style" and obviously wanted no part of
farm living. After finding a likely prospect,
Harry would go to bed with her and be
joined by Alma. Afterwards, Alma would
regale Harry about being a cheapskate and
insist he give the girl $10. Later the girl
would be invited to visit Chicago. Once
again, she would end up in bed with the couple, but this time a male friend of Harry's
would show up and the threesome would
become a foursome. Upon leaving, Harry's
friend would insist on giving Alma and the
girl $10 each. Generally, by the next day the
girl was working in a whorehouse. The
Guziks sold each recruit for $100 plus
expenses and a percentage of the girl's future
earnings. They often procured some 10 girls
a month in an attempt to keep up with the
demand for "fresh bodies."

In 1921 the Guziks had trouble convincing a farm girl to turn prostitute; so they
made her a prisoner, took away her clothes
and had her forcibly indoctrinated. After
many months the girl got word out to her
family and was rescued by her brothers. The
couple tried to fix things by bribing the
father of the girl, now a mental and physical
wreck, not to press charges. But the attempt
didn't work and they were convicted and
sentenced to the penitentiary. Out on bail
while the case was being appealed, the
Guziks stepped up their recruiting activities
to raise a large sum of money. These funds
found their way to Illinois Gov. Len Small,
who abruptly granted them a full pardon
before the judicial process was completed.

After Harry Guzik joined the Capone syndicate, he was put in charge of prostitution
and procuring and became the chief funnel
for much of the mob's payoffs to police and
politicians. Eventually, brother Jake Guzik
handled even bigger payoffs for the Capone
gang, and upon Harry's death the Greasy
Thumb monicker passed on to him.

Two Chicago newspapermen once over-
heard a conversation between Guzik and a
young Willie Bioff, then primarily a procurer
known for slugging whores who attempted
to hold out on him. It was Guzik's observation that "they're so dumb (prospective prostitutes) you have to teach them never to give
away what they can sell." The pair then discussed the best technique for convincing
women to "go horizontal." The first step was
to seduce a woman, then lavish money on
her and finally wake up one morning and
declare bankruptcy. Bioff told Guzik: "Then
I hint that if she really loved me, she'd lay a
friend of mine who wanted to give me a hundred dollars if he could just get in her pants
once. She always cries. She always tells me
she loves me and she could not possibly lay
anybody else. But I tell her I wanted to buy
such wonderful things for her—and here we

are without even breakfast money. She comes around."

"And," rejoined Harry Guzik, "once she's laid one other guy for money, she's hooked. After that you can put her right into a house and she'll turn over her earnings to you every night. If she tries to hold out, you just slap her around a little."

A mistaken belief today is that most procurers are black, a perception fostered, according to Richard Milner, coauthor of *Black Players,* perhaps the most definitive study of black pimps, by the fact that the blacks are primarily street operators and thus more visible than white procurers. In New York the role of black procurers in recruiting runaway girls around the Port Authority bus terminal on Eighth Avenue has been the subject of numerous studies.

According to Milner, most important procurers are whites. It is they who recruit women for the legalized whorehouses in Nevada and for the "massage parlors" in various major cities. By abandoning the streets to the blacks, the same as has occurred in drug distribution, the white procurers have been able to shift attention away from their activities.

See also: NEW ORLEANS PROCURESSES.

Purvis, Will (1874–1943) wrong man

Will Purvis' escape from execution in Mississippi in 1894 has long been cited by opponents of capital punishment as an example of the danger of error in dealing out the death penalty.

A 19-year-old farmer in Mercer County, Miss., Purvis was arrested and charged with the murder of Will Buckley in what appeared to have been an internal dispute within the White Caps, a Ku Klux Klan–type organiza-

tion of the period. Purvis had joined the White Caps some three months before Buckley was shot to death. After Buckley's murder bloodhounds traced a cold trail to near the Purvis farm. Jim Buckley, the dead man's brother, identified Purvis as the murderer, and he was indicted and quickly found guilty.

Purvis' execution by hanging was scheduled for February 7, 1894, and on that day about 3,000 persons jammed the area around the scaffold to watch the events. Many in the crowd, however, still insisted Purvis was being executed for a crime he had not committed and were there to show their support for him. At the moment a preacher implored heaven, "God save this innocent boy," the hangman severed the rope holding the trapdoor shut, but Purvis just tumbled to the ground below, as the rope around his neck unwound.

His hands still tied, Purvis jumped back up the gallows steps, crying, "Let's get this over with!" Officials were about to oblige, but the crowd grew unruly. The preacher asked for a show of hands of "all who are opposed to hanging Will Purvis a second time." A sea of hands rose and hundreds of men moved forward menacingly. Purvis was then returned to his jail cell.

After a time, the Mississippi Supreme Court ruled that Purvis had to be executed, but before the second attempt could be made, friends of the condemned man helped him to escape. He remained in hiding until 1896, when a new governor, A. J. McLaurin, took office. McLaurin had campaigned on a promise to reduce Purvis' sentence to life imprisonment. In 1898 Purvis was pardoned when Jim Buckley admitted he was not sure Purvis had been the killer.

Then in 1917, 24 years after the murder, an old man named Joe Beard came forward at a religious revival meeting to purge his soul before taking to his deathbed. He said he and another White Capper, Louis Thornhill, had been chosen by lot to kill Will Buckley. Beard offered enough independent proof to indicate he had information about the crime that only the real murderer or murderers would have. In 1920 the Mississippi legislature awarded Will Purvis $5,000 compensation "for a great wrong done you" and removed "all stain and dishonor from your name."

Rablen, Carroll (1895–1929) murder victim

The murder of Carroll Rablen in 1929 resulted in one of California's most sensational murder trials, so sensational it had to be held in an open-air dance pavilion to accommodate all those eager to attend.

Carroll Rablen of Tuttletown, Calif. was deaf because of an injury received during World War I. His wife Eva was a vivacious, fun-loving woman who enjoyed dancing. While Carroll didn't dance, he took her to affairs and didn't object to her dancing with other men. On April 29, 1929 the couple went to the town's weekly ball. Carroll stayed outside in their car while Eva went inside to enjoy herself. About midnight Eva pushed through the crowd to bring her husband a cup of coffee and then returned to the dance. Moments later, Carroll was writhing in agony on the floor of the car; his cries brought his father and several others to his side. He complained of the way the coffee had tasted. A doctor was summoned but Carroll died before he arrived.

Carroll's father was sure Eva had poisoned her husband for his insurance, but when the contents of the dead man's stomach were sent to a chemist for analysis, no trace of poison was found. However, a subsequent search of the dance hall area uncovered a bottle marked, "Strychnine." The bottle was traced to a pharmacy in a nearby town, where records showed it had been bought by a Mrs. Joe Williams, allegedly to kill some gophers. The druggist identified Eva Rablen as Mrs. Williams. She was charged with her husband's murder and her trial drew one of the largest crowds ever to attend a formal judicial hearing in the state. The weakness in the prosecution's case was that no poison had been found in Carroll Rablen's body. Consequently, the prosecutor called in one of the most famous chemists in the nation, Dr. Edward Heinrich, who was recognized as a brilliant forensic expert.

Heinrich found traces of strychnine in the dead man's stomach as well as in the coffee cup. He also theorized that since Eva Rablen had carried the coffee through a packed dance hall, she might have spilled some on the way. An appeal for help produced a woman who remembered that Eva had bumped into her and spilled coffee on her dress. The coffee stains on the dress also contained traces of the poison. Faced with this damning evidence, Eva Rablen changed her plea to guilty and was sentenced to life imprisonment.

Ragen's Colts   Chicago gang

One of Chicago's huge Irish gangs, Ragen's Colts achieved their height of power during the first two decades of the 20th century. The gang's fate was typical of the pattern of absorption of Irish gangs into what became part of the national crime syndicate.

Dominating Chicago's South Side around the stockyards, the Colts were political sluggers, racists, jingoists, bootleggers and killers. Formally called Ragen's Athletic and Benevolent Association, the gang started, as did a number of others in that era, as a baseball team. Frank Ragen was the star pitcher and also the star political operator. He soon was offering the gang's services to Democratic Party candidates throughout the entire city. With the Colts' muscle and firepower, elections proved easy to win and many members of the city council and state legislature owed their victories to the gang. "When we dropped into a polling place," one Colt bragged, "everybody else dropped out."

By 1902 Ragen's Colts numbered 160, and by 1908 the gang's motto was "Hit Me and You Hit 2,000." Over the years the gang launched the careers of aldermen, sheriffs, police brass, county treasurers and numerous other officeholders as well as some notable ballplayers. Ragen himself became city commissioner. However, the Colts' main product was accomplished criminals. Its notables included Gunner McPadden, who committed a long string of homicides; Harry Madigan,

the owner of the notorious Pony Inn, a Cicero saloon, who was charged—but never tried because of the Colts' political connections—with several kidnappings and assaults during various elections; Dynamite Brooks, another saloon keeper who often killed in a drunken rage; Danny McFall, who was made deputy sheriff, in the mysterious ways of Chicago politics, despite having murdered a couple of business competitors; Stubby McGovern, a deadly triggerman whose assignment to a hit was a guarantee of success; Yiddles Miller, a boxing referee and notorious white supremacist who once called the members of the Ku Klux Klan "nigger lovers"; and Ralph Sheldon, a fearless bootlegger and hijacker.

In addition to furnishing political strong-arm services and running a number of South Side rackets, the Colts took it upon themselves to defend the white race, provoking a great race riot in 1919. It started one day when a black youth swimming off a South Side beach encroached on segregated waters. He was stoned and drowned by white bathers. As tensions mounted between the races on the South Side, members of Ragen's Colts baited blacks. Later that night the Colts stormed through the Black Belt, shooting blacks on sight, firing and dynamiting homes and looting shops. Black war veterans dug out their service weapons and returned the fire. Rampaging blacks overturned autos and streetcars carrying whites and destroyed property belonging to whites. Before the fury on both sides subsided from sheer exhaustion after four days, 20 whites and 14 blacks were dead and the injured toll stood at 1,000, about equally divided between the races.

After the riot the Colts turned to more profitable pursuits, namely bootlegging, although a contingent of the gang under

Ralph Sheldon exhibited little interest in making booze, preferring simply to hijack it from others. Despite having to fight a number of bootlegging wars with the gang, Al Capone showed considerable patience toward the Colts and eventually a large portion of the gang was absorbed into his organization. The descendants of the original Colts are important members of organized crime today.

Restell, Madame (1812–1878) Madame Killer

"The wickedest woman in the city," Ann Trow Lohman, better known as Madame Restell, was New York's most infamous abortionist in the 19th century.

Born in poverty in England, she emigrated to the United States in 1831 with her first husband, a tailor named Henry Summers who died two years later as a result of yellow fever, typhoid and alcoholism. In 1836 she married "Doctor" Charles R. Lohman, a former compositor who had prospered as a quack physician selling medication that supposedly inhibited conception and aborted unwanted fetuses. Soon, Lohman's new wife turned up in newspaper advertisements as "Madame Restell, female physician and professor of midwifery."

Madame Restell opened an establishment on Greenwich Street where she sold various contraceptive devices, performed abortions and delivered babies who were later put up for adoption by their single mothers. To stay in business, Madame Restell paid enormous sums to the police. The superintendent of police, George W. Matsell, was widely believed to have been on her payroll. Concurrently, Matsell's private company was proprietor of the *National Police Gazette*, which regularly ranted about Madame Killer and her establishment. Clearly, Matsell used his publication as leverage to raise the ante on his bribes. Madame Restell became so notorious that while Boss Tweed allowed her to operate, he refused, in a rare burst of virtue, to take her money and declined invitations to parties at her lavish Fifth Avenue mansion.

Madame Restell prospered despite her numerous expenses. It was said, for example, that more than 100 wealthy men paid regular tribute to her establishment for the right to send young girls there for various forms of "treatment." She was arrested on a number of occasions, especially when a young girl sent to her died from an abortion, but she never served more than a year in prison for any offense. A far more serious threat to her were the angry mobs that frequently gathered outside her establishment and threatened to destroy it. Whenever she went forth in her carriage, street boys followed it shouting: "Yah! Your house is built on babies' skulls!"

While Madame Restell could hardly stand as a tragic heroine, she was probably less of an abortionist than a purveyor of contraceptives and the operator of an undercover maternity hospital and adoption center. In the 19th century there was a great semantic confusion concerning abortion and contraception, both officially viewed as the same evil.

After her husband died in 1876, Madame Restell led a lonely life. Because of her notoriety she was abandoned by her brother and a stepdaughter by her first marriage. She lived for the affection shown her by her two grandchildren, for whom she entertained high social ambitions. She was elated when her granddaughter married extremely well in 1878.

The following month, however, Madame Restell was trapped by Anthony Comstock of the New York Society for the Suppression of Vice, who purchased a number of contraceptive items from her. He then had her arrested for possession of articles used for "immoral" purposes. Facing a sensational trial and fearing the publicity would lead to estrangement from her grandchildren, Madame Restell climbed into her bathtub and slit her throat with a carving knife. She left an estate of $1 million, a stupendous sum for that era.

Riley, James "Butt" (1848–?) San Francisco hoodlum

Butt Riley grew up as a hoodlum in New York and then, after a stint as a sailor, ended up in San Francisco, where police soon labeled him King of the Hoodlums. Certainly, he was one of that city's principal, if less sophisticated, criminals. He never led any specific gang, but most of the city's toughs would flock to join him whenever he called.

Riley was known as a vicious fighter who was always armed with a long knife, brass knuckles, a slungshot and a hickory bludgeon. However, his principal weapon was his head, which he claimed had the thickest skull in Christendom. He would disable a foe by charging him and butting him in the stomach or on the chin, rendering the man helpless. When Butt Riley led raids on Chinese opium houses or slave dens, he always batted the doors down with his head, and when his men grabbed a Chinese victim, Riley would see how far he could butt him. Records were kept on such matters, and according to them, Riley once butted a 160-pound man exactly 10 feet. Riley has been described as an extraordinarily handsome man, and it is a matter of record that he was eagerly sought

James "Butt" Riley was frequently used by contemporary newspaper artists as a model for what the "more exquisite-type" hoodlum looked like.

after by prostitutes and that when he bestowed his favors, the usual procedure was reversed and he collected a fee. He even sold female admirers his photograph for 25¢; for his favorite harlots only, a photo of him in the nude was available for 50¢. It was quite common for clients of some of the city's most popular prostitutes to find themselves making love under an autographed picture of the King of the Hoodlums. Riley would have new photos taken of himself each week and on Mondays he would make a picture-selling tour of the red-light areas, his merchandise in a black satchel slung over his shoulder.

In 1871 Riley butted the wrong victim, a 22-year-old carriage painter named John Jordon, who took two vicious butts to the stomach and then pulled a revolver and shot Riley in the chest. Doctors at the county hospital said the wounds were fatal but Riley recovered. Unfortunately, his health was poor thereafter, and he lost the strength and beauty the harlots admired. He also lost his standing with the hoodlums and degenerated to a common housebreaker. In 1876 he was caught breaking into a house and sent to San Quentin Prison for 15 years. After that San Francisco's King of the Hoodlums disappeared.

Roger's Barracks   underworld refuge and vice area

In the 1850s a diminutive Englishman from Yorkshire, Roger Plant, came up with the idea that what Chicago needed was the Compleat Underworld Refuge, which he set about establishing at the northeast corner of Wells and Monroe streets. He started with just a single two-story house and then expanded straight down the block, adding one rookery after another until he had what a journalist of the day called the "very core of corruption." By the mid-1860s Plant's dives lined both sides of the street for almost a block. The police came to call the conglomeration Roger's Barracks. Journalist Frederick Francis Cook described it as "one of the most talked about if not actually one of the wickedest places on the continent" and as "a refuge for the very nethermost strata of the underworld—the refuse of the Bridewell."

A tunnel led from Roger's Barracks under Wells Street to the various underworld strongholds between that street and the Chicago River. All sorts of stolen goods were funneled through it and out the various dives. It was said that the underworld's first bomb was manufactured in a room in the barracks, leading the *Chicago Times* to comment in December 1870, "Such a discovery in a civilized community seems almost incredible, but there is not the slightest doubt of its truth."

Plant collected exorbitant rents for making his premises available for such nefarious purposes, but he also garnered considerable revenues from so-called straight rackets, including dance halls, brothels and deadfalls, i.e., saloons that specialized in robbing strangers. Special cubicles were rented out to streetwalkers, male degenerates and procurers, who would have young girls raped in the cells by a half-dozen men as a preparation for their assignment to bordellos.

Plant weighed barely over 100 pounds but was known as a vicious fighter. Although always armed with knife, pistol and bludgeon, his favorite weapon was his own teeth, which he would readily use on a foe's ears or nose with maiming efficiency. The only person Plant could not control was his wife, a fearsome creature of 250 pounds who would often pick him up with one hand and spank him with the other. Mrs. Plant ran the family's brothel interests and lent a hand herself during peak hours. She also produced an estimated 15 children, all of whom were cunning little rascals credited by journalists with being able to pick a pocket almost before they could walk.

Roger's Barracks was seldom bothered by the police because, as Cook recorded, "Roger paid his toll with exemplary regularity." By 1870 Plant had collected a fortune, and he abruptly shuttered all his establishments and moved to the country to become a gentleman of leisure and patron of the turf. The Plant children, however, appear to have carried on the criminal tradition of the family, several finding their way onto the police blotters for robbery and sundry other crimes while in their teens. In 1894 English journalist William T. Stead published the *Black List* of Chicago property, which named Roger Plant, Jr., as the operator of three saloons and two bordellos and listed two sisters, Daisy and Kitty Plant, as the operators of adjoining brothels on South Clark Street. It was said that a secret passage allowed harlots to pass from one of these establishments to the other as needed and that it was quite possible a customer venturing from one place to the next might well find himself being entertained by the same female clad in a different colored wig.

Russian Bill (1855–1881) outlaw

William Tattenbaum was a colorful character who turned up in Tombstone, Arizona Territory in 1880 claiming to be the son of Countess Telfrin, a wealthy Russian noblewoman. He also said that as a young lieutenant he had deserted the Czar's Imperial White Hussars when faced with a court-martial for striking a ranking officer. Decked out in the finest and flashiest Western clothing and gear, Tattenbaum was quickly dubbed Russian Bill by the citizens of Tombstone, who did not believe a word he said about himself. Nevertheless, Russian Bill managed to ingratiate himself with Curly Bill Brocius, the head of the notorious Clanton gang, and rode with the outlaws for about a year. There is no record of Russian Bill engaging in any overt banditry and he seems to have served mainly as a "horse holder," but Curly Bill insisted on keeping him around so that he could watch him groom his own hair for hours "just like a Chinaman" and listen to him quote the classics. Russian Bill comes down to us, thanks to Hollywood depictions, as a comic character. Quite possibly to escape that very reputation in Tombstone, he struck off for the New Mexico Territory on a horse-stealing enterprise of his own. The result was not a happy one, as he was soon captured by the Law and Order Committee of Shakespeare, New Mexico Territory. Russian Bill and another malefactor named Sandy King were given a fast trial by the committee in the banquet room of a local hotel. In keeping with the group's reputation for quick justice, he was hanged from a beam in the room without further ado.

In 1883 inquiries from the Countess Telfrin about her son confirmed that all of Russian Bill's tales had been true. The town of Shakespeare was a mite chagrined about having hanged "an honest-to-God son of a countess." To spare the Countess' feelings and a troublesome investigation by Washington, it was duly reported to the authorities that Russian Bill had met with an accidental death.

Sands Chicago vice area

In the 1850s the worst vice district in Chicago was called the Sands, lying just about where the Tribune and Wrigley buildings are now situated. At the time, the Sands consisted of about 40 buildings, every one of which was a brothel, a gambling den, a thieves' hideout or a saloon partly used for prostitution. The *Chicago Tribune* called the Sands

> the vilest and most dangerous place in Chicago. For some years past it has been the resort or hiding place of all sorts of criminals, while the most wretched and degraded women and their miserable pimps [are] there in large numbers. A large number of persons, mostly strangers in the city, have been enticed into the dens there and robbed, and there is but little doubt that a number of murders have been committed by the desperate characters who have made these dens their homes. The most beastly sexuality and darkest crimes had their homes in the Sands. . . .

Typical of the establishments found there was a saloon-bagnio operated by Freddy Webster. It was noted for both its viciousness and vileness. One of Webster's inmates was a prostitute named Margaret McGuinness, who was described as never having been sober or out of the house in five years and never having had clothes on in three years. She entertained anywhere from 15 to 40 men a night. When she died on March 8, 1857 of "intemperance," hers was the seventh death to occur in the Sands in the previous seven days.

The Sands, or at least its women, were the cause of the so-called Whore War of 1857, when a group of madams on State Street attempted to lure away some of the area's star prostitutes. Led by a brutal young prostitute, Gentle Annie Stafford, the forces of the Sands prevailed.

Numerous political figures vowed to wipe out the Sands but never did, mainly because its inhabitants insisted they would fight to the death to remain there. Finally, in 1857 Mayor Long John Wentworth accomplished the deed on a day when all the men and many of the women had left the Sands to attend a great dog fight at a nearby racetrack. Accompanied by some 30 policemen and two horse-drawn wagons loaded with hooks and chains, the mayor ordered the flimsy structures of the Sands pulled down. As the work progressed, a fire company arrived and destroyed several shanties with streams of water. Some of the buildings were burned, and by the time the inhabitants of the Sands returned, they found nothing left but rubble and ashes. The area eventually became a prime business location, but whether the destruction of the Sands represented civic progress is debatable. Its several hundred undesirable residents simply spread themselves around Chicago.

See also: ANNIE STAFFORD, WHORE WAR.

shanghaiing

The custom of kidnapping seamen to fill out a ship's crew was practiced worldwide, but nowhere was the art so perfected as along the San Francisco waterfront.

In early times there were no ships sailing directly from San Francisco to Shanghai and back to San Francisco; the round trip involved a long dangerous cruise, which became known as a Shanghai voyage. When a man in San Francisco was forcibly impressed into a ship's crew, he was thus described as being "sent to Shanghai." This in time was shortened to just plain shanghaied.

By 1852, 23 known gangs in San Francisco were engaged in the shanghai trade. Some, of course, would waylay men foolish enough to walk the shadowy waterfront alone, but few shanghai gangs would wait so patiently for a fly to enter their web. The gangs employed runners to board incoming ships and induce sailors to come to boardinghouses they operated. As the *San Francisco Times* of October 21, 1861 reported:

They swarm over the rail like pirates and virtually take possession of the deck. The crew are shoved into the runners' boats, and the vessel is often left in a perilous situation, with none to manage her, the sails unfurled, and she liable to drift afoul of the shipping at anchor. In some cases not a man has been left aboard in half an hour after the anchor has been dropped.

The runners would all carry the standard gear of their trade: a pair of brass knuckles, a blackjack or slungshot, a knife, a revolver, obscene pictures, several bottles of rum and whiskey spiked with Spanish fly and a flask of liquid soap. If the runners swarmed aboard at meal time, the soap would be slipped into soup or stew simmering on the galley stove. When this awful mixture was served, the seamen would be disgusted and much more receptive to the runner's spiel. First, the runners would offer the sailors some doctored liquor. After that began to take effect, the seamen would be shown obscene pictures and given an enticing, graphic description of what awaited them at a certain boardinghouse as well as the brothels of the Barbary Coast.

Usually, this was enough to convince at least one sailor, and he would be ushered to a runner's boat, where the boatman would give him more to drink. If the sailor showed signs of wavering or attempted to fight, the runner and boatman would club him into silence. Sailors who insisted on staying with their ship were often brass-knuckled or threatened with knives or guns. Often competing runners would settle on the same sailor and each would seize an ear with his teeth and bite down until the frightened man shouted out the boardinghouse he wished to go to. It was considered a serious violation of the runner's code for one runner to steal another's victim.

Some captains would try to protect their crew, but they were helpless when as many as a score of armed men stormed aboard. In addition, shipmasters were often warned by "certain interested parties," as the *San Francisco Times* put it in 1861, meaning the politicians and city officials who received payoffs from the boardinghouse masters, to look the other way or they would not be allowed to raise a crew when they were ready to sail.

Once a sailor reached the boardinghouse, his bag of possessions would be locked up and he would virtually be held prisoner until he was resold to an outgoing vessel. Captive sailors were sold whiskey laced with opium to keep them docile and, on occasion, prostitutes would be brought in to service them; the boardinghouse master would get a percentage of the prostitutes' fees and whatever they could steal from the sailors. A shipmaster would pay the boardinghouse master between $25 and $100 for each crewman he supplied plus a customary two-months' advance salary to cover the seaman's bill in the boardinghouse. There was seldom any money left over for the sailor when the boardinghouse master figured out the bill.

Shanghaiing could exist on such an organized basis only because most sailors were brutalized men, long subjected to harsh treatment aboard ship and thus conditioned to receiving the same when ashore. Finally, with the rise of unions and a federal law against shanghaiing, the vicious practice began to disappear after 1906.

See also: JOSEPH "BUNCO" KELLY, SHANGHAI KELLY.

Shinburn, Mark (c. 1833–?) aristocrat of bank burglars

Perhaps the most colorful of all New York criminals in the 1860s, Mark Shinburn was a dapper bank burglar who complained at length that he was at heart an aristocrat and that he was repelled by the crooks with whom he was forced to associate. Shinburn was a particular favorite of Marm Mandelbaum, the great fence, and would attend her famous dinner parties, where she entertained society's better half with a number of underworld personalities mixed in for spice. Shinburn always acquitted himself perfectly when the wife of a judge or an important City Hall figure happened to be sitting next to him. He would inform them, with somber earnestness, that he was involved in banking.

Some of Shinburn's crimes were truly spectacular. After he and a confederate robbed a bank in Saint Catharines, Ontario, they found all routes across the border blocked by Canadian police. The only unguarded point was a half-constructed suspension bridge over Niagara Falls. The pair started across on a snowy and sleety night after tying ropes around their waists and securing another rope to a girder. If one slipped off, his partner was to try to pull him back, but if the task proved impossible, each agreed to cut the other loose, letting him drop into the chasm below rather than letting him remain suspended in the air to freeze to death. Twice Shinburn slipped over the side but was pulled back to safety by his partner. Amazingly, the pair made it across to American soil and escaped.

Shinburn was also a member of the infamous Bliss Bank Ring, which corrupted the New York Police Department detective bureau and paid off officers following every big caper pulled by the gang. However, Shinburn did not like sharing in big operations because he wanted to accumulate as much loot as he could in the shortest possible time in order to return to his native Prussia. He engaged in several two-man jobs, the largest being a $170,000 Maryland bank caper with gang leader George M. Bliss, one of the few criminals he respected. Shinburn then announced his retirement from crime and, after being bid a fond farewell from Bliss and Marm Mandelbaum, set sail for Europe.

Using some of his loot, Shinburn managed to buy a title and became Baron Shindell of Monaco. He lived quite well for many years, but his lavish lifestyle eventually took its toll and he was forced to return to crime. He was caught attempting to rob a Belgium bank and imprisoned. When finally released he managed to scrape up enough money to return to the United States, where he apparently intended to return to his version of the bank business. However, he soon discovered that some of his real estate holdings in Chicago had grown enormously in value, and he was once more able to retire in luxury under another assumed name. Since no more was heard of him, it is assumed his second retirement was permanent.

See also: BLISS BANK RING, FREDERICKA "MARM" MANDELBAUM.

Shotgun Man (?–?) unidentified Black Hand hit man

America's best-known murderer, in the sense that literally thousands of people could have identified him—but didn't—was Chicago's infamous Shotgun Man, an assassin who worked for Black Hand extortionists. If the police were aware of his name and identity, no case could be built against him, and little of his past was known in Chicago's Little Italy, even though he openly plied his trade there. Most Black Hand gangs did not do their own killings but farmed them out to free-ance hit men who owed no loyalty beyond doing the job they were paid for. Between January 1, 1910 and March 26, 1911, the Shotgun Man

killed 15 Italians and Sicilians on orders from various Black Handers. By comparison, the total number of unsolved Black Hand murders during that period was 38. In March 1911 the Shotgun Man assassinated four victims within a 72-hour period, all at the intersection of Milton and Oak streets. Before and after his killings he walked freely through the streets of Little Italy, his gun always for rent to the highest bidder. Although he was well known, no one in Little Italy identified him to the Chicago police. It was generally believed that the Black Handers who hired him had considerable political influence and that if arrested, the Shotgun Man would be back on the streets within a short time, a prospect likely to give any potential informer second thoughts. Black Handers supposedly paid the Shotgun Man extremely well for his services, since he made a fearsome walking advertisement for them. It may have been that he had accumulated all the wealth he wanted or just that the Black Hand menace was starting to recede anyway, but after a period of eight or nine years the Shotgun Man left Little Italy.

See also: DEATH CORNER.

Small, Len (1862–1936) "pardoning governor" of Illinois

It would be futile to attempt to single out the most dishonest politician ever to hold office, but Len Small, governor of Illinois during the 1920s, stands as the most blatantly corrupt. A Kankakee farmer and puppet of Chicago Mayor Big Bill Thompson, Small took office in 1921 and was indicted a short time later for embezzling $600,000 during his previous term as state treasurer, an activity that before and after Small was a time-honored tradition in Illinois.

Facing trial, Small said he had an abiding faith in the jury system. As it turned out, he had very good reason to. While his lawyers fought the standard courtroom defense, Small's behind-the-scenes support came from Walter Stevens, then regarded as the dean of Chicago's gunmen; Jew Ben Newmark, a former chief investigator for the state's attorney who found greater prosperity as a counterfeiter, extortionist and all-around thief; and "Umbrella Mike" Boyle, a corrupt Electrical Workers' Union official. This trio successfully molded the jurors' opinions with bribes and, when that technique did not work, with threats against them and members of their family. Small was acquitted.

Duly grateful, the governor shortly thereafter was able to repay his debt to the three by granting all of them pardons for sundry offenses—Boyle and Newmark for jury tampering and Stevens for murder. Thereafter, Small ran up a pardon-granting record unparalleled in American history.

During his first three years in office, he pardoned about 1,000 felons. And that was only the warm-up. Over the next five years Small freed another 7,000 on a strictly cash basis. A longtime Chicago newspaperman, George Murray, explained the operation most succinctly:

> *The Republican party machinery of the state was then in the hands of Len Small as governor, Robert E. Crowe as state's attorney of Cook County, and William Hale Thompson as mayor of Chicago. . . . When Crowe would convict a wrong-doer the man could buy a pardon from Small. Then Small and Crowe would split the take and Crowe would go into court for more convictions. The voters returned this team to office year after year.*

That incredible electoral streak came to an end in the infamous Pineapple Primary of 1928. Despite the support of the Capone

mob, the Small-Crowe ticket went down to a resounding defeat, as enraged voters turned out in record numbers. "It was purely a revolt," concluded the Illinois Crime Survey, "an uprising of the people, expressing themselves through the ballot. The birth of 'Moral Chicago' was hailed throughout the world."

The accolade may have been somewhat overly enthusiastic but with the removal of Small from office, the citizens of Chicago and the rest of Illinois could at least entertain the hope that a convicted felon might actually be required to put in some time behind bars.

See also: PINEAPPLE PRIMARY.

Soldier of Fortune hit man want ads
magazine's liability

In 1985 Robert Black, 35, a former U.S. Marine Corps captain decided he had to be rid of his wife, Sandra, and so hired a hit man to carry out the crime. How did Black locate such a character? He simply consulted the ads in *Soldier of Fortune*, a right-wing publication devoted to the art of force to, among other things, defend the American way of life, and in this case, death.

The plot was successful, but afterward uncovered, and the killer, John Wayne Hearn, plea-bargained a life sentence for himself and testified against Black. Black was executed in 1992.

In 1990 businessman Richard Braun was murdered by gunman Michael Savage. In this case as well the plot did not remain undetected. However, in a sense the solutions to both murders became secondary to whether or not there was a degree of guilt beyond that of the plotters themselves. Braun's sons ended up suing *Soldier of Fortune*, claiming business associates of their father hired Savage to kill the senior Braun through a "gun-for-hire" advertisement in the publication. Similarly the victim's estate in the Black case had sued on the same grounds.

Initially both suits against the magazine were successful, but these decisions were later overturned. In the Black case an appeals court overruled the previous finding, holding that the ad in question was ambiguously worded, and therefore cleared the magazine against having to pay damages. In 1992 a judgment for $4.37 million for the Braun family was upheld by the U.S. 11th Circuit Court of Appeals. The court ruled that Savage's ad had implied a willingness "to use his gun to commit crimes," and therefore was outside the commercial free-speech protections of the First Amendment.

Stafford, Annie (1838–?) Chicago madam

Annie Stafford, better known as Gentle Annie in her younger, more voluptuous days, was the leading fighter in Chicago's Whore War in 1857, representing the forces of the Sands, a sinkhole of vice, against an incursion by the madams of the better State Street district, who were looking for attractive talent to stock their house with. Annie at the time was merely a 50¢ prostitute in the house of Anna Wilson, but she nevertheless took on the brunt of the fighting, which eventually resulted in a victory for the Sands area. Somewhere along the line Annie got tired of doing all the work while others were making the money. She resolved to become the madam of her own establishment, and by the early 1860s she was running what she described as a "classy place with 30 boarders."

For close to two decades Annie was a principal figure in Chicago vice and her lovelife and business enterprises were duly recorded by the newspapers. Annie had been the longtime mistress of Cap Hyman, a lead-

ing Chicago gambler, who enjoyed her company and charms but didn't see the need for making it legal—until one September day in 1866 when Annie stormed into his gambling house carrying a rawhide whip. She found Hyman sleeping on a sofa, threw him down the stairs and chased him up the street, her whip cracking on his shanks with every stride. Shortly thereafter, Cap Hyman proposed marriage. The wedding was an elegant affair that attracted not only the Chicago underworld but also representatives from as far away as Cincinnati and New Orleans. Immediately following the ceremony, Cap Hyman announced he was giving his wife a very special present, a tavern outside the city limits called Sunnyside, which would be turned into "a high-toned roadhouse."

The opening of Sunnyside was a gala event, with guests of honor including city and county officials, young businessmen with sporting interests, big-time gamblers and reporters from each of the newspapers. Also invited were other leading Chicago madams, while some three dozen of Annie's young ladies were trained thoroughly on the proper etiquette for the occasion. The reporters were brought to Sunnyside in a huge four-horse sleigh.

Frederick Francis Cook, there as a reporter for the *Chicago Times*, reported that the festivities started in a most decorous fashion. "You were ceremoniously introduced, engagement cards were consulted, and all the rest of the little formalities that distinguish like functions in the *haut monde* were strictly observed. Yes, the make-believe was quite tremendous." One young redheaded lady of Annie's staff walked around looking gentlemen in the eye and asking, "Who's your favorite poet? Mine's Byron."

The tone couldn't last. Before the night had finished, case after case of champagne had been consumed, Cap Hyman had shot out the lights, Annie had had to reprimand other madams for passing out business cards, and several harlots had set up business on a freelance basis in a number of the upstairs rooms.

While Sunnyside was a great social success, it flopped as a commercial enterprise. Annie Stafford noted that gentlemen just wouldn't travel that far even for high-class strumpets. So the couple returned to their Chicago haunts. In 1875 Cap Hyman suffered a complete physical and mental collapse. He died the following year, with Annie at his bedside. Annie continued to run a brothel until about 1880, when she dropped from sight.

See also: SANDS, WHORE WAR.

Standard Oil Building, Battles of the

Probably more than any other events, the two so-called Battles of the Standard Oil Building in 1926 were what people thought of when they heard the words "Chicago gangsters."

On the morning of August 10 Hymie Weiss and Schemer Drucci, who took control of Dion O'Banion's North Side Gang after O'Banion's assassination, were on their way to make a payoff to Morris Eller, political boss of the 20th Ward, in order to secure protection for their numerous speakeasies. The meeting was to take place at 910 South Michigan Avenue, the new 19-story Standard Oil Building. Just as the pair reached the bronze Renaissance-style doors of the building, four Capone gunmen, the North Siders' sworn enemies, jumped from a car and charged at them. Seeing the attackers' drawn guns, Weiss and Drucci ducked behind a parked car and pulled their own weapons from shoulder holsters. The area, which at

that hour teemed with pedestrians, erupted in gunfire. One pedestrian was hit in the volley of 30-odd shots, as bystanders either dived for cover or stood frozen with horror.

Weiss started to retreat from car to car, but Drucci headed for his hated foe. The Capone gunmen backed off to a sedan parked on the other side of the avenue and then pulled away, with a still-angry Drucci firing after them. He jumped on the running board of a passing car, put his gun to the driver's temple and ordered, "Follow that goddamn car." Just then a police flivver pulled up and officers yanked the crazed Drucci to the pavement.

Drucci told the police there had been no gang battle, that it had merely been a case of some punks "trying for my roll." The police brought Louis Barko, whom they had recognized as one of the Capone gunners, before Drucci for identification. In keeping with underworld tradition, Drucci shrugged, "I never seen him before." Barko and all other suspects were released.

Five days later, on August 15, Weiss and Drucci were again attacked at almost the same spot. This time they were driving in a sedan when rival gangsters trailing in another auto opened up on them. Although their car was riddled with bullets, the two gangsters were not hit. They dashed from their car to the sanctuary of the Standard Oil Building, firing wild shots over their shoulders.

On September 20 Weiss and Drucci retaliated with the famous attack on the Capone headquarters at the Hawthorne Inn in Cicero. A convoy of eight cars loaded with gunmen poured lead into the building in a vain effort to kill Al Capone. In addition to wounding some pedestrians, the gunmen shot Louis Barko in the shoulder. Later, police picked up Drucci on the suspicion that he had fired the shot which downed Barko. When asked if he could identify Drucci as his assailant, Barko returned a past favor by announcing, "Never saw him before."

About this time Lucky Luciano, Capone's Brooklyn schoolmate, visited Chicago on crime business. "A real goddam crazy place!" he told associates upon returning to the quiet of New York. "Nobody's safe in the streets."

Stevens, Walter (1867–1939) hit man
One of the most proficient killers in a city of killers, Walter Stevens was known as the Dean of Chicago Gunmen.

Stevens turned up first in Chicago shortly after the turn of the century as a slugger and killer for Mossy Enright's union-busting mob. After Enright was murdered in 1920, Stevens became a freelance hit man, often renting his guns out to Johnny Torrio and Al Capone. There was direct evidence linking Stevens with more than a dozen murders (although it was believed he had committed at least 60), but he only went to prison for one, the killing of a policeman in Aurora, Ill. However, he was pardoned shortly after his incarceration by Gov. Len Small, evidently for past services rendered. Years before, Small had been accused of embezzling more than $500,000 while serving as state treasurer. Stevens bribed and threatened a number of jurors and Small was acquitted.

While Stevens can only be described as ferocious in his profession—he once did a killing as a favor for a mere $50—he displayed an entirely different manner in his home life. Well-educated, he enjoyed the works of Robert Burns, Robert Louis Stevenson and Jack London. He neither drank nor smoked until he was 50, and for 20 years he took excellent and doting care of his invalid wife. He adopted three children and gave them a good education. Stevens was also a prude. He censored his children's reading material, tearing out pages of books that he considered immoral. When he found stage plays and movies not up to his puritanical standards, he ordered his children not to attend them. His daughters were not allowed to wear short skirts or use lipstick or rouge.

After an attempt was made on his life, Stevens retired, earning the same description as Johnny Torrio: "He could dish it out but he couldn't take it." Still, no one ever said it to Stevens' face during the last dozen years of his life.

Storyville New Orleans red-light district
For 20 years, from 1897 until 1917, Storyville in New Orleans was the most famous red-light district in the United States.

Long before Storyville emerged, New Orleans had achieved the "almost universal reputation as the promised land of harlotry," as social historian Herbert Asbury put it. Prostitutes from all over the country flocked there. Eventually, the entire citizenry realized that unless prostitution was somehow suppressed or regulated, the entire city would become one vast brothel. However, all the proposed solutions were shot down in the cross fire between what might be called the brothel lobby and the equally powerful lobby representing the clergy and respectable southern womanhood, which argued that a law licensing prostitutes would legitimatize vice. Finally, in January 1897 the city council adopted an ordinance introduced by Alderman Sidney Story, a leading broker, that provided for the containment of prostitution in a prescribed area. After considerable maneuvering, including lawsuits by landlords in other parts of the city who would be left tenantless if the harlots moved elsewhere, a quasi-legal red-light district was established. It consisted of five blocks on Customhouse, Bienville, Conti and St. Louis streets and three on North Basin, Villere, Marais, North Franklin, North Robertson and Treme streets. As a result, a total of 38 blocks were to be occupied exclusively by brothels, assignation houses, saloons, cabarets and other types of businesses that depended on vice for their prosperity. It was Alderman Story's misfortune that the area took his name.

Inside of a year Storyville became the top attraction of the city. Tours took visitors "down the line" so that they could see the richly furnished parlors of the plush, even palatial mansions of sin. Inside the cabarets they could be shocked by the bawdy shows and dancing and later they could peek through the shutters of the hundreds of cribs in the cheaper houses where naked girls lay waiting for customers. Actual pleasure seekers could find houses to meet any purse. In most of the crib-type brothels, flimsy one-story wooden shanties, the price varied from 25¢ up to $1. These establishments dominated St. Louis and Franklin streets and others could be found on Conti, Customhouse and North Robertson. A step up in class, $2 and $3 houses were located on Villere, Marais, Customhouse and North Liberty streets. Most of the $5 establishments were on North Basin Street. A good number of them were imposing mansions, where liaisons were conducted with great ceremony and elegance. Customers were expected to refrain from any rudeness or bawdy behavior and no drunken gentlemen were accommodated. Naturally, these finer houses sported such trappings as rooms with mirrored walls

and ceilings, ballrooms with fine hardwood floors and curtained platforms for special circuses, indecent dancing and other forms of erotic entertainment. Top houses had bands, consisting of two to four musicians, who played in the ballrooms from about seven o'clock in the evening until dawn. It was these musicians who created jazz in the brothels on North Basin Street.

Storyville even developed its own newspapers. One such publication was the *Mascot*. A 5¢ tabloid that appeared weekly starting in 1882, the *Mascot* was a vigorous weekly on the liberal end of the political spectrum. While it devoted considerable space to crime and scandal in the vein of the *Police Gazette*, the newspaper also performed valued service in exposing high-level corruption. In the 1890s, however, the *Mascot* shifted more toward a Storyville orientation, instituting a column called "Society," which consisted of personal items about prostitutes, a sort of harlot gossip column. The column reported such news as:

> Madame Julia Dean has received a draft of recruits, and the fair Julia is bragging loudly of her importation. She seems to forget that the ladies played a star engagement here last winter at Mme. Haley's, and they all carry their diplomas with them.

> It is safe to say that Mrs. (Madeleine) Theurer can brag of more innocent young girls having been ruined in her house than there were in any other six houses in the city.

> Several amateurs have been enjoying quite a good time of late in the residence at the rear of a grocery store on Derbigny Street.

The *Sunday Sun* was perhaps more explicit in covering bawds. The following excerpts were taken from the column "Scarlet World":

Miss Josie Arlington is suffering with a bad cold, but she is on deck all the same attending to business.

Jessie Brown is expecting two girls from Atlanta, Ga.

Stella Clements, who now calls herself Stella Moore, has taken the name of a performer in Haverly's Minstrels. Are you going to do the couche-couche, Stella?

Lou Raymond, better known as Kackling Lou, ought to attend to her own business and quit poking her nose into her neighbors' affairs. The way Kackling Lou has put the devil in a couple of young girls, who were doing nicely with a neighbor of hers, was a caution. Such conduct on the part of a woman as old as Kackling Lou is most mortifying. Now will you be good, you naughty old girl, and attend to your own business?

Storyville's most famous publication was the *Blue Book*. It was published regularly from 1902 on and had a complete list of all prostitutes in residence in Storyville. The girls were coded by race, sometimes listed alphabetically and sometimes by street. There was a special listing of "Late Arrivals." The publication was 40 to 50 pages in length and sold for a quarter. It was on sale at hotels, railroad stations and steamboat landings and was of course available in saloons. The *Blue Book* was read as much for its advertisements as for its editorial content. The ads went straight to the point:

Martha Clark, 227 North Basin. "Her women are known for their cleverness and beauty. Also, in being able to entertain the most fastidious of mankind."

Diana and Norma, 213–215 North Basin. "Their names have become known on both continents, because everything goes as it will, and those that cannot be satisfied there must surely be of a queer nature."

Eunice Deering, corner of Basin and Conti Streets. "Known as the idol of the society and club boys. . . . Aside from the grandeur of her establishment, she has a score of beautiful women."

The Firm, 224 North Villere Street. Kept by Miss Leslie. "The Firm is also noted for its selectness. You make no mistake in visiting The Firm. Everybody must be of some importance, otherwise he cannot gain admittance."

Mary Smith, 1538 Iberville. "A pleasant time for the boys."

Taps was sounded for Storyville when America entered World War I. The army and navy issued orders forbidding open prostitution within five miles of any army cantonment or navy establishment. Federal agents visited Storyville and ordered it closed. When New Orleans mayor Martin Behrman went to Washington to lodge a protest, he was told that if the city didn't close Storyville, the army and navy would. After all manner of legal appeals—by city officials, madams, whores—failed, a final appeal was made to the Supreme Court, but it too was rejected and Storyville passed into history.

Further reading: *The French Quarter* by Herbert Asbury.

suicide by cop   deliberately seeking to be shot
While the news media in the 1990s devoted itself to reporting allegations of police brutality that often resulted in death and inevitably led to charges of police out of control, there was another growing phenomenon that put officers in a bad light. The baffling concept is known to police and psychologists as "suicide by cop."

While firm statistics are not available on the frequency of such suicides, it has been estimated that of the 600-odd fatal police shootings per year, about 10 percent are clearly provoked by individuals seeking to make a police officer shoot—usually under threat of shooting the officers.

Item: A 46-year-old cancer patient who was shot and wounded after pulling a gun on two Jersey City, N.J., police officers eating in a pizza parlor. Clearly, he wanted to die.

Item: A 19-year-old college student with a destructive gambling problem was shot and killed after he pulled a toy gun on officers who had pulled him over for driving erratically on the Long Island Expressway.

Item: A security guard brandished two guns outside a police station in Shelby, S. C., and screamed at officers, "Do your job! It's going to end here." It did.

Perhaps persons who opt for suicide by cop are essentially no different in motivation from other suicides, but what remains a matter of some bafflement is why they single out cops as their executioners. There are documented cases of persons planning such acts of self-destruction actually telling loved ones or friends that they intended to get the police to shoot them. About one-third of suicides by cop leave notes apologizing to the police for intentionally making them their executioners.

Dr. Deirdre Anglin of the University of Southern California points out, "Suicide is still socially taboo. This way you're not actually killing yourself." Dr. Anglin cites other possible motivations: cowardice, religious prohibitions against suicide, not wishing to jeopardize their families' inheriting insurance money because of policy restrictions, and

being simply incapable of committing the act themselves.

Additionally, Clinton R. Van Zandt, a former chief negotiator for the FBI, notes, "What it all comes down to is that people know the police have weapons. If you drive your car into a bridge abutment, you may not die. But provoking a cop—there's good reason to believe that's going to kill you."

Studies of suicide conducted by researchers at the Harvard Medical School and in British Columbia have helped pinpoint the typical suicide by cop figure. He is a white man in his mid-20s with a record of drug and alcohol abuse. His acts are often triggered by a deterioration of an important personal relationship.

A recent study on suicide by cop analyzed by Sgt. John Yarbrough of the L.A. County Sheriff's homicide bureau indicates "a breakup or a divorce with no belief that there can be a reconciliation is often the significant contributing factor. They are helpless to change their situation and they often suffer the frustration of, 'I can't get it back, it's over.'"

One of the chief victims of suicide by cop actions are, although it is often not known to the public, the cops themselves. It is one thing to get involved in a shooting with a real or even a perceived sense of duty or at least self-preservation; however, suicide by cop plots leave the officers with, says expert Bill Geller, "feelings of powerlessness, feelings of being manipulated." Geller, author of *Deadly Force: What We Know,* adds that most officers in suicide by cop incidents tend to retire prematurely.

tong wars

The origins of the tongs date back roughly 2,000 years. In ancient China the tongs were bandit or rebel organizations. When first imported into the United States, they served as mutual aid societies. Unfortunately, aiding someone meant attacking someone else and the result was the great tong wars in American cities.

From about the 1860s more than 30 tongs appeared and prospered along the West Coast. San Francisco's Chinatown supported six great tongs. As the Chinese migrated east so did the tongs. Almost all these organizations derived their main incomes from such illegal enterprises as opium dens, gambling, smuggling of aliens, especially slave girls, and prostitution. The tongs tended to concentrate on the same illegal activities, making conflict inevitable. This gave rise to numerous small strong-arm gangs, or enforcers, known as highbinder societies, which were composed of hit men available for hire to tongs that wanted the competition eliminated. The Chinese called these fighting men *boo how doy* and the American newspapers dubbed them hatchet men, in honor of their favorite weapon. The tong wars raged on and off for more than 50 years, occasionally over the loss of face but far more often over the loss of profits. Great wars were fought at different times between the tongs, although tongs not infrequently changed from one side to the other. It made no matter, skulls were still split and pitched battles fought, while the white man's law proved incapable of stopping them.

When the tong wars got completely out of hand, white society tried unique tactics to restore the peace. After the great tong warrior Fung Jing Toy, better known as Little Pete, was assassinated in San Francisco in 1897, his tong, the Sum Yops, was decimated by the Sue Yops. Finally, some white Americans appealed to the emperor of China, Kwang Hsu, for help, and he called in the great Chinese statesman Li Hung Chang. "The matter has been attended to," Li Hung Chang reported in due course. "I have cast into prison all relatives of the Sue Yops in China, and have cabled to California that their heads will be chopped off if another

Sum Yop is killed in San Francisco." Suddenly, one of the greatest tong wars ended. The Sue Yops and the Sum Yops signed a peace treaty that was never violated.

By 1922 the San Francisco Police Department had learned how to apply pressure to the Chinese community as a whole and in that year the presidents of the six great tongs put their signatures on a treaty of lasting peace.

As fierce as the San Francisco tong wars were, they were equaled in intensity and bloodshed by numerous battles in New York City, especially the Hip Sings and On Leongs. One war in 1909–10 over the murder of a beautiful slave girl called Bow Kum, or Little Sweet Flower, resulted in 350 casualties. Lesser wars occurred in Boston and Chicago.

See also: BLOODY ANGLE, BOW KUM, LITTLE PETE, MOCK DUCK.

Wall, Tessie (1869–1932) San Francisco madam

The best-known parlor house madam in San Francisco from 1900 to 1917, Tessie Wall was described as a "flamboyant, well-upholstered blonde." Her most famous brothel, at 337 O'Farrell Street, was regarded as the Golden Gate City's greatest fun palace. She stocked it with beautiful, slightly plump girls, remarkably all of them blondes. She charged what was then an outrageous price, $20, for an assignation. But the clients seemed to feel it was worth it and said Tessie Wall's services were "super." Overnight guests could expect to find their clothes pressed and shoes shined when they awoke in the morning. Those who were not staying and had to get back across the bay to Oakland would be interrupted by Tessie and informed, "You just have time to catch the last ferry."

As was true of many famous madams, Tessie Wall in later life was invested with perhaps more colorful accomplishments than she deserved, such as the journalistic credit for inventing the phrase, "Company, girls!"; those words were probably first uttered by an earlier madam, Bertha Kahn. In Tessie's case, this sort of embroidery was pointless since her own legitimate achievements were quite sufficient to make her famous. An incredible drinker, she once drank boxer John L. Sullivan under the table. Tessie was amazingly generous with the police and generally led off the Grand March at the annual policemen's ball on the arm of Mayor Sunny Jim Rolph. She started things rolling at such affairs by slapping a $1,000 bill down on the bar and shouting, "Drink that up, boys!"

Long married to Frank Daroux, a gambler and owner of a number of brothels, she resisted his entreaties that she leave the business and become a country housewife on a lavish estate that he had bought for her in San Mateo County. Once, Tessie told him, "I'd rather be an electric light pole on Powell Street than own all the land in the sticks." After Daroux finally divorced her, Tessie begged him to return. When he refused, she sent word to him that she would fix him so no other woman would ever want him. She did her best to keep her word in the summer of 1916 by firing three bullets into his body from a .22-caliber revolver. When the police arrived, she was standing over him crying, "I shot him because I love him—damn him!"

Daroux survived, and although the shooting permanently weakened him, he refused to testify against Tessie and she was released. Tessie retired from the business in 1917 during a wartime wave of reform that wiped out the Barbary Coast and most of the sordid features of her bailiwick, the so-called Upper Tenderloin, which was the city's best theater and restaurant district. Years of wild living and gambling had reduced her fortunes considerably, but she had enough left to establish herself comfortably in a nice flat on Eighteenth Street, taking with her many of the furnishings from her O'Farrell Street place, including a needlepoint wall motto that read, "If every man was as true to his country as he is to his wife—God help the U.S.A." Tessie died in April 1932.

Walsh School feud

Undoubtedly, the most remarkable schoolboy feud in American history occurred in Chicago at the Walsh School on Johnson Street. A war between two rival gangs of schoolboys broke out in 1881 and continued for almost three decades, during which several boys were killed and more than a score were shot, stabbed or severely beaten with clubs or brickbats. A number of pitched gun battles were fought both inside and outside the school by the two gangs, which were known as the Irishers and the Bohemians, although ethnic origin was not the real touchstone of allegiance. Place of residence was the important factor, with boys living east of Johnson Street constituting the Irishers and those west of Johnson making up the Bohemians.

For years the boys came to school armed with revolvers and knives and on many occasions they would take pot shots at one another in the classrooms. Some of these little gangsters were only 10 years old and so small that they had to use both hands to even lift their weapons to firing position. The last major gunfight between the rival gangs occurred in December 1905, when 25 Irishers and an equal number of Bohemians blazed away at each other outside the school until police arrived. Finally, authorities launched daily searches of all pupils going into or leaving the school and confiscated all weapons found. This continued for several years until the level of violence dropped.

Whore War   Chicago prostitutes' feud

Jurisdictional disputes as well as ownership of "goods" have always dogged organized prostitution, but never has the business been more marked by violence than during the so-called Whore War in Chicago in 1857.

Pitted against each other were the forces of the Sands, the lowest center of vice in the city, and those representing the more "refined" houses of State Street, such as Julia Davenport's Green House and Mother Herrick's Prairie Queen. The spark that ignited the war was a provocative act by Mother Herrick, who lured away from the Sands the fairest specimen in Madame Anna Wilson's brothel with an offer of more money and a clean dress. Madame Wilson operated the only 50¢ brothel in the Sands, twice the standard rate for that area, and, as such, was considered the natural leader of the bordello forces there. Several pitched battles with harlots and pimps on each side were fought on city streets, as newspapers duly warned their readers to seek cover whenever a large gang of "strumpets and their men" appeared.

The Sands' forces had an advantage in having on their side a pugnacious young prostitute named Annie Stafford. Totally misnamed Gentle Annie, she was recognized as one of the most brutal fighters in Chicago, male or female. The war continued indecisively for a number of months until April 3, when Gentle Annie, with the aid of a number of henchwomen and their pimps, made a surprise attack on the Prairie Queen. They battered down the door, destroyed furniture and forced customers to flee in varying states of dishabille. Mother Herrick and her supporters were beaten, and Gentle Annie marched back in victory to the Sands, personally driving before her the stolen harlot as well as Mother Herrick's prize prostitutes as the spoils of victory. The State Street houses never again tried to raid the Sands.

See also: SANDS, ANNIE STAFFORD.

Whyos last great 19th-century ruffian gang

A ruffian gang that was to dominate the New York crime scene for two decades after its formation in 1874, the Whyos recalled all the viciousness of such early marauder bands as the Chichesters and the Dead Rabbits. They, like their predecessors, were Irish to the core, but whereas the early gangs reveled in robbing, assaulting, maiming and killing Englishmen, the Whyos would victimize anyone. In fact, the gang functioned as a primitive Murder, Inc., ready to perform any sort of mayhem for a set fee. When one of the top Whyos, Piker Ryan, was apprehended in 1883, he had in his possession what the newspapers called the "official" Whyo price list for services. It read:

Punching	$ 2
Both eyes blacked	$ 4
Nose and jaw broke	$ 10
Jacked out [knocked out with a blackjack]	$ 15
Ear chawed off	$ 15
Leg or arm broke	$ 19
Shot in leg	$ 25
Stab	$ 25
Doing the big job	$100 and up

So powerful were the Whyos that they exacted tribute from many other gangs for permission to operate. The names of Whyo members constituted a full roster of the most vicious thugs of the period: English Charley, Denver Hop, Hoggy Walsh, Big Josh Hines, Fig McGerald, Bull Hurley, Dandy Johnny Dolan, Baboon Connolly, Googy Corcoran and Red Rocks Farrell.

Big Josh, who had the franchise for collecting protection money from the various stuss games, an illegal form of gambling of the era, would parade from one game to another armed with two revolvers to take out the Whyos' portion of the revenues. When some of the stuss operators complained he took too much, Big Josh peevishly told a detective: "Them guys must be nuts. Don't I always leave 'em somethin'? All I want is me share!"

Because membership in the Whyos meant higher income, the more lethal criminals in the city naturally gravitated to it. In the 1880s the gang's two most-celebrated leaders, Danny Driscoll and Danny Lyons, enforced an edict reserving membership only to those who had killed at least one man. Both Driscoll and Lyons were hanged in 1888. Driscoll had been convicted of shooting to death a young prostitute and Lyons of killing another gangster in a street shoot-out. Shortly after Lyons' death, two young prostitutes—Gentle Maggie and Lizzie the Dove—who had toiled hard and long to keep him in the style to which he had become accustomed got into a boisterous argument about which of them missed Lyons the most. Gentle Maggie won the dispute by slitting Lizzie the Dove's throat.

The Whyos headquartered at a low Bowery dive aptly called the Morgue, whose proprietor proudly boasted his liquid refreshments were equally potent as either a beverage or an embalming fluid. It was at the Morgue that one of the gang's most brutal members, Dandy Johnny Dolan, would often display proof of his latest crime. In addition to flashing the appropriate bankroll, he would display his victim's eyes, which he carried around in a pocket. Dolan was the inventor of a new and efficient eye gouger, an apparatus worn on the thumb and available for instant use. He also designed special fighting shoes with sections of a sharp ax blade imbedded in the soles, so that a Dolan stomping was always particularly gory.

The Morgue was the scene of the Whyos' last battle. The gang members were notorious for fighting as much among themselves as with their victims. It started when Denver Hop and English Charley got into an argument over the division of some loot. Suddenly, both started shooting, and soon, at least 20 other Whyos joined in the gun battle. No one was injured, however, since all were drunk; the press reported that the proprietor felt the Whyos had been rather silly to expect to hit anything after imbibing his liquor.

The incident perhaps best explained why the Whyos were to disappear from the scene. While they were certainly the most efficient killers and maimers in town, they did not understand the full value of political influence. A powerful gang, the Eastmans, that came to the fore upon their decline was just as brutal, but its members learned to work with the Tammany Hall powers, providing efficient services at election time. The Whyos simply wanted to crack skulls and, as such, fell victim to the changing times. Without political protection, they were open to arrest and imprisonment.

See also: DANNY DRISCOLL.

Yorky of the Great Lakes murderer who became a legend

For over a century now Yorky Mickey the Clam Man has scoured the Great Lakes on a mission of murder, and, the story goes, he will not give up until vengeance is his.

Yorky Mickey was a real person well-known to the denizens of Buffalo's Canal Street vice area, a jutting piece of land segregated from the rest of Buffalo by 40 feet of murky water called the Erie Canal. In the 1860s and 1870s Yorky ran a clam stand there that offered two main attractions. Yorky, a man of amazing strength, could crush a man's fingers with his grip and often did. Patrons flocked to his stand to watch in wonder as he opened clams with his fingers. After a patron filled up on clams, he could avail himself of the stand's second attraction: women. Yorky was also a procurer, leasing out women by the evening. It was a good deal for his patrons because Yorky was an honest man and never allowed his women to rob a customer.

Everyone liked Yorky and they were happy for him when love came into his life.

He fell for one of his own women, a lass known as the Thrush, and they had a wedding that Canal Street—indeed the entire Great Lakes—long remembered. The Thrush, who was famed for her figure, performed at times as a singer in a bar called the Peacock. Her voice was not particularly good but no one seemed to notice.

It was in the Peacock that the pair joined in tragic wedlock. All Canal Street was there—the leading prostitutes, the rival saloon owners, the sporting men and the cooperative politicians. Liquor and beer flowed freely and food was plentiful. A brass band blared without letup. Finally, Yorky and his lady were married by a Canal Street character named Preacher Dobie, a minister who had deserted his flock for the ways of the fleshpots. Preacher Dobie ran through the words in a drunken stupor, but then everyone else was drunk as well—Yorky, his bride and the guests.

The newlyweds were hustled to the bar as soon as the ceremony was over and served more liquor. Yorky was so happy he couldn't seem to get enough. As a result, the Thrush was being deserted by her groom only minutes after their marriage. The more Yorky drank the less likely it appeared he would be leaving soon. At first the Thrush didn't seem to mind. She had no aversion to the brew herself, but the more she drank, the more her eye would rove.

The Thrush drank until her eye settled on a rakish young sailor who'd just wandered into the Peacock. The fact that the Thrush was garbed in a wedding dress did not deter the young sailor. He was right off his ship, his pockets bulged with a month's pay and he ached to spend some of it. Yorky was so far gone he failed to notice his bride and the sailor slip out of the Peacock.

It took another two hours before Yorky noticed his bride's absence. He stormed forth to look for her, and his anger soared when he heard from others that she had been seen carousing with a young sailor. Yorky lurched from bar to bar, clenching his powerful fists

tighter each passing minute. Finally, he found the Thrush. She was sprawled in a drunken stupor on the bed of the two-room flat Yorky had furnished for her. Her lipstick and clothing were in disarray and there was some money pinned to the rumpled pillow.

Later, when others ventured into the flat, they found the Thrush still lying on the bed, but her head had been twisted and she looked like a chicken whose neck had been wrung. She was dead and Yorky was gone.

He was never seen again on Canal Street, but lakers coming in from other ports reported having observed him scouring all the ships of the Great Lakes looking for the young sailor. A couple of times, it was said, Yorky had just missed catching his man.

Apparently he never did. Even today when a dim light is seen in the mist over the Great Lakes, there are some lakers who say it is Yorky still hunting for the sailor who seduced his new bride.

PHOTO CREDITS

BIBLIOGRAPHY

Following is a bibliography of selected resources for further reading on strange crimes and criminals as well as the history of crimes in America in general.

Adams, Ramon F. *Burs Under the Saddle*. Norman: University of Oklahoma Press, 1964.

Adler, Polly. *A House Is Not a Home*. New York: Popular Library, 1954.

Allen, Frederick Lewis. *Only Yesterday, An Informal History of the Nineteen Twenties*. New York: Harper & Bros., 1931.

———. *Since Yesterday*. New York: Harper & Bros., 1940.

Asbury, Herbert. *The Gangs of New York*. New York: Alfred A. Knopf, Inc., 1927.

———. *The Barbary Coast, An Informal History of the San Francisco Underworld*. Garden City, N.Y.: Garden City Publishing Company, Inc., 1933.

———. *Sucker's Progress*. New York: Dodd, Mead and Company, Inc., 1938.

———. *Gem of the Prairie*. New York: Alfred A. Knopf, Inc., 1940.

———. *The French Quarter, An Informal History of the New Orleans Underworld*. New York: Alfred A. Knopf, Inc., 1940.

———. *The Great Illusion: An Informal History of Prohibition*. New York: Doubleday & Co., 1950.

Berger, Meyer. *The Eighty Million*. New York: Simon & Schuster, 1942.

Block, Eugene B. *The Wizard of Berkeley*. New York: Coward-McCann, 1958.

———. *Great Train Robberies of the West*. New York: Coward-McCann, 1959.

———. *Great Stagecoach Robbers in the West*. New York: Doubleday & Co., Inc. 1962.

———. *Fifteen Clues*. Garden City, N.Y.: Doubleday & Co., Inc., 1968.

Bolitho, William. *Murder for Profit*. New York: Harper & Bros., 1926.

Bonanno, Joseph. *A Man of Honor, The Autobiography of Joseph Bonanno*. New York: Simon & Schuster, 1983.

Boswell, Charles, and Lewis Thompson. *The Girls in Nightmare House*. New York: Gold Medal, 1955.

———. *Practitioners of Murder*. New York: Collier, 1962.

Brynes, Thomas. *Professional Criminals in America*. New York: Chelsea House, 1969.

Burns, Walter Noble. *The One-Way Ride*. Garden City, N.Y.: Doubleday, Doran & Company, 1931.

Caesar, Gene. *Incredible Detective: The Biography of William J. Burns*. Englewood Clifs, N.J.: Prentice-Hall, 1968.

Chandler, David. *Brothers in Blood: The Rise of the Criminal Brotherhoods*. New York: Dutton, 1975.

Churchill, Allen. *A Pictorial History of American Crime.* New York: Holt, Rinehart & Winston, 1964.

Coates, Robert M. *The Outlaw Years: The History of the Land Pirates of the Natchez Trace.* New York: The Literary Guild of America, 1930.

Collins, Ted, ed. *New York Murders.* New York: Sloan & Pearce, 1944.

Crouse, Russell. *Murder Won't Out.* New York: Pennant Books, 1953.

Croy, Homer. *He Hanged Them High.* Duell, Sloan & Pearce, 1952.

DeFord, Miriam Allen. *Murders Sane & Mad.* New York: Abelard-Schuman, Ltd., 1965.

Demaris, Ovid. *Captive City.* New York: Lyle Stuart, Inc., 1969.

DeVol, George. *Forty Years a Gambler on the Mississippi.* New York: H. Holt & Company, 1926.

Drago, Harry Sinclair. *Outlaws on Horseback.* New York: Dodd, Mead & Company, 1964.

Eisenberg, Dennis; Uri Dan; and Eli Landau. *Meyer Lansky, Mogul of the Mob.* New York & London: Paddington Press Ltd., 1979.

Elman, Robert. *Fired in Anger.* Garden City, N.Y.: Doubleday & Company, Inc., 1968.

Emrich, Duncan. *It's an Old Wild West Custom.* New York: The Vanguard Press, Inc., 1949.

Emery, Edward Van. *Sins of New York.* New York: Frederick A. Stokes, 1930.

———. *Sins of America as "Exposed" by the Police Gazette.* New York, Fredrick A. Stokes Co., 1931.

Frank, Judge Jerome, and Barbara Frank. *Not Guilty.* Garden City, N.Y., Doubleday & Company, Inc., 1957.

Godwin, John. *Alcatraz 1868–1963.* New York: Doubleday & Co., 1963.

———. *Murder USA.* New York: Ballantine Books 1978.

Gosch, Martin A., and Richard Hammer. *The Last Testament of Lucky Luciano.* Boston: Little, Brown, 1975.

Hammer, Richard. *Playboy's Illustrated History of Organized Crime.* Chicago: Playboy Press, 1975.

Hecht, Ben. *A Child of the Century.* New York: Simon & Schuster, 1954.

———. *Charlie, The Improbable Life and Times of Charles MacArthur.* New York: Harper & Bros., 1957.

Horan, James D. *Desperate Men.* New York: G. P. Putnam Sons, 1949.

———. *Pictorial History of the Wild West.* New York: Crown Publishers, Inc. 1954.

———. *The Desperate Years.* New York: Crown Publishers, Inc., 1962.

———. *The Pinkertons, The Detective Dynasty That Made History.* New York: Crown Publishers, Inc. 1967.

Hynd, Alan. *Murder, Mayhem and Mystery.* New York: A. S. Barnes & Co., 1958.

Jackson, Joseph Henry. *San Francisco Murders.* New York: Duell, Sloan and Pearce, 1947.

Johnston, James A. *Alcatraz Island Prison.* New York: Charles Scribner's Sons, 1949.

Karpis, Alvin, with Bill Trent. *The Alvin Karpis Story.* New York: Coward McCann & Geoghegan, Inc., 1971.

Katcher, Leo. *The Big Bankroll, The Life and Times of Arnold Rothstein.* New York: Harper & Bros., 1959.

Katz, Leonard. *Uncle Frank: The Biography of Frank Costello.* New York: Drake, 1973.

Kefauver, Estes. *Crime in America.* New York: Doubleday & Co., 1951.

Kilgallen, Dorothy. *Murder One.* New York: Random House, 1967.

Klein, Alexander, ed. *Grand Deception.* New York: J. B. Lippincott & Company, 1955.

———. *The Double Dealers.* Philadelphia and New York: J. B. Lippincott & Company, 1958.

Kobler, John. *Capone.* New York: G. P. Putnam's Sons, 1971.

Kohn, George C. *Encyclopedia of American Scandal.* New York: Facts On File, 1989.

Lawes, Warden Lewis Edward. *Twenty Thousand Years in Sing Sing.* New York: R. Long & R. R. Smith, Inc., 1932.

Lewis, Alfred Henry. *The Apaches of New York.* New York: G. W. Dillingham Company, 1912.

———. *Nation-Famous New York Murders.* G. W. Dillingham Company, 1914.

McLoughlin, Denis. *Wild and Wooly.* Garden City, N.Y.: Doubleday & Company, Inc., 1975.

Maas, Peter. *The Valachi Papers.* New York: G. P. Putnam's Sons, 1968.

Messick, Hank. *Lansky.* New York: G. P. Putnam's Sons, 1971.

Morrel, Ed. *The Twenty-fifth Man.* Montclair, N.J.: New Era Publishing Co., 1924.

Murray, George. *The Legacy of Al Capone.* New York: G. P. Putnam's Sons, 1975.

Ness, Eliot, with Oscar Fraley. *The Untouchables.* New York: Julian Messner, 1957.

Newton, Michael. *Hunting Humans.* New York: Avon Books, 1992.

Pearson, Edmund L. *Studies in Murder.* New York: MacMillan Company, 1926.

———. *More Studies in Murder.* New York: Harrison Smith & Robert Haas, Pub., 1936.

Peterson, Virgil. *Barbarians in Our Midst.* Little, Brown & Co., 1936.

———. *The Mob.* Ottawa, Illinois: Green Hill Publishers, Inc., 1983.

Radin, Edward D. *12 Against the Law.* New York: Bantam Books, 1952.

———. *12 Against Crime.* New York: Collier Books, 1961.

Reid, Ed. *Mafia.* New York: Random House, 1952.

———. *The Grim Reapers.* Chicago: Henry Regnery Co., 1969.

Reid, Ed, and Ovid Demaris. *The Green Felt Jungle.* New York: Trident Press, 1963.

Rodell, Marie F. *New York Murders.* New York: Duell, Sloan and Pearce, 1944.

Salerno, Ralph, and John Tompkins. *The Crime Confederation.* New York: Doubleday & Co., 1969.

Sann, Paul. *The Lawless Decade.* New York: Crown Publishers, Inc., 1957.

Scott, Gini Graham. *Homicide: 100 Years of Murder in America.* Lincolnwood, Illinois: Roxbury Park, 1998.

Smith, Alton. *Syndicate City.* Chicago: Henry Regnery Co., 1954.

Sondern, Frederic, Jr. *Brotherhood of Evil: The Mafia.* New York: Farrar, Straus & Cudahy, 1959.

Stone, Irving. *Clarence Darrow for the Defense.* New York: Doubleday & Co., 1941.

Tallant, Robert. *Ready to Hang.* New York: Harper & Bros., 1952.

Teresa, Vincent, with Thomas C. Renner. *My Life in the Mafia.* Garden City, New York, Doubleday & Company, 1973.

Teresa, Vincent. *Teresa's Mafia.* Garden City, New York: Doubleday & Company, Inc., 1975.

Toland, John. *The Dillinger Days.* New York: Random House, 1963.

Touhy, Roger, with Ray Brennan. *The Stolen Years.* Cleveland: Pennington Press, Inc., 1959.

Turkus, Burton B., and Sid Feder. *Murder, Inc.: The Story of the Syndicate.* Farrar, Straus & Young Co., 1951.

Turner, Wallace. *Gambler's Money.* Boston: Houghton Mifflin Co., 1965.

Wendt, Lloyd, and Herman Kogen. *Lords of the Levee.* New York: Bobbs-Merrill, 1943.

Wilson, Frank J., and Beth Day. *Special Agent.* New York: Holt, Rinehart & Winston, 1965.

Whitehead, Don. *The F.B.I. Story.* New York: Random House, 1956.

Wolf, Marvin J., and Katherine Mader. *L.A. Crime.* New York: Facts On File Publications, 1986.

Wooldridge, Clifton R. *Hands Up! In the World of Crime or Twelve Years a Detective.* Chicago: Police Publishing Co., 1901.

Index

Boldface page numbers indicate main headings.